SMALL FIRM

FINANCE

AN ENTREPRENEURIAL PERSPECTIVE

Jerome S. Osteryoung
Jim Moran Professor of Entrepreneurship
and Professor of Finance
Florida State University, Tallahassee

Derek L. Newman
Senior Lecturer in Finance
Lincoln University
New Zealand

Leslie G. Davies
Professor of Business Administration
Bodo Graduate School of Business
Norway

SOUTH-WESTERN
TM
THOMSON LEARNING

Australia · Canada · Mexico · Singapore · Spain · United Kingdom · United States

Executive Editor	Mike Reynolds
Acquisitions Editor	Shana Lum
Developmental Editor	Yvette Rubio
Project Editor	Sandy Walton
Production Manager	Serena Manning
Executive Product Manager	Craig Johnson
Art Director	Jeanette Barber
Art & Literary Rights Editor	Adele Krause
Production and Editorial Services	Seaside Publishing Services
Text Type	10/12 Palatino
Cover Image	©2001 by South-Western

Address for Editorial Correspondence:
South-Western/Thomson Learning
5191 Natorp Boulevard
Mason, Ohio 45040

1-800-543-0487

ISBN: 0-03-098220-0

Library of Congress Catalog Card Number: 95-67390

Printed in the United States of America

1 2 3 4 5 6   039   9 8 7 6 5

To our families, friends, and colleagues who have encouraged and supported us.

PREFACE

Small businesses pervade the fabric of all business economies. In every country small businesses play a pivotal role in economic activity and the growth of employment. In the United States eleven million of the sixteen million new jobs created over the last decade are believed to have originated with small business. This increase in employment in small businesses was triggered by the partial reorientation of the U.S. economy from an industrial to a service focus. Similar reorientation has also been occurring in most developed economies.

Small business can be considered as the cauldron in which employment is brewed. The growth of employment is both a reflection and a cause of economic success. Thus the performance of small businesses is a measure of economic confidence. Small businesses generate employment by focusing on those sectors that have growth potential and which are more labor intensive than larger capital intensive industries.

THE PURPOSE OF THIS BOOK

The purpose of this textbook is to present in a clear and concise way the role of finance in the small business. There are many textbooks which describe corporate finance, but, unfortunately, these textbooks do not adequately describe the nature of finance in its application to the small business. Small businesses have very different attributes from large businesses, and, therefore, their requirement for financial management differs from those of their larger counterparts.

The specialty of small business finance is relatively new to the finance discipline. However, while our knowledge of small firm finance is in a development stage, it does have the advantage of being able to call on the established disciplines of finance and economics as aids to the student or the owner/manager of the small business.

The text will take the reader through the essential tenets of small business finance, distinguishing it appropriately from its larger relation, corporate finance, and focusing its examples and cases specifically on the smaller business. Not all of the generally accepted doctrines of corporate finance are inappropriately applied in the case of the small business. The reader will notice considerable areas of overlap with the general theory of finance. In a number of critical areas, however, there are major differences between the two bodies of knowledge. The financial alternatives available for selection by the management of the small firm will be entirely different from those available to the management of the larger firm.

The textbook is aimed at undergraduate and graduate students of business, at the owner-managers of small firms, and at consultants and others seeking knowledge in the area of small firm and entrepreneurial finance. While some prior knowledge of accounting and/or finance is not essential for the user of this textbook, readers with some prior knowledge of these disciplines will be able to follow its arguments more easily. Prior familiarity with a spreadsheet application such as Lotus 1–2–3, QuattroPro, or Excel will also be of assistance for those wishing to undertake the assignments presented at the end of each chapter.

CHAPTER LAYOUT

+ Chapter 1 of this book introduces the small firm, its organizational form and its objectives, and describes the fundamental differences between the larger and the smaller firm in the context of its financial management.
+ Chapter 2 describes the nature of the income statement and the balance sheet.
+ Chapter 3 describes the accounting process by considering the accounting conventions and the nature of financial statements that focus on cash flows.
+ Chapter 4 extends chapter 2 and chapter 3 by explaining how accounting-generated information can be used to determine the performance of the business through the examination of critical relationships disclosed in the financial reports of the business.
+ Chapter 5 describes the process of financial planning and introduces the notion of risk.
+ Chapter 6 discusses the working capital policies of the small firm that are so critical to its survival.
+ Chapter 7 introduces the elements of capital budgeting including the cash flow forecast and the choice of a discount rate.
+ Chapter 8 demonstrates the application of project evaluation in the context of the small firm.
+ Chapter 9 explains how the small firm is funded and the nature of its capital structure.
+ Chapter 10 describes the methodology involved in the valuation of the small firm.
+ Chapter 11 seeks to place the small firm in the international environment.

✦ Chapter 12 describes the nature of franchising and its role in the financing of the business. This chapter also examines sources of new equity funding and the problems faced by the owners of the small firm with respect to harvest and succession issues.

PEDAGOGY

Pedagogically, the text contains concept checks at the end of each major section of a chapter. It is suggested that at these points, the reader pause and consider the concepts described before progressing with further reading. End-of-chapter questions are presented for the student to use in reinforcing the material contained in the chapter. These largely relate to a case study that is developed throughout the text using the same small firm as an example. The questions relate the principles suggested in the relevant chapter to the solution of realistic problems faced by the management of the study business. Key terms are highlighted throughout the book, with a glossary of these terms contained at the end of the book.

ACKNOWLEDGMENTS

Many colleagues have contributed to this book. They recommended many suggestions that greatly enhanced this text. For their insightful reviews of the manuscript we would like to thank:

John Dunkelburg	Wake Forest University
Robert Hopley	University of Massachusetts—Amherst
Shirley Love	Idaho State University
Richard McMahon	University of South Australia
William Meggison	University of Georgia
William Petty	Baylor University
Warren Purdy	University of Southern Maine
Charles Ramser	Midwestern State University
Fredrick Scherr	West Virginia University
Timothy L. Thomas	Midwestern State University
Howard Toole	San Diego State University
Walt Wilson	University of Georgia

Additionally, we would like to thank our students who have encouraged us to write this textbook and were willing participants to test early versions of the manuscript.

BRIEF CONTENTS

CONTENTS

Preface   vii

CHAPTER   3   FINANCIAL STATEMENTS: CONVENTIONS AND CASH FLOWS   44

CHAPTER 4   PERFORMANCE ANALYSIS   57

CHAPTER 5   FINANCIAL PLANNING   91

CHAPTER 6 WORKING CAPITAL POLICY   126

CHAPTER 7   LONG TERM ASSET DECISIONS   183

SMALL FIRM
FINANCE

AN ENTREPRENEURIAL PERSPECTIVE

CHAPTER 10   BUSINESS VALUATION   268

        Changes in the Ownership of a Business   270
        Ascertaining If Goals Are Being Met   271
        Taxation   271
        Seeking Finance   271
        Legal Reasons   272

10.2   The Role of Comparables   272
        Comparable Sales   272

10.3   General Factors Influencing Value   273
        The Economy   273
        The Industry   273

10.4   Methods of Valuation   275
        Asset-Based Valuation Methods   275
        Income-Based Methods   276
        Which Cash Flow Should Be Capitalized?   279
        Revenue Multiplier Method   280

10.5   Steps in the Valuation Process   281
        Estimating Cash Flows   281
        XYZ Corporation Example   284
        Free Cash Flow and Taxation   285
        Estimating the Discount Rate   286

10.6   Types of Values   288
        Fair-market Value and Investment Value   288
        Price versus Value   288

10.7   The Key-Person Discount   289

10.8   The Minority Discount and the Control Premium   290

10.9   Example   292

       Summary   292

       The Case–Part Ten   294

       Assignment 10.1   294

       Assignment 10.2   294

       Assignment 10.3   295

       Assignment 10.4   295

       Selected Additional Readings   296

INTRODUCTION

1

OBJECTIVES

1. *Introduce the range of opinions concerning the differences between a small and a large business*

2. *Introduce the notion that the personal liability of the owners of a small business distinguishes it from a large business*

3. *Describe the organizational structure forms of small businesses: sole proprietorships, partnerships, sub-chapter S corporations, corporations, and limited-liability companies*

4. *Discuss the objectives of the small business*

1.1 WHAT IS SMALL BUSINESS?

Small businesses have existed since time immemorial and probably began in the caves with the first barter between our skin-clad ancestors. It is also not unrealistic to suggest that, even at a very early stage of human behavioral development, a bargain would have been appreciated. We do know for certain that specialization of labor existed very early in human evolution, and that primitive organizational structures resulted from that role allocation. Today's small business is merely a more sophisticated version of this suggested early scenario. Businesses in general have a long-term profit motive, an organizational structure, and utilize the specialized skills of the contributors to the success of the business. Small firms comprise a subset of businesses in general, and are the focus of this particular book.

But, what is small business? It is critically important that one understand what a small business is. First, its definition must be agreed upon so that communication can take place without any ambiguities. Secondly, researchers require a consistent definition so they know just what it is they are looking at when they study the small business. Thirdly, policymakers, both government and non-government, must define the small business in such a way that their policies can be evaluated for effectiveness. For example, if the government is considering a tax reduction for small business to encourage employment, then the definition of the small business is critical in the measurement of the effectiveness of this policy. Adequately defining the small business has exercised the minds of academics and policymakers for a considerable period of time.

The definition of a small business has changed over time in response to the desires of governments to target policies of certain types of business and the attentions of academics who have considered the principles that distinguish between larger and smaller firms. The following discussion relates to the development of thought in the United States about the nature of the small business. It is provided as an example of the way in which American thinking has evolved and also exemplifies similar developments in other countries.

One of the earliest attempts to define a small business was a Philadelphia social history project written during the period from 1850 to 1880. This project defined the small firm as one with fewer than fifty employees. In 1938, Ernest G. Draper, assistant treasurer of the U.S. Commerce Department, defined a small business as one with fewer than five hundred employees; by this definition over 90 percent of manufacturing firms in the United States were considered to be small. One year later, in 1939, the U.S. Bureau of Census published the Census of Business and defined a small business in manufacturing as one employing less than forty-three persons and earning less than $20,000 in annual sales. During the 1940s, several other definitions were suggested. In 1944, a U.S. Senate committee defined a small business as one employing fewer than five hundred persons. In the same year, Congress passed the War Mobilization Act and defined a small business as one employing less than two hundred fifty persons.

At the same time that government agencies were attempting to adequately define the small business, academics were also interested in its characteristics.

COLE AND TEGELER'S ANALYSIS

Basis of Definition	Percentage of Proprietors Surveyed
Annual revenue	32.0 %
Number of employees	23.0 %
Business characteristics	14.0 %
Industry characteristics	12.0 %
Annual revenue + number of employees	10.0 %
Geographic area served	2.0 %
Company assets	0.5 %
Miscellaneous measures	6.5 %
	100.0 %

Source: Roland J. Cole and Philip D. Tegeler, *Government Requirements of the Small Business* (Lexington, MA: Lexington Books, 1980), 120.

In the *American Economic Review* of 1944 Theodore W. Beckman suggested that a small business is one that meets any one of the following three criteria:

♦ less than two hundred fifty employees
♦ $225,000 in total assets
♦ $100,000 in net worth

During the period from 1950 to 1980, many other variations of definitions were suggested and, in the 1980s, Cole and Tegeler surveyed small businesses and asked their proprietors how they would define a small business in their particular industry. The results of this study are shown in Exhibit 1.1 grouped by generic type of definition.

The definition applied by the Small Business Administration (SBA) determines whether or not a business will be considered eligible for one of the SBA guaranteed loan programs (see Chapter 9 for a discussion of these programs) or qualifies to bid for certain government contracts. Also, when the government reports statistics, it usually accepts the definition of a small business used by the SBA.

The definition currently used by the SBA is that a small business is one that does not dominate its industry, and in which the capital is owned by a few individuals. These general tenets are further constrained by the application of the following industry standards (note that there is some flexibility depending on the particular industry):

Wholesale firms: maximum of one hundred employees

Manufacturing firms: maximum of five hundred employees (flexible to fifteen hundred)

Retail businesses: sales not exceeding $5 million (flexible to $21 million)

Service businesses: sales not exceeding $1.5 million (flexible to $21.5 million)

This brief historical overview of the definition of the small business demonstrates that policymakers, academics, and the owners of small businesses themselves have suggested widely varying versions of a definition. While this definition has varied over time, it has also been arbitrary—a firm with 999 employees is small; a firm with 1,000 employees is large. In addition, definitions that are based on such characteristics as sales or number of employees are not consistent across national boundaries. What is a large business in one economy may constitute a small business in another.

In 1993, Osteryoung and Newman attempted to circumvent this problem and suggested a definition for a small business that does not rely on operating characteristics as a basis. They argue that any definition of a small business must have three attributes: (1) the definition must be measurable and observable; (2) the definition must be congruent with the market system (e.g., financial markets cannot delineate between a firm having a revenue of $2,000,000 and one having a revenue of $1 less than $2,000,000); and (3) the definition must be meaningful (e.g., while a firm might be defined as large because it has a commanding share of the market, if the total revenue of such a firm is only $5,000, then it can hardly be described as a large firm—market share in such circumstances is not a meaningful discriminator). With these requirements in mind, they define a small business as one exhibiting:

1. no publicly traded equity, and
2. an actual or potential need for the owners of the firm to personally guarantee any existing or planned borrowing.

The first element of their definition states that a small business is one that does not, or potentially cannot, have publicly traded equity. When a firm has publicly traded equity, it has many government regulatory bodies controlling its activities. Also, the nature of the investor in a publicly traded firm is different from the nature of the investor in a small firm: an investor in public equity knows that the equity is readily negotiable—it can be sold on the stock exchange. In addition, the valuation of public equity is easily ascertained by examining the financial section of most newspapers. The valuation of the private firm is much more difficult.

The need to exclude those firms that are potentially publicly traded is best exemplified by a large public firm that is "taken private." In this case, there is no doubt that the firm is large; its ownership is merely so closely held that public trading of its equity is unnecessary. Should such a firm require additional funding, however, the option of issuing common stock on a stock market is readily available. In the case of the small business, such an option is not available.

The second element of the Osteryoung–Newman definition recognizes the nature of the personal exposure of the owner of the smaller firm to the creditors of the business. In many circumstances personal guarantees are required by banks when such a business applies for a loan. With this guarantee the bank will look to both the firm's assets and to the personal assets of the owner as security for its loan. The actual or potential presence of a **personal guarantee** significantly increases the risk of the small-business owner when compared to the risk accepted by the owner of equity in a publicly traded (i.e., large) firm.

Personal guarantees can be either formal or informal. In the case of a formal personal guarantee to a bank, for example, collateral security over the personal assets of the guarantor is offered. In the case of an informal personal guarantee, the creditors of a firm know that they have access to the personal assets of the proprietor because of the organizational structure of the firm itself. Sole proprietorships and partnerships are not limited-liability corporations, and it follows that the owner of such a firm offers a personal guarantee to all the creditors of the business. An example of the extent of personal liability occurs with a partnership borrowing $50,000. Assume the partnership comprises two individuals; they are jointly and severally liable for the entire debt themselves—each partner is liable for the entire $50,000 loan.

With small businesses that are corporations, banks will still require a formal personal guarantee as additional collateral for the loan.

Some of the possible major differences between large and small businesses are listed in Exhibit 1.2.

◆ EXHIBIT 1.2

DIFFERENCES BETWEEN LARGE AND SMALL BUSINESSES

	Larger Firms	Smaller Firms
Size Factors		
Asset size	Larger	Smaller
Number of employees	More	Less
Objectives		
Objective of the firm	Wealth maximization	Income, lifestyle
Personal and business mix		
Separation from personal assets	Separate	Not separate
Use of family labor	Rare	Common
Intergenerational transfers of ownership	Easy	Difficult (generally due to personality issues)
Personal risk of management	Low	High
Fringe benefits to owners	Few	Potentially high
Personal guarantees	Not present	Present
Likely life of the business	Longer	Shorter
Ownership		
Equity ownership	Public	Private
Equity negotiability	Easy	Difficult
Ownership vehicle	Public company	Proprietorship, partnership, corporation, or limited-liability company
Number of owners	Many	Few
Valuation		
Ease of valuation	Easy	Difficult

CONCEPT CHECK

1. *Why has the definition of the small business changed over time?*
2. *Why were definitions of small businesses prior to 1993 arbitrary in their classification?*
3. *With respect to the public trading of equity, what is the major difference between a large and a small firm?*

1.2 THE NEED FOR PERSONAL GUARANTEES

Why do financial institutions require personal guarantees?

In some cases the security offered to the bank involves real estate held by the owner of the business. Thus the owner is automatically a guarantor of the loan. In other cases, the bank wants to be sure that *all* of the resources of the owner, both income and assets, can be called upon to support the business; in other words, the bank cannot recognize any difference between the small business and its owner. To ensure its own security, a bank usually wants to make the owner personally responsible for the obligations inherent in the loan contract and does so by requiring the owner to personally guarantee the advance. Clearly, the bank is reducing its risk by requiring personal guarantees but it must be recognized that this increases the exposure of the small-business owner in the case of default.

In the rare circumstance that a firm has no public equity but its owners are not required to furnish personal guarantees as security for its borrowings, Osteryoung and Newman consider these firms to be either medium-sized businesses or indeed, large businesses. As introduced in the previous section of this chapter, examples include such businesses as those that have been listed but have been "taken private" or large firms that desire to remain private.

CONCEPT CHECK

1. *What is a personal guarantee?*
2. *Why might a personal guarantee be needed in the case of a small firm and not in the case of a large firm?*

1.3 SMALL BUSINESS AND ENTREPRENEURIAL ACTIVITY

Small businesses can be divided into two types: lifestyle and entrepreneurial. Both types of businesses are important and both are necessary.

Lifestyle businesses are firms that are not growth-oriented; their goals are to survive and to provide a living for their owners. Individuals who own and manage these organizations are frequently trying to provide employment for themselves and for others. Lifestyle businesses are frequently referred to as "mom-and-pop" businesses. A quick glance up and down your town's main street will demonstrate the myriad of lifestyle businesses. Typical examples include a local pet store and a local restaurant.

On the other hand, **entrepreneurial businesses** are growth- and profit-oriented. They typically appeal or hope to appeal to a national market. These firms attract outside investors willing to risk their investment in the firm's product, market, services, and management team. Clearly, in the early phases, Apple Computer was an entrepreneurial firm, as were Kodak and Xerox. Individuals who start franchises (franchisors) are entrepreneurial in outlook.

Lifestyle firm management is typically concerned with the personal goals of the owner. Take, for example, the owner of a small vineyard; such a person enjoys the lifestyle, and the goal of the business is congruent with the personal agenda of the owner. Entrepreneurial firms are concerned primarily with profits and growth. This is not to say that the owners of lifestyle firms necessarily turn down the opportunities to grow; they just don't actively seek growth. Neither is it true that "lifestylers" are not wealth maximizers; this objective is just more constrained than in the case of the entrepreneur. Nobody wants to lose wealth, and everybody prefers more wealth to less; lifestylers are less driven by objectives such as wealth maximization and growth than are entrepreneurs.

Petty and Bygrave[1] estimate that 95 percent of all small (non-public) firms are lifestyle and 5 percent are entrepreneurial. In many cases the problems and decisions the firms have to face are different. For example, most entrepreneurial firm funding will come from outsiders to the firm, whereas lifestyle firms receive most of their funding from the owner. This text will be concerned with both lifestyle and entrepreneurial firms.

 CONCEPT CHECK

1. *Distinguish between entrepreneurial firms and lifestyle firms.*
2. *What are the objectives of the lifestyler, and how do they differ from those of the entrepreneur?*

1.4 FORMS OF SMALL BUSINESS

Depending on the method of ownership, small businesses can be organized into one of five types:

✦ Sole proprietorships
✦ Partnerships

---

[1]See W. J. Petty and W. D. Bygrave, "What Does Finance Have to Say to the Entrepreneur?" *Journal of Small Business Finance* 2(2)(1993): 125–138 for a full discussion about entrepreneurs and lifestylers.

✦ Sub-chapter S corporations
✦ Limited-liability companies
✦ Corporations

SOLE PROPRIETORSHIPS

The majority of small businesses are **sole proprietorships,** businesses that are owned by one person. Most small businesses start out with this form of organization. There were 15.1 million sole proprietorships in the United States in 1993.[2] The advantage of a sole proprietorship is that it is very inexpensive to start, operate, and terminate. It is the most flexible of the various ownership forms. With respect to taxation, there is no distinction between income arising as the result of the business activity and that derived from personal activity; a proprietorship is taxed at the rate of the owner without any type of additional taxes that corporations may have to pay.

Sole proprietorships have two large disadvantages. First, if a firm seeks growth, then a sole proprietorship does not offer a suitable foundation. Growth in this case must be funded solely from the savings of the proprietor (including business profits) together with additional borrowing. As soon as equity is raised from outside investors to fund business growth, by definition, the sole proprietorship becomes a multiple proprietorship either in the form of a partnership or in the form of a corporation. Secondly, the owner of the sole proprietorship and the business itself are deemed to be a single entity for both taxation and other commercial activities. For example, if a sole proprietorship is sued by a customer for some reason, then both the assets and income of the business and the owner will be applied to any settlement.

PARTNERSHIPS

A **partnership** is an organizational form of business owned by two or more individuals. In 1993 there were 1.6 million partnerships in the United States.[3] It is easier for a partnership to raise capital than it is for a sole proprietorship simply because there is more than one person providing the capital and collateral security. A partnership is more expensive to form and administer than a sole proprietorship.

A partnership is not a **legal entity** as such—it cannot sue or be sued, although its existence is legally recognized. Instead, the partners are jointly and severally liable for all of the obligations of the partnership. This means that each partner is liable for all of the obligations. Like the sole proprietorship, the owners and the business are considered one and the same and the liability of the partners is unlimited.

---

[2]See *The State of Small Business: A Report of the President* (Washington, D.C.: U.S. Government Printing Office, 1994) p. 37.

[3]Ibid.

The exposure to full liability provides a very good reason why a person should choose a partner very carefully, and why partnerships are often an ownership structure of short duration. Additionally, each time the composition of the partnership changes, the old partnership must be dissolved and a new one formed. This may be costly if it is a regular occurrence. Many professionals, such as accountants and doctors, form partnerships (in some cases because the law prevents them forming limited-liability companies).

As with the sole proprietorship, the income of a partnership is deemed to be that of its owners; they must each pay income tax on their full share of the partnership income whether or not it is fully distributed. Taxation in such circumstances is at the individual partner's income-tax rate.

Limited partnerships are a special kind of partnership (and, indeed, in some countries they are known as "special partnerships"). With this type of organization there is normally one general partner who is personally liable for the obligations of the partnership. Additionally, there are limited partners who cannot take an active role in the management of the business and are not personally liable for its obligations. The risk faced by the limited partners is only the risk associated with their initial investment. Many real-estate and cable TV partnerships have been set up under a limited partnership form of organization.

SUB-CHAPTER S CORPORATIONS

The third type of organization listed has many different names, depending on the country in which the organization is registered. The common characteristic of this type of ownership form is that while owners maintain the legal fabric of a corporation, they are treated as partnerships for many other purposes, often including taxation. In the United States, these firms are called **sub-chapter S corporations** or **S-corporations,** the latter is the terminology that will be used throughout this book.

One way for many small-business owners to possibly reduce their risk of exposure, while maintaining some of the flexibility of the partnership with respect to taxation, is through the formation of a sub-chapter S-corporation. This is an entity that has the limited-liability attributes of a corporation but maintains the nature of a partnership for the purposes of taxation. That is, any income is deemed to be the direct income of its owners, and no corporate income tax is levied on the organization itself, thus avoiding the double taxation of corporations. The onerous paperwork required of any corporation may also be reduced in the case of the S-corporation. The United States requires that an S-corporation have thirty-five or fewer shareholders and that corporations and partnerships cannot be equity owners.

One big advantage of an S-corporation is that the limited liability of the corporation can protect the owners, their liability is limited to the amount of their investment if the corporation is sued (e.g., due to a product malfunction). However, despite the implied limitation of liability accruing to the owners of the S-corporation, it must be remembered that this characteristic will be ineffective in the instance when personal guarantees have been furnished to secure credit.

LIMITED-LIABILITY COMPANIES

Limited-liability companies (LLCs) are a relatively new phenomenon in the United States, where, in 1988, the Internal Revenue Service (IRS) ruled that LLCs would be taxed as partnerships. Currently there are forty-three states that have passed laws allowing the formation of LLCs. Limited-liability companies are corporations that are taxed as partnerships, and so for tax reasons they act similarly to S-corporations. However, they overcome many of the deficiencies of S-corporations. For example, with S-corporations there can be no foreign owners and the number of owners is limited to thirty-five. Neither of these limitations apply to LLCs. LLCs probably will replace the currently popular S-corporations as LLCs offer the business owner more flexibility.

In countries other than the United States, the term *limited-liability company* refers to what is known in the United States as the corporation. To save the reader confusion, U.S. limited-liability companies will be referred to as LLCs throughout this book. All other references to companies or corporations will refer to corporations (which also exhibit limited liability). The reader should be aware of these differences in terminology because the increasing globalization of trade necessitates such distinctions.

CORPORATIONS

A **corporation** is a true legal entity with the right to sue and be sued distinctly from its owners (and can in fact be sued *by* its owners). Approximately 4,500,000 of all of the tax returns filed in the United States in 1993 were from corporations. This represented approximately 25 percent of all business forms according to Internal Revenue Service data.[4]

A corporation is the form of organization to which most small businesses advance as they grow. Corporations offer several advantages over both proprietorships and partnerships. First, the maximum loss for an owner of a small business with a corporate form of organization is the value of the equity investment (i.e., limited liability exists). Obviously, if any personal guarantee exists, then the risk exposure of the guarantor is increased commensurately. Financial institutions are well aware of the limited liability associated with corporate ownership, and in the case of smaller firms, the lender may defray this limitation by requiring personal guarantees. Forming a corporation, therefore, is not an effective way for a small business to avoid personal exposure.

---

[4]Ibid.

A major advantage of the corporate structure is the relative ease with which additional equity can be raised. Individual investors may be more willing to contribute funds to a corporate form of organization that ostensibly protects their personal assets from the claims of creditors. Unfortunately diverse multiple ownership may also be a constraining influence on the operations of the firm if additional funding is necessary and personal guarantees are sought to secure this funding. However, individual shareholders are unlikely to want to proffer personal guarantees unless they are very confident in the behavior of their co-owners, that is, unless all owners contribute similarly (as is often the case when the owners are all family members). Another advantage of a corporation is that it will outlive the lives of the individual owners. If one equityholder should die, the corporation will continue.

One large disadvantage with a corporate form of organization is that the government levies income tax on the income of the corporation and then again on income received by any shareholder as a dividend. For example, if a sole proprietorship earned $50,000 before taxes and its owner was in the 31 percent income-tax bracket then the total taxation paid would be $15,500. However, if a U.S. corporation earned $50,000, it, too, would have to pay $15,500 in taxes, assuming the same tax rate for corporations and individuals. Then, if the firm paid out the difference ($50,000 − $15,500 = $34,500) as a dividend, its owners would have to pay $10,695 (31% × $34,500) in additional taxes on the dividends received. In this case, the proprietorship paid $15,500 in taxes while the corporation's owners paid $26,195 in taxes.

THE CHOICE OF ORGANIZATIONAL FORM

The choice of organization for a small business is an important decision and depends on many factors. Some of the factors that need to be considered include:

+ the expected viable life of the business
+ the number of owners desired
+ tax implications
+ the need for growth
+ the need to raise equity funds

CONCEPT CHECK

1. *What is the difference between the liability of the sole proprietor and the liability of partners in a partnership?*
2. *What is the difference between a partnership and an S-corporation?*
3. *What is the difference between an S-corporation and a limited-liability corporation?*

1.5   THE OBJECTIVES OF A SMALL BUSINESS

Any firm, large or small, needs **objectives**. They are required to develop business plans and to measure accomplishments. Given the fragility of small firms, it is absolutely critical that small businesses specify their objectives.

Corporate finance theory assumes that the objective of the firm (and thus its owners) is to maximize owners' wealth. This is accomplished in one or more of the following ways:

+ maintaining net income and reducing risk
+ increasing net income while keeping risk constant
+ increasing net income to such an extent that it more than counters the consequences of an increase in risk

The owners of a large firm increase their wealth via the dividends received together with changes in the value of the firm's shares.

On the other hand, in the case of the small business, **wealth maximization** is not necessarily the most appropriate objective. Most small businesses have (at least) a dual objective: to provide after-tax income to their owners and to grow (if they can). With respect to growth, the objective is usually oriented toward increasing the future after-tax income stream rather than the value of the business (although obviously the latter follows the former). In the case of the small business, the increase in the after-tax income stream is often more facilitated by manipulation of the effective income-tax rate than by increasing the pre-tax income stream itself. For example, small businesses in corporate form (where double taxation exists) frequently pay either excessive salaries, directors' fees, or perquisites (fringe benefits, such as cars or entertainment) to their owners rather than face double taxation.

Additionally, because small firms are not publicly traded, objective measurement of the value of equity (and therefore increases in that value) becomes more difficult.

If the wealth-maximization objective assumed for publicly traded firms is an inadequate specification of the reason for existence of the small business, then what is the correct objective? If one considers the various small firms that one transacts business with on a day-to-day basis, tremendous differences in their objectives can be seen. Many people start businesses just to have a job. There has been a recent trend in many countries for the government and large public firms to reduce the size of their work force. These recently unemployed individuals often start small businesses as a way to provide employment. Other individuals start or purchase a business because of the lifestyle associated with that business. For example, people who love dogs start businesses breeding dogs because they want the lifestyle associated with this type of activity.

It is very difficult to simply and generically state the goals of the small-business owner. Osteryoung et al. suggest that goals for a small business should be some combination of financial goals and non-financial goals.[5] While these goals may not appear to be very specific, the behavior of the small-firm owner does suggest that both financial goals and non-financial goals exist. Some possible non-financial goals include:

+ achieving independence
+ surviving financially
+ maintaining a chosen lifestyle
+ helping families (dynastic arrangements)
+ rendering a needed service
+ participating in a challenging or creative endeavor
+ acquiring position in the community

Some possible financial goals include:

+ maximizing profit
+ making a reasonable profit
+ increasing the future value of the business
+ increasing the number of locations of the business
+ becoming a large public firm

While these lists are not comprehensive, they do give an idea of the range of objectives, both financial and non-financial, that a small business may have. Regardless of its goal choice, there must be some aim associated with the existence of every small business. It is only through the identification and implementation of these objectives that the financial management of the small business can be operationalized and controlled.

The financial goals of the small business can differ considerably from those of its larger counterpart. The preceding discussions describe how the individual plays a much larger part in the focus of the smaller firm than is the case with the individual owner of the larger firm (especially when the tradeoffs between long-term and short-term gains are considered).

 CONCEPT CHECK

1. *In what ways is the wealth-maximizing objective an insufficient predictor of the behavior of the small firm?*
2. *What effect does lifestyle considerations have in the case of the goals of the small firm?*

---

[5]See J. S. Osteryoung, R. J. Best, and D. A. Nast, "On the Size Differences of Small Businesses," paper presented at the Southern Finance Association meeting in Jacksonville, Florida, November 1992.

3. *What differences might there be with respect to non-financial goals between the large and the small firm?*

4. *What differences might there be with respect to financial goals between the large and the small firm?*

SUMMARY

✦ The purpose of this chapter is to show the importance of small business and to review some of the critical elements relating to small-business finance. The presence of an environment in which small businesses can flourish is critical to the success of most economies. Small businesses underpin job growth and general economic activity.

✦ Small-business finance differs from the more general corporate finance; for example, small firms tend to have funds limitations, high debt in their capital structure, and a high failure rate.

✦ A small business is defined as one in which the owners are actually or potentially liable for the obligations associated with the debts of the business, and for which the equity of the firm is not publicly traded. These characteristics infer that the risks faced by the owner of the small business are considerably larger than those faced by the shareholders of a large business. They also infer that the funding activity of the small business is significantly constrained.

✦ There are five basic forms of organization for a small business: sole proprietorship, partnership, sub-chapter S corporation, corporation, and limited-liability company. The choice depends on many factors, including the foundation for growth and tax implications.

✦ With respect to the objective of the smaller firm, the commonly accepted wealth-maximization objective is inadequate. At best, the objective can be regarded as maximizing the satisfaction of the owners of the business including both financial goals and non-financial goals. The goals must be identified in each case so that a realistic financial plan can be generated that is congruent with the goals of the firm's owners and so that the firm's performance can be measured in some realistic context.

THE CASE

The following narrative introduces the case study of a small business that will be followed throughout the remainder of this book. At the end of each chapter, the progress of Dave and his business activities will be followed. New elements will be introduced as the book proceeds to reflect the nature of material introduced in the text.

THE CASE—PART ONE

It is 1998 and Dave, who graduated from State University four years ago, is a competitive sportsman with a particular interest in mountain biking. As a student he set up a small bicycle-assembly plant, but it did not prove profitable enough to provide him with a living once he graduated.

During a trip overseas last year to compete in an international mountain-biking race, he was introduced to state-of-the-art bicycle technology that he had never seen at home, and that he had not seen advertised anywhere.

At a meeting with a couple of the owners of the latest technology, Dave began talking about the business opportunities associated with the new technologies. His new friends decided that they liked Dave's style enough to supply him with a domestic franchise for their company.

On his return home, Dave set up a local assembly plant, complete with a small showroom, and began to assemble mountain bikes from the components forwarded to him by his overseas suppliers.

Among the early tasks that Dave undertook were decisions about the name of his business and its form of organization: proprietorship, partnership, or limited-liability corporation. At the time, Dave's parents were very supportive of his move into the bicycle business and were seriously considering being partners if Dave was unable to raise the necessary funding from his own and borrowed resources.

After discussing the advantages and disadvantages of each form of organization with his finance mentor at University, Dave decided to form a corporation to be known as Dave's Bikes & Co.

On the basis of his initial budget, Dave decided that the company would need $89,000 to adequately fund its initial operations. He began in business on January 1 by investing $25,000 of his own money in the business (for fifty thousand fifty-cent shares), borrowing $20,000 from his bank as a long-term loan secured against the assembly plant and an additional $30,000 secured against his family home. He also organized a line of credit with the same bank for fluctuating working-capital needs and immediately drew down the full $9,000 against this line. Dave also transferred some plant of his own from his previous involvement in the assembly business to the company, which he valued at $5,000 (exchanging it for another ten thousand fifty-cent shares in the company).

Dave sells the completed bikes both to the general public and to other retailers (at a lower price). Sales were relatively slow at the start, but there was a lot of general inquiry, and before long the orders were rolling in. In fact, Dave realized very early on that he could repay the debts of the business far more quickly than he had budgeted because the business was going better than anticipated.

As far as his own personal requirement for cash is concerned, Dave draws from the company as much as he needs after he has deducted tax on his wages. The financial statements include these wages as operating expenses.

ASSIGNMENT 1.1

Required

1. What type of organizational form should Dave select? What are the advantages and disadvantages of the various alternatives, such as the partnership, corporation, and sub-chapter S corporation?

ASSIGNMENT 1.2

Required

1. Would Dave's business be considered large or small by current definitions? Explain your answer.
2. The business borrowed $50,000 from the bank by way of a long-term loan secured against the assembly plant and against Dave's house, plus $9,000 in the form of a current account advance (or overdraft), so Dave received $59,000 from

his bank. How much of this would you expect to be secured by way of a personal guarantee? Does this change your answer to question 1?

3. In what ways would you consider Dave's objectives to differ from those of the business?

SELECTED ADDITIONAL READINGS

Cole, Roland J., and Philip D. Tegeler. 1980. *Government requirements of the small business.* Lexington, MA: Lexington Books.

Cooley, P., and C. E. Edwards. 1983. Financial objectives of small firms. *American Journal of Small Business* (July–September): 27–31.

Osteryoung, J. S., R. J. Best, and D. A. Nast. 1992. On the size differences of small businesses. Paper presented at the Southern Finance Association meeting in Jacksonville, Florida, November.

Osteryoung, J. S., and D. L. Newman. 1993. What is a small business? *Journal of Small Business Finance* 2(3) (Summer): 219–232.

Petty, W. J., and W. D. Bygrave. 1993. What does finance have to say to the entrepreneur? *Journal of Small Business Finance* 2(2): 125–138.

Walker, E. W., and W. J. Petty, 1986. *Financial management of the small firm.* 2d ed. Englewood Cliffs, NJ: Prentice-Hall.

FINANCIAL STATEMENTS: INCOME STATEMENT AND BALANCE SHEET

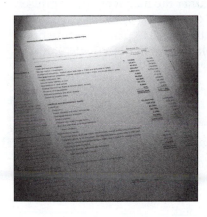

OBJECTIVES

1. *Introduce the reasons for financial reporting*
2. *Describe the structure of financial reports, their foundation in cash transactions, and the necessity for an accrual process*
3. *Describe the structure and components of the income statement and the balance sheet and the alternative layouts that are commonly utilized in their presentation*
4. *Describe the relationships that exist between the components of the income statement and the balance sheet and how the management of one component will affect others*

2.1 INTRODUCTION TO FINANCIAL REPORTING

The purpose of this chapter is to introduce the reader to the nature and purposes of accounting. For the student of small-business finance, it is important to recognize what the figures in a set of financial reports mean and how they were established because the financial reports form the objective basis on which many of the tasks undertaken by either the manager, the appraiser, or the business analyst are based. Without financial reports, one would be unable to determine the performance of the business, to plan its future operations on anything other than subjective beliefs, and to objectively value its worth or that of its owners.

WHY THE ACCOUNTING STATEMENT?

A business starts its life when its owners provide resources to undertake an enterprise from which they hope to profit. Accounting is necessary to inform the owners and other interested people, such as bank managers, about the level of that profit. At the end of a period, usually on an annual basis, the amount of the profit for the period is determined.

Net worth is the difference between the total **assets** of the business (how much the business owns) and the **liabilities** of the business (how much it owes). Net worth can be increased by increasing the assets of the business (without a corresponding increase in liabilities), or by decreasing the liabilities of a business (without a corresponding decrease in the assets of the business), or a combination of both. Without the business borrowing or its owners injecting more money, the only way that the assets of a business can grow is if the operations of the business are profitable and the business itself generates the additional funds required to finance the additional assets that represent the growth of the firm.

The profits of a business are just revenue minus costs. This profit is known as the **net income** of the business. Accounting is the mechanism by which the net income of the business is determined and the net worth of its owners' contributions is measured.

From the perspective of the analyst or user of the financial information, it must always be remembered that figures in financial statements only represent the opinion of the person who prepared the report. The accuracy of the report depends on the type of accounting system used, the methodology applied in its preparation and the adequacy of the data provided to the preparer. The analyst must verify the financial data and accounting sources before assessing any value of the firm.

Accountants prepare financial reports using several methods.

✦ **Audited statements,** as will be described in more detail later in this chapter, refer to reports in which the methodology used in their preparation has been examined, and the accuracy of transaction recording

◆ **EXHIBIT 2.1**

COMPILED STATEMENT: COVER LETTER

SEED, SALDANA & JAWORSKI
Certified Public Accountants
Tallahassee, Florida
March 2, 1997

Ajax Distribution Company
Tallahassee, Florida

The accompanying income statement of Ajax Distribution Company for the period to December 31st 1996 and the related statements of income and changes in financial position for the year then ended have been compiled by us.

A compilation is limited to presenting the form of financial statement information that is the representation of management. We have not audited or reviewed the accompanying financial statements and, accordingly, do not imply any form of assurance about them.

Rowena Seed, CPA
Managing Partner

has been verified. The analyst would prefer to work with audited financial reports as much as possible, but, unfortunately for the analyst, most smaller businesses cannot afford the expense of an auditor. The analyst of the unaudited report must perform her own check on the accuracy of the reports and, where necessary, make adjustments to the reports before offering an opinion as to the performance of the business.

◆ **Reviewed statements** are based on management-supplied information, but are certified as to their reasonableness by a certified public accountant. While glaring irregularities are noted in reviewed statements, no verification of source data is required.

◆ **Compiled statements** contain unaudited information provided by the firm's management. They are commonly used in small businesses because they do not involve the expense associated with a more sophisticated approach. Unfortunately, compiled statements also tend to be the least accurate of the formally presented reports because the data has not been verified. Exhibit 2.1 displays an accountant's cover letter for a compiled income statement for the Ajax Distribution Company indicating the limitations of the compilation.

✦ In many cases, the only financial statements available to the analyst of the smaller business is the **tax return** because, either through ignorance or frugality, the owner of the business did not have any other report prepared. However, the analyst should be aware that the owners of the business will frequently attempt to minimize the reported profit in a tax return to minimize the tax that they will have to pay and, in so doing, will understate the financial performance of the business.

THE FORMAL STRUCTURE OF ACCOUNTING REPORTS

Accounting reports may contain up to five different statements. They are the **income statement,** the **balance sheet,** the **cash-flow statement,** the **notes to the accounts,** and the **auditor's opinion**. The formal financial report of a corporation that is listed on the stock exchange will usually also contain a notice of meeting, a list of the directors of the corporation, a directors' report, and a statement of the major shareholders' interests, among other things. However, in contrast to a large publicly held corporation, the financial reports of smaller businesses will not necessarily contain all of these statements.

Because of its contribution in the planning process, a statement of cash flows is increasingly becoming an essential addition to the financial reports of the smaller firm. The advent of computers makes its generation simple and its potential use as a basis for cash-flow budgeting is encouraging its presentation. The statement of cash flows will be discussed further in Chapter 3.

CASH AND ACCRUAL ACCOUNTING

While all financial reports are prepared using data concerning the firm's financial activities, there are two possible bases for the preparation process: the **cash basis** and the **accrual basis**. In the case of the former, revenues are recognized only when collected, and expenses only when paid. In the case of the latter, revenues and expenses are recorded in the period in which they are committed; they are not necessarily received or paid in that period. Many smaller businesses prefer cash-basis accounting because revenues are easier to record at the point of sale and expenses at the point of payment.

Business analysts generally prefer financial statements that have been prepared from data recorded under the accrual method of accounting because, as will be shown, the cash basis distorts the measurement of profitability and financial condition. Revenues earned but not yet received are ignored with cash-basis accounting, as are expenses incurred but not yet paid. The analyst must adjust for such discrepancies in these instances, a subject that will be addressed later in this chapter. However, the majority of small businesses generate financial statements on a cash basis.

DONNELLY & CO.: FIRST-YEAR TRANSACTIONS

Cash inflows:	
Sales to customers	$460,000
Borrowings	100,000
Contributions from the owners	82,000
	$642,000
Cash outflows:	
Payments to suppliers	$509,000
Interest	11,000
Purchase of assets	120,000
	$640,000

CASH TRANSACTIONS: THE FOUNDATION

Financial reports summarize the **financial transactions** of a business for the period under consideration. A starting point in the explanation of accounting reports is to consider those transactions that are cash-based. For each of these transactions, there will be an increase or decrease in the cash balance held by the firm.

There are two basic types of cash flows. First, there are those that are related to the ongoing activities of the business; for example, sales of **finished goods,** purchases of **raw materials,** or payments of **interest**. Second, there are those transactions related to other more capital-oriented activities, such as the purchase of assets or the repayment of **long-term debt**. The basic difference between the two classes of transactions is that, in the case of the former, the transactions relate to the profitability of the business, while in the case of the latter, the transactions relate to the asset structure of the firm and to the manner in which the assets are financed.

By way of demonstration, the rest of this chapter (and, in some instances, subsequent chapters) will use the case of Donnelly & Co. as an example. Donnelly & Co. is a light fabrication plant in a city that is owned by Jim and Imelda Donnelly. The business was previously owned by a publicly listed firm that, for strategic reasons, moved out of light industry and offered various business units to the managers at the time. Jim was one of the managers who benefited from this change.

Jim and Imelda used all of their surplus cash together with money raised by using their family home as collateral to purchase the assets of the business. They organized a line of credit at the local bank, leased premises in which the plant was to be located, and went into business. In their first year of business, they experienced the set of transactions depicted in Exhibit 2.2.

◆ EXHIBIT 2.3

INCOME STATEMENT TRANSACTIONS

Sales		$460,000
Cost of goods sold	$509,000	
Interest	11,000	
Total expenses		520,000
Net income		$ (60,000)

◆ EXHIBIT 2.4

BALANCE SHEET TRANSACTIONS

Assets:		
Final	$120,000	
Cash	62,000	
		$182,000
Liabilities:		
Borrowings	$100,000	
Assets – liabilities = owners' equity		$ 82,000

THE INCOME STATEMENT AND THE BALANCE SHEET

To determine how profitable the enterprise is, the accounting process groups together those items that are relevant to the determination of profitability. In this case, the relevant transactions are presented in Exhibit 2.3.

To ascertain the financial condition of the business, accountants group together those items that are relevant to the determination of the productive capacity of the firm and the manner of financing. Exhibit 2.4 presents the transactions relevant to this grouping.

The business at first glance seems to have lost $60,000 in its business activities, but, on closer inspection, it can be seen that the owners maintain the business through the contributions of **debtholders** and **equityholders** (owners). Whether or not the business is in a good or a bad position after this result depends upon the future prospects of the business. Many firms in their first year of operations suffer a loss for a myriad of reasons, ranging from slow initial start-up to the high initial costs associated with primary market penetration. The **budget** for next year's cash flows would provide more information needed before commenting on the firm's ability to succeed.

There is one other possibility: *All* of the relevant transactions may not be represented by cash flows. There may be other relevant transactions that are *not* included in the cash-flow transactions. For example, there may have been a large order that was sold on credit, or some of the bills may not have been paid for a month or two. This is where the analysis of cash flows *alone* breaks down and provides the reason why accountants apply an accrual basis to their calculations. The accrual basis involves adjusting the cash flows to recognize transactions that rightly belong to the **accounting period** under consideration, but for which there is no *cash* transaction during the period.

 CONCEPT CHECK

1. *What are the different types of financial reports?*
2. *What are the five major components of a financial report?*
3. *Distinguish between cash accounting and accrual accounting.*

2.2 THE INCOME STATEMENT

THE STRUCTURE OF THE INCOME STATEMENT

The statement that describes the results of the income-generating operations of the business for the period under examination, which is usually (but not always) one year, is called the income statement. The objective of this statement is to exhibit the way in which the profit of the business is calculated. Income statements are the foundation of business performance.

Elements of the income statement include sales revenue, various categories of expenses, and profit for the period under consideration. Terminology for each element often varies with the nature of the business and with the person who compiles the report, but the concept that revenue less expenses equals profit remains the same. For example, Donnelly & Co. sold 10,000 items at $52 each that cost $32.50 each to manufacture. The firm paid administration costs of $142,000 to maintain its operations along with $13,000 in interest and it paid taxes at a rate of 30 percent.

A convenient starting point is to establish the level of sales: $520,000 worth of goods were sold. Next, it is useful to establish the cost of those sales: they cost $325,000. The difference between sales and the cost of sales ($195,000 in this case) is known as the **gross profit.** Gross profit reports how much money the items themselves have generated.

If the business was run from home and had no other administrative costs and had to pay no interest, it would obviously have cleared $195,000. In order to calculate the profit, though, it is also essential to deduct the other expense items listed. If administration costs of $142,000 are deducted from the gross profit of $195,000, the **net operating income** of the business, regardless of the way in which it was financed, is $53,000. The net operating income is also often known as the **operating income** or the **earnings before interest and tax** (or **EBIT**).

If the $13,000 paid in interest is deducted from the operating income, a figure of $40,000 can be reported as being earned during the period before any allowance for paying tax. This figure is known as the **earnings before tax (or EBT).**

◆ EXHIBIT 2.5

INCOME STATEMENT FOR THE YEAR

Sales revenue		$520,000
Cost of goods sold		(325,000)
Gross profit		$195,000
Operating expenses	$130,000	
Depreciation expense	12,000	
		(142,000)
Net operating income		$ 53,000
Interest expense		(13,000)
Earnings before tax		$ 40,000
Income tax expense		(12,000)
Net income		$ 28,000

If income tax is to be paid at a rate of 30 percent, then the firm will eventually have to pay 30 percent of $40,000 as taxes (i.e., $12,000), and this will leave the business with $28,000 as the net income or net profit.

COMPONENTS OF THE INCOME STATEMENT

Sales Revenue
Revenue is the stream of benefits accruing to the firm from the sales of products or services **(operating revenue). Non-operating revenue** can be derived from interest earned or some other non-operations-related items, such as depreciation recovered on the sale of an asset.

Cost of Goods Sold
The stock of goods on hand ready for processing or sale is known as **inventory**. The **cost of goods sold (COGS)** is the inventory cost associated with a particular sale. Cost of goods sold includes the cost of raw materials and certain costs of processing (depending on the accounting methodology used). The estimation of cost of goods sold is based on the following relationship:

beginning inventory + purchases – ending inventory
= cost of goods sold

For example, if the firm purchases $45,000 during the period and its beginning inventory was $5,000 and its ending inventory is $10,000 then its cost of goods sold for the period is $40,000.

Gross Profit
Gross profit margin or **gross margin** describes the relationship between gross profit and sales. In the case of Donnelly & Co. (Exhibit 2.5), the corpo-

ration earned a gross profit equal to 37.5 percent of its sales revenue. The gross margin is calculated as:

$$\text{gross margin} = \frac{\$195,000 \text{ gross profit}}{\$520,000 \text{ sales revenue}} = 37.5\%$$

The term **mark-up** describes the relationship between profit and sales in an alternative way by comparing the gross profit with the cost of sales.

$$\text{mark-up} = \frac{\$195,00 \text{ gross profit}}{\$325,000 \text{ cost of sales}} = 60\%$$

Operating Expenses

Operating expenses are those costs incurred by the firm in its operations. Because higher operating expenses lead to lower profitability, in the case of closely held businesses there is often a problem with the intermingling of business and personal expenditures. Excessive "perks" and the personal use of business assets do not constitute realistic operating expenses and their inclusion in the financial report distorts reality. As with the cost of goods sold, comparison with industry norms can often signal the presence of excessive intermingling. Institutions such as Dun & Bradstreet and the Financial Research Associates provide information relating to such norms.

Items of expense, often exhibited separately under the general heading of operating expenses, include:

+ *Salaries and wages.* While these will include all wages and benefits *paid* to the owners and the employees of the business, two problems arise in the case of the closely held firm. First, there may be relatives who are employed at above-market rates or who are paid fringe benefits that are not commensurate with their positions and contributions. The second area of concern relates to the owner's salary. Many small-business owners do not specifically identify a salary for themselves in the financial report. This is because, at least in the case of the sole proprietorship, the net income *is* the salary of the owner. In other cases, the owner's salary may be more a function of income-tax planning than reality. Of course, the reverse of these scenarios is also possible. The owners of a small business, especially in its formative stages, may work very long hours for very little formally reported reward.
+ *Travel and entertainment.* These expenses must be business-related.
+ *Utilities.* The cost of telephone, water, and electricity should only be included insofar as they represent expenses related to genuine business activity.
+ *Vehicle expenses.* Regarding costs relating to the repairs, maintenance, and running costs of vehicles, personally related costs must be removed from business expenses.

✦ *Advertising.* The lack of advertising expense may be one indication that a small firm is having financial problems. This is because advertising is a key element in some types of firms' ability to attract new and continuing sales, and yet it is an easy expense to defer in order to access immediate liquidity.

Depreciation Expense

Depreciation is the name given to the cost allowance applied to use of a firm's long-term assets. The cost of such an asset is paid at the time the asset is first purchased and it would be economically irrational to offset this cost entirely against revenues in the period that the asset was purchased. Instead, the asset is gradually "written off" by the depreciation mechanism.

Generally accepted accounting principles (GAAP) suggest that firms apportion an equal amount of the cost of the asset to each year of its use. In other words, if an asset costs $5,000 and has a life expectancy of five years, then $1,000 will be allocated to each of the first five years of its life, and will be added to the expenses of the firm each year. This is known as **straight-line depreciation.** The other type of depreciation is **accelerated depreciation.** This type of depreciation accelerates annual depreciation. Common types of accelerated depreciation are sum-of-the-years or double-declining balance methods. With these techniques the depreciation charge in the earlier years is much higher than under straight-line depreciation.

Net Operating Income

The net operating income is the difference between the revenues of the business and the expenses, with the exception of interest and taxes. As stated earlier in this chapter, this figure is also widely known as earnings before interest and taxes, or EBIT. It is a figure that is critically important in the analysis of performance, as shall be seen throughout this book, because it signals whether or not the owners of the business should be borrowing to invest in the business.

Interest

Interest is always separated from other operating expenses because it arises from the way in which the business is financed, rather than the way in which the business is operated; it is a financial charge against the revenues of the firm rather than a charge associated with the firm's operating activities. Interest is a cost associated with the way in which the firm's assets have been financed and does not have anything to do with the value of the assets themselves.

Earnings before Taxes

This figure is the difference between the adjusted revenues of the business and the associated expenses. The figure reported as earnings before taxes forms the basis for the determination of any income taxes relating to the firm for the period.

Income Tax

In the case of many small businesses, especially sole proprietorships and partnerships, the taxation figure may not be evident. This is because the income for the particular business under consideration may be combined with other personal and business income of the owner before the owner's taxation is computed. In the instance of these two ownership systems, the business *itself* does not pay income tax; only the owner pays income tax. In the instance of the corporation, however, the firm itself does pay income tax, and this figure should be evident.

Net Income

The net income of the business is the earnings after payment of taxation in the case of the corporation (in the case of the proprietorship or partnership there will be no such figure). If the business is structured as a corporation, these profits either can be paid out to the owners of the corporation by way of a **dividend** or they can be retained by the business, in which case they are known as **retained earnings.**

Dividends

The amount of net income of the corporation paid out to its owners is called dividends. As explained earlier, small firms that are organized as sole proprietorships, partnerships, and sub-chapter S corporations do not pay dividends; instead, all net income flows to the owners as income.

Many small corporate businesses likewise will never pay a dividend. This is not for any legal reason (as is the case with the sole proprietorship) but because many such businesses rely on retained earnings to fund their growth, and secondly because dividends (on which tax has already been paid) are taxed (again) in the hands of the shareholder. Thus, the owner–manager of the small business, given the choice of withdrawing money as either wages or dividends will generally use the former mechanism. For example, assume that the corporate tax rate is 40 percent, the owner pays personal tax at a rate of 20 percent, and the corporation earns $100,000 before taxes and prior to paying its owner any money. If the corporation pays tax on $100,000 ($40,000 paid in corporate taxes leaves $60,000 for the owner's salary, which, in turn, is taxed $12,000 at the personal rate) and then distributes the balance as a dividend, the total tax paid will equal $52,000, whereas if the $100,000 is taken by the owner as wages, the total tax paid would only equal $20,000. The former circumstance would leave the owner with $48,000 available for personal consumption, the latter with $80,000. However, the Internal Revenue Service frequently reviews corporate returns to insure that income is not being paid in wages that should be taxed as corporate income.

In summary, the dividend policy of the small corporation is inextricably intertwined with other mechanisms, such as the payment of wages, in an attempt to minimize taxation.

CONCEPT CHECK

1. *What is the difference between a gross profit margin and a mark-up?*
2. *Why is it not possible for a sole proprietor to extract amounts from the business that can properly be designated as wages?*
3. *What is the purpose of depreciation?*

4. *Why is interest not included along with all of the other expenses of the business?*

5. *Why are the owners of a small business in corporate form better off paying themselves wages (or salaries) than dividends?*

2.3   THE BALANCE SHEET

LAYOUT OF THE BALANCE SHEET

A cash receipts and payments summary for the year does not reveal the financial condition of the corporation. The financial statement that describes the financial condition of the business, what it owns, to whom it owes money, how much the owners have contributed *on one particular date*, is known as the balance sheet.

As was the case with the income statement, the analysis of the balance sheet is essential if the performance of the firm is to be appraised. Not all small businesses present a balance sheet though. For example, where the financial reports are compiled on a cash basis and purely for income-tax purposes, it would be extremely rare to find a balance sheet. In these circumstances the analyst must compile a balance sheet from other information provided by the owners of the business.

Exhibit 2.6 reflects the financial position of Donnelly & Co. at the end of its first year of operations and depicts the following scenario: The Donnellys' contributed $82,000 to start the business and selected the corporate form of ownership. They borrowed $80,000 on a long-term basis from their bank. This loan was secured by a mortgage of their family dwelling plus a debenture over the assets of the corporation plus the personal covenants (i.e., guarantees) of Mr. and Ms. Donnelly. The money was used to buy $120,000 of manufacturing equipment, which generated a profit of $28,000 after allowing for $12,000 depreciation. The Donnellys withdrew nothing for their personal use during the period and lived on the rent paid to them by their older children, who were still living at home. At the end of the year there was $2,000 in the bank, accounts receivable were $60,000, and there was $80,000 in inventory on hand. During the year, the business prepaid $10,000 of next year's expenses. Trade creditors were owed $30,000 and the taxation authorities were owed $3,000. The business had accrued $17,000 in expenses and owed the bank $20,000 in short-term borrowing.

One side of the balance sheet lists assets. On the other side it lists the claims on those assets. These claims comprise external liabilities and owners' equity.

ACCOUNTING FOR THE BALANCE SHEET

Each separate asset, liability, and owners'-equity item reported in the balance sheet is called an **account**. Every account has a name and a dollar amount, which is called its **balance**. For instance:

♦ EXHIBIT 2.6

BALANCE SHEET AS OF DECEMBER 31, 1997

Current assets:			Current liabilities:		
Cash		$ 2,000	Accounts payable		$ 30,000
Accounts receivable		60,000	Accrued expenses		17,000
Inventory		80,000	Notes payable		20,000
Prepaid expenses		10,000	Income tax payable		3,000
Current assets		$152,000	Current liabilities		$ 70,000
Long-term assets:			Long-term liabilities:		
Equipment	$120,000		Bank loan @ 13% interest		80,000
Depreciation	(12,000)				
Net fixed assets		108,000	Owners' equity:		
			Paid-in capital	$82,000	
			Retained earnings	28,000	
			Total owners' equity		110,000
Total assets		$260,000	Total liabilities & owners' equity		$260,000

Name of account	Balance of account
Inventory	$80,000
Bank loan	$20,000

Other dollar amounts shown in the balance sheet are not accounts; they are subtotals or totals from adding (or subtracting) balances of accounts.

The balance sheet is prepared at the close of business on the last day of the income-statement period. If, for example, the income statement is for the year ending June 30, 19XY, the balance sheet is prepared as of midnight on that date (known as the **balance date**). The balances of accounts reported in the balance sheet are the amounts at that precise moment in time. The financial situation of the business is "frozen" for one split second, and captured in the financial statements.

The balance sheet does not show the cash flows into, or out of, assets and liabilities during the period. Only the ending, or closing, balance at the balance date is reported for each account. For example, the business has an ending cash balance of $2,000. One cannot tell the cash receipts and disbursements for the year from the balance sheet.

The manager of any business needs to know the composition of the assets and liabilities of the business. Lenders and investors are interested in the same things. These interested parties need to know the values and quantities of receivables, inventory, and other assets the firm has and the amounts of its debts.

The manager of a business has two basic responsibilities. First, there is the responsibility for keeping the corporation in a position to pay its liabilities as they come due. Second, there is the responsibility for insuring that the firm's assets are being used effectively and efficiently; that is, whether the assets are too large (or too small) relative to the sales volume of the business.

COMPONENTS OF THE BALANCE SHEET

Assets

An asset is something that is owned. Accountants usually divide assets into two groups: those that are of a permanent nature, such as real estate, or plant and machinery, and those that are of a more temporary nature, such as cash or inventory (trading goods) on hand. These two groupings are known as **fixed assets** and **current (or short-term) assets,** respectively. Sometimes it is difficult to decide into which of these groups certain assets fall. To a certain extent, it depends on the nature of the business—what is a permanent asset to one business may well be a temporary asset to another.

Liabilities

A liability is something owed; it is a claim against assets. As with assets, some liabilities are more permanent than others. A mortgage borrowed against real estate is usually regarded as a permanent, or long-term, liability, as is a debenture or bond secured against the assets of a business. On the other hand, monthly trade credit, or accounts payable, is a good example of a more temporary obligation. More permanent forms of liability are usually grouped together as **long-term liabilities** and more temporary liabilities are usually grouped as **current liabilities**.

There are two groups of people with claims against the assets of a business. One is people who are not involved with the ownership of the business, but who have advanced credit in some form to the business. The other is people who *are* involved with the ownership of the business. The former group includes mortgagees, bankers, and those who advance trade credit for supplies to the business. The latter group comprises the owners of the business. They have contributed money to the business and so are owed this money by the business; they are shown in a balance sheet as part of its long-term financing. These two groups of claims are thus divided into the **debt** and **equity** components of the liabilities of the business, the debt being owed to "outsiders," the equity being owed to the owners.

Equity

Equity is also known as **owners' equity, capital,** or **net worth,** and it can arise in two ways. First, equity can arise directly from the capital contributions of the owners of the business. In the case of a non-corporate ownership form, this may occur where the owners personally contribute to the assets of a business. In the case of the corporate ownership form, equity occurs when the owners of the firm buy the shares that the corporate form of business issues. This does not necessarily mean that if an individual buys shares on the stock exchange then that person is contributing to the capital of a business; in that case the person is merely buying someone else's record of contribution—the transaction does not affect the total claims on the business at all.

The second way in which equity can arise is through the retention of profits by the business. Profits are amounts generated above expenses and belong to the owners of a business. Where these (or part of these) are paid out to the owners, they are known as dividends in the case of a corporation or

drawings in the case of a non-corporate ownership form, such as a sole proprietorship or partnership. If only part of the profit of a business is paid out
to its owners, then the undistributed balance (known as retained earnings)
can be regarded as a further contribution to the equity of the business by its
owners.

One point that should be made clear at this stage is that the balance sheet
of a business shows the amount that has been contributed to the business by
the owners. This is not necessarily the same as the value of that contribution.
In other words, cost is not necessarily value. Financial reports do not directly
provide the value of equity, instead they show the recorded historical contributions to equity.

Current Assets

The current assets of a business are assets of a short-term nature that will be
collected during the next accounting period. The major types of current assets include cash, accounts receivable, inventory, marketable securities, and
prepaid expenses.

Cash   The cash item shown in the balance sheet reflects cash in the bank as
well as any petty cash held by the business at balance date.

Accounts Receivable   Whenever a business sells goods or services on credit,
the purchaser's obligation to the business is recorded as **accounts receivable**. The balance in accounts receivable at any time reflects the amount that
people owe the business as a result of its sales.

If customers do not pay their accounts on time, then the business will
have less cash coming in. This has two side-effects: first, interest is foregone
on the money "advanced," and, second, the cash needs of the business must
be funded from other sources, such as borrowing, and this costs the firm interest. However, a trade-off needs to be made by the owners of the business
between refusing to advance credit to potential customers (and losing the
profit that would have been made on those sales) and carrying the cost of the
receivables.

Inventory   The **inventory** account displays the book value of inventory on
hand at balance date. There are three different types of inventory: raw materials, work in process, and finished goods. The valuation of inventory is a
specialized process much debated by accountants. Different methods of valuation will provide different amounts to be reported in the balance sheet,
and because the cost of goods sold is closely related to the valuation of raw
materials inventory, it will also affect the profit reported by any accrual accounting system.

Marketable Securities   One of the problems with cash is that it earns no interest. If a business has large amounts of cash on hand at a particular time, it
makes sense for that business to invest that money temporarily in readily negotiable securities. These are known as **marketable securities**. Marketable securities range from temporary investments in government or corporate debt
to certificates of deposit with a bank. The prime requirement of marketable

securities is that they should be easily negotiable back into cash; in other words, they need to be **near cash**. The most common investments of this type for small businesses in the United States include Treasury bills, bank certificates of deposit, and money-market mutual funds.

Prepaid Expenses Prepaid expenses include all of those payments that have been made in one period that actually cover part of a subsequent period as well. Payment of fire insurance is a good example. In this case, assume that the balance date is December 31 and an insurance payment of $1,000 is paid on July 1. Obviously, one-half of the premium "belongs" to the current year while the other half "belongs" to the next year. Including the total premium in this year's expenses would overstate the costs of running the business this year. Prepaid expenses are a bit like longer term assets, but instead of depreciating them over a number of future periods, in the case of long-term assets, they are generally expensed in the subsequent period. Nevertheless, in some extreme cases, prepaid expenses may have an effect far longer than the subsequent period. For example, a **front-end loan fee** paid for a loan that has a five-year duration would be classed as a prepaid expense but should be **amortized** over the term of the loan, i.e., written off in a similar manner to straight-line depreciation.

Fixed Assets
These assets often are not itemized in the balance sheet, which only reports a summary of all assets. The value of the assets reported is usually a book value, which is calculated by deducting the accumulated depreciation figure from the historical cost of the assets. Accumulated depreciation in turn is computed as all of the depreciation recorded for the assets up to the current balance date.

For example, assume that an asset was purchased three years ago for $10,000 and is being depreciated over five years with straight-line depreciation. Its book value today would be $4,000, as shown in Exhibit 2.7.

Current Liabilities
The current liabilities of the business refer to liabilities that are due to be paid during the next accounting period. This usually means that all liabilities due during the next year, including those portions of any long-term debt that will fall due for payment during the next year will fall into this category. The major subgroups of current liabilities include accounts payable and accrued expenses.

Accounts Payable Accounts payable result from credit purchases by the business. Delaying the payment of accounts payable is one way to create liquidity for a business and it may be costless in the short term (although the firm's reputation may be at stake in the longer term if a formal arrangement to defer payment is not made with the creditor). However, in many cases, discounts are available for prompt payment, and these can be very expensive to ignore (see Chapter 6 for a full discussion on the cost of discounts foregone).

COMPUTATION OF BOOK VALUES

Year	Historical cost	Annual depreciation	Accumulated depreciation	Book value
1	$10,000	$2,000	$2,000	$8,000
2		$2,000	$4,000	$6,000
3		$2,000	$6,000	$4,000

Because the owner of the small business usually finds funding business activities difficult and trade credit is one way of funding those activities, the availability and use of trade credit is critical to the success of the business. As a principle, the payment of trade credit should be slowed down as much as possible (once the discount for prompt payment is lost, the only way to reduce the cost of such borrowing is to lengthen the period over which the money is borrowed) while the collection of accounts receivable should be sped up as much as possible.

Accrued Expenses Accrued expenses is a summary account that records all of those expenses that are due at balance date but for which no invoice has yet been received. These expenses usually comprise those items for which invoices are received on a less-than-monthly basis and may include such items as holiday pay, property taxes (or rates), electricity, interest, and taxation accrued. They can total a significant amount for a business that is labor intensive and that has debt financing that is serviced, for example, on a quarterly basis.

Notes Payable **Notes payable** are securities resulting from the formal short-term borrowing activities of the business. They are often not due for full repayment during the subsequent accounting period, but will be relatively short term in nature. Notes payable are often used to finance inventory purchases.

Short-Term Bank Debt There are two ways in which funding can be advanced from a bank. The first is an advance of the total loan approved. This is usually secured by a personally guaranteed note in the case of a small business. The second way is for the bank to offer a **line of credit** similar to personal credit cards. The business uses the line of credit as needed by drawing against it.

Long-Term Liabilities

The **long-term liabilities** of a business include all of those debts that are not due for a relatively long period of time. The most common form of this financing activity in the case of the small business is the **mortgage** over real estate. Because most small businesses are unable to issue **bonds** or **debentures** in the public market, the lender usually takes collateral security over not

✦ EXHIBIT 2.8

EQUITY: THE SOLE PROPRIETOR

Contributed equity	$50,000
Retained earnings	10,000
Total equity	$60,000

only business assets, such as land, buildings, plant, machinery, and other chattels like inventories, but also over the personal assets of the proprietors of the business, such as their homes.

Chapter 9 will have more to say regarding the sources of finance for the small business. At this stage, however, it is enough to recognize that the balance sheet will record all of the liabilities existing at the balance date.

Owners' Equity

Owners' equity records the financial contributions to the business of its owners. These contributions can be in the form of contributions from outside the business itself or from profits that are generated by the business that its owners elect not to pay out to themselves (in dividends), but rather to reinvest in the business to fund its future activities.

One of the major differences between the smaller business and its larger counterpart is that all of the contributions of the owners to the business may not be reflected in the balance sheet. Initially, many of the assets of the small business may have been "donated" by the owners to the business, and therefore have never been captured by the formal accounting process. Secondly, the contribution of time in the development of a small business is rarely recognized in the recorded equity of such a business. In other words, the accounting reports may understate the correct asset and equity positions of small businesses.

The way in which the equity of the small business is reported in the balance sheet will depend on the ownership structure of the business. Chapter 1 explained how small businesses range in ownership structure from sole proprietorships through partnerships and sub-chapter S corporations to corporations. To exemplify the different ways in which such businesses would display the equity portions of their balance sheets, assume that there has been an initial contribution by the owner or owners of the business of $50,000 and that the business has earned and retained $10,000 in its first year of operations. Equity for a sole proprietorship, a partnership, and a corporation would be shown as in Exhibits 2.8, 2.9, and 2.10 respectively.

Notice that, regardless of the form of ownership, the amount of equity reported is the same: $60,000; and, in the case of the partnership, the contribution of each partner is reported. But, in the case of the corporation, the relative shareholdings of the owners are not reported in the balance sheet.

◆ EXHIBIT 2.9

EQUITY: THE PARTNERSHIP

Contributed equity—Ms. Velasquez	$30,000	
Retained earnings	6,000	
Ending equity		$36,000
Contributed equity—Mr. Kouri	$20,000	
Retained earnings	4,000	
Ending equity		$24,000
Total equity		$60,000

◆ EXHIBIT 2.10

EQUITY: THE CORPORATION

Paid-in capital	$50,000
Retained earnings	10,000
Total equity	$60,000

Retained Earnings One other thing that should be noted is that retained earnings is not an asset. It is a liability. Retained earnings is the accumulation of net income, and net income is not simply money in the bank.

Retained earnings should be considered as that part of the increase in the net worth of the owners' investment in the corporation since the firm began (due to profits having been earned rather than supplied via additional capital inputs). Retained earnings should *never* be regarded as a pool of cash, waiting to be disbursed.

CONCEPT CHECK

1. *Why is equity reported together with the liabilities of a business?*
2. *What is the difference between assets and liabilities?*
3. *In what ways can the owners of a business remove money for their personal consumption? What affects the choice of method?*
4. *Why are retained earnings not an asset?*

SUMMARY

◆ This chapter introduced the structures and components of the income statement and the balance sheet and examined the relationships between them.

✦ The basis of accounting in cash transactions was described, and the need for an accrual process was identified as necessary to correctly determine the net income of a business.

✦ The nature of depreciation and the computation of the book values of assets were outlined.

✦ The structures of reported equity for the sole proprietor, the partnership, and the corporation were summarized, and the nature of retained earnings was discussed.

THE CASE—PART TWO

Dave's banker was a little skeptical about the ability of the corporation to generate enough income from bicycle assembly alone to provide a contribution toward covering overhead costs, but she was prepared to give Dave six months to prove that the business would be profitable. She believed that Dave would need to assemble other items in addition to bicycles in order to survive.

Early in April 1998 (his first year of operations), Dave made an appointment to visit his banker to discuss progress. The banker asked him to provide, among other things, statements of the accounts payable and accounts receivable as of April 15, the date of the appointment. During the visit, she asked Dave to send her the business results after six months in business, and thereafter on a quarterly basis.

The beginning balance sheet for Dave's Bikes & Co. was described in Chapter 1 and is exhibited below in abbreviated form:

DAVE'S BIKES & CO.: BALANCE SHEET AS OF JANUARY 1, 1998

Assets:		Liabilities and equity:	
Cash	$24,000	Bank short-term loan	$ 9,000
Vehicles	24,000	Bank long-term loan	50,000
Plant	41,000	Equity	30,000
Total assets	$89,000	Total liabilities and equity	$89,000

One of Dave's discoveries about the world of accounting and cash flow is that amounts received from customers and amounts paid to suppliers do not always match up, either as to amount, or as to time of payment, and that the determination of periodic profit is not quite as simple as he had at first thought.

The following details applied to Dave's business *for the first six-month period*, to June 30:

✦ ABC Bicycles purchased $40,000 worth of cycles from Dave on January 1 and agreed to pay the bill on March 1.

✦ Alias Industries purchased $20,000 worth of cycles from Dave on February 1 and agreed to pay by May 1.

✦ Barn's Bikes purchased $30,000 of cycles on April 1 and arranged to pay on June 1.

✦ Ladybird Distributors purchased $45,000 of cycles on February 28 and arranged to pay on June 30.

✦ Dave purchased $10,000 worth of materials on January 1 and paid for them on April 1.

✦ He purchased $15,000 worth of materials on March 1 and arranged to pay for them on April 1.

✦ He made another purchase of materials on February 28 worth $18,000 and paid for it on May 31.

✦ Finally, Dave purchased $12,000 worth of materials on April 1 and paid for them on June 1.

Dave's business transactions *for the first nine-month period* (to September 30) of business were:

Cash received from customers for products sold to them	$164,060
Payments made by Dave for shares issued	25,000
Cash received from long-term borrowing	50,000
Sale of surplus plant	1,000
Operating expenses	65,000
Purchase of a motor vehicle	24,000
Purchase of raw materials	107,100
Cash received from short-term borrowing	9,000
Interest paid	3,540
Purchase of plant and equipment	37,000

ASSIGNMENT 2.1

Required

1. If Dave and his parents formed a partnership, what would their beginning balance sheet look like?
2. How would this differ from Dave's Bikes & Co.'s beginning balance sheet shown previously?

ASSIGNMENT 2.2

Required

1. From the information given about Dave's *first six months of business,* identify the amounts of accounts receivable and accounts payable *as of April 15.*
2. Calculate the cash contribution that the sales of bicycles makes toward the payment of other expenses after payment for raw materials *for the six months prior to June 30.* Is this the same as the "actual" profit made by Dave?
3. Prepare a summary of cash receipts and payments *for the nine-month period.* Show whether there has been an increase or decrease in cash for the period.

ASSIGNMENT 2.3

In early 1999, Dave's second year of business, his banker suggests that they meet and examine progress again. She asked Dave to calculate the business's profit for its first year and to provide a statement of assets and liabilities as of December 31, 1998. At this stage Dave hasn't actually prepared his accounts for the year, but Sandy, the firm's accountant, produced the following figures:

Operating expenses	$ 80,000
Income-tax expenses	3,414
Cost of goods sold	125,000
Sales revenue	250,000
Personal drawings (wages to Dave)	20,000

Interest expense	4,720
Cash	111
Bank short-term loan	7,000
Bank long-term loan	50,000
Vehicle (cost)	24,000
Depreciation expense on vehicle	4,800
Plant & equipment (cost)	41,000
Inventory	23,438
Accrued liabilities	9,000
Depreciation expense on equipment & plant	4,100
Accounts receivable	31,250
Accounts payable	11,250
Prepaid expenses	5,000
Paid-up capital	30,000
Income tax payable	683

Dave is always in a hurry because the business is booming. He decides that he is a specialist in assembly and not in accounting, and he asks you to prepare the statements for his banker.

Required

1. Prepare the income statement and balance sheet for Dave's Bikes & Co. for the banker.

ASSIGNMENT 2.4

When Dave first examines the statements that you prepared for his banker, he notices that the profit shown in the income statement is the same figure as the retained earnings figure in the balance sheet. He wonders whether this is because the two figures just happened to be the same amount, or whether the two are, in fact, linked. And, having seen the profit for the year, Dave also wonders whether he could have taken more out of the business for his own personal use.

Required

1. What is the relationship between the profit shown in the income statement and the retained earnings figure in the balance sheet?
2. If Dave wants to take an additional $5,000 out of the corporation for his own use, what will be the effect on retained earnings if he takes it out as:
   a) wages, in the manner that he has done for other drawings, or
   b) a dividend?
3. If Dave draws a dividend of $5,000, where does the money come from? What changes to the balance sheet, other than to retained earnings, will occur?

ASSIGNMENT 2.5

While the business progresses successfully, Dave always believes that it is possible to "fine tune." Dave's accountant, Sandy, is concerned about the firm's liquidity, and that the credit policy that Dave has adopted is too long.

Sandy asks Dave to consider changing his credit policy and Dave agrees that he will do so. As usual though, Dave asks you to determine what effect reducing the average sales credit period will have upon accounts receivable.

From the accounting statements that you have already prepared, you know what the annual sales have been. By examining the debtors' ledger, you are also able to establish the average sales credit period. The relevant figures are:

Annual sales revenue	$250,000
Average sales credit period	five weeks

Required

1. Calculate Dave's average accounts receivable.
2. What is the potential profitability of reducing the current credit policy by two weeks if Dave can earn 6 percent interest on cash deposited in the local bank?
3. What are the disadvantages to Dave of reducing the credit period?

ASSIGNMENT 2.6

Dave discovers that his raw-materials holding period is quite short due to the demand created by the interest in biking sports, and that most of his raw materials inventory turns over within two weeks.

However, knowing he only has one chance to make it in business, Dave is determined to minimize the capital tied up in raw materials. He believes that this will enable him to minimize the idle capital that is not directly involved in generating income.

He notices that the demand for bikes falls over the winter months and that raw materials inventory accumulates during this period. This has the effect of increasing the amount of money tied up in inventory. By cutting back on purchasing bike parts and by being more efficient, he will be able to reduce the overall inventory holding period from two weeks to one week over the winter months.

Dave comes to you to undertake some analysis for him. He wants to know all about inventory holding costs and what he should do in this respect.

Required

1. If the current cost of goods sold is $125,000 per annum, what would be the reduction in the value of raw materials held if the inventory holding period was decreased to one week?
2. What are the advantages and disadvantages of holding
   a) high inventory levels of raw materials?
   b) low inventory levels of raw materials?

ASSIGNMENT 2.7

Dave has always paid for most of his raw materials on delivery, as it seems the appropriate way of doing business. But he notices that many of his clients pay their accounts less frequently.

Sandy mentions purchasing raw materials on credit so that the bank debt can be reduced more quickly since trade credit is free.

When he mentions to his supplier the possibility of trade credit for a $9,000 tire order to be delivered on July 1, he is offered the following terms:

1. Pay $7,950 for the tires at the end of the month, but pay the freight and handling costs of $1,000 once the tires have arrived (cash on delivery) on July 1, or

2. $9,000 to be paid in full, but on a "drip-feed" basis at the start of the next month in the following schedule:

Date	Aug. 1	Sept. 1	Oct. 1	Nov. 1	Dec. 1	Jan. 1
Payment	$4,000	$1,000	$1,000	$1,000	$1,000	$1,000

Required

1. What would you advise Dave regarding any excess cash balances that he might have if any money he has on hand can be deposited in the local bank at 6 percent per annum or 0.5 percent per month (assuming simple interest applies)?

ASSIGNMENT 2.8

On September 15, 1999, Dave calculates that the following expenses were incurred by the corporation:

Telephone rental	$ 96.50
Transportation expense	75.25
Monthly depreciation of office equipment	37.75
Advertising expense to be paid before the end of the month	110.00
Purchase of components for assembly	520.00

Required

1. Calculate the amount of accounts payable at the end of the month that arises from operating expenses. Remember that not all expenditures are operating expenses.
2. Calculate the total accounts payable.

ASSIGNMENT 2.9

The following are a few transactions that took place over the month of February 1999.

✦ Paid January's wages amounting to $4,000.
✦ Purchased $12,000 worth of inventory on credit from Hoban & Co. Import Supplies.
✦ Received $3,500 (accounts receivable) from Drayton Brothers factory.
✦ Paid the quarterly county tax payment of $2,500.
✦ Paid the electricity bill of $2,000.
✦ Paid the telephone bill of $1,000.
✦ Spent fourteen hours talking to Sandy about accounting procedures. She will bill this at the year end together with other accounting costs. She charges $80 per hour.

Dave knows that the total operating expenses for the year were calculated in Assignment 2.3 of this case study to be $100,000. If the average time before Dave pays these accounts is 6.4 weeks, then at any time there is a build-up of unbilled accounts.

Required

1. Do the transactions listed above affect accrued expenses payable?
2. What should the size of accrued expenses payable be for balance-sheet purposes?

ASSIGNMENT 2.10

Dave now has a substantial asset base to his business, and Sandy advises him to insure his assets against loss by fire, theft, or natural disaster.

A complete general insurance policy costs $6,000 per year.

Required

1. Assume the policy is taken out on April 1. What amounts will be included in the balance sheet as part of prepaid expenses when Dave prepares his accounts for the bank (i.e., quarterly as of June 30 and then quarterly thereafter)?
2. Insurance expense is also included in the income statement. What amounts will be included at the quarterly balance dates and under what heading will they be included?

ASSIGNMENT 2.11

When Dave set up the business, he purchased $37,000 worth of plant and equipment. In addition, he transferred $5,000 worth of plant that he already owned into the business. $1,000 worth of plant was found to be surplus to what he required, and was sold early in the year. In addition, the business bought a motor vehicle for $24,000.

For accounting purposes, the plant and equipment is depreciated at the rate of 10 percent per annum, the car at 20 percent (both straight-line).

Required

1. Calculate the depreciation applicable to these assets for three years.

ASSIGNMENT 2.12

Early in 1999 Dave decides to extend his retail business by refurbishing part of the warehouse from which he operates and convert it into a small shop. His accountant has arranged yet another loan with Dave's bank. The loan agreement this time stipulates that the bank will lend $10,000 for a five-year term at 8 percent interest payable quarterly. The bank will begin charging interest on March 14, and will automatically deduct the interest from Dave's current account with the bank on the fifteenth of every quarter from that date. Dave will continue to produce quarterly reports as in the past.

Dave's accountant will record the additions as "furniture and fittings" in the corporation's financial statements and will depreciate them on a straight-line basis at 10%.

Required

1. Calculate the quarterly interest payments made by Dave to the bank.
2. How much interest should Dave accrue at December 31, 1999, for this particular loan?

ASSIGNMENT 2.13

While Dave does not take too much interest in the actual presentation of his corporation's annual accounts, he wonders just how much information, other than the figures themselves, he should disclose. He can see both good and bad sides to full disclosure, but he is not too sure whether he is right.

Required

1. List the advantages that an investor would gain from full disclosure, and the disadvantages of full disclosure that Dave could face as an entrepreneurial owner.

ASSIGNMENT 2.14

The fact that there is a variety of different accounting treatments possible for some transactions ensures that it is often possible to place alternative values on assets and liabilities and to recognize costs and revenues at different times.

Some business friends of Dave told him that he could reduce his income, and therefore his taxation liability, solely by changing his method of accounting. He found all the talk of conservative and liberal accounting policies confusing.

He asks you to look at the following transactions to see whether there is a best way of recording them for accounting purposes.

✦ The corporation purchased a patent for a mountain bike design. Dave wants to charge it as an expense against income rather than charging it over the expected useful life of the patent.

✦ The business has not taken into account any bad debts that are applicable to sales made on credit for the year.

✦ There was a possibility of union action being taken against Dave, and the possibility that some materials could become obsolete during the strike period. Dave wants to expense these materials immediately rather than wait and see.

✦ Dave has been using an attorney in connection with his real-estate proposals. The lawyer told Dave that he would be charged "at some point" for the advice. Dave wants to estimate this charge immediately and include it in his expenses.

✦ Toward the end of the year, Dave re-insures his plant. He pays the new insurance premium and wants to include the full expense this year.

Required

1. For each situation listed above, is Dave being conservative or liberal?

ASSIGNMENT 2.15

Early in his third year of business, Dave purchases a new van. This cost $20,000 for the basic machine, plus $10,000 for special fittings. Dave's banker is getting worried about the corporation's debt level, but Dave's projections look good and Dave's personal assets (which back his personal guarantee) are worth much more than the sum of the bank's exposure to the corporation. The bank advances another $30,000 to the business.

Under normal circumstances, Dave would expense the fittings to the van in the first year, but he has heard a rumor that the corporate tax rate is to be increased from the present level of 30 percent to 50 percent for the year after next. He thinks that there might be some advantage in delaying the expense by capitalizing it and depreciating it. Depreciation on the fittings can be expensed on a straight-line basis at a rate of 10 percent.

Required

1. Advise Dave as to the best option.

SELECTED ADDITIONAL READINGS

Bernstein, L. 1989. *Financial statement analysis: Theory, application, and interpretation.* 4th ed. Homewood, IL: Irwin.

Gordon, G. 1992. *Understanding financial statements.* Cincinnati, OH: South-Western.

Osteryoung, J. S., R. L. Constand, and D. L. Nast. 1982. Financial ratios in large public and small private firms. *Journal of Small Business Management* (July): 35–46.

FINANCIAL STATEMENTS:
CONVENTIONS AND CASH FLOWS

OBJECTIVES

1. *Introduce accounting conventions and the results of their adoption*
2. *Discuss the role of book values in financial performance and introduce alternative measures of value*
3. *Describe the statement of cash flows and other commonly presented reports of a similar nature*

3.1   THE TERMINOLOGY AND PROCESS OF ACCOUNTING

People who have no formal training in accounting often perceive accounting as a large black box of debits and credits, assets and liabilities. These perceptions and the associated difficulties that non-accountants have with accounting are often due to a lack of understanding regarding three areas. First, accounting statements have a very formal structure. Second, the figures that are exhibited in a set of accounting statements are underpinned by a set of accepted conventions that have developed over the past five hundred years. And third, there is a set of commonly used analytical measures that are used to compare and contrast different accounting statements.

To fully comprehend the nature of the information that is available in financial statements, one must be aware of the conventions that determine the nature of accounting information.

THE ACCOUNTING CONVENTIONS

There are a large number of principles, concepts, conventions, and doctrines that underpin the theory of accounting. One need not understand these conventions in order to *read* a financial statement, but should understand the conventions in order to *recognize the limitations of the data provided* in the statement. Some of these accounting conventions are listed below with a brief explanation of their impacts on the reader of a financial statement.

The Accounting-Entity Concept
The **accounting entity** is the entire organization to which the financial statement applies. The entity can be large or small, single or multidivisional.

The Going-Concern Assumption
Accounting assumes that the entity will continue in operation for a period of time sufficient to carry out its commitments. The term **going-concern assumption** means that the accounting process can ignore liquidation values and current market values.

The Accounting-Period Principle
The financial statement provides a periodic measurement of performance (the **accounting-period principle**). The need for a frequent measurement can cause problems with the allocation of expenses that affect the business beyond the period under consideration. Depreciation is one example of how these expenses are allocated between periods.

The Constant-Money Principle
Accounting assumes that money is the common denominator that can be used for financial reporting (the **constant-money principle**). Unfortunately, the relative value of money changes over time due to economic pressures

such as inflation. Under such circumstances, the analyst may not always be able to add, for example, the costs of two assets purchased in different time periods to provide guidance as to the total value of the assets.

The Doctrine of Objectivity

Financial reports ought to be unbiased and independently verifiable. The **doctrine of objectivity** means that all accounting data is provided from the records of actual transactions; it provides reliability in the process of accounting. Two resulting principles arise from this doctrine: the usage of historical cost as a basis for accounting and the matching of revenues with their associated costs.

The Historical-Cost Convention

All of the information included in a financial statement is based on the **historical-cost convention** (the historical cost of a transaction). Allocations of expenses over time are based on the original cost of the expense (or asset) and not on its current value, nor on its current replacement cost. This does cause some analytical problems, but at least the analyst can be confident about the figures on which any analysis is based.

The Matching Principle

The **matching principle** is the basis of accrual accounting. In the previous chapter, the nature of accrual accounting was discussed, but by way of a brief review, assume that a retailer is purchasing a stock item for $50 and selling it for $80. During the period under consideration, one hundred items were purchased and thirty were sold. What was the profit? Obviously $5,000 worth of stock was purchased and only $2,400 has been recorded as sales, but has the business really made a loss of $2,600 when it still has seventy items on hand? After all, it might be able to return these to the supplier and receive a refund of $3,500 (which would turn the loss of $2,600 into a profit of $900). Conventional accounting assumes the latter position. Sales revenues should be matched with the costs of those sales.

Another dimension of the matching process occurs when the acquisition of an asset that will slowly be used up over a number of periods is considered. Is it fair to offset the entire cost of this asset against the profits of the period in which it is purchased, even though there is no doubt that the cash was paid out during the period under consideration? Accounting principles apportion the cost of the asset in some way to the number of periods covered by its lifetime through the depreciation allowance mechanism.

Wherever the matching process is used, there will be a difference between the profit that would have been shown if cash transactions only were considered, and the profit calculated on a matched basis, more commonly known as an "accrual basis."

Accrual-basis accounting is necessary to get a realistic view of the profitability of a business. It is also necessary for the realistic appraisal of the firm's assets, liabilities, and other sources of capital.

CONCEPT CHECK

1. *What are the basic accounting conventions?*
2. *How do these accounting conventions impact the financial statements?*

3.2   THE NATURE OF BOOK VALUES

The **book values** of long-lived assets rarely reflect their market values. They are based on the artificial reduction of an historical cost by a model-determined depreciation allowance. Book values generally do not reflect replacement costs either.

From the perspective of the analyst, the book values of assets are of little importance. While they are of use in the determination of future depreciation (and therefore taxation), they are of little relevance in an appraisal/valuation context. What is of more value in these circumstances is the computation of either the **replacement cost** of the assets, or their **net realizable value**. Replacement costs are of value to the analyst wishing to plan for the maintenance of the productive capacity of the business or for expansion. Net realizable values reflect the **disposal prices** of the assets and are accordingly useful for assessing the **liquidation value** of the firm so that management and investors are aware of the amount of cash that could be generated from the sale of the firm's assets, either as part of a total liquidation, or merely as part of a general asset-replacement plan.

 CONCEPT CHECK

1. *Why is each of the accounting conventions critical in the preparation of financial reports?*
2. *Describe the different ways in which assets can be valued and consider the occasions in which each method would be appropriate.*

3.3   WORKING CAPITAL AND CASH FLOWS

STATEMENT OF CASH FLOWS

The third statement present in the financial statement of most businesses (the first two are the balance sheet and the income statement) summarizes the cash movements of the business. There is no international consensus concerning the presentation of the reporting of cash flows. Some countries prefer to report a **statement of cash flows,** others a **statement of movements in working capital.** Both reports disclose not only the cash generated from operations but also the cash raised from additional financing and the expenditure of cash on additional assets of the business. The difference between the two types of reports results from their fundamentally different viewpoints. In the case of the statement of cash flows, the focus is on cash; in the case of the statement of movements in working capital, the focus is on working capital (of which cash is merely one component).

What would be the outcome if a firm was to offer customers twelve months' free credit? No doubt the level of sales would increase, but what would happen to the cash situation? Despite a potential increase in profit, the increase in sales would not bring in any cash. Business managers must not only earn a profit, but must also convert the profit into cash within a reasonably short time. Over a long time, say ten to fifteen years, the total increase in cash would be very close to the total net income earned. But in any one year, because financial reports are constructed using accrual-based accounting procedures, the cash flow can be considerably less or more than the amount of net income reported in the income statement for that year.

The cash flow statement divides all cash flows into three groups:

1. those associated with operations such as the receipts and disbursements arising from sales;
2. those associated with financing activities, such as the raising and servicing of debt and equity; and
3. those associated with investment activities, such as asset purchases.

First, there are those transactions associated with the operations of the business: the net operating income, income-tax expense, and all of those items that contribute to the net operating income, but which are neither received nor paid in cash. These items include, for example, the increase in accounts receivable that is added to cash sales to provide the true sales revenue for the period. The cash-flow statement reverses this adjustment to show the original cash situation. It also reverses all of the other accruals that the business has made in relation to the calculation of net operating income.

For example, in the case of Donnelly & Co., sales were reported in the income statement as $520,000 while accounts receivable were reported in the balance sheet as increasing by $60,000 (see Exhibits 2.5 and 2.6). Thus $60,000 of the sales revenue was not received in cash during the year; only $460,000 of the sales revenue was received in cash. Similarly, Donnelly's income statement shows that there was an allowance for depreciation of $12,000. This was clearly not a cash item. Exhibit 3.1 summarizes the changes to the net operating income in order to compute the cash flow from operations.

Second, there are those transactions associated with the financing activities of the firm. Additional borrowings and additional equity contributions increase the supply of cash; interest paid and dividend payments made decrease the supply of cash.

Donnelly & Co. borrowed $100,000 during the year and Mr. and Ms. Donnelly contributed $82,000 to the business at its inception. In addition, the income statement shows interest of $13,000 but $2,000 of this was accrued leaving cash interest paid of $11,000. Exhibit 3.2 summarizes these adjustments.

CASH FLOW FROM OPERATIONS

Net operating income		$ 53,000
Less: income tax		(12,000)
		$ 41,000
Plus: increases in current liabilities		
Accounts payable	$30,000	
Accrued expenses	15,000	
Income tax payable	3,000	
		48,000
Plus: depreciation		12,000
Less: increases in current assets		
Accounts receivable	60,000	
Inventory	80,000	
Prepaid expenses	10,000	
		(150,000)
Cash flow from operations		$ (49,000)

CASH FLOW FROM FINANCING

Short-term borrowing		$ 20,000
Long-term borrowing		80,000
Equity contributions		82,000
		$182,000
Interest expense	$(13,000)	
Less: accrued interest	2,000	
		(11,000)
Cash flow from financing		$171,000

Third, there are those transactions that are associated with the investment activities of the business. Assets are sold to supply cash, and cash is disbursed on asset purchases. Donnelly & Co. bought assets for $120,000. This is the cash flow from investing and is depicted in Exhibit 3.3.

The cash-flow statement itself begins with the cash-flow effects of the operations of the firm, and includes all those operating activities (as distinct from financing and investing activities) that contribute directly to making a profit. In other words, "operations" refers to those transactions involved in making sales and incurring expenses. Operating cash flows do *not* include

CASH FLOW FROM INVESTING

Asset purchases	$ 120,000
Cash flow from investing	$ (120,000)

CASH FLOW SUMMARY

Funds used:			
Operating activities (from Exhibit 3.1)		$ (49,000)	
Investing activities (from Exhibit 3.3)		(120,000)	
			$(169,000)
Funds raised:			
Financing activities (from Exhibit 3.2)			
Debt raised	$100,000		
Equity raised	82,000		
		182,000	
Interest paid		(11,000)	
			171,000
Increase (decrease) in cash:			$ 2,000

interest expense, which is regarded as a cost of financing rather than an operating cost. The cash flow from operations is then adjusted to reflect the cash flows associated with financing activities (such as the raising of new debt or equity, the repayment of old debt or the retirement of equity, the payment of interest and dividends, and so on), and with investment activities such as the sales and purchases of old and new assets, respectively.

Exhibit 3.4 summarizes the cash flows associated with Donnelly & Co. The final result reported in the cash-flow statement ($2,000 increase in cash) matches exactly the summary of transactions that the accounting process began with at the start of this chapter. Why then go through this rather complicated process? Because, in many circumstances, the analyst does not have the information that the accounting process began with—often the analyst will have only the most recent income statement and balance sheet to work with. The determination of the cash flow is also critical to the planning process. The information used to prepare cash budgets for future periods is usually extracted from the cash results of prior periods. Also, in a performance appraisal context, the substantial differences that may occur between the cash flows and the income for the period need to be explained.

As with the income statement and the balance sheet, there are many different ways in which the cash flow statement can be organized. The layout used here has been chosen because it integrates well with the income state-

ALTERNATIVE CASH-FLOW STATEMENT LAYOUT

Cash flow from operations:			
Received from customers		$ 460,000	
Paid to suppliers and taxation		(509,000)	
Cash flow from operations			$ (49,000)
Cash flow from investing:			
Purchases of assets			(120,000)
Cash flow from financing:			
Borrowings		100,000	
Capital issues		82,000	
Less: interest paid	$11,000		
Dividends paid	0		
		(11,000)	
Cash flow from financing:			171,000
Increase in cash			$ 2,000

ment and the balance sheet layouts that have already been used in this chapter. An alternative layout is shown in Exhibit 3.5.

THE STATEMENT OF CHANGES IN FINANCIAL POSITION

While many analysts prefer to receive a statement of cash flows, others prefer instead a **statement of changes in financial position**. The statement of changes in financial position reports the sources and uses of **working capital** during the period. Working capital is not cash; it is defined as the difference between current liabilities and current assets. Alternative terms for *working capital* are **net working capital** and (the more confusing term) **funds**.

Exhibit 2.6 depicted Donnelly's balance sheet at the end of its first year. Using that balance sheet, the company's working capital is determined as shown in Exhibit 3.6.

While the cash-flow statement focuses on cash flows, the statement of changes in financial position focuses on working capital.

Exhibit 3.7 shows how the statement of changes in financial position is divided into two parts: the *sources* of working capital, and the *uses* of working capital. Notice in Exhibit 3.7 that the short-term bank borrowing, classified as a current liability in the balance sheet, affects the amount of working capital.

In some countries, the working-capital approach is the more popular way of presenting investment and financing information in external financial reports. However, in other countries, dissatisfaction has been voiced over the

✦ **EXHIBIT 3.6**

WORKING CAPITAL

Current assets:		
Cash	$ 2,000	
Accounts receivable	60,000	
Inventory	80,000	
Prepaid expenses	10,000	
Total		$152,000
Current liabilities:		
Accounts payable	$ 30,000	
Accrued expenses	17,000	
Income tax payable	3,000	
Short-term bank loan	20,000	
Total		(70,000)
Working capital		$ 82,000

statement of changes in financial position and its working-capital focus. Because the cash-flow statement presents the same information in a more appropriate way, professional accounting associations of many countries now require this statement as part of the reporting process. In the United States, the Financial Accounting Standards Board (FASB) Standard 95 mandates that, for fiscal years ending after July 15, 1988, a firm's financial statements must include a statement of cash flows.

HOLDING PERIODS AND CASH FLOW

Delay in the collection of customers' receivables or a deliberate shift in business policy allowing longer credit terms would cause accounts receivable to increase. In these circumstances, additional capital would have to be secured or else the business would have to get by on a smaller cash balance.

Similarly, slowing down the payment of accounts payable and the rate at which inventory is purchased (and held, pending its use in the production of sales) obviously will improve the firm's cash position. Also, because there is usually no interest charge levied on trade credit, it is a very cheap source of financing.

 CONCEPT CHECK

1. *Why is it so important to be able to construct a statement of cash flows from an income statement and a balance sheet?*
2. *Why is net income alone not an adequate predictor of periodic performance?*
3. *Why is the cash-flow statement important in the planning process?*

◆ EXHIBIT 3.7

STATEMENT OF CHANGES IN FINANCIAL POSITION

Sources of working capital:		
Operating income	$ 53,000	
Less: income tax expense	(12,000)	
Less: interest expense	(13,000)	
Net income as per income statement	$ 28,000	
Plus: depreciation expense	12,000	
Working capital provided from net income	$ 40,000	
Long-term borrowing	80,000	
Stock issue	82,000	
Total sources of working capital		$ 202,000
Uses of working capital:		
Cash dividends	- 0 -	
Purchases of long-term assets	120,000	
Total uses of working capital		(120,000)
Increase of working capital during the year		$ 82,000

Changes in current assets and current liabilities during the year:

	Working capital
Cash	$ 2,000
Accounts receivable	60,000
Inventory	80,000
Prepaid expenses	10,000
Accounts payable	(30,000)
Accrued expenses	(17,000)
Income tax payable	(3,000)
Short-term bank loan	(20,000)
	$ 82,000

4. *What are the fundamental differences between the statement of cash flows, the statement of working capital, and the statement of changes in financial position?*

3.4 OTHER STATEMENTS

NOTES TO THE ACCOUNTS

The fourth statement present in the financial statements of certain classes of companies helps the reader to understand the conventions used in the preparation of the statement and explains how some of the more important figures were calculated. The notes to the accounts are very important from the perspective of the financial analyst because they often disclose items such as the contingent liabilities associated with leases and debt repayments that the analyst needs for use in future cash-flow projections.

The financial statements of a sole proprietorship, a partnership, and most small corporations will contain minimal notes. The note that is most prevalently disclosed relates to the basis for the valuation of inventory and thus the determination of the cost of goods sold.

THE AUDITOR'S OPINION

The fifth item present in a financial statement is that of an independent person who provides an opinion concerning whether, in that person's opinion, the financial report was prepared in a proper fashion and accurately represents the true state of affairs of the business. The auditor's opinion should always be read carefully. It is *not* a guarantee that the firm is doing well. Rather, it merely confirms (or not, as the case may be) that proper accounting procedures were followed in the preparation of the accounting statement that is attached.

The majority of small businesses rarely furnish an auditor's opinion. However, in special circumstances, such as might pertain in the event of the potential sale of a business, an external audit may be undertaken. An example of an auditor's opinion was depicted in Exhibit 2.1 of the previous chapter.

SUMMARY

+ This chapter introduced the assumptions and conventions that underpin the construction of the financial statements of a business.
+ The structure and components of the cash-flow statement were identified and examined.
+ Alternatives to the cash-flow statement, such as the statement of working capital and the statement of changes in financial position, were described and compared to the cash-flow statement.
+ Deficiencies in the ability to interpret these statements (from a performance-analysis viewpoint), such as the use of historical cost and book values in the financial statements, were identified.
+ While the focus on net income was not played down, the importance of cash flow, especially in the case of the small business, was reinforced consistently.

THE CASE—PART THREE

When Dave looked at his income statement and balance sheet, he was surprised to see that the reported net income was not reflected in his bank account. The difference sparked his curiosity and he became very interested in how a reported profit does not necessarily increase the cash in the bank because, while he knows that the business is profitable, he is just a little worried that the cash levels might continue to decrease.

ASSIGNMENT 3.1

At the end of Dave's first year, he decides to prepare a statement of cash flows based on his income statement and balance sheet (see Assignment 2.3 of the case study in Chapter 2).

Required

1. Assume that the total taxes accrued for 1998 ($2,731) was paid and calculate the cash flow for the operations of the business for the year.

ASSIGNMENT 3.2

When you provide Dave with your calculation of the cash flows arising from operations, he looks at it briefly, and then realizes that he does not actually have that amount of cash in the bank. He apologizes for not instructing you more accurately. He also tells you that he paid $2,000 toward the loan from the bank (i.e., reduced the amount owed to $7,000).

Required

1. Prepare a full cash-flow statement for 1998.

ASSIGNMENT 3.3

Dave's second year in business went like a charm. In addition to the successful opening of his shop, early in the year he opened a second plant. The equipment for this cost $38,000 and was financed by increasing the current account advance with the bank, which took security over the new plant. By the end of 1999, Dave has managed to reduce the advance to $30,000. His income statement and balance sheet for 1999 are shown below.

Required

1. Identify the changes in the balance sheets of the first and second years.
2. If cash on hand at the start of the second year was $111 and income tax payable was $683 (as in Assignment 3.1), provide Dave with a statement of cash flows for the second year.

INCOME STATEMENT FOR THE YEAR ENDING DECEMBER 31, 1999

Sales revenue	$ 337,500
Cost of goods sold	(172,125)
Gross profit	165,375
Operating expense	(125,000)
Depreciation expense	(12,330)
Operating income	28,045
Interest expense	(4,554)
Earnings before tax	23,491
Income tax expense	(7,048)
Net income	$ 16,443

BALANCE SHEET AS OF DECEMBER 31, 1999

Assets			Liabilities and Owners' Equity		
Cash		$ 79	Accounts payable		$ 14,856
Accounts receivable		42,188	Accrued expenses		11,886
Inventory		32,273	Income Tax payable		1,409
Prepaid expenses		6,250	Bank loan		30,000
Current assets		$ 80,790	Current liabilities		$ 58,151
Vehicle	$ 24,000		Term loan		60,000
Less: depreciation	(8,640)	15,360	Total liabilities		$118,151
Plant & equipment	79,000		Paid-in capital	$ 30,000	
Less: depreciation	(11,590)	67,410	Retained earnings	24,409	
			Owners' equity		54,409
Other fixed assets	10,000				
Less: depreciation	(1,000)	9,000			
Total assets		$172,560	Total liabilities & owner's equity		$172,560

ASSIGNMENT 3.4

As Dave enters his third year of operations, his overseas suppliers become very interested in pursuing a closer relationship with their successful local distributor. Their bank asks for a statement of changes in financial position.

Required

1. Adapt your answer to Assignment 3.3 of this case study to construct a statement of cash flows for the company for 1999 and provide Dave with the required statement of changes in financial position.

SELECTED ADDITIONAL READINGS

The readings suggested in Chapter 2 apply equally well to this chapter.

PERFORMANCE ANALYSIS

OBJECTIVES

1. *Describe the performance indicators that arise from the analysis of the financial reports of the business*
2. *Define trend, comparable, and structural analyses*
3. *Define and describe the use of short-term solvency ratios, activity ratios, financial leverage, and profitability ratios*
4. *Introduce some of the relationships that can be applied in the valuation of the private firm*
5. *Introduce the concept of financial leverage and describe the circumstances under which it is favorable*
6. *Introduce the concept of risk in the context of its business and financial components*

4.1 MEASURING PERFORMANCE

Now that we understand just what the financial statements of a business contain, it is possible to consider the use of financial statements in measuring the performance of the business, its progress over time, and its comparability with other similar firms. The determination of relevant ratios from the information provided in a financial report enables the comparison of businesses that differ widely in orientation, size, and scale.

The following section briefly explains the basic financial-statement ratios used by analysts, creditors, and investors and uses the case of Donnelly & Co. as a basis for analysis. The income statement and balance sheet for Donnelly & Co. is reproduced in Exhibit 4.1. The ratios are the basic "scores" by which managers are judged by the suppliers of capital to the businesses. Among other uses, ratios determine the borrowing capacity of the business.

Financial statements are needed to demonstrate whether or not the business is performing as well as it should be. They are part of the control mechanism of any business organization. However, financial statements, in and of themselves, disclose very little without further analysis. Without determining relationships within a report and comparing them with other information, the analyst cannot decide whether the situation, as reported, is good or bad. Even a loss may not be "bad" if it is known, for example, that every other business in the economy did worse and that next year is likely to be a boom year. Alternatively, if the loss was caused by some planned but extraordinary event, or if the loss was only a fraction of the previous period's, the firm's performance might not be considered to be poor.

Financial statements disclose three things. The income statement reports the profit for the accounting period. The balance sheet reports the financial condition of the firm at the *end* of the period. The statement of cash flows exhibits the liquidity of the firm. However, this is not enough. It is necessary to compare items or groups of items in the financial statement with similar items or groups of items from either different time periods (known as **trend analysis**), different businesses, or an industry analysis before the level of performance of the business can be gauged.

This should not be construed as meaning that the analyst must always have another financial statement handy to make comparisons; there are also relationships within a single financial statement that can cast insight on the performance of the business. **Structural analysis** is the process of examining relationships within a report and determining the relative importance of particular items or groups of items as compared to the business as a whole. Structural analysis can help the management of a business plan to defend against threats or to take advantage of opportunities. It can expose the sensitivity of a business to a change in some critical area.

In addition to the objective measures and ratios of business performance related to the financial statement, which could be used by the management

♦ **EXHIBIT 4.1**

DONNELLY & CO. FINANCIAL STATEMENTS FOR ITS FIRST YEAR OF BUSINESS

INCOME STATEMENT FOR THE YEAR

Sales revenue		$520,000
Cost of goods sold		(325,000)
Gross profit		$195,000
Operating expenses	$130,000	
Depreciation expense	12,000	(142,000)
Net operating income		$ 53,000
Interest expense		(13,000)
Earnings before tax		$ 40,000
Income tax expense		(12,000)
Net income		$ 28,000

BALANCE SHEET AT END OF YEAR

Current assets:			*Current liabilities:*		
Cash	$ 2,000		Accounts payable		$ 30,000
Accounts receivable	60,000		Accrued expenses		17,000
Inventory	80,000		Income tax payable		3,000
Prepaid expenses	10,000		Bank loan at 13%		20,000
Total current assets		$152,000	Total current liabilities		$ 70,000
			Long-term liabilities:		
			Long-term bank loan at 13%		80,000
Fixed assets:			Total liabilities		$150,000
Machinery, equipment					
Furniture and fixtures	$120,000		*Shareholders' equity:*		
Accumulated depreciation	(12,000)		Paid-in capital	$82,000	
Book value		108,000	Retained earnings	28,000	
			Total shareholders' equity		110,000
Total assets		$260,000	Total liabilities and shareholders' equity		$260,000

of a business to guide their future plans, investors use the information provided by the financial statement to develop their perceptions of the performance of the business, its risk, and its worth.

 CONCEPT CHECK

1. *Why are financial statements needed?*
2. *What basic types of comparisons can be made using the information provided in financial statements?*

4.2 STRUCTURAL, COMPARABLE, AND TREND ANALYSIS

STRUCTURAL ANALYSIS: COMMON-SIZE STATEMENTS

Structural analysis involves the comparison of items, or groups of items, within a single financial statement. Often this type of analysis requires more physical information about the business than is available in the financial statement alone.

Two types of structural analysis exist. First, there are those ratios that can be directly deduced from the financial report itself, such as all of those relationships based on the proportion of sales revenue (or on the proportion of total assets) represented by an individual item. This is called a **common-size statement.** Exhibit 4.2 depicts the structural relationships that can be deduced from the common-size financial reports of Donnelly & Co. This type of analysis can provide the basis for future planning and budgeting, and can also be used to show the sensitivity of an item to a change in sales. For example, if all of the relationships remain the same, a $100,000 increase in sales would result in a $10,200 increase in operating earnings (10.2 percent of $100,000). It can also be used as a control device to check that costs are not getting out of line.

The second type of structural analysis is one that relies on additional information about the firm. Such input/output relationships as sales per salesperson, labor hours per dollar of sales, inventory turnover, and interest coverage assist management with their planning and control functions.

COMPARABLE ANALYSIS

Comparable analysis involves the comparison of items, or groups of items, in the financial statements of different organizations. This type of analysis endeavors to answer the question: How good is this particular firm in comparison to other firms in the industry? Managers must be responsive to their competition and should be prepared to take advantage of the opportunities that arise when they recognize some advantage that they have over others. Naturally, this form of ratio analysis is more meaningful when the ratios of one business are compared with similarly sized firms in similar industries.

TREND ANALYSIS

Trend analysis is the comparison of items, or groups of items, within the same organization's financial reports for different time periods. Cartoons of offices invariably show a trend chart on the wall. The early recognition of a trend has assisted many businesses to either capitalize on good performance, or conversely, to take appropriate action over poor performance.

"YES KRAUSE, I'D QUIT THIS JOB IN A SEC IF IT WASN'T FOR THE PRESTIGE, POWER AND MONEY."

© 1996 Lo Linhert

◆ EXHIBIT 4.2

STRUCTURAL ANALYSIS: DONNELLY & CO. (COMMON-SIZE STATEMENT)

			Percent of sales
Sales revenue		$520,000	100.0%
Cost of goods sold		(325,000)	62.5%
Gross profit		$195,000	37.5%
Operating expenses	$130,000		
Depreciation expense	12,000		
		(142,000)	27.3%
Operating earnings		$ 53,000	10.2%
Interest expense		(13,000)	2.5%
Earnings before tax		$ 40,000	7.7%
Income tax expense		(12,000)	2.3%
Net income		$ 28,000	5.4%

Four categories of performance measures exist within these types of analyses. They are:

1. Short-term solvency (liquidity)—ability of the business to meet its short-term financial obligations
2. Activity (efficiency)—ability of the firm to control its investment in assets
3. Financial structure (leverage)—financial stability and reliance on debt
4. Profitability—profit performance of the firm

Financial statements provide the base data from which these measures can be determined. They do not provide the strategies that a firm must follow, but they do provide the information from which appropriate strategies can be formulated.

CONCEPT CHECK

1. *What are common-size statements and what is their purpose?*
2. *Discuss comparable and trend analyses and suggest when you would use each.*

4.3 SHORT-TERM SOLVENCY (LIQUIDITY) RATIOS

THE CURRENT RATIO

The **current ratio** suggests to the analyst the ability of the firm to meet its short- and medium-term commitments. It reflects the number of times the current liabilities of the business are covered by its current assets. The higher the current ratio, the more liquid a firm is. The current ratio for Donnelly & Co. can be computed as shown below.

$$\text{Current ratio} = \frac{\text{total current assets}}{\text{total current liabilities}}$$

$$= \frac{\$152,000}{\$70,000} = 2.17$$

Some current assets are very liquid (easily sold) and some are not. Within the current assets category, one can find a wide range of assets, both in terms of value stability, and in terms of their liquidity. In other words, there are differences in the *quality* of current assets. Obviously, in selecting an appropriate current ratio for a business, the quality of the current assets must be considered.

THE ACID-TEST (QUICK) RATIO

The **quick ratio** (or **acid-test ratio**) represents the ability of the business to meet its immediate obligations as they fall due and reflects a much shorter time horizon than the current ratio. The lower the acid-test ratio, the more probable it is that the firm will have liquidity problems. The quick ratio for Donnelly & Co. can be calculated as shown below.

$$\text{Quick ratio} = \frac{\text{cash} + \text{marketable securities} + \text{accounts receivable}}{\text{current liabilities}}$$

$$= \frac{\$2,000 + \$60,000}{\$70,000} = 0.89$$

This ratio, .89, is below an industry guideline of 1.0 and signals to the owners of the business that they face a potential liquidity problem unless they can restore the balance. One simple way of doing this would be to replace some of the short-term bank debt with a more permanent source of financing, known as **re-financing.** Of course, the owners may decide to do nothing at all because the problem is over a short term only—the improved cash flow (and/or profitability) of the following period might correct the problem without the need to do anything formal at all. This is a good example of how ratio analysis can identify a potential problem and provide a warning to the owner and the analyst.

CONCEPT CHECK

1. *Why is it necessary to analyze the short-term solvency of a business?*
2. *Which ratios can be used to analyze the short-term solvency of a business, and how do they differ?*

4.4 ACTIVITY (EFFICIENCY) RATIOS

One of the ways that analysts target problems and gauge efficiency is to examine closely the effectiveness of the firm's asset management. Turnover ratios provide information about the management of these items. These ratios will be introduced in this chapter and then revisited later in Chapter 6 when the management of working capital is discussed in more depth. At this stage, though, the intention is merely to explain the calculation of the ratios themselves.

Because Donnelly & Co. is in its first year of operation, the following activity measures are based on the premise that the end-of-year balance sheet items represent the average of activity for the whole year. When, for example, accounts receivable is used as a denominator, the figure used should really be the "average" accounts receivable (i.e., the beginning and ending receivables added together, and divided by 2). If this premise was not assumed, some nonsensical answers would occur, due to the beginning balances being zero.

ACCOUNTS RECEIVABLE TURNOVER

The accounts receivable turnover for Donnelly & Co. is computed as:[1]

$$\text{Accounts receivable turnover} = \frac{\$520{,}000 \text{ sales revenue for the year}}{\$60{,}000 \text{ accounts receivable}} = 8.67$$

In other words, accounts receivable are collected or "turned over" 8.67 times per year. If the **accounts receivable turnover** ratio is high, the firm is generally using its accounts receivable effectively in generating sales. If the ratio is low, the firm is generally not using the asset (accounts receivable) effectively; it should reduce the size of the asset by tightening credit policy. Unfortunately, this strategy might cause a further decrease in the level of sales, thus compounding the inefficiency. In addition, a high account receivable turnover does not always indicate that a firm is utilizing its accounts receivable effectively, as this will vary between industries and will depend on how aggressive the firm is in extending credit.

The value of the accounts receivable turnover ratio will directly reflect the firm's credit policy. A liberal credit policy will have the effect of increasing the size of accounts receivable (and probably sales), other things being equal.

The **average collection period** (also known as the **average sales credit period**) for Donnelly & Co. is forty-two days and is calculated as follows.

$$\text{Average collection period} = \frac{365 \text{ days}}{\text{accounts receivable turnover ratio}}$$

$$= \frac{365}{8.67} = 42 \text{ days}$$

This is the average length of time for which the business extends credit to its customers. One commonly used rule of thumb is that the average collection period should not be more than ten days in excess of the normal credit period. So, if the usual terms of credit are thirty days, the average collection period should not exceed forty days (or approximately six weeks). Donnelly & Co. is right on target with forty-two days.

---

[1]Note that the denominator in this equation *should be* expressed as the *average* of the beginning and ending figures, which is more representative of the average for the period. However, in this case, only one year's financial statements are presented and thus the closing figure is used. It should also be noted that, in the case of the first year of operation of a business (in which the beginning figure is zero), it is customary to apply the closing figure only, the assumption being that the beginning and ending figures would have been equal.

What would happen if Donnelly & Co. could increase its accounts receivable turnover ratio to 10.4 times per year without losing any sales? The average collection period can now be computed as thirty-five days, as shown below.

$$\text{Average collection period} = \frac{365 \text{ days}}{\text{accounts receivable turnover ratio}}$$

$$= \frac{365}{10.4} = 35 \text{ days}$$

What would be the advantage of increasing the accounts receivable turnover ratio? The firm would collect the cash owed to it more quickly.

Note that one week's receivables for Donnelly & Co. is $10,000. Speeding up the collection process will reduce the accounts receivable by $10,000 and increase the cash on hand by a like amount. This cash can then be used for other productive purposes; it could be used to repay debt and therefore permanently reduce the amount of interest the firm is paying.

INVENTORY TURNOVER

The **inventory turnover** for Donnelly & Co. is calculated as:[2]

$$\text{Inventory turnover} = \frac{\$325,000 \text{ cost of goods sold for the year}}{\$80,000 \text{ inventory}} = 4.06$$

Donnelly & Co.'s inventory is "turned over" approximately four times per year.

Inventory turnover is greatly affected by the nature of the business. A property-development business will have a much slower turnover than a retail grocery store. Discount chain-stores have a much faster turnover than their specialty counterparts.

The calculation of inventory turnover is also obviously affected by the basis of valuation of inventory.

Donnelly & Co.'s **average inventory holding period** can be estimated as being ninety days. This is the average length of time the business takes to receive, process, and ship its inventory.

$$\text{Average inventory holding period} = \frac{365 \text{ days}}{\text{inventory turnover ratio}}$$

$$= \frac{365}{4.06} = 90 \text{ days}$$

---

[2]See footnote 1.

What would happen if Donnelly & Co. could increase its inventory turnover to five times per year? In this circumstance, the business would save seventeen days' worth of cost of goods sold (the new holding period would be only seventy-three days), or $15,137.

$$\frac{\$325,000}{365} \times 17 = \$15,137$$

At 13 percent interest being paid on its debt, this would save the business $1,968 in interest payments (13 percent of $15,137).

Accounts Payable Turnover

The **accounts payable turnover** for the firm is obviously closely related to the accounts receivable turnover of the supplier, and is also related to the rates at which inventory is used and operating expenses are committed. The relevant rates for Donnelly & Co. are:

Average inventory usage	$6,250 per week
Average operating expenses	$2,500 per week
Total expenses	$8,750 per week

Accounts payable of $30,000 therefore represents 3.4 weeks' worth of expenses ($30,000 divided by $8,750).

Using similar information from the financial statements, the accounts payable turnover can also be calculated:[3]

$$\frac{\text{Cost of goods sold} + \text{operating expenses}}{\text{Accounts payable}} = \frac{\$455,000}{\$30,000} = 15.2 \text{ times}$$

In other words, Donnelly & Co.'s accounts payable is turned over approximately fifteen times per year.

The management of accounts payable can be considered to be the reverse of the accounts receivable. The aim with accounts payable is to *extend* the payment period and to increase the turnover. What would happen if the company could increase its accounts payable turnover to thirteen times per year?

The **average purchase credit period** can be computed as:

$$\text{Average purchase credit period} = \frac{365 \text{ days}}{\text{accounts payable turnover}}$$

$$= \frac{365}{13.0} = 28 \text{ days}$$

Now, twenty-eight days or four weeks of payables at $8,750 per week totals $43,750—an increase of $13,750 over the existing level of accounts

[3]See footnote 1.

payable. At 13 percent interest being paid on its debt, this would save the business $650 in interest payments (13 percent multiplied by $5000).

One way of achieving this higher level of payables is to pay labor on a monthly basis, rather than on a weekly or bi-weekly basis. Because wage payments are delayed, labor is effectively lending money on an interest-free basis to the business and, therefore, in an opportunity sense at least, is paying (at least approximately) what the company is earning in interest.

ASSET TURNOVER

The **asset turnover ratio** reflects the inherent ability of the firm to use its assets in the generation of sales. The higher the asset turnover, the more effective the use of the firm's asset in generating sales; and sales are the "cornerstone of profits." The asset turnover ratio for Donnelly & Co. is:[4]

$$\text{Asset turnover ratio} = \frac{\text{sales revenue}}{\text{total assets}} = \frac{\$520,000}{\$260,000} = 2$$

It should be noted that, while the denominator in this case represents the book value of the assets of the business, a far more meaningful result would be gained if the total asset value was, in fact, the market value of the assets of the firm. This fact applies to all of the other ratios that will be examined in the rest of this chapter. For the purposes of demonstrating the ratios themselves, however, the book value of the firm's assets will be used as a surrogate for their market value. This assumption is not entirely unrealistic; one of the great difficulties faced by any analyst of a small business is the determination of market value, and many analysts continue to use book values of assets where they appear to be similar to market values. Preferably though, market values should always be used.

 CONCEPT CHECK

1. *What is the use of computing activity ratios?*
2. *Turnover ratios are closely related to holding periods. Describe the mathematical relationship between the two types of computations, and distinguish between their uses.*

4.5 FINANCIAL LEVERAGE RATIOS

Financial-leverage ratios provide the basis for the analysis of the capital structure of the firm. They measure the extent to which the firm relies on debt as a source of financing.

---

[4]See footnote 1.

If a firm has too much debt, it risks insolvency, financial distress, and possible bankruptcy. If it has too little debt, it is probably not growing as fast as it could if it borrowed money to finance profitable expansion, and is probably not taking advantage of all the profitable opportunities offered in its relevant industry.

Borrowing money is not a bad thing. Borrowing too much, too expensively, is bad. In most business environments, it is usually possible to find assets that promise with relative safety to yield amounts that exceed the cost of debt. If a business doesn't have the spare cash to invest in these opportunities, then it must either pass them by or must borrow to finance the acquisition. If the return exceeds the cost of borrowing (with relative safety), then the owners of the firm will be far better off by borrowing and investing than by doing nothing.

There are two groups of financial-leverage ratios. The first deals with the structure of the balance sheet, while the second deals with numbers that measure the firm's ability to service debt and are related to the income statement. Examples of the former include the debt-to-assets ratio and the debt-to-equity ratio. The interest coverage ratio provides an example of the latter.

Debt-to-Assets Ratio

The **debt-to-assets ratio** is a measure of a firm's debt level. It is also known as the **debt ratio** or the **leverage ratio.** Donnelly & Co.'s debt-to-assets ratio is computed as follows:[5]

$$\text{Debt-to-assets ratio} = \frac{\text{total liabilities}}{\text{total assets}}$$

$$= \frac{\$150,000}{\$260,000} = 0.58$$

This means that 58 percent of the total financing of the firm has been undertaken by borrowing; and, of course, that 42 percent has been financed from equity.

Debt-to-Equity Ratio

There are many different forms of leverage ratio. While the debt-to-assets ratio is the favorite of finance academics, bankers tend to use an alternative, known as the **debt-to-equity** (or just debt:equity) **ratio**. Other alternatives,

---

[5]It should be noted that, in this case, and with other cases of financial leverage ratios, the debt-to-assets ratio is a measurement of a financial situation *at a point in time*. Therefore, there is no need to use the average of the beginning and ending figures.

such as the **net-worth ratio** (equity divided by assets), also known as the **ownership ratio,** are commonly used.

The debt-to-equity ratio for Donnelly & Co. is as follows and shows that for every dollar of equity in the business, Donnelly & Co. has borrowed $1.36.

$$\text{Debt-to-equity ratio} = \frac{\text{total liabilities}}{\text{total equity}}$$

$$= \frac{\$150,000}{\$110,000} = 1.36$$

TIMES INTEREST EARNED (INTEREST COVERAGE) RATIO

The **interest coverage ratio** is an example of the second type of financial-leverage ratio (that is, it is related to the income statement). It tells an analyst how many times the net operating income of a firm covers its interest expense. For Donnelly & Co., this is:

$$\text{Interest coverage ratio} = \frac{\text{earnings before interest and tax}}{\text{interest expense}}$$

$$= \frac{\$53,000}{\$13,000} = 4.1$$

In other words, interest expense will account for approximately one-fourth of the operating income of the business. This ratio is very important for creditors to see the safety of their loan. Obviously, the higher this ratio is, the less risk they face.

Ways to adjust the interest coverage ratio include adjusting the numerator (adding back depreciation), and the denominator (adding debt principal repayments and/or lease rentals). For example:

$$\text{Interest coverage} = \frac{\text{EBIT} + \text{depreciation}}{\text{interest expense}}$$

$$\text{Interest coverage} = \frac{\text{EBIT}}{\text{interest expense} + \text{debt principal repayments}}$$

$$\text{Interest coverage} = \frac{\text{EBIT} + \text{depreciation}}{\text{interest} + \text{debt principal payments} + \text{lease rentals}}$$

The fact that the same ratio can be calculated in so many different ways can lead to obvious confusion. Each of these ratio computations suits a different circumstance, and all may be used by the same analyst. It always pays to check which version is being applied.

CONCEPT CHECK

1. *Leverage ratios include both those of a structural nature and those of a coverage nature. Specify which ratios are structural and which are coverage and distinguish between their uses.*
2. *Determine the relationship between the debt-to-asset ratio and the debt-to-equity ratio.*

4.6 PROFITABILITY RATIOS

Equity investors take the risk of whether the business can earn a profit and sustain its profit performance over the years. The value of their shares depends on the profitmaking record and potential of the business measured by calculating the business's **profitability ratios**.

RETURN ON EQUITY

Donnelly & Co.'s **return on equity ratio** is calculated as follows:[6]

$$\text{Return on equity} = \frac{\text{net income}}{\text{total shareholders' equity}}$$

$$= \frac{\$28,000}{\$110,000} = 25.5\%$$

Return on equity (ROE) is one of a number of ways of reporting the **return on investment (ROI)**. The word *return* refers to the gain made, and the word *investment* refers to the amount invested. For example, a $100,000 annual net income relative to $250,000 shareholders' capital base is very good, and represents a 40 percent return on equity. $100,000 annual net income relative to $2,500,000 shareholders' capital base is very poor at 4 percent.

In some circumstances, ROE will be calculated on the basis of pre-tax earnings. For Donnelly & Co., the pre-tax earnings (from Exhibit 4.1) is $40,000 and the pre-tax ROE (or **gross ROE**) is then 36.4 percent ($110,000 divided by $40,000). This figure is more directly comparable with the cost of borrowing, which is always quoted on a pre-tax basis.

Financial analysis often requires that the analyst convert pre-tax to after-tax measures and vice-versa:

pre-tax measure (1 − tax rate) = after-tax measure

---

[6]The figure used in the denominator of profitability ratios is the ending figure because one only has a single set of statements from which to work. It is a point of contention as to whether the figure should reflect the beginning figure, or the average of the beginning and ending figures. It is customary to apply the average figure.

or,

$$\text{pre-tax measure} = \frac{\text{after-tax measure}}{(1 - \text{tax rate})}$$

For example, if after-tax ROE is 25.5 percent, and the tax rate is 30 percent, then

$$(1 - \text{tax rate}) = 70\%$$

and

$$\text{pre-tax ROE} = \frac{25.5\%}{70\%} = 36.4\%$$

While, for the purposes of exposition, Donnelly & Co. pays tax at a rate of 30 percent, in reality, firms pay tax at widely varying rates, depending on a host of circumstances relating to the regulation of taxation. Under normal circumstances, an analyst can determine the appropriate tax rate directly from the financial report by dividing the tax expense by the earnings-before-tax figure.

$$\text{Tax rate} = \frac{\text{income-tax expense}}{\text{earnings before tax}}$$

RETURN ON ASSETS

Return on assets (ROA) is another very important return on investment (ROI) measure. Using Donnelly & Co. as an example, it is calculated as follows:[7]

$$\text{Return on assets} = \frac{\text{net income}}{\text{total assets}} = \frac{\$28,000}{\$260,000} = 10.8\%$$

This measure tells us that the Donnelly & Co. earned almost eleven cents after tax on each dollar invested in assets. While it is an adequate method of calculation for simple comparisons between businesses, *this measure of ROA is not at all suitable* for the type of analysis that managers and others with a real interest in the efficiency of the firm require. The problem with this measure is that, while the numerator reflects the gain made by the owners of the business, the denominator reflects the assets that are funded by both debtholders and equityholders. As seen later in this chapter, depending on the source and cost of these funds, the measure may not tell quite all that the analyst needs to know. Nevertheless, it is a commonly used "quick and dirty" measure of performance.

The **gross ROA** is the measure that is needed for a *proper* financial analysis. The analyst cannot establish the gross ROA directly from the ROA

---

[7]See footnote 6.

because it entails more than merely adjusting for tax—one must also adjust for interest expense, so it is easier to recalculate the gross ROA directly from the financial statements.

The gross ROA is the relationship between the productive assets of the business and the amount that they earn irrespective of financing considerations. It is the quotient of the net operating income, also known as earnings before interest and tax (EBIT), and the asset base. For Donnelly & Co., the gross ROA is calculated as follows:[8]

$$\text{Gross ROA} = \frac{\text{EBIT}}{\text{assets}} = \frac{\$53,000}{\$260,000} = 20.4\%$$

The gross ROA is a very important figure in financial management for two reasons: first, it indicates the operating performance of the firm by representing the earning power of the assets of the firm irrespective of financial-leverage considerations. Second, it can be compared directly with the annual interest rate on borrowed funds.

The **net ROA** is another equally useful measure. It is calculated by first computing the **after-tax EBIT**:

$$\text{After-tax EBIT} = \text{EBIT}(1 - \text{tax rate})$$

Then the net ROA is calculated by dividing this figure by the assets of the business:[9]

$$\text{Net ROA} = \frac{\text{EBIT}(1 - t)}{\text{assets}} = \frac{\$53,000(0.7)}{\$260,000} = 14.3\%$$

Notice that one could also move directly from the gross ROA to the net ROA merely by multiplying gross ROA by $(1 - t)$:

$$\text{Gross ROA}(1 - t) = 20.4\%(0.7) = 14.3\%$$

The only reason for calculating the ROA in both gross and net form, is that the analyst must often compare these figures with the yield on other investments, which in turn could be either before-tax or after-tax. For example, we know that the bank interest rate for Donnelly & Co. is 13 percent pre-tax. The assets of Donnelly & Co. earn 20.4 percent pre-tax. Therefore, there is a margin of 7.4 percent pre-tax. Donnelly & Co.'s assets earn 7.4 percent more than the bank's source of financing. Comparing the net ROA of 14.3 percent with the bank rate of 13 percent is meaningless (unless we compare it with the after-tax bank rate of 9.1 percent, or 13 percent multiplied by 0.7.

---

[8]See footnote 6.
[9]See footnote 6.

Both the gross ROA and the net ROA provide us with a very effective measure of operating performance. The numerator reflects what the assets are earning regardless of the chosen capital structure, while the denominator values the assets themselves.

CONCEPT CHECK

1. *Distinguish between the four general classes of ratios (short-term solvency ratios, activity ratios, financial-leverage ratios, and profitability ratios).*
2. *What are the component ratios that comprise the four general classes of ratios?*
3. *What is the objective in calculating financial ratios?*
4. *Why is the net income-to-assets ratio likely to be an inadequate measure of comparative performance?*

4.7 VALUATION MEASURES

One thing that the financial statements of a business cannot disclose is its **market value**. In the case of a public company, the market value of the equity of a company equals the market price per share times the number of shares in the company. Unfortunately, small businesses are not publicly traded, and, therefore, the valuation of equity is much more of a problem. However, while valuing businesses that are not publicly listed is a much more difficult process, the principles of valuation remain the same.

Valuation measures are generally based on two types of factors: **yield factors** and **asset factors**. Yield factors reflect the earnings of the business and the level of its distributions. Asset factors represent the differences between the book values of the assets and liabilities of the company and their market values. Market value, more than anything else, depends on the earning ability of the business. Therefore, market value is compared to net income (earnings after interest and income tax, or the final bottom-line earnings of the business).

Yield factors for publicly traded companies commonly comprise the **earnings yield**, the **dividend yield**, and the **price–earnings multiple**. While these cannot be directly compared with the smaller business, given some adjustments of the information provided by the financial reports of the small business, these factors can provide some guidelines to its valuation.

The following discussions relate more to the public equity arena than to the small private firms, but given some adjustment to reflect the lack of negotiability of the equity of the private firm, valuation measures derived from public markets can still be used to provide guidelines in the appraisal of the small business.

EARNINGS PER SHARE

In the case of the corporate form of ownership, market value and net income are usually referred to on a per-share basis.

So far, the discussion has been based on the premise that there is only a single **class of shares**. Under this circumstance, it is appropriate for the analyst to merely divide whatever is to be measured (earnings, dividends, assets, etc.) by the number of shares. However, where there are two or more classes of shares, each with different rights to income or assets (or indeed subcategories of income or assets), it may be necessary to adjust the figures so that the analyst matches the class of income or asset with the class of equity. In the instance of Donnelly & Co., its eighty-two thousand shares comprise a single class of equity and **earnings per share (EPS)** is calculated as follows:[10]

$$\text{Earnings per share (EPS)} = \frac{\text{net income}}{\text{number of shares with a claim on net income}}$$

$$= \frac{\$28,000}{82,000 \text{ shares}} = 34.2 \text{ cents per share}$$

In many circumstances, however, family companies are set up with more than a single class of shares. The different classes may vary with respect to their rights to vote or their rights to residual income. An example of the former might occur when a parent gives children some shares in the company but wishes to restrict their control: the shares held by the parent include voting rights, whereas those of the children do not. While this may appear inequitable at first glance, unless such provisions were possible, the children would probably not be given shares in the first place. In time, such non-voting shares are usually exchanged for voting shares. An example of this might occur where the holders of one class of shares require income from the business for their maintenance, while others do not. Again, this arrangement may be merely temporary, and on the occurrence of some contingent event, non-participating shares could convert to fully participating shares.

DIVIDENDS PER SHARE

In the case of the company that is paying dividends, **dividends per share (DPS)** is a function of the EPS and the dividend-payout ratio. The **dividend payout ratio** refers to the proportion of the available net income that is paid in the form of dividends to ordinary shareholders.

$$\text{Dividend payout ratio} = \frac{\text{dividend paid}}{\text{net income}}$$

Many firms attempt to maintain a "stable" dividend policy by maintaining a stable dividend-payout ratio. While Donnelly & Co. paid no dividend at the end of the first year of operations (due to a shortage of cash), assume

---

[10]See footnote 6.

for a moment that the directors decided to maintain, if possible, a constant dividend policy based on a dividend-payout ratio of 40 percent.

From this information the amount that would be paid as a dividend can be determined as follows:

$$\text{Dividend paid} = \text{net income} \times \text{dividend-payout ratio}$$

$$= \$28{,}000 \times 40\%$$

$$= \$11{,}200$$

By dividing the total dividend by the number of ordinary shares issued, the dividend per share can be calculated:[11]

$$\text{Dividends per share (DPS)} = \frac{\text{dividend for the year}}{\text{number of shares claiming the dividend}}$$

In this case, DPS is:

$$\text{DPS} = \frac{\$11{,}200}{82{,}000 \text{ shares}} = 13.7 \text{ cents per share}$$

EARNINGS YIELD

The total return that a shareholder receives as a return on investment in a company is called the earnings yield. The dividend forms only part of the return on investment. Money retained by a business creates growth for the business (if it doesn't, the money should be paid out) and, commensurately, causes an increase in the business's worth. Therefore, the dividend only goes part way toward explaining the return that the investor receives. The dividend can be considered as the short-term gain, while the growth in value of the shares is part of a longer-term gain resulting, in turn, from increased future net income.

If, for example, the shares of Donnelly & Co. were trading on the stock exchange for $2.73 per share, the earnings yield would be:[12]

$$\text{Earnings yield} = \frac{\text{earnings per share}}{\text{current market price}} = \frac{\text{net income}}{\text{equity market value}} = \frac{\$28{,}044}{\$224{,}000}$$

$$= \frac{\$0.342}{\$2.73} = 12.5\%$$

---

[11]See footnote 6.

[12]Despite the fact that (technically) one should relate the earnings to either the initial (beginning) value of the investment, or perhaps the average investment for the period, it is customary to utilize *today's* market price in the instances of the earnings yield, the dividend yield, and the price–earnings ratio.

Growth in value results from either an increase in net income (other things, such as risk, being equal), a decrease in risk (other things, such as net income, being equal) or a combination of both. Later chapters will address these issues in much more depth than is needed at this point. The reinvestment of profits in the business is one of the causes of growth. In the case of a large company that is listed on a stock exchange, this growth in value can be realized periodically by selling shares. In the case of the small business, however, despite the simple lack of negotiability of equity, value does increase with the retention of earnings. For this reason, the earnings yield can be considered a superior measure of performance than the dividend yield, which is subject to the whims of directors and dividend policy.

Unfortunately, small businesses do not have access to a stock exchange to facilitate the market valuation of their equity. In these cases, unless there is evidence that the market value and the book value of equity differ, the analyst of the small business will probably use the book value of assets and equity in yield calculations. Donnelly & Co.'s book earnings yield is calculated as follows:

$$\text{Book earnings yield} = \text{ROE} = \frac{\text{net income}}{\text{equity book value}}$$

$$= \frac{\$28,000}{\$110,000} = 25.5\%$$

Notice that, if the market value of the firm's assets and liabilities equated their book values, the earnings yield would be identical to the ROE, as determined earlier in this chapter. The reader's attention is again drawn to the earlier comment that, in order to simplify the presentation of ratio analysis in this chapter, one should assume that there is no difference between the book value and the market value of the assets of the business in most of the computations.

Market value depends on the perceived risk inherent in any investment. A rational investor will want to earn a greater return on investment in a business with a high-risk nature than in a business that is regarded as safer. So, the earnings yield can be used to assist with valuing the equity of a firm. The relationship between value and earnings yield can be expressed as:

$$\text{Current market price} = \frac{\text{expected EPS}}{\text{required earnings yield}}$$

This method of valuing shares is called the **earnings capitalization method** and it is closely related to the use of the price–earnings multiples that are presented later in this section.

DIVIDEND YIELD

As opposed to the owner of a small business, the shareholder in a publicly listed company may be more interested in the cash return on investment than in the (partially, at least) non-cash earnings per share. The difference between the earnings of the firm and the dividend paid is the retained earnings. Of course in the case of the small business, for reasons that were explained earlier in this chapter, ratios based on the analysis of the dividend rarely apply because first, the dividend decision is too intertwined with other reward mechanisms and, second, because the majority of small businesses do not pay dividends simply because they are sole proprietorships and partnerships (which, by definition, cannot pay a "dividend").

However, for those firms for which the dividend *is* a relevant factor, the relationship between the current market price of a share and the dividend paid is called the dividend yield; it is computed as:[13]

$$\text{Dividend yield} = \frac{\text{dividend per share}}{\text{current market price}}$$

$$= \frac{40\%(\$0.342)}{\$2.73} = 5\%$$

$$\text{Dividend yield} = \text{earnings yield} \times \text{dividend-payout ratio}$$

$$= 12.5\% \times 40\% = 5\%$$

Notice that the dividend yield could be obtained in two ways—either by dividing a known dividend by a known share price, or merely by multiplying the earnings yield by the dividend-payout ratio if those figures are known.

PRICE–EARNINGS RATIO

One of the other measures of performance commonly used in the case of large publicly held firms is known as the **price–earnings (P/E) ratio**. This ratio presents another way by which EPS can be compared with the market price of the share of a publicly traded company.

The P/E ratio is the reciprocal of the earnings yield. It tells the analyst the number of years' earnings it will take to pay for the share at its current market price and given the risk class of the share (although if earnings are expected to grow, investors will get their money back in less years than the P/E multiple suggests). If investors want to get their money back more quickly on a high-risk investment than on a safer investment, the P/E ratio will be lower for the more risky investment. However, it must be recognized that the P/E ratio is analogous to the payback measure,[14] as used in investment appraisal, and contains all of the deficiencies associated with that

---

[13]See footnote 12.

[14]See Chapter 8 for a discussion of the payback period and other techniques used to appraise investments.

measure in that it ignores the timing of cash flows and the nature of post-payback-period cash flows.

$$\text{Price-earnings ratio} = \frac{\text{current market price}}{\text{earnings per share}}$$

If the shares of the company are trading at $2.73 per share, and the EPS for the most recent year is 34.1 cents, the P/E ratio is 8. Note that 8 is the reciprocal of the earnings yield (1 divided by 0.125).

$$P/E = \frac{2.73}{0.341} = 8$$

What should the P/E be? If the industry that the firm is in goes into decline (i.e., becomes more risky), then the P/E ratio might drop to, say, 5. This means that investors would want their money back in five years, rather than in eight years as before. Another way of thinking about this is to consider the investor raising the required rate of return from 12.5 percent (at a P/E of 8) to 20 percent (at a P/E of 5) as the perceived risk increases.

The P/E ratio (as with other relevant ratios) can be used as a signal to investors and analysts. If it is dramatically different than the P/E ratio for other firms in the same industry, further investigation is warranted.

So, analysts can use either the P/E ratio or the earnings-capitalization method to value shares. The P/E ratio is often called the P/E multiple when it is used in this fashion. Along with other market-trading information, analysts can find the P/E ratios for all ordinary shares listed by the stock exchange, in many local newspapers from time to time, and in various specialist financial newspapers that publish the information daily.

The availability of P/E ratios for listed shares enables the simple valuation of other shares:

Current market value = EPS × P/E ratio

Does the P/E ratio apply to smaller private firms? The P/E ratio is generally not regarded as a very accurate way of valuing small firms. In part, this is purely because analysts lack suitable information regarding comparable P/E ratios, and, in part, it is because the earnings declared or projected by many small firms vary too widely to be able to ascertain a reasonable earnings figure to which one might apply such a measure. Finance experts are not convinced that P/E multiples can be used for the valuation of the small firm. However, many of the appraisers of small businesses would admit that, while stock-exchange-originated P/E multiples are not *directly* applicable to small firms, they are, nevertheless, frequently used to provide a basis for inter-industry comparisons and for placing upper bounds on applicable P/Es for small firms. Also, if the P/Es are known for comparable firms that have recently been sold, then, obviously, they can be a very effective guide to that

FINANCIAL RATIOS SUMMARY

Current ratio	=	current assets / current liabilities
Quick ratio	=	(cash + marketable securities + accounts receivable) / current liabilities
Accounts receivable turnover	=	sales / accounts receivable
Average collection period	=	(365 × accounts receivable) / sales
Inventory turnover	=	cost of goods sold / inventory
Average inventory holding period	=	(365 × inventory) / cost of sales
Accounts payable turnover	=	(cost of goods sold + operating expenses) / accounts payable
Average purchases credit period	=	(365 × accounts payable) / (cost of goods sold + operating expenses)
Asset turnover	=	sales / assets
Debt-to-assets ratio	=	debt / assets
Debt-to-equity ratio	=	debt / equity
Times interest earned ratio	=	EBIT / interest
Return on equity	=	net income / equity
Gross ROA	=	EBIT / assets
Net ROA	=	EBIT(1 − t) / assets
Earnings per share	=	net income / number of shares
Earnings yield (market)	=	EPS / market value per share
Earnings yield (book)	=	EPS / book value per share
Dividend yield (market)	=	dividend / market value per share
Price-to-earnings ratio	=	market value per share / EPS

which should apply to the business under consideration. One of the major problems in the small-business environment is obtaining relevant and comparable information.

Finance experts believe that the size of the dividend paid by a company may not affect the value of its shares. Value may be more closely related to total earnings than to how those earnings are returned to the shareholders. Lower dividends mean more earnings retained by the firm; this leads to more growth by the company, and from there to capital growth in the value of the company's shares. Many firms that pay very small dividends have a relatively high share value.

Exhibit 4.3 presents a summary of the financial ratios defined above. Exhibit 4.4 presents a summary of the financial ratios of Donnelly & Co.

OTHER RATIOS

In addition to the ratios specifically discussed in this chapter, there are a host of other ratios that might be applicable in any given circumstance. In fact, an analyst can design a ratio that will lead to the solution of a given problem, providing that comparable ratios are available for other firms or time periods, and as long as they are consistently applied. For example, in an agricultural context, measures such as debt servicing per gallon of milk or fertilizer as a percent of gross income might be appropriate. For hotels,

✦ EXHIBIT 4.4

FINANCIAL RATIOS: DONNELLY & CO.

Short-term solvency ratios

Current ratio	2.17
Quick ratio	0.89

Activity ratios

Accounts receivable turnover	8.67
Average collection period	42 days
Inventory turnover	4.06
Average inventory holding period	90 days
Accounts payable turnover	15.2
Average purchase credit period	28 days
Asset turnover	2

Financial structure ratios

Debt-to-assets ratio	0.58
Debt-to-equity ratio	1.36
Times interest earned ratio	4.1

Profitability ratios

Return on equity	25.5%
Return on assets (gross)	20.4%
Return on assets (net)	14.3%

Valuation measures

Earnings per share	34.1 cents
Earnings yield (market)	12.5%
Earnings yield (book)	25.5%
Dividend yield (market)	5%
Price-to-earnings ratio	8

total expenses per night per room or bar income as a percent of total income could be of use.

One thing of which the analyst should be aware, though, is the vast range of different names for the same ratio (and in some circumstances the same name for different ratios). When communicating, always be aware that the ratio that you are talking about may be misunderstood by another person and vice versa.

 CONCEPT CHECK

1. *What are the major sources of difficulty in applying valuation ratios of the type discussed in this chapter to the small business?*
2. *What is meant by the term* growth?
3. *How does retained earnings cause growth?*
4. *Why do different classes of shares exist?*

4.8 FINANCIAL LEVERAGE

A firm's return on assets usually differs from the cost of its borrowed funds, and this difference leads to the analysis and meaning of financial leverage. To understand the basic principles relating to financial leverage, ask the following questions: Would I borrow at 15 percent if I could only earn 12 percent on the investment that I am planning? Would I borrow at 12 percent to invest at 15 percent? Would I borrow at 12 percent to invest in an asset that would return 15 percent *on average*, but the income would vary above and below 15 percent? Would I borrow more or less if this variability was to increase?

In the case of Donnelly & Co. (see Exhibit 4.1), the company's annual rate on its interest-bearing short-term and long-term debt is 13 percent, but as well as the interest-bearing debt, the company has other current liabilities on which no interest is paid. In total, its liabilities total $150,000 and the total cost for the use of this capital is the $13,000 interest expense for the year. Thus, the **average cost of debt (K$_i$)** is:[15]

$$\text{Average cost of debt (K}_i) = \frac{\text{interest}}{\text{liabilities}}$$

$$= \frac{\$13,000}{\$150,000} = 8.7\%$$

It should be noted that, in the average cost of debt equation, *all* liabilities are included in the denominator.

Recall that Donnelly & Co. had an ROA of 20.4 percent. So, while the company is paying 8.7 percent for its debt financing, it can earn 20.4 percent on the money borrowed. There is a favorable **spread** of 11.7 percent between the two. The difference between these two rates is the basis of **financial leverage** analysis.

Exhibit 4.5 summarizes the **before-tax** and **after-tax measures** relating to ROA, ROE, and the cost of interest.

Why does the gross ROE exceed the gross ROA? It occurs due to the **favorable financial leverage** that occurs when a business uses debt capital on which it can earn a higher gross ROA than the annual interest rate paid on the debt. Allowing for some approximations due to rounding, if the $110,000 shareholders' equity earned 20.4 percent before tax, this would equal $22,440. Donnelly & Co.'s income statement discloses that the earnings before tax was actually $40,000 (see Exhibit 4.1). The difference is $17,560. But where did this extra $17,560 come from? It is the gain due to favorable financial leverage. If the company was 100 percent equity financed, the shareholders would earn 20.4 percent. But by financing some of the assets ($150,000 worth) with lower-cost debt, they increase their own returns commensurately.

---

[15]Because the interest charge is levied across the period under consideration, the denominator should reflect the average liabilities—it does not in this case.

BEFORE- AND AFTER-TAX RETURNS

Ratio	After-tax	Before-tax
Return on assets	14.3%	20.4%
Return on equity	25.5%	36.4%
Cost of debt (K_i)	6.1%	8.7%

FINANCIAL LEVERAGE GAIN FOR THE YEAR

$150,000 × 20.4% = $ 30,600	Proportion of operating earnings due to debt financing
(13,000)	Interest expense
$ 17,600	Financial leverage gain

Exhibit 4.6 displays the origins of Donnelly & Co.'s financial leverage gain. The $150,000 of assets financed by low-cost debt earned $30,600 at an interest cost of $13,000 to provide a gain of $17,600. Financial leverage provided $17,600 (about one-third) of the $53,000 operating earnings for the year.

It does not always work this way, though. If the gross ROA is less than its annual interest rate, financial leverage works against the business.

Another way of looking at the effect of financial leverage is to consider the gross ROA divided between the debt and the equity holders in the firm. If the average after-tax cost of Donnelly & Co.'s debt is 14.3 percent, and the **leverage ratio** was 0.5, there would be no gain from financial leverage, and both the debt holders and the shareholders would earn 14.3 percent:

Assets earn	14.3%	Debtholders earn	14.3%
		Equityholders earn	14.3%

For example, consider a firm with a debt-to-equity ratio of 1 to 1 that earns a 10 percent after-tax ROA on assets of $200,000. Its equity is therefore $100,000, as is its debt. Its debt also costs 10 percent after-tax. Thus, its earning power is divided as follows:

		Return			Return
Assets earn	$20,000	10%	Debtholders earn	$10,000	10%
			Equityholders earn	10,000	10%
	$20,000	10%	Total earnings	$20,000	10%

As shown, the assets and the claims on assets both earn $20,000 on $200,000 (or 10 percent), which is divided between debtholders who earn $10,000 on $100,000 (10 percent) and equityholders who also earn $10,000 on $100,000 (or 10 percent).

If, however, the after-tax cost of debt was only 5 percent, then the effect of favorable financial leverage can be seen. The assets remain earning 20 percent after-tax, or $20,000. This is divided between the debtholders who earn 5 percent of $100,000 (or $5,000) and the equityholders, who receive the balance of $15,000 (15 percent of their $100,000 investment).

The $20,000 total earnings provides an after-tax ROA of 10 percent. The returns to the stakeholders (debtholders and equityholders) in the business, weighted by the proportion of the capital structure that they have contributed, also equals this figure (known as the **weighted average cost of capital, or WACC**). In this case, the weightings are each 0.5 for the return to the debtholders and the return to the equityholders. Therefore the WACC is:

$$WACC = 0.5 \times 10\% + 0.5 \times 10\% = 10\%$$

		Return			Return
Assets earn	$20,000	10%	Debtholders earn	$ 5,000	5%
			Equityholders earn	15,000	15%
	$20,000	10%	Total earnings (WACC)	$20,000	10%

Under these circumstances, favorable financial leverage is increasing the ROE by $5,000 to 15 percent. This $5,000 is the financial leverage gain.

As before, the equityholders and the debtholders each hold 50 percent of the capital of the business, and therefore:

$$WACC = 0.5 \times 5\% + 0.5 \times 15\% = 10\%$$

Now assume that the owners of this firm decide to take $80,000 of their capital out of the firm and replace it with debt; i.e., there is now $180,000 of debt costing $18,000 (5 percent), and only $20,000 equity. The equityholders receive the residual income of $11,000 as a return on their investment of $20,000 (or 55 percent):

		Return			Return
Assets earn	$20,000	10%	Debtholders earn	$ 9,000	5%
			Equityholders earn	11,000	55%
	$20,000	10%	Total earnings (WACC)	$20,000	10%

In this case, the debtholders are providing 90 percent of the capital of the business, while the equityholders provide only 10 percent. Therefore, the weighted average cost of capital, which can be seen is *the same* as the average return (of 10 percent), is:

$$\text{WACC} = 0.9 \times 5\% + 0.1 \times 55\% = 10\%$$

While the shareholders have only earned an additional $1,000 as a financial leverage gain, their earnings are now generated by a much smaller investment base ($20,000 instead of $100,000). Obviously, the more financial leverage employed in these circumstances, the greater the ROE. This is known as the **magnification factor** associated with financial leverage.

This leads to the *first rule*:

If ROA > K$_i$ then ROE > ROA

If financial leverage is favorable, the more debt the firm has, the greater the return on equity invested.

But, with increasing degrees of financial leverage comes the increased risk that, if profitability or cash flows decline (or interest rates increase), then leverage could very easily become *unfavorable*, and the magnification factor could work to the detriment of the equityholders. This risk arises from the requirement to service the interest charge (a **fixed cost**) associated with debt financing regardless of the level of net operating income.

For example, assume that a downturn in the business of the highly leveraged previous example (in which $200,000 of assets was 90 percent leveraged) caused a reduction in after-tax ROA to 2 percent ($4,000). The interest (after-tax) of $9,000 must still be paid, and the residual income accruing to the equityholders is thus a loss of $5,000.

		Return			Return
Assets earn	$4,000	2%	Debtholders earn	$9,000	5%
			Equityholders earn	(5,000)	−25%
	$4,000	2%	Total earnings (WACC)	$4,000	2%

The weighted average cost of capital is now:

$$\text{WACC} = (0.9 \times 5\%) + [0.1 \times (-25\%)] = 2\%$$

In this circumstance, the equityholders have lost 25 percent of their $20,000 capital. If the ROA dropped even further, say, to 1 percent, they would suffer a loss of 35 percent (or $7,000) of their capital.

The *second rule* is, therefore:

When financial leverage is unfavorable, the greater the degree of financial leverage, the lower the return on equity

If financial leverage is favorable, why don't firms borrow more? There are two very good reasons for this. First, as the amount of debt in the firm's capital structure increases, lenders recognize that, interest being a fixed cost, the greater the amount of interest that needs to be paid, the greater the probability of the firm being unable to meet its commitments. To counter this additional risk, they increase the cost of debt, which has the direct effect of reducing the gain from financial leverage. Second, as the debt ratio increases, the owners of the firm recognize that they, too, are facing greater risk, and the owners of most small businesses are not prepared to commit themselves (and their personal assets, which are providing the collateral security to the lenders) to too much risk.

At this point, it is appropriate to examine the concept of risk, which is closely linked to the ROA and the ROE. The next chapter will revisit these notions when the nature of break-even analysis is discussed.

 CONCEPT CHECK

1. *Why is it necessary to distinguish between ROA on a before- and after-tax basis?*
2. *Describe the circumstances in which favorable financial leverage occurs.*
3. *What is the basis for the weighted average cost of capital?*

4.9   RISK

In addition to growth, the other universal problem in small-business finance is the management of **risk**.

What is risk? There are many definitions—risk can be regarded as the difference between an expected and an actual outcome. Statistically, risk can be defined as variability; the greater the variability, the higher the risk. Some of the factors that cause risk in business to change include changes in time, competition, and technology.

Risk can be divided into business risk and financial risk. **Business** (or **operating** or technical) **risk** is related to the variability of operating income. It is the variability that arises due to the nature of the business and its asset intensity. It is present even when there is no financial leverage. It is the risk that earnings before interest and taxes will vary due to changes in sales revenue and the costs of expenses other than interest.

Financial risk is related to the variability of net income. It is the added variability that is due to the presence of financial leverage. Even if EBIT remains constant, net income will vary with changes in interest rates. If EBIT varies, the net income of a leveraged firm will vary more markedly than the net income of an unleveraged firm. Financial risk is the additional variability of leveraged returns over the variability of unleveraged returns that reflect business risk only. It is the probability that leverage will be favorable, i.e., that the ROA will exceed the cost of debt. The potential variability in the ROA and in the cost of debt causes financial risk.

Business risk relates to the type of business and its asset structure (and thus to the nature of its fixed costs and break-even point), while financial risk relates to the additional risk contributed by the increase in fixed costs associated with the contractual costs associated with borrowing.

Small businesses are considered as more risky than large businesses for a number of reasons. The following list is not exhaustive, neither does it apply in all cases, but it shows the main causes of the problem:

✦ small businesses are normally not very diversified in their activities
✦ they typically maintain relatively high levels of debt in their capital structure
✦ they do not have access to public markets for debt and equity
✦ they often rely largely upon the expertise of a single person

Because of the importance of risk and the unlimited obligation of the owner in the case of default, small-business owners must manage their risk-taking very carefully.

In summary, there are two components to financial risk: the cost of debt and the degree (or amount) of financial leverage.

 CONCEPT CHECK

1. *Why does financial leverage occur?*
2. *Under what circumstances does favorable financial leverage occur?*
3. *How does magnification work?*
4. *Distinguish between business risk and financial risk.*

4.10 PERFORMANCE: THE CRITICAL ELEMENTS

There are two sides to the efficiency measures that can be applied to any business. These sides relate to the perspective that is being considered. The analyst wants to know not only how efficient the business is in the use of its assets, but also whether or not this level of efficiency is translated into gains for the owners of the business.

These perspectives lead to the concepts of **operating efficiency** and **financial efficiency**. The measures of these two types of efficiency can conflict, and a firm can be operating efficiently without being financially efficient, and vice versa.

For example, Firm A and Firm B both have identical asset structures and make the same products. Both have invested $1 million in assets, but while Firm A has after-tax earnings of $65,000, Firm B has earnings of only 60 percent of this figure. Both firms pay tax at a rate of thirty-five cents on the dollar. While the two firms have identical asset structures, they are financed differently. Firm A is all equity financed, while Firm B is 50 percent leveraged

PERFORMANCE MEASURES

		Firm A	Firm B
Step 1:	Reported earnings	$ 65,000	$ 39,000
	Add back: tax	35,000	21,000
	Earnings before tax	$ 100,000	$ 60,000
Step 2:	Assets	$1,000,000	$1,000,000
	Debt		(500,000)
	Equity	$1,000,000	$ 500,000
Step 3:	Debt		$ 00,000
	× interest rate		15%
	Interest paid		$ 75,000
Step 4:	Earnings before tax	$ 100,000	$ 60,000
	Add back: interest		75,000
	Operating earnings	$ 100,000	$ 135,000
Step 5:	Gross return on assets	10%	13.5%
	Gross return on equity	10%	12%

at a cost of 15 percent per annum. An investor has decided to invest in only one of these firms and wants to know which firm performs better.

Exhibit 4.7 shows that Firm B is more efficient technically, or operationally (i.e., uses its assets more effectively), because it has the higher ROA, but is less efficient financially because, despite its higher ROE, the use of debt is unfavorable due to the cost of interest exceeding the ROA.

Firm B could replace its debt through a new issue of equity, in which case its ROE would increase to 13.5 percent. Or Firm B could refinance its debt at a cost lower than 13.5 percent and thus increase its ROE above the ROA. Either way, Firm B is the better firm, both now and potentially, but the investor still needs to look at its financial structure.

If a financial analyst was asked to define the three key factors associated with the measurement of business performance, he would probably agree on the following indicators:

1. Asset turnover—the maximization of the sales-to-assets ratio is critical to the performance of the business. This does not mean that sales should be increased beyond a point where profitability declines, but, without sales, there is no income.

2. Gross margin—sales is one thing, *profitable* sales is another. The gross margin represents the contribution of sales to the operating income of

◆ EXHIBIT 4.8

THE duPONT EQUATION

$$ROE = \frac{\text{net income}}{\text{equity}} = \frac{\text{sales}}{\text{assets}} \times \frac{\text{net income}}{\text{sales}} \times \frac{\text{assets}}{\text{equity}}$$

the business. Assuming that overhead expenses are incurred wisely (and they are usually closely related to the level of assets), maximizing the gross margin will maximize net income.

3. Financial leverage—the comparison between ROA and the cost of debt signifies whether or not the business should be financed with debt. Indeed, if the analyst considers that a small business is a risky venture and the cost of debt is relatively riskless, then unless the ROA exceeds the cost of debt, a good case can be made for liquidating the firm and investing the money so generated in a debt instrument of some type.

One of the major guidelines for running a business, whether it be large or small, is to maximize the firm's return on equity. Using this premise, a group of analysts "invented" what has become known as the **duPont expression**. This neat piece of mathematic juggling is presented in Exhibit 4.8. From this expression it can be seen why the three factors mentioned (asset turnover, gross margin, and financial leverage) are critical to the successful operation of the business.

The duPont expression is of considerable use as an analytical technique when trying to determine which components of the return on equity figure can be improved upon. The fact that the ROE overall is acceptable tells only part of the story. It may be that one component is very good, while the other two can be markedly improved. The major advantage of the duPont expression is its simplicity, and it contains the basic elements that analysts consider. The asset-turnover ratio (sales/assets) indicates the efficiency with which assets are utilized, the net income/sales ratio indicates operating (input/output) efficiency, and the assets/equity ratio refers to financial leverage. While the duPont expression does not provide all of the answers, it certainly provides an initial indication of where to look for improvement.

 CONCEPT CHECK

1. *How is it possible for one firm to be technically more efficient than another and yet financially less efficient?*
2. *What are the key factors in performance analysis and how does the duPont equation incorporate these factors?*

SUMMARY

+ This chapter introduced the concept of performance evaluation using the financial reports of the business as a basis for analysis. A number of comparative ratios were defined and their use exemplified. Of particular interest are those ratios that measure the liquidity and financial stability of the business.

+ In conjunction with other market information, some ratios can be used to assist in the valuation process. While the use of these ratios should be strictly confined to larger firms, they can still be used to guide the valuation process for the smaller business.

+ Financial leverage reflects the presence of debt in the capital structure of the business. Where the return earned by the assets of the business exceeds the cost of borrowing, the favorable spread is reflected in increased returns on the equity invested by the owners of the firm. The greater the spread and the greater the leverage the more magnified the advantage becomes. However, where there is a possibility that losses will occur, these losses will be magnified with leverage; it works both ways.

+ Risk derives fundamentally from two sources: the capital intensity of the business activity (the type of business) and the way in which it is financed (the amount of financial leverage). Acceptance of financial leverage adds financial risk to business risk.

+ Lastly the duPont expression was introduced. It focuses attention on the critical relationships that comprise performance: the ability of the assets to generate sales, the profit margin in the sales and the amount of financial leverage.

THE CASE—PART FOUR

At the end of 1999 Dave's banker informed him that, as part of the normal review process, the affairs of Dave's Bikes & Co. will be re-evaluated. She has the feeling that, while on the face of it, Dave's Bikes is a very profitable business, the amount of debt being borne by the company might be too high given the economic outlook. Without applying too much pressure, she suggests that the business is now quite valuable, and that if Dave wants to, he could probably issue some new shares in the company and use the money to reduce the bank's exposure.

Because of your past services to Dave, he approaches you to see if you would be interested in buying a share of the business.

ASSIGNMENT 4.1

Using the information presented in Assignment 3.3 and knowing that the price/earnings ratio of the shares of a similar small firm had recently been established to be 4 to 1, advise Dave about the following:

Required

1. Estimate the book value per share of Dave's shares.
2. Calculate the market value of Dave's equity.
3. If, during the financial year to December 31, 1999, Dave bought and sold a piece of real estate at a profit of $45,000 and replaced that with another piece of real estate for which he paid $60,000 and is now valued at $75,000, what would the value of Dave's shares be on a per-share basis?

ASSIGNMENT 4.2

Dave has asked you to examine his 1999 financial statements (see Assignment 3.3) and provide him with some performance-appraisal figures.

Required

1. Using average figures where appropriate, determine the following relationships:
   a) Acid-test ratio
   b) Current ratio
   c) Debt-to-assets ratio
   d) Debt-to-equity ratio
   e) Earnings per share
   f) Asset turnover
   g) Gross return on assets
   h) Return on equity

2. Applying both the book value of equity and market value of equity (as determined in Assignment 4.1) to the denominator, calculate the:
   a) Earnings yield
   b) Dividend yield

3. Create the duPont expression for Dave's Bikes & Co. for its second year of operation. How is Dave doing? Where is the profitability arising?

ASSIGNMENT 4.3

Required

1. What was the average cost of Dave's Bikes & Co.'s debt in 1999?
2. What was the gain due to financial leverage in 1999?
3. Assuming that the bank would have allowed it, should the company have borrowed more to finance even more expansion in 1999?
4. Using the market value of equity determined in Assignment 4.1(2),
   a) compile a market-value balance sheet for Dave's Bikes & Co.
   b) determine the weighted average cost of capital for Dave's Bikes & Co. for 1999 using the market values as weights

SELECTED ADDITIONAL READINGS

The readings suggested in previous chapters apply to the material in this chapter as well. In addition, the following are useful:

Masulis, R. 1988. The debt/equity choice. *The Institutional Investor Series in Finance.* Cambridge, MA: Ballinger.

Myers, S. C. 1984. The search for optimal capital structure. *Midland Corporate Finance Journal* 1 (Spring):1.

Pratt, S. 1989. *Valuing a business: The analysis and appraisal of closely held companies.* 2d. ed. Homewood, IL: Irwin.

FINANCIAL PLANNING

OBJECTIVES

1. *Demonstrate that financial planning is a necessary technique for the effective management of the small business*
2. *Introduce break-even analysis and its variants that apply in the case of the smaller firm*
3. *Discuss budgeting both with and without information*

5.1   INTRODUCTION

Financial planning is critical for the small business. Planning is part of the risk-reduction strategy that is designed to improve the certainty of outcomes in an uncertain business environment.

A business faces two fundamental forms of risk. First, there is that type of risk that is associated with the type of business: there is less risk in manufacturing common t-shirts than there is in running a fine French restaurant; there is less risk in servicing bicycles than there is in selling pet rocks; there is less risk in providing accounting services than there is in manufacturing. "Business risk" is associated with the capital intensity of the business—the type of industry and the relative level of its fixed costs.

There is also risk associated with funding the activities of the business with borrowed money. It is obvious that a business is safer when it has no debt. The reason for this, however, is not the debt itself, but the need to service the interest and the principal payments regardless of whether the business is performing well at the present time or not. This is defined as "financial risk."

There are many different approaches that can be taken to financial planning in practice, but those approaches generally fall into two basic categories: break-even analysis and budgeting. Both of these take a structured approach to looking into the future and planning the physical and financial flows of the business. At some future date actual performance can be compared with the plan to identify areas that performed better or worse than anticipated. Once this has been done, those areas that performed worse than anticipated can be subjected to remedial action, while those that performed better than anticipated can be expanded.

5.2   BREAK-EVEN ANALYSIS

At this stage it is necessary to review some of the terminology that is commonly used in financial management of businesses:

✦ Net operating income (or operating profit) equals sales revenue less all operating expenses, including cost of goods sold. Another name for operating income is earnings before interest and taxes, or EBIT.

✦ Operating expenses can be classified as fixed or variable. **Fixed operating expenses** are those that are constant regardless of sales volume. Examples of fixed operating expenses are depreciation, general administration expenses, and rent. **Variable operating expenses** are those expenses that change in direct proportion with the level of sales and production. The largest variable operating expense is usually the cost of goods sold but other examples might include sales commissions and distribution costs; if there are no sales, there are no commissions.

The division between fixed and variable operating expenses depends on the type of business under consideration. What is fixed in one business may be variable in another. In the long run, *all* expenses are variable, including asset purchases, because in the long run, even assets can be structured to fit the volume of production of the business. For example, for a business that relies on door-to-door sales, selling and distribution expenses are variable, while for a business that sells to retailers using permanently employed and salaried salespersons, these same expenses could be considered fixed, although obviously in the long run, they too are variable. So, the division between fixed and variable expenses depends on the type of business and the period under consideration.

Financial planners need to determine which expenses are fixed and which are variable so that they can calculate how much the firm needs to sell in order to just cover its costs. This is the amount that should ensure the firm's survival; it answers the question "How bad can things get before the firm has to close down?" Planners can use a technique known as **break-even analysis** to assist them with answering not only this question, but also a host of other questions relating to planning the firm's future, such as:

✦ What if the competition cut the price of their product? How much extra does the business have to sell at the lower price to make the same profit?

✦ What if the owners are considering a new campaign to boost sales that will cost $50,000? How much will sales have to increase in order to break even on the new venture?

The level of sales where revenue equals the sum of fixed plus variable costs is known as the **break-even point**. If one considers for the moment that the business does not have any debt (thus ignoring interest because it is part of the financing policy rather than the operating policy), then, at the break-even point, sales revenue exactly equals the total operating expenses, including the cost of goods sold.

The break-even point for a firm is determined by the relationship between the firm's sales revenues, its fixed costs, and its variable costs. These relationships can be depicted graphically. Exhibit 5.1 shows production volume on the horizontal axis and dollar sales on the vertical axis.

It is apparent from this exhibit that sales varies directly with volume, as do variable costs. Fixed operating costs are represented by a horizontal line because of the assumption that they don't change when the sales volume changes. It is also evident that when sales equal zero, variable costs equal zero, but the fixed cost still exists. Under these circumstances, the firm would incur a loss equal to the fixed costs. The total cost line in Exhibit 5.1 represents the sum of the fixed and variable costs for each level of sales.

The vertical distance between the sales revenue line and the total costs line represents the operating earnings. The break-even point occurs where the sales revenue line meets the total costs line. Below the break-even point, the vertical distance between the sales and total costs lines represents an operating loss. Beyond the break-even point, it represents an operating profit.

If the fixed costs of the firm increased, the fixed costs line would rise vertically on the graph, and increase the break-even volume.

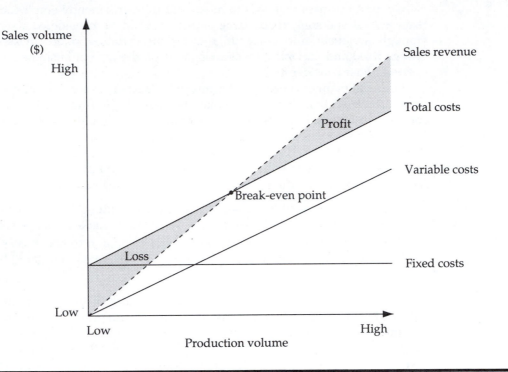

If the fixed costs of the firm increased, and at the same time the variable costs decreased, perhaps as the result of substituting a new machine (fixed cost of depreciation) for labor (variable labor cost per unit of production), the fixed cost line would be lifted vertically, the slope of the variable costs line would decrease, and, as a result, the slope of the total costs line would also decrease. What would happen to the break-even volume under these circumstances would depend on the substitution relationship—it might increase, or it might decrease.

The relative angle of the sales revenue line to the total cost line is an important feature of the graphical representation of break-even analysis. Consider that the vertical distance between the sales revenue line and the variable cost line represents the contribution margin, the greater the angle between the two lines (and consequently between the sales revenue line and the total cost line) the greater the contribution margin as a percent of sales and the greater the extent of the **operating leverage** of the business.

Break-even analysis can be approached algebraically:

Let:

Q	=	Sales volume in units		
P	=	Selling price per unit		
S	=	Sales dollars	=	PQ
NOI	=	Net operating income		
V	=	Unit variable cost		
VC	=	Total variable costs	=	VQ
FC	=	Fixed operating costs		

At the break-even point in units of production:

$$S = VC + FC$$

$$PQ = VQ + FC$$

$$Q = \frac{FC}{P - V}$$

or:

$$\text{Break-even sales in units} = \frac{\text{Fixed operating costs}}{\text{Unit contribution margin}}$$

where the unit contribution margin is the unit selling price less the unit variable cost.

For example, if Jiminez Backpack, Inc., manufactures and sells backpacks to retailers for \$100 each, the backpacks have a variable cost of \$70 per unit, and the company has fixed costs of \$60,000, then the company's break-even point is:

$$Q = \frac{FC}{P - V} = \frac{60,000}{100 - 70} = 2,000 \text{ backpacks}$$

The problem with this form of analysis is that determining the break-even sales in units is impossible where sales revenue is made up of many different items. In these circumstances one has to determine the break-even point in dollar sales. To do this, begin with what is known:

NOI	=	S	−	VC	−	FC

Net operating income = Sales in dollars − Variable costs − Fixed costs

And, at the break-even point, where the net operating income equals zero:

$$S = VC + FC$$

If we let

$$VC = \frac{VC}{S}(S)$$

and

$$FC = S - VC$$

then

$$FC = S - \left[\frac{VC}{S}(S)\right]$$

thus it can be said:

$$\mathbf{FC = S\left[1 - \left(\frac{VC}{S}\right)\right]}$$

So, the break-even level of sales will be:

$$\mathbf{S = \frac{FC}{1 - \dfrac{VC}{S}}}$$

The denominator $[1 - (\frac{VC}{S})]$ is known as the **contribution margin**. It is the amount of every sales dollar that goes to pay off or *contributes* to covering the fixed costs.

For Jiminez Backpack, Inc., the variable operating cost per sales will be 70 percent. In other words, the first seventy cents of every dollar in sales in the example above goes toward covering the variable costs of production. That is, every dollar of sales incurs seventy cents of variable costs. The next thirty cents ($1.00 – $.70) goes toward recouping the fixed operating costs.

$$S = \frac{FC}{1 - \dfrac{VC}{S}} = \frac{\$60,000}{1 - .7} = \$200,000$$

So, Jiminez Backpack, Inc., must sell $200,000 worth of products to cover its fixed costs and break even. Note that this is the same way of saying that two thousand units must be sold at a price of $100. Dividing the fixed costs by the contribution margin gives the amount of dollar sales needed to just break even.

If this same analysis is applied to the first year of operation of Donnelly & Co. (the income statement for which is reproduced in Exhibit 5.2) and assuming that 30 percent ($39,000) of the $130,000 operating expenses are fixed, fixed costs will be the sum of the fixed operating expenses ($39,000) and the depreciation expense ($12,000), or $51,000.

At this point it should be decided whether to include interest as a fixed cost or not. The majority of the interest expense will be fixed. To the extent that fluc-

◆ **EXHIBIT 5.2**

INCOME STATEMENT FOR THE FIRST YEAR OF OPERATION: DONNELLY & CO.

Sales revenue		$520,000
Cost of goods sold		325,000
Gross profit		$195,000
Operating expenses	$130,000	
Depreciation expense	12,000	
		142,000
Net operating income		$ 53,000
Interest expense		13,000
Earnings before tax		$ 40,000
Income tax expense		12,000
Net income		$ 28,000

◆ **EXHIBIT 5.3**

TOTAL FIXED COSTS

Fixed operating expenses	$39,000
Depreciation	12,000
Fixed costs	$51,000
Interest	13,000
Total fixed costs	$64,000

tuating seasonal needs are included, these will naturally be variable; nevertheless, it is customary to consider interest as fixed. However, there are two things that the analyst generally wants to know: the break-even point of this business *with* debt financing, and the break-even point *ignoring* financing. The latter may appear irrelevant where the owner of the small business is unable to adjust the capital structure of the business, but it is an important starting point to ascertain whether or not the business can break even irrespective of financing.

First the break-even point (ignoring financial leverage and based on fixed costs of $51,000) must be determined. Then the break-even point must be calculated given the present financial structure of the business with total fixed costs of $64,000 (interest expense of $13,000 plus fixed costs of $51,000) as depicted in Exhibit 5.3.

Ignoring financial leverage and assuming that total variable costs will be the sum of cost of goods sold and variable operating expenses, break-even point in sales will be $255,000, as shown in Exhibit 5.4—the firm must sell $255,000 of its products to break even. Since this is approximately one-half of its present sales volume, one can be reasonably sure that the firm, in the absence of financial leverage, can survive quite a large downturn in the demand for its products.

$$S = \frac{FC}{1 - \dfrac{VC}{S}} = \frac{(30\% \times 130{,}000) + \text{depreciation}}{1 - \dfrac{(70\% \times 130{,}000 + \text{cost of goods sold})}{\text{sales}}}$$

$$= \frac{39{,}000 + 12{,}000}{1 - \dfrac{(91{,}000 + 325{,}000)}{520{,}000}} = \$255{,}000$$

Why look at an artificial situation by ignoring the interest component of fixed costs? Inclusion of interest in the fixed costs has the obvious effect of increasing the break-even point (the actual figure will be calculated later in the chapter). Assume that achieving such a level of sales would be impossible. Does this mean that the business has no future? Not necessarily: it could merely mean that there is too much debt in the capital structure. Under these circumstances, the fixed cost associated with the payment of interest must be reduced. The business itself could be quite sound, while the financing is out of balance. Bearing in mind that the cost of equity always exceeds the cost of debt (because it is more risky), the advantage inherent in a situation where the owner finds a partner to replace debt with equity would be short term. While the fixed cost would be reduced, so would the value of equity (the new owner would demand an adequate return on investment, and if the potential cash return is low, the only way that the ROE can be increased is if the price of the investment is low). In the extreme case, the owner will have to sell the business to a new owner at a price that provides an adequate return on the required level of equity.

Break-even analysis does have some assumptions built into it, though, and, as in most cases where assumptions exist, this can cause some weaknesses in its application. The assumptions are as follows:

◆ Break-even analysis assumes that the relationship between sales and variable costs is linear. This means it also assumes the contribution margin is constant. This may not always be so.
◆ It assumes that fixed costs do not change. In practice, fixed costs vary with sales volume, but in a rather "lumpy" fashion. For example, as sales increase, administration costs may increase.
◆ It assumes that the selling price of goods sold stays the same. In practice, a firm may have to decrease the selling price of its products in order to increase the volume of products sold.

Break-even analysis can be adapted to deal with these situations by "bending" the lines on the graph, or by utilizing more complex algebra, but the principle remains the same.

The break-even analysis that has been considered here has ignored interest thus far. Consider that the total fixed costs will include not only the fixed operating expenses ($39,000) but also depreciation ($12,000) and interest ($13,000), the break-even point for Donnelly & Co. becomes $320,000, or 62 percent of present sales volume.

$$S = \frac{\text{Total fixed costs}}{1 - \dfrac{VC}{S}}$$

$$= \frac{64,000}{1 - \dfrac{(91,000 + 325,000)}{520,000}}$$

$$= \frac{64,000}{1 - 0.8} = \$320,000$$

One of the more common adaptations is to include a targeted pre-tax profit in the numerator along with the fixed costs. For example, if the Donnellys wanted to target a $20,000 profit, the numerator would increase to $84,000, and the break-even sales (including a profit of $20,000) becomes $420,000, or 81 percent of present sales volume.

$$S = \frac{FC + \text{interest} + \text{profit}}{1 - \dfrac{VC}{S}} = \frac{64,000 + 20,000}{1 - 0.8}$$

$$= \frac{84,000}{1 - 0.8} = \$420,000$$

Note that if Donnelly & Co. had targeted a pre-tax profit of $40,000 (the present earnings before tax) the break-even point would become $520,000, which is the present sales volume.

$$S = \frac{104,000}{0.2} = \$520,000$$

This step is especially important for the smaller business in which the owner is reliant on the profit of the business to provide a living. Cash flows are likely to be much tighter in the case of the small business, and if break even is not achieved (including an allowance for the owner's consumption needs), then the money has to be borrowed, which is not always possible.

✓ CONCEPT CHECK

1. *What is break-even analysis?*
2. *What is the purpose of break-even analysis?*
3. *Why is break-even analysis undertaken—with and without the inclusion of interest expense?*

4. What problems are faced in the division of costs into their fixed and variable components?
5. What assumptions are made in linear break-even analysis and how can these assumptions be relaxed?

5.3   BUDGETING

Because the owners of a business want to be able to predict whether the firm will make a profit or a loss, whether the firm will survive and grow, and whether the firm will generate enough income to service its debt, they must plan. However, before they can produce such a plan, they must decide on an effective planning period. This will depend on the reason for the forecast. It is not much use preparing a five-year forecast of daily cash positions. That forecast might be more effectively prepared on a weekly basis with daily updates.

Developing a business plan requires the analysis of general business conditions and market conditions so that some estimate of likely sales volume can be determined. In addition to the determination of likely market conditions, a planner should examine the likely cost of borrowing and the feasibility of raising new equity and should also analyze inventory availability and scheduling. She should probably also consider pricing and credit strategies, likely capacity limitations, and product promotion and might also look at likely effects of new product launches on both the firm's and competitors' marketing strategies.

Development of the sales forecast is probably the single most important step in the process of financial planning; sales volume influences most of the other items in the plan, so the accuracy of the sales volume estimate is crucial to the firm's success. If sales estimates are too high, there will be unsold inventory, if they are too low, there are likely to be disgruntled customers.

Financial forecasting finds its nexus in what is known as the **budgeting process**. A budget is a formal statement of expectations of production volume, sales, expenditures, and other financial transactions. It is used to provide an estimate of a firm's future financial requirements. There are many types of budgets, because a budget is merely a forecast of some future relationship. The types of budget that are most important in financial planning are the **pro forma financial reports** (i.e., income statement, balance sheet and cash flow statement that have been projected into the future). The figures used in the budgeting process obviously will depend on such policies and relationships as the sales credit policy, the accounts receivable collection policy, inventory purchase and payment patterns, taxation payments, as well as capital expenditures and receipts.

There are three types of financial planning:

◆ **Profit planning** is the estimation of the sales forecast, the production volumes necessary to meet the sales forecast, and the operating expenses to be incurred in production and administration. Profit planning determines not only the predicted level of profit, but also the sensitivity of that profit to changes in sales and/or expenses. This type of financial planning results in the production of the pro forma income statement and the pro forma balance sheet.

+ **Short-term financial planning** is the development of the **annual cash budget** and the use of this to forecast the cash flow of the firm, cash surpluses and deficits, and any resulting financial effects. There are usually two components to short-term financial planning. First, there is the annual budget, which should relate closely, in a pro forma sense, to the statement of cash flows. Second, there are the monthly (or less) cash-flow budgets. In practice, it is very difficult to compile the first without compiling the second (and vice versa), principally because, in order to ascertain the interest component of the annual budget, it is necessary to predict the likely pattern of cash flows into and out of the business throughout the year. Only then can the interest component of the annual budget be determined.

+ **Long-term financial planning** assists management in planning the funding needs for the future growth of the firm. Long-term financial planning also comprises two major intertwined components. First, there is the process of determining the likely cash flows from the business in its present state. This indicates how much cash is available for reinvestment in the business. Second, there is the capital budgeting process that appraises the various investment possibilities available to the firm and suggests the likely financing needs of those projects. Unlike big business, which is the subject of standard financial texts that assume that both debt and equity are both accessible in public markets, the small firm is constrained in its funding (Chapter 9 addresses this issue in more detail). This means that long-term financial planning, in the case of the smaller firm, must be an iterative process. We establish the funds available from the existing operations of the firm; we measure the outcomes of a set of investment projects; we compare the costs of the projects with the funds available; then we decide which investments are acceptable with and without raising new debt or equity; and, finally, we decide what funds are likely to be available from all sources and prepare the long-term plan.

CONCEPT CHECK

1. *Why does a business need a budget?*
2. *What are the three types of financial planning?*

5.4   PRO FORMA STATEMENTS

As with financial reports, every budget can be divided into two components, operating and financial.

An **operating budget** is a comprehensive plan of the physical product within the business, the interrelationships of all of the physical and financial factors involved, and the determination of planned income. Before a planner can prepare the operating budget, he must first determine lower-level budgets for such items as sales, production, inventory, direct materials, direct labor, production-unit overhead, and selling and administration expenses.

Once these lower-level budgets have been completed, the **pro forma income statement** can be produced. The **financial budget** adds items of a capital nature to the operating budget and results in the presentation of the **pro forma balance sheet** and the annual cash budget.

When available, a previous year's ratios and relationships can be used as a basis for the future. These relationships naturally would be updated for any obvious changes in components such as depreciation or interest.

A pro forma balance sheet relates to a pro forma income statement and an annual cash budget in much the same way that a balance sheet relates to an income statement and a statement of cash flows.

When the analyst/planner begins the budgeting process, she will be in one of two positions: either prior information in the form of financial reports will be available, or it won't. Previous reports may not be available in a number of common circumstances: it may be the first year of operation of the business or the owner may be considering investment in a new project or an existing business for which the current owner is not prepared to provide the previous financial reports.

The next few sections of this chapter examine the budgeting process with and without prior information for both growth and non-growth situations.

 CONCEPT CHECK

1. *What are some of the critical elements in preparing a pro forma budget?*

5.5   GROWTH AND FAILURE: THE BUSINESS LIFE CYCLE

The management of **growth** is one of the major financial-management issues relating to small-business financial management. Without growth, small businesses wither away; with too much growth they have trouble marshaling necessary resources. Lack of growth is evident in the high rate of failure among small firms. In order to understand the problems of growth in a small business, it is important to understand the different phases of growth through which small firms pass.

One of the best discussions of growth is offered by Churchill and Lewis[2] in which they describe five stages of growth:

Stage 1: Existence

Stage 2: Survival

---

[2]See N. C. Churchill, and V. L. Lewis, "The Five Stages of Small Business Growth," *Harvard Business Review* (May–June 1993): 30–34, 38–40, 44, 48, 50.

Stage 3: Success

Stage 4: Take-off

Stage 5: Resource maturity

Stage 1, the existence stage, occurs during the start-up phase of the firm. It is during this stage that the firm must ascertain if it has a customer base and if it can deliver the product or service. During this phase the objective of the small business is to maintain its existence and thus to acquire the option of entering subsequent stages.

In Stage 2 the firm has demonstrated a demand for its products and an ability to provide the service or product. In this phase there is a shift to more sophisticated objectives. **Cash flow** and **profitability** become important. This is the critical phase for most small businesses. Firms can either grow in size and profitability (and move on to further stages) or they can remain at this stage. "Mom and pop" stores are in the category of firms that do not grow, either voluntarily or involuntarily, beyond this stage.

In Stage 3 the firm has demonstrated its ability to survive by its growth in size and profitability. Cash flow is not the pervasive problem it was during Stages 1 and 2. The firm has an accepted product in the marketplace and can deliver the product with consistent profits. In this stage the owners must make a critical decision to either set the foundation for future growth or to remain at this level.

Stage 4 is the take-off stage. In this phase the firm's financial resources are going to be pushed to the limit so its owners must decide how fast the business is to grow and how to acquire the necessary financial resources to support the growth. The firm will need a relatively substantial infusion of funds to finance the necessary build up of current and fixed assets so that cash flow becomes critical again. With respect to their behaviors, the business and its owners can now be considered as being separate. This is evidenced by the replacement of the original owner by more business-cognizant management. Typical financial considerations at this stage are venture capital (capital provided by outsiders who are willing to take large risks) and initial public offerings (IPOs).

In Stage 5 the company becomes a mature firm and attempts to retain the advantages brought on by rapid growth. The support staffs are large enough to allow the firm to compete with almost any size firm. Exhibit 5.5 depicts these stages.

Small businesses comprise the majority of those firms in Stages 1 through 4, although it is possible for a large publicly funded firm to exist temporarily in these stages. Only large businesses typically exist in Stage 5. Growth, with its associated funding requirements, is one of the major problems faced by the small business. The problem is twofold: first, the decision as to whether growth is to be a goal, and, second, if growth is to be a goal, how is it to be funded? The management of growth is a critical and universal problem that the small business must address. As one progresses through this text, the financial implications of growth on the small business in many different areas will be explored.

EXHIBIT 5.5

GROWTH STAGES

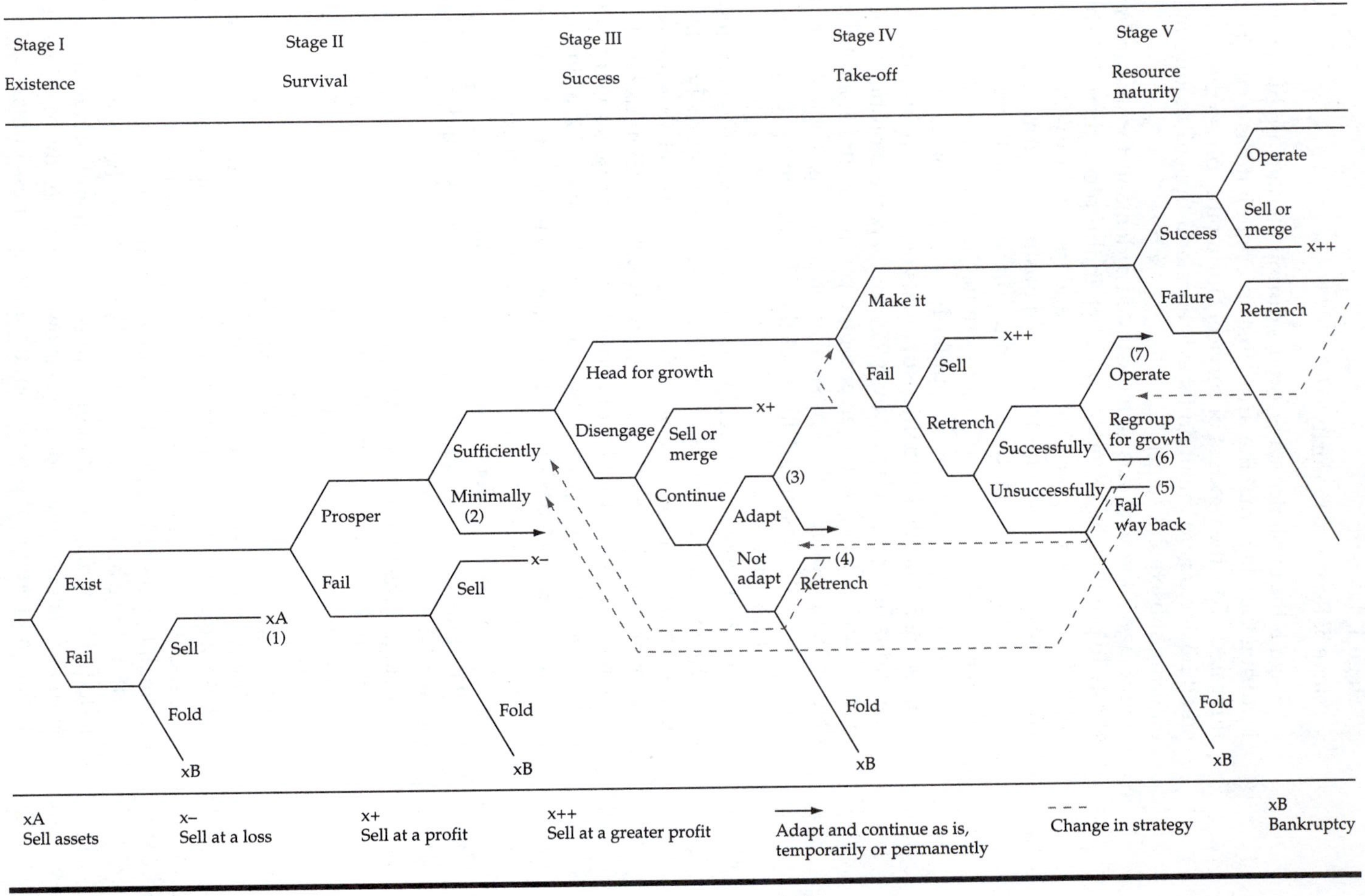

Stage I	Stage II	Stage III	Stage IV	Stage V
Existence	Survival	Success	Take-off	Resource maturity

Exist

Fail

Sell

Fold

xB

xA (1)

Prosper

Fail

Sell

Sufficiently

Minimally (2)

Sell

Fold

xB

x–

Head for growth

Disengage

Sell or merge

Continue

x+

Adapt (3)

Not adapt

Retrench (4)

Fold

xB

Make it

Fail

Sell

Retrench

x++

Successfully

Unsuccessfully

Operate (7)

Regroup for growth (6)

Fall way back (5)

Fold

xB

Success

Sell or merge

Operate

x++

Failure

Retrench

Bankruptcy

xB

xA Sell assets

x– Sell at a loss

x+ Sell at a profit

x++ Sell at a greater profit

xB Bankruptcy

→ Adapt and continue as is, temporarily or permanently

– – – Change in strategy

CONCEPT CHECK

1. *Why does a small business need to manage growth?*
2. *What are the stages of growth in a business?*

5.6   BUDGETING WITH PRIOR FINANCIAL INFORMATION

Examining the financial reports from previous periods provides a very good starting point for the budgeting process. Even if records from the existing business are not available, the planner may be able to gain access to information relating to similar businesses. One of the advantages that professional analysts have over others is that their own experiences provide prior information.

Assume that an analyst is being asked to analyze the performance of Donnelly & Co. and to plan for its future. Information is available in the form of its financial reports for its first year of operation. The income statement for Donnelly & Co. was depicted in Exhibit 5.2, and its statement of cash flows is portrayed in Exhibit 5.6.

◆ EXHIBIT 5.6

STATEMENT OF CASH FLOWS: DONNELLY & CO.

Operating income	$ 53,000	
Less: income tax	(12,000)	
		$ 41,000
Plus: positive cash-flow factors:		
Accounts payable increase	30,000	
Accrued expenses increase	15,000	
Income tax payable increase	3,000	
Depreciation	12,000	
		60,000
Less: negative cash-flow factors:		
Accounts receivable increase	60,000	
Inventory increase	80,000	
Prepaid expenses increase	10,000	
		(150,000)
Cash flow from operations		$(49,000)
Short-term borrowing	20,000	
Long-term borrowing	80,000	
Equity contribution	82,000	
	182,000	
Interest	(11,000)	
Cash flow from financing		171,000
Cash flow from investing		(120,000)
Increase in cash		$ 2,000

There are a number of things that the planner must do. The following list reflects the process in general, although it must be pointed out that there are as many different ways of budgeting as there are planners. The critical thing to remember is that budgeting is an iterative process, i.e., the planner does something, looks at it, makes a decision, and that decision will affect the next step of the process. While there are many highly sophisticated computer-based budgeting packages, the skill and judgment of the planner is more critical to the success of the process than is the type of template or package used.

1. The planner decides whether or not the firm is likely to grow in the subsequent period, because if not, as we shall see, the subsequent period's performance will be very similar to the prior period's.
2. Financial information, where it is represented in accrual form, such as in Exhibit 5.6, is converted to cash form. If a statement of cash flows is presented together with the other financial statements, this step becomes much easier.
3. The budgets are prepared and, in an iterative process, decisions (such as the level of the dividend payout, wages paid to the owners, or debt repayment) can be incorporated prior to presentation of the final version.

The best framework to use in the budgeting process is that which forms the basis for the preparation of a statement of cash flows. As has been pointed out earlier, businesses are funded in three different ways. **Operating activities** include all of those activities associated with the earning of operating income, or EBIT. **Financing activities** are those that are associated with the raising, servicing, and redemption of debt and equity. **Investment activities** are those associated with the sale and purchase of the productive assets of the business and of marketable securities.

BUDGETING FOR NO GROWTH (WITH INFORMATION)

The easiest budget to compile is the one that plans for no growth and when there are previous financial reports to assist with the process. "No growth" refers to the level of activity of the firm; the no-growth firm will have similar sales to the previous period, similar margins, and similar assets and liabilities (and thus net worth).

With respect to the cash flow from operating activities, if there is no growth in sales and neither internal nor external credit policies change, then there should be no change in the level of current assets, such as accounts receivable, or current liabilities, such as **accounts payable.** This means that the firm will not have to invest more heavily in its current assets, but neither will it realize its current liabilities; i.e., as fast as accounts receivable are received, new debtors are accrued; the same principle applies to accounts payable. This means that the majority of the items reported as revenues and expenditures will be represented similarly in the subsequent period, not only by an accrual accounting basis, but also on a cash basis. This assumption is the starting point in the planning process.

♦ **EXHIBIT 5.7**

BUDGETED OPERATING CASH FLOWS

Sales	$ 520,000
Less: cost of sales	(325,000)
Gross profit	195,000
Less: operating expenses	(142,000)
Operating earnings	53,000
Plus: non-cash depreciation	12,000
Before-tax cash flows from operations	65,000
Less: taxes	(12,000)
After-tax cash flows from operations	$ 53,000

♦ **EXHIBIT 5.8**

TAX SHIELD ON DEPRECIATION EFFECT

Operating income	$ 54,000
Less: income tax expense	(12,300)
	41,700
Plus: depreciation	11,000
Cash flow from operations	$ 52,700

In the case of Donnelly & Co., the analyst can assume that the budget will be based on a gross profit of $195,000 and a pre-tax cash flow from operations of $65,000, as shown in the **cash-flow budget** in Exhibit 5.7.

Notice that depreciation is accounted for in two places. It is initially included in the operating expenses and then it is added back. Even though it may seem unnecessary to undertake the two steps separately, it is important that depreciation be identified so that taxation can be determined accurately. Of course, the amount of depreciation budgeted may be quite different from that of prior periods, but any increase or decrease in depreciation will only affect the taxation cash flow, nothing else.

For example, if depreciation was expected to be $1,000 less in the subsequent year (e.g., $11,000) this would add $1,000 to Donnelly's operating income (increasing it to $54,000) and consequently adding $300 to taxation (to $12,300).

Exhibit 5.8 demonstrates how this will change the cash flow from operations if all other things are held equal.[3]

---

[3]It should be noted that taxes are *not* 30 percent of the firm's operating income. The level of taxes is derived from the accounting process. In this example, taxes are computed on 30 percent of $40,000 (see Exhibit 5.2), *not* 30 percent of $53,000. Rather than complete a pro forma income statement at this stage, one can adjust for the tax effects of the changes independently.

If you compare the after-tax cash flow from operations shown in Exhibit 5.7 ($53,000) with the equivalent figure in Exhibit 5.8 ($52,700) one can see that the difference between the two is the $300 taxes paid; the amount of depreciation allowed by the accounting process has been relevant only for the tax computation. The tax shield on depreciation reduced by $300 because the allowance for depreciation was reduced by $1,000 at a tax rate of 30 percent.

For Donnelly & Co., Exhibit 5.7 shows the before-tax operating cash flows to be $65,000. At some point we need to deduct taxation from this figure, and it is at this point that the budgeting approach and the accounting approach (i.e., the statement of cash flows) part company. It is just not possible to establish the budget for taxes without considering some other expenses and making other adjustments. In reality, in order to establish an accurate tax figure, the planner needs to prepare the pro forma income statement. Only in this way can future taxes be accurately represented.

In the no-growth situation there will be some slight changes to funds arising from operations. There may also be changes in investing and financing activities.

Consider the investing activities. It is one thing to show a cash surplus in the absence of any investment activity, it is quite another to show a surplus after allowing for the maintenance of capital assets. While depreciation is ignored in the budgeting process (except in the calculation of taxation) undertaking no capital replacement presents a very short-term view of business existence. Why would the no-growth firm need to purchase new assets? In order to continue to produce the revenues of the business, its assets must be maintained at their **productive capacity**. For example, consider the case of a delivery business. If the vehicle that forms the basis of the business is not replaced from time to time, the business will inevitably decline. The no-growth scenario, which applies to a very large number of small businesses, implies that sales revenue is not increasing; but it also implies that the productive value of the firm's assets is maintained. If business assets are not maintained, net worth will decline.

If the objective of the cash-flow budget is short term, then no allowance for capital maintenance need be included (unless it will actually be spent—after all, the main purpose of the budget is to reflect reality). However, if the purpose of the budget is to fit into the wider scenario of long-term planning, then capital must be maintained. How is this reflected in the budget? Some planners "beef-up" the repairs and maintenance provisions of the budget, others prefer to include a cash item for plant replacement either nominally or as a sinking fund (an account set up to store funds in anticipation of needs). Which method is used will depend very much on the circumstances. If the plant is new, then there will be little need for formal recognition of plant maintenance in the near term. On the other hand, if it is old, the problem becomes much more immediate. It is interesting to note that many planners dodge the problem completely by including the depreciation allowance as a sort of nominal sinking-fund payment.

The analyst also needs to consider the cash flows associated with financing activities. Financing relates to three elements: interest, debt repayment (or additional borrowing), and dividend payments. First, with respect to interest, even in the no-growth situation it is unlikely that the amount of interest paid will be identical across all periods. Only in the limited circumstance of absolute stability of interest rates and identical cash flows into and out of the business would the interest paid be identical. The preparer of an annual budget can often take a fairly accurate guess at the interest that is likely to be paid because the majority of interest is usually contractual. However, to be really accurate in circumstances of current-account borrowing, the planner should prepare a cash-flow budget by the week (or at least by the month) so that the actual likely cash-flow patterns can be measured. An example of cash-flow budgeting will be given later on in this chapter.

The second element of the financing activity is the change in debt. Most firms with debt reduce that debt. All formal repayments should be budgeted.

The third element to consider regarding the funds associated with the financing activity of the business relates to equity. In the case of corporate ownership and the payment of a dividend, the dividend should be included as an outflow of funds associated with the financing activity. Owners of a business may also introduce or withdraw equity from time to time and this must also be planned for.

If one assumes that, for Donnelly & Co.,

+ depreciation for the coming year will be $11,000,
+ $12,500 will be spent on interest,
+ gross profit will be $195,000,
+ operating expenses will be $130,000,
+ the Donnelly proprietors will pay themselves a dividend equal to the firm's net income, and
+ there will be no other cash flows associated with financing or investing, then

the ending cash balance will be forecasted at $13,000 (as depicted in Exhibit 5.9).

This budget tells a considerably different story than the cash flows exhibited by Donnelly & Co. in its first year of operation. Notice that in the no-growth situation the increase in cash is solely due to depreciation being non-cash. If one merely adds back depreciation to the net income projected for the period, the period's cash flow would be determined.

Exhibit 5.10 presents the pro forma income statement and balance sheet for Donnelly & Co. for the period budgeted. Notice that the only changes from the previous period are that the book value of plant and equipment has declined by the $11,000 in depreciation for the year, and that cash has increased by an identical amount.

BUDGETING FOR GROWTH (WITH INFORMATION)

"Growth" in the context of this chapter refers to the circumstance in which sales are expected to increase. When sales increase, many of the items in both the income statement and the balance sheet increase at the same time. In fact,

ANNUAL BUDGET (NO GROWTH)

Sales	$ 520,000
Less: cost of sales	(325,000)
Gross profit	195,000
Less: operating expenses	(130,000)
Less: depreciation	(11,000)
Operating earnings	54,000
Less: interest	(12,500)
Earnings before taxation	41,500
Less: taxes	(12,450)
Net income	29,050
Plus: depreciation	11,000
	40,050
Less: dividend	(29,050)
Increase in cash	11,000
Plus: beginning cash balance	2,000
Ending cash balance	$ 13,000

as sales increase, many of the current asset and current liability accounts also increase spontaneously at the same rate. For example, if sales were to increase by 50 percent, other things being equal, one could expect accounts receivable to increase by 50 percent. Of course, it is always possible that some of the increase in activity arises as a conscious decision to change working-capital policy. In those cases the discussion that follows would have to be amended to suit those particular circumstances.

Whether growth entails an increase in other assets and liabilities is a function of whether or not there was unutilized capacity in the original assets (in which case the purchase of additional assets would not be necessary) and of the business policy relating to financing. Growth causes liquidity problems in small businesses. How that problem is funded is a function of the rate of growth, the amount of money involved, the financial slack (surplus cash) of the business, and the owners' access and attitudes to various sources of both debt and equity.

Where the analyst has access to prior information, life is made much easier. Again, the starting point is to construct the pro forma income statement and balance sheet and then adjust those to present the budgeted cash flows. As was the case with budgeting for no growth, the only way to prepare the budget effectively for the growth situation is by using all of the information available and breaking down the annual budget into predicted monthly or weekly cash flows to accurately predict the interest expenditure.

By way of an example, use Donnelly & Co. again as the basis for the previous period and assume that sales will increase by 20 percent while other critical relationships, such as the gross margin and receivables turnover, re-

✦ EXHIBIT 5.10

PRO FORMA FINANCIAL STATEMENTS: NO GROWTH (DONNELLY & CO.)

INCOME STATEMENT FOR THE YEAR

Sales revenue		$520,000
Cost of goods sold		(325,000)
Gross profit		$195,000
Operating expenses	$130,000	
Depreciation expense	11,000	(141,000)
Operating earnings		$54,000
Interest expense		(12,500)
Earnings before tax		$41,500
Income tax expense		(12,450)
Net income		$ 29,050

BALANCE SHEET AT END OF YEAR

Current assets:			*Current liabilities:*		
Cash		$ 13,000	Accounts payable		$ 30,000
Accounts receivable		60,000	Accrued expenses		17,000
Inventory		80,000	Income tax payable		3,000
Prepaid expenses		10,000	Short-term bank loan at 13%		20,000
Total current assets		$163,000	Total current liabilities		$ 70,000
			Long-term liabilities:		
			Long-term notes payable at 13%		80,000
Fixed assets:			Total liabilities		$150,000
Machinery, equipment					
Furniture and fixtures	$120,000		*Shareholders' equity:*		
Accumulated depreciation	(23,000)		Paid-in capital	$82,000	
Net fixed assets		97,000	Retained earnings	28,000	
			Total shareholders' equity		110,000
Total assets		$260,000	Total liabilities and shareholders' equity		$260,000

main the same. Also assume that the firm was operating at full capacity in the previous period and, therefore, any increase in production will have to be accompanied by a proportionate increase in plant size.

The first step is to produce a pro forma income statement. Exhibit 5.11 presents the pro forma statements for the circumstance of 20 percent growth for the business, assuming that it was previously operating at full capacity.

This exhibit shows every item in the income statement being increased by 20 percent including depreciation and interest. With respect to depreciation in this case it is assumed that straight-line depreciation is being used (so accumulated depreciation equals the $12,000 incurred in the prior period plus 10 percent of $144,000 in assets). Generally, the depreciation expense should be that used in the accounting process. There is less justification for increasing

PRO FORMA STATEMENTS: 20 PERCENT GROWTH

Pro Forma Income Statement

Sales revenue		$624,000
Cost of goods sold		(390,000)
Gross profit		234,000
Operating expenses	156,000	
Depreciation expense	14,400	
		(170,400)
Operating income		63,600
Interest expense		(15,600)
Earnings before tax		48,000
Income tax expense		(14,400)
Net income		$ 33,600

Pro Forma Balance Sheet

Assets:		
Cash		$ 16,000
Accounts receivable		72,000
Inventory		96,000
Prepaid expenses		12,000
Current assets		$196,000
Fixed assets	144,000	
Accumulated depreciation	(26,400)	
Net fixed assets		117,600
Total assets		$313,600
Liabilities:		
Accounts payable		$ 36,000
Accrued expenses		20,400
Income tax payable		3,600
Short-term bank loan		30,000
Current liability		$ 90,000
Shareholders' equity:		
Long-term debt		80,000
Paid-in capital		82,000
Retained earnings		61,600
Total shareholders' equity		$223,600
Total liabilities & shareholders' equity		$313,600

the interest bill by 20 percent because this figure depends largely on the magnitude of the associated borrowings necessary to support this sales growth.

When one looks at the projected current assets and current liabilities of Donnelly & Co. it can be seen that, with the exception of the cash figure,

CASH FLOW FROM OPERATIONS: 20 PERCENT GROWTH

Operating income	$ 63,600	
Less: income tax	(14,400)	
		$ 49,200
Plus: positive cash-flow factors:		
Accounts payable increase	$ 6,000	
Accrued expenses increase	3,000	
Income tax payable increase	600	
Depreciation	14,400	
		24,000
Less: negative cash-flow factors:		
Accounts receivable increase	$ 12,000	
Inventory increase	16,000	
Prepaid expenses increase	2,000	
		(30,000)
Cash flow from operations		$ 43,200

these too have been "spontaneously" increased by 20 percent along with the fixed assets. This increase includes an increase in accrued interest (included in accrued expenses) of $400.

The second stage of the budgeting process is to convert Donnelly & Co.'s pro forma statements into cash-flow form. As described in Chapter 2, this is done by adjusting the net income figure for changes in current assets and current liabilities. Exhibit 5.10 shows the forecasted income statement and balance sheet under the no-growth scenario, while Exhibit 5.11 shows them for a 20 percent growth assumption. Exhibit 5.12 shows the cash flow from operations derived from these forecasts given the assumption that accrued expenses includes an increase in accrued interest of $400, which will be accounted for as a financing adjustment. From this analysis it can be established that the 20 percent increase in Donnelly & Co.'s sales will generate an increase in positive cash flow of $43,200 compared with an analogous amount under a no-growth scenario of $53,000. The difference is the amount that has had to be invested immediately in working capital.

We now need to graft the fund flows from investing and financing activities onto this amount. The cash flow from investing activities reflects the $24,000 expenditure on new assets. If Donnelly & Co. had been operating with excess capacity in the past, this investment may not have been necessary. The decision to invest in surplus capacity is part of the strategic planning process and it is always possible that there could be a decision made at any time as part of that process to add to the assets of the business. Deducting the $24,000 from the $43,200 leaves a surplus of $19,200.

✦ EXHIBIT 5.13

BUDGETED CASH FLOWS: 20 PERCENT GROWTH

Cash flow from operations	$ 43,200
Cash flow from investments	(24,000)
Cash flow from financing	(5,200)
Increase in cash	$ 14,000
Beginning cash balance	2,000
Ending cash balance	$ 16,000

The third stage of the budgeting process is to determine the budgeted cash flows from financing activities so that the cash balance can be determined. Obviously, this part of the process is also iterative. Interest of $15,600 has been budgeted of which $400 is accrued, so interest paid in cash will be $15,200. It is also obvious from the pro forma balance sheet that an additional $10,000 in short-term financing has been raised. Therefore, the cash flows from financing activities will consume $5,200—leaving an overall increase of $14,000 in cash on hand to add to the $2,000 beginning balance.

Exhibit 5.13 displays the final budgeted cash flows of Donnelly & Co. as extracted from the pro forma income statement and balance sheet.

The difficulty that the analyst now faces is that, while the level of cash on hand at the end of the period has been forecasted effectively and has been presented on the pro forma income statement and balance sheet, these are not in the form usually presented as an annual budget. The analyst needs to regroup this information in the form depicted in Exhibit 5.10 for the no-growth situation.

To undertake this step requires some additional information. Assume that, of the $60,000 increase in accounts payable, $10,000 will relate to operating expenses and the balance to inventories; also assume that, of the increase in accrued expenses, $3,000 will relate to operating expenses with the balance relating to interest. Now the pro forma income statement can be adjusted to reflect the components of the cash flow. The full result is depicted in Exhibit 5.14.

In practice, this pro forma format is summarized still further by condensing the increases and decreases in current assets and current liabilities into their relevant components, as shown in Exhibit 5.15. However, it is critical that changes in these items are not ignored and, at least in the initial stages of the reporting process, should be included as shown.

CONCEPT CHECK

1. *Justify the provision of the statement of cash flows in the financial reports of a business from the perspective of its use in the budgeting process.*

◆ EXHIBIT 5.14

PRO FORMA STATEMENT OF CASH FLOWS: 20 PERCENT GROWTH

Sales revenue	$624,000	
Less: accounts receivable increase	(12,000)	
Collections of sales		$ 612,000
Cost of goods sold	(390,000)	
Less: accounts payable increase	5,000	
Plus: inventory increase	(16,000)	
Cost of sales paid		(401,000)
Cash gross profit		$ 211,000
Operating expenses	(170,400)	
Less: accounts payable increase	1,000	
Less: accrued expenses increase	3,000	
Less: depreciation	14,400	
Plus: prepaid expenses increase	(2,000)	
Cash operating expenses		(154,000)
Cash operating income		$ 57,000
Income tax	(14,400)	
Less: accrued tax increase	600	
Income tax paid		(13,800)
Cash flow from operations		43,200
Interest expense	(15,600)	
Less: accrued interest increase	400	
Interest paid		(15,200)
Cash income prior to capital adjustments		$ 28,000
Cash flow from investments	(24,000)	
Cash flow from financing	10,000	
Capital cash flows		(14,000)
Cash flows budgeted for the period		$ 14,000
Beginning cash balance		2,000
Ending cash balance		$ 16,000

2. *How is the depreciation of fixed assets handled in a cash-budgeting context?*
3. *When is the assumption that increases in production activity will require proportionate investment in plant and equipment (and perhaps other fixed assets) valid?*
4. *What are "spontaneous increases" in working-capital items and when do they arise?*
5. *We often hear that "growth causes funding problems." How can an increase in profitability be accompanied by a decrease in liquidity?*

◆ EXHIBIT 5.15

ANNUAL CASH BUDGET: 20 PERCENT GROWTH

Cash receipts:		
Cash sales		$612,000
Cash expenditures:		
Purchases	$401,000	
Selling and administration	154,000	
Interest	15,200	
Income tax	13,800	
Total cash expenditures		(584,000)
Cash flow before capital items		$ 28,000
Capital receipts:		
Short-term borrowing	(10,000)	
Capital expenditures:		
Asset purchases	24,000	
Net capital cash flow		(14,000)
Increase in cash during the year		$ 14,000
Beginning cash balance		2,000
Ending cash balance		$ 16,000

5.7   BUDGETING WITHOUT PRIOR INFORMATION

In the case of many small-business budgeting exercises, prior information will not be available. In these cases it may be possible to obtain information about similar businesses to guide the forecasting process, but, if not, the analyst must start by predicting the sales figure and the relevant ratios and then constructing the types of reports that have been considered above. The second step in this process is to adjust the figures so determined to reflect changes in current assets and current liabilities—thereby allowing for such things as sales not paid by customers (an increase in accounts receivable) and expenses not paid (an increase in accounts payable) by the business itself.

The process is not entirely different from that followed where prior information is available, but the planner needs to "create" the same type of information before the forecasts can be begun.

BUDGETING FOR NO GROWTH (NO INFORMATION)

For reasons explained previously in this chapter, if a firm's sales are static and the relationships between sales and expenditure patterns are also static, then changes in current assets and current liabilities can be ignored; the collections and payments of prior periods will be exactly matched by the accruals of the future period.

Gan Enterprises is an importing and distribution business. The business is not growing, but has provided the Gan family with a good living. The family

ANNUAL CASH FORECAST

Sales receipts	$180,000
Cost of sales	(30,000)
Cash gross profit	$150,000
Operating expenses	(24,000)
Depreciation	(24,000)
Operating income	$102,000
Interest	(12,000)
Earnings before taxation	$ 90,000
Taxation	(27,000)
Net income	$ 63,000
Plus: depreciation	24,000
	$ 87,000
Loan repayment	(20,000)
Cash surplus for the year	$ 67,000

is considering selling the business, but is not prepared to provide potential purchasers with previous accounting reports. The Goh family is considering buying the business and while they have not been given any previous financial reports, they have managed to estimate the following:

- ◆ Sales — $15,000 per month
- ◆ Inventory purchases — $2,500 per month
- ◆ Operating expenses — $2,000 per month
- ◆ Tax rate — 30 percent
- ◆ Interest to be paid — 12 percent on a $100,000 loan
- ◆ Principal payments per year — $20,000 per year
- ◆ Assets consist of vehicles and equipment that will cost the Gohs $120,000 and that can be depreciated on a straight-line basis at a rate of 20 percent

Exhibit 5.16 shows the cash forecast resulting from these projections. One can see that this circumstance is very easily modeled following the normal accounting rules for the preparation of an income statement because there are no changes in the accruals. Unfortunately, it is not always so easy, especially when growth is involved.

BUDGETING FOR GROWTH (NO INFORMATION)

Remember that the cost of goods sold and many of the operating expenses can be expected to increase directly with sales. Costs that do this are known as **variable costs**. However, some operating expenses might not increase directly with sales.

- ◆ Interest expense depends more on the level of debt than on the level of sales.

✦ Depreciation does not increase unless the company has to purchase additional plant to service an increase in sales. If the business is not operating at **full capacity** (i.e., has unutilized capacity) the existing asset base might well be able to absorb an increase in sales volume without the need to expand.

✦ **Overhead** expenses, such as general administration expenses, may be fixed costs **(fixed overheads).** For example, there is only one chief executive's salary paid.

The problem with growth in the small business, as already seen, is that, even though net income is growing, the cash flow from operations is considerably less than that in the no-growth case. In the case of the small business that often has difficulty locating permanent financing on reasonable terms, this phenomenon results in very conservative cash management. The owners of the growing small business will usually err on the side of conservatism by limiting extra payments to themselves (either as bonuses or dividends) and will often neglect plant replacement. Unless credit lines are organized in advance to match the extra funds needed, the quick ratio of the small growing business can deteriorate rapidly, with potentially disastrous results.

Without prior information, the budgeting process must begin from scratch. The following section of this chapter describes the determination of the cash-flow budget that can form the basis for the preparation of the annual cash budget and that will identify the timing and pattern of extra funds needed.

 CONCEPT CHECK

1. *What are some problems with growth in small businesses?*

5.8   BUDGETING: THE PERCENT-OF-SALES TECHNIQUE

The cash-flow budget shows the timing of cash inflows and outflows, usually based on the weekly (or monthly) sales forecasts, and is an important tool for short-term financial management because it gives the owner of the business a prediction of the timing and amount of cash surpluses and shortages. If the owner is aware of potential liquidity bottlenecks well in advance, then some action for extra credit can be undertaken before any checks bounce. Likewise, if the owner is aware of surpluses of cash well in advance, then some optimal investment decision can be made in an attempt to match the amount of time for which the surplus will exist and the term of the investment selected.

There are two basic methods of preparing the cash-flow budget:

✦ The division of the annual cash budget into shorter periods is based on past experience and records. This method suits those types of business with "lumpy" cash flows and extreme seasonality, and those for which the cash flows associated with the cost of goods sold and the sales themselves are only weakly related. It also suits the prior-information circumstance best.

◆ EXHIBIT 5.17

EXTRA FUNDS NEEDED

+	Increases in fixed assets to allow production
	Spontaneous increases in current assets
=	Funding required for additional assets
−	Spontaneous increases in current liabilities
−	Retained earnings increase (net income less dividends)
=	Extra funds needed

◆ The percent-of-sales forecasting technique is an alternative method of preparing a cash-flow budget. This technique is based on the assumption that current assets, current liabilities, and perhaps fixed assets vary proportionately with sales. It is very well suited to circumstances in which planners find it necessary to build the budget "from the bottom up," such as when there is little prior information available. While the technique described assumes that the relevant ratios are known in advance (perhaps from information derived from "industrial espionage" of comparable businesses). On the other hand, where such relationships are not available, estimates of the amounts of the items themselves can be used in the place of the ratio-based methodology.

The basic technique is the same as that applied in projecting the growth scenario earlier in this chapter. For example, if for comparable businesses, the current and fixed assets are 40 percent of sales, it can be assumed that this relationship will approximately be maintained into the future in the business being planned. This means that every $100 increase in sales will need a $40 increase in assets; in other words, the analyst naively assumes that costs and assets vary linearly with sales (as in the basic break-even-analysis assumptions).

It is easy to see how current assets, such as accounts receivable, increase spontaneously with an increase in sales, and how if the manufacturing plant is at full capacity now, a 10 percent increase in sales will require a 10 percent increase in manufacturing capacity. These increases in assets must be financed somehow; either by an increase in equity, or by an increase in borrowing. Some of this financing also occurs spontaneously. If accounts payable and accrued expenses vary directly with sales, say at a 40 percent rate, then every extra $100 in sales will generate $40 in spontaneous increases in liabilities. Therefore, only the difference between the increase in assets and the spontaneous increase in liabilities has to be funded. Exhibit 5.17 depicts how the **extra funds needed (EFN)** arises.

How is the cash-flow budget determined? In the two examples that follow assume monthly figures are required. The first example concentrates on the relationship between sales-collection policy and cash flow.

Example 1 Gloria's Repairs is an automotive-repair shop. While some of the work carried out is for individuals, Gloria has concentrated more on contractually servicing the fleets of larger firms. Gloria estimates that sales for the next three months will be:

March sales	$100,000
April sales	$120,000
May sales	$ 80,000

Analysis of Gloria's Repairs' sales and accounts receivable shows that 70 percent of all sales are made on credit while 30 percent are made in cash. Of the credit sales, 20 percent will be collected in the month of the sale, 70 percent in the following month, and the final 10 percent in the third month. Gloria's bank wants to know how much cash will be collected in May.

	March	April	May
Total sales	$100,000	$120,000	$80,000
Cash sales (30%)	$ 30,000	$ 36,000	$24,000
Credit sales (70%)	$ 70,000	$ 84,000	$56,000

To answer this question, not only May's sales, but also the sales made in other months that will affect the cash collections made in May must be considered. The first step is to determine the credit sales and cash sales for every month that affects May's collections.

The second step is to allocate the collections of each month's sales:

Collections:					
Cash sales	in	May	=	30% of $80,000	$ 24,000
Credit sales	in	May	=	20% of $56,000	11,200
	in	April	=	70% of $84,000	58,800
	in	March	=	10% of $70,000	7,000
Total collections in May					$101,000

The following example demonstrates how the collection analysis shown above can also be applied to accounts payable. The example also adds a number of other relationships from the past to provide clues as to the future.

Example 2 Plumbers' Supplies sells plumbing supplies. All of its sales are on credit and the owners' bank is worried about the firm's liquidity and has asked for monthly cash budgets for the months of March and April. The following information is known:

Current assets at Feb. 28:	Inventory	$28,000
	Accounts receivable	83,000

Bank debt:	Line of credit	$20,000
	Short-term loan	5,000
Sales prior to Feb. 28:	December	$70,000
	January	40,000
	February	60,000
Forecasted sales:	March	$80,000
	April	80,000
	May	100,000

Expected collections:	60 percent in the month following sale
	30 percent in the second month
	8 percent in the third month
	2 percent uncollectible bad debts

Cost of goods sold:	70 percent of sales
	All purchases are on credit
	Expected payment to suppliers:
	80 percent in the month following purchase
	20 percent in the second month

| Fixed overhead: | $6,000 per month, paid in the month incurred |

| Variable overhead: | 10% of sales |

| Expected payment: | Half in the month incurred |
| | Half in the following month |

| Inventories: | At the first of each month, inventories should be one-half of the forecasted cost of sales for the month |

| Other expenditures: | During March income tax of $12,000 will be paid |
| | During April dividends of $20,000 will be paid |

When this data is analyzed and reported in the format shown in Exhibit 5.18 one can see that the business has financing problems in both March and April. If the bank's line of credit was renegotiated upward to $50,000, then there would be no solvency problems in either March or April. Accelerating the collections of accounts receivable or slowing down the payment of accounts payable would also help the firm's solvency during this period.

It should be noted that, in Exhibit 5.18, the ending inventory for each month equals the beginning inventory for the following month (in turn, equal to one-half of the cost of sales for the month).

The cash-flow budget for Plumbers' Supplies (Exhibit 5.19) can now be derived from the information presented in Exhibit 5.18. One can see from the bottom line that this business requires extra funds of $2,600 in March and an additional $19,400 in April. Without organizing these amounts in advance, the owners of the business could be sorely embarrassed.

✦ EXHIBIT 5.18

COLLECTIONS AND PAYMENTS

	December	January	February	March	April	May
Sales and collections:						
Sales	$70,000	$40,000	$60,000	$80,000	$80,000	$100,000
Collections:						
First month 60%		42,000	24,000	36,000	48,000	48,000
Second month 30%			21,000	12,000	18,000	24,000
Third month 8%				5,600	3,200	4,800
Total collections				$53,600	$69,200	$ 76,800
Purchases and payments:						
Purchases:						
COGS (70% of sales)	49,000	28,000	42,000	56,000	56,000	70,000
Ending inventory	14,000	21,000	28,000	28,000	35,000	
	63,000	49,000	70,000	84,000	91,000	
Beginning inventory		14,000	21,000	28,000	28,000	
Purchases needed		35,000	49,000	56,000	63,000	
Purchases payments:						
First month 80%			28,000	39,200	44,800	
Second month 20%				7,000	9,800	
Total payments				46,200	54,600	
Variable overhead:						
Budgeted 10% of sales			6,000	8,000	8,000	
Payments:						
Same month 50%			3,000	4,000	4,000	
Next month 50%				3,000	4,000	
Total Payments:				$ 7,000	$ 8,000	

✦ EXHIBIT 5.19

CASH FLOW BUDGET FOR MARCH AND APRIL

	March	April
Receipts:		
Collections from sales	$53,600	$69,200
Payments:		
Purchases	46,200	54,600
Fixed overhead	6,000	6,000
Variable overhead	7,000	8,000
Taxation	12,000	
Dividends		20,000
Total payments	(71,200)	(88,600)
Net cash flow during the month:	(17,600)	(19,400)
Beginning short-term bank debt	(5,000)	(22,600)
Cumulative bank debt if no financing:	(22,600)	(42,000)
Present credit limit	(20,000)	(20,000)
Cumulative financing needs	$ 2,600	$22,000

CONCEPT CHECK

1. *What added problems are faced when budgeting without prior information?*
2. *How realistic is the percent of sales technique?*
3. *Why should a business undertake a monthly cash-flow budgeting process?*

SUMMARY

- ✦ Financial planning is critical for all businesses, but even more so for the smaller business because its owners are more exposed to risk personally than are the owners of large public companies.
- ✦ Break-even analysis, and variants of it that apply more in the case of the smaller firm, can be used to provide insight into the sales requirements of the business in order to break even. Sales are the cornerstone of planning; once they are known, other items in the budgetary process can be ascertained.
- ✦ Budgeting can be undertaken with or without prior information. While budgeting without prior information is technically more difficult, the processes for the two situations are similar in principle. The statement of cash flows assists the budgetary process immeasurably because the annual cash budget is merely a pro forma statement of cash flows. Given the pro forma income statement and balance sheet, the annual cash budget can be compiled in a similar manner to the determination of the statement of cash flows.
- ✦ Growth causes funding problems, especially in the case of the smaller business, which does not have effective access to capital markets. Calculating the funding needed to allow the effective continuance of the business in an environment where constraints are placed on the amount that can be borrowed is a necessary part of the planning process.

THE CASE—PART FIVE

Dave's Bikes had a good year in its fourth year of operations (2001). Dave and his overseas suppliers consolidated their relationship as Dave's Bikes & Co. increased its sales and approached its existing capacity. Dave not only totally cleared his current account advance, but also repaid $10,000 of his term loan with the bank and even managed to put $3,000 in a savings account (earning 5 percent) with the bank. He also managed to maintain the 40 percent dividend-payout ratio that he had begun the previous year. While Dave had undertaken a considerable amount of informal planning, it had always occurred to him that he should undertake some sort of formal financial planning.

ASSIGNMENT 5.1

Dave's Bikes sold 1,500 bicycles in 2001. Fixed operating costs were $52,000. An abbreviated income statement for Dave's Bikes & Co. for 2001 shows:

Sales revenue	$504,562	
Cost of goods sold	(267,723)	
Gross profit		$236,839
Operating expenses	173,094	
Depreciation expense	12,535	(185,629)
Net operating income		$ 51,210
Interest expenses (net)		(7,593)

Earnings before tax	$ 43,617
Income tax expense	(13,085)
Net Income	$ 30,532
Dividend	(12,213)
Retained Earnings	$ 18,319

Required

1. Calculate:

    a) Total fixed costs (including interest and depreciation)

    b) Total variable costs

    c) Contribution margin

    d) Unit contribution margin

    e) Contribution margin percent

    f) The buffer against a decline in sales

    g) Break-even sales in units

    h) Break-even sales

ASSIGNMENT 5.2

Dave uses his financial reports for the year ending December 31, 2001, to generate the following expectations for 2002:

Cash sales	$592,861
Cash purchases	366,732
Operating expenses	196,994
Interest expenses	6,380
Income tax paid	15,426
Plant purchases	60,000
Line of credit from bank	20,000

He wants to use these figures in the preparation of the business's budget for the year ending December 31, 2001, especially because he wants to know if it is possible to pay a dividend of $15,000 that year despite the need to increase the capacity of the plant. Dave can realize his $3,000 deposit at the bank to aid his cash flow.

Required

1. Prepare an annual cash budget for Dave's Bikes & Co. for the year ending December 31, 2002, and determine the increase in cash projected during the year with and without a dividend payment of $24,000.

ASSIGNMENT 5.3

In February 2001 Dave forecasted sales for the next six months as shown below:

March	$40,000	June	$35,000
April	$50,000	July	$30,000
May	$40,000	August	$30,000

Using past collections as a guide, 20 percent of sales are expected to be for cash. Of the credit sales, 16 percent are expected to be collected during the month of sale; 56 percent in the following month; and 4 percent in the second month following; leaving 4 percent as uncollectible.

Required

1. Prepare the sales and collections portion of the cash-flow budget for the months of May to August.
2. Prepare the sales and collections portion of the cash-flow budget if 50 percent of sales are for cash and all credit sales are paid in the month following.
3. Comment on the difference in cash collected.

ASSIGNMENT 5.4

Toward the end of 2001 Dave begins to prepare his estimates for the year 2002. He guesss that the level of sales will be:

November 2001	$40,000
December 2001	$40,000
January 2002	$50,000
February 2002	$60,000
March 2002	$70,000

He guesses that expected collections will be 70 percent in the month following and 30 percent in the second month.

There was $401 cash in the bank at the beginning of January 2002.

Cost of goods sold will equal 55 percent of sales, all on credit. Expected payments will be 80 percent in the month following and 20 percent in the second month.

Variable operating expenses will be 20 percent of sales, all paid in the month following accrual. Fixed operating expenses will be $7,000 per month, paid in the month incurred.

Beginning inventory will equal 120 percent of the cost of goods sold for that month.

Tax expense will be $4,160, to be paid in February.

Required

1. Prepare a cash-flow budget for January and February 2002.
2. Estimate Dave's financing requirements for the first two months of 2002.
3. What methods could be used to overcome any financing problems?

SELECTED ADDITIONAL READINGS

Ang, J. S. 1991. Small business uniqueness and the theory of financial management. *Journal of Small Business Finance* 1(1): 1–13.

Churchill, N. C., and V. L. Lewis. 1983. The five stages of small business growth. *Harvard Business Review* (May–June): 30–50.

Dodge, R. H., and J. E. Robbins. 1992. An empirical investigation of organizational life cycle models for small business development and survival. *Journal of Small Business Management* (January): 27–37.

Higgins, R. C. 1991. Sustainable growth under inflation. *Financial Management* 10(4): 36–40.

McMahon, R. G., and L. G. Davies. 1994. Financial reporting and analysis practices in small enterprises: Their association with growth rate and financial performance. *Journal of Small Business Management* (January): 9–17.

WORKING CAPITAL POLICY

OBJECTIVES

1. *Define working capital and introduce the concept of the working-capital cycle*
2. *Distinguish between permanent and temporary working capital*
3. *Describe the management of cash, accounts receivable, and inventory*
4. *Describe cash forecasting and management practices*
5. *Describe the management of current liabilities*

6.1   INTRODUCTION

While financial management is a critical element of the management of a business as a whole, within this function the management of its assets is perhaps the most important. In the long term, the purchase of assets directs the course that the business will take during the life of those assets, but the business will never see the long term if it cannot plan an appropriate policy to effectively and efficiently manage its working capital.

Working-capital management or **policy** is *that set of principles governing the management of the current assets and current liabilities in the balance sheet.* The terms *working-capital policy* and *working-capital management* will be used interchangeably in this chapter.

As indicated in Chapter 1, an owner/manager in particular operates a business for a wide variety of reasons and that person's objective function (or reason for running the business) is not always in accordance with optimal financial practices. Where a person owns and manages their own business, there is no requirement to account for their actions (other than, perhaps, to lenders). They can therefore either operate in an aggressive manner, "sailing close to the wind," or be very conservative. This attitude is, in turn, a function of the **risk profile** of that owner/manager. This attitudinal feature has a direct bearing on whether the various elements of working capital are managed aggressively or conservatively.

In addition to the division of assets and liabilities in a traditional balance sheet, assets and liabilities can be divided further into short-term and long-term categories. This division is represented in Exhibit 6.1.

The current assets specified in Quadrant 1 of Exhibit 6.1 are typical of those found in most businesses. Cash is the most liquid asset and is therefore listed first. The remaining current assets are listed in descending order of their liquidity from most to least liquid: marketable securities, prepayments, and accounts receivable. The least liquid asset is typically inventory and is listed last. It should be noted that the current assets of smaller enterprises differ from those of their larger counterparts in that they are typically more cash-oriented.

Quadrant 2 contains the short-term liabilities of the business, including taxes payable (if any).

Quadrant 3 contains assets with a typical life span of greater than one year. The arbitrary period of one year is used as it usually conforms with the period between two balance sheet dates and with accounting conventions. Clearly, such assets must be purchased from the firm's present or future capital sources, a process known as the **capital-budgeting decision**. This decision is dealt with further in Chapters 7 and 8.

Quadrant 4 contains the firm's long-term financing. It reflects the claims of the long-term stakeholders in the firm, including the capital contributions of its owner(s) and the contributions of its debtholders. It may also include long-term accruals. It is therefore not surprising that this section of the balance sheet describes the firm's **capital structure**.

REPRESENTATIONAL BALANCE SHEET

Quadrant 1	Quadrant 2
Current assets:	*Current liabilities:*
Cash	Accounts payable
Marketable securities	Accruals
Prepayments	Short-term debt
Accounts receivable	Taxes payable
Inventory	
Quadrant 3	**Quadrant 4**
Fixed assets:	*Long-term liabilities:*
Investments	Debt
Plant and machinery	Equity
Land and buildings	

The top two quadrants depict the firm's short-term assets and liabilities. The collective term for decisions regarding short-term assets and liabilities is *working-capital management*, the subject of this chapter.

CONCEPT CHECK

1. *How does the risk profile of the owner/manager affect asset management?*
2. *Reconcile Exhibit 6.1 with the various balance-sheet formats presented in Chapter 2.*

6.2 TERMS AND CONCEPTS RELATED TO WORKING CAPITAL

There are a number of terms and concepts related to working capital that are fundamental to an accurate appreciation of working-capital policy. These are briefly outlined below.

THE WORKING CAPITAL CYCLE

Imagine a firm that operates very simply: its assets are comprised of only cash, inventory, and receivables. It makes cash purchases of inventories for processing, sells them on credit, and duly receives payment. In its simplest form, this cycle, known variously as the working-capital cycle or the cash-conversion cycle, is depicted in Exhibit 6.2.

The owner(s) of the firm may withdraw funds, but the size of such withdrawals must leave sufficient cash in the business to finance the pur-

THE WORKING-CAPITAL CYCLE

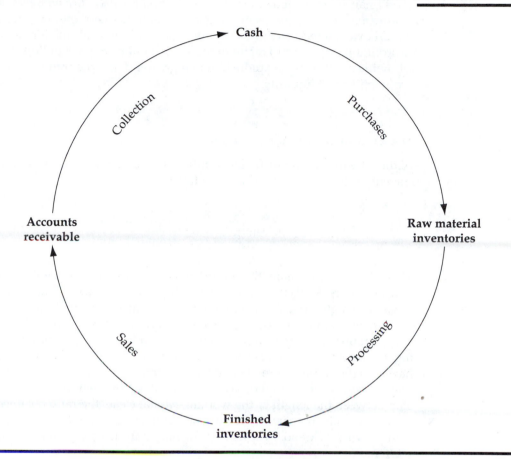

chase of further inventories so that the process is continuous. The model is simplistic to the extent that it is totally deterministic and does not allow for the element of risk, e.g., non-payment for goods supplied. Nevertheless, the exhibit effectively represents the principle of the working-capital cycle.

PROFITABILITY VERSUS LIQUIDITY

One of the most important tenets of small-business financial management is that profitability and **liquidity** are not the same thing, in fact, they may be in direct conflict with one another. Profitability is an accounting concept that relates to the income statement. Liquidity is the ease in which assets can be converted into cash. Frequently, a small business may increase its profitability by extending credit to customers who might not be able to make payment. In this case, the owner/manager of a small business must try to reconcile these two distinct elements. The basic tenet, however, of good financial management is to *maximize profits subject to a minimum level of required liquidity*. In the example given, small-business owners/managers should extend credit to those customers that will produce the highest levels of profitability subject to maintaining some minimum level of liquidity. The following sections will explore in much greater detail the trade-off between profitability and liquidity.

MEASURES OF LIQUIDITY

Within the discussion of financial ratios in Chapter 4, there was noted the current (or liquidity, or working-capital) ratio:

$$\text{Current ratio} = \frac{\text{Current assets}}{\text{Current liabilities}}$$

This ratio tells how many times current assets cover current liabilities. If current assets are $250,000 and current liabilities are $100,000, the ratio is 2.5 times. The higher this figure the more liquid a firm is deemed to be.

Years of dealing with businesses have taught financiers and analysts that a current ratio of 2:1 is the ballpark figure to be looking for, but will vary according to type of industry and even type of business. Manufacturing firms tend to have a higher ratio where the ballpark figure may be, say 3:1, while retailers may well have a lower ratio, say 1:1. As may be observed, there is a relationship between the length of the working-capital cycle, the ratio obtained, and the type of industry. Significant variance from either the industry norm or the firm's own past trends, warns that further analysis of the business may be warranted.

It may be of importance to the analyst of the financial statements of the smaller firm that the business has sufficient cash and short-term assets to cover its short-term liabilities. The ratio used for this type of analysis is called the acid-test (or quick) ratio, the formula for which is:

$$\text{Acid-test ratio} = \frac{\text{Current assets} - \text{inventory}}{\text{Current liabilities}}$$

The reason for calling this ratio the "acid test" is because it does not include inventory. The same numerator term may also be expressed as:

$$\text{Cash} + \text{Marketable securities} + \text{Accounts receivable}$$

Chapter 4 also introduced the concept of accounts receivable turnover, represented as:[1]

$$\text{Accounts receivable turnover} = \frac{\text{Annual sales}}{\text{Average accounts receivable}}$$

However, there are hidden problems that can occur with receivables. For example, there may exist a high proportion of bad or doubtful debts or particularly slow payers.

The other significant ratio is inventory turnover:[2]

$$\text{Inventory turnover} = \frac{\text{Cost of goods sold}}{\text{Average inventory}}$$

While standard accounting practice follows the principle of including inventories at the lower of cost or net realizable value in the audited statements, the value realized for such inventories on the liquidation of a firm rarely achieves the balance-sheet figure and liquidators are often fortunate to realize 10 percent of the figure. If slow-moving items contribute a disproportionate element of the inventory figure, this will merely exacerbate the problem. Therefore inventories are a notoriously unreliable figure. In larger firms, the external auditor has some control over the figure reported but internal (management) accounts usually prove to be a relatively unreliable source of information.

The point is that ratios can usefully be used as a comparative guide in working-capital management but there may exist a significant variation between book and actual values. For the small business, this may not be too much of a problem as a mental correction is often undertaken by the internal management, if they use the ratio at all, and many small businesses do not. More problematic is the use by external third parties, who tend to place greater emphasis on the ratio, and arguably on reliability, than the figures sometimes warrant. Due care must be exercised in comparative analyses.

However, this is not the end of the problematic nature of the above measures. It has been argued that the current and acid-test ratios have inherent flaws. For instance, the composition of assets and liabilities in the current ratio take no account of the *time* element except that they are "current," i.e., less than one year. The current ratio makes no distinction between a debt

---

[1] In Chapter 4 we simplistically used the ending balance in the denominator (for reasons explained in footnotes at that point). The analyses that follow, however, will use the more accurate application of the average of the beginning and ending balances.

[2] See footnote 1.

payment due in ten days or ten months. Clearly, the definition of a "near-cash asset" is significantly different in each case.

In addition, inventory and receivables are composed of items that include obsolete or slow-moving stock and slow or non-payers respectively. The acid-test ratio removes one relatively illiquid measure, inventory, but still includes receivables, which may not be "quick."

The receivables and inventory measures are very specific and ignore the time element. At best, liquidity ratios can give a reasonable approximation of the firm's overall liquidity position, but, at worst, they give a totally contradictory evaluation of the true position.

In response to these criticisms, a number of aggregate liquidity measures have been developed. The **cash-conversion cycle** is one such measure.

The Cash-Conversion Cycle

In its simplest form, the cash-conversion cycle is merely a measure of the length of time it takes between incurring a cash expenditure and the receipt of cash associated with the sale of the goods or services created by the initial expenditure. It measures the length of the working-capital cycle (illustrated in Exhibit 6.2).

The shorter the cycle, the less time taken in conversion, and the more liquid the firm. The number of days to be supported from the firm's own working capital equals:

> (I) days in inventory-conversion process + (II) days in accounts receivable − (III) days in payables

In this model (I) represents the time element associated with the physical process of purchasing raw materials, transformation into finished goods, and storage of those goods pending sale; (II) represents the time between the sale of the goods and the receipt of cash for the goods; and (III) represents the time between the purchase of inputs and payment for those inputs.

Exhibit 6.3 depicts these elements in a diagram.

Reconsider the circumstance of Donnelly & Co., encountered in Chapter 4. The income statement and balance sheet for Donnelly was shown in Exhibit 4.1, and, using the ratios developed in that chapter, it is possible to calculate the cash-conversion cycle for Donnelly & Co. Exhibit 6.4 summarizes these ratios and their associated time periods.

Exhibit 6.5 demonstrates the computation of the cash-conversion cycle for Donnelly & Co. From Exhibit 6.5 it can be seen that it takes, on average, one hundred thirty-two days from the beginning of the operating cycle to the receipt of cash. However, to partially offset the funding needs of this situation, the firm has twenty-four days of credit from the suppliers of its inputs. The remaining one hundred eight days requires that funding come from working capital. The lower this figure, the more liquid a firm may be considered. Thus the cash-conversion cycle is merely the net time period between having to pay the costs associated with production and the receipt of money related to the sale and collection of that same production. The objective is to minimize the time period associated with the conversion cycle.

THE CASH-CONVERSION CYCLE

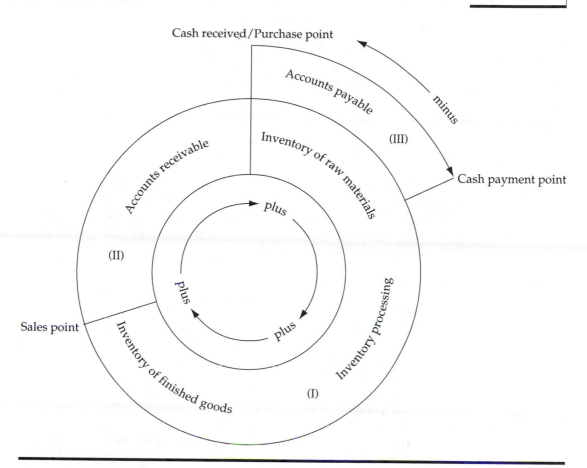

◆ EXHIBIT 6.4

RATIO SUMMARY: DONNELLY & CO.

	Turnover ratio	Weeks	Days
Inventory	4.06	12.8	90
Receivables	8.67	6.0	42
Payables	15.10	3.4	24

   Notice that the cycle is calculated in terms of days and not in terms of cash. In fact, the balance of cash is not considered at all. This is the weakness of the model: it does not give an accurate overall view of the firm's total liquidity position. Nevertheless, the approach provides a useful measure for internal-management purposes.

THE CASH-CONVERSION CYCLE

Average sales credit period	42 days
Inventory holding period	90 days
Operating cycle	132 days
Less: days in payables	24 days
Cash-conversion cycle	108 days

ACTUAL VERSUS OPPORTUNITY COST

The cost attached to all current assets can be described in either actual terms or **opportunity cost** terms. Cash has no actual holding cost other than physical security, but it does have an opportunity cost. Cash that is surplus to immediate requirements earns no return unless it is placed on short-term deposit or in marketable securities. The opportunity cost arises when cash is not put to some interest-bearing use. During inflationary periods cash will actually lose value and it is therefore essential that the rate of return on short-term investments exceeds the rate of inflation.

Similarly, a firm that holds too much inventory will unduly deplete its cash resources and thus incur an opportunity cost. The reverse side of the coin is that where too little inventory is held, there is a risk of running out of inventory to sell (a **stock-out**) thereby losing not only customers but also perhaps **goodwill.**

Allowing the accounts receivable to remain outstanding beyond the due date means that the business cannot use that cash for other purposes, such as purchasing inventory or paying off loans. The alternative argument is that harassing customers for early payment may subsequently cause the loss of those customers and engender ill will. As usual, it is a matter of balance.

There is also a cost attached to holding insufficient cash. In this circumstance, the firm will be unable to meet its financial obligations when they become due. The firm then loses a certain amount of favored customer status and drops down on the priority lists of suppliers, which may then result in late deliveries or partial shipments, etc.

Even worse, the firm may see the removal of credit terms altogether, which means purchases must be on a cash-on-delivery basis. The delinquent firm will then see its credit rating drop dramatically. This affects not only the ability to obtain credit from suppliers, but will probably also affect the terms of credit and interest rates charged. In addition, banks will upwardly adjust the rate charged to the business due to a worsened credit rating (if they continue to supply money at all). For instance, a large favored customer with a good credit rating may obtain financing at the prime rate plus 1 percent, whereas a firm that exhibits laxity in its financial management will soon find

PERMANENT CURRENT ASSETS

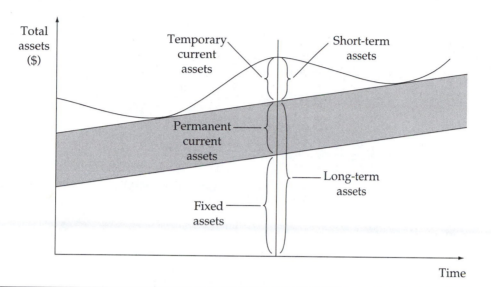

that the rate becomes prime plus 2 percent, 3 percent, etc., depending on its credit rating. In the extreme case, the firm faces the possibility of closure.

The aim of liquidity management is therefore to achieve an optimal *balance*, neither too much cash nor too little, in a commercially dynamic environment.

PERMANENT AND TEMPORARY CURRENT ASSETS

At first glance the term **permanent current assets** might appear to be contradictory. If current assets change at least once every twelve months, how can they be permanent? Clearly, it is not any specific asset that remains constant, but the *minimum aggregate level* of current assets needed for the efficient running of a going concern during its trading cycle. Permanent current assets represents the minimum amount of working capital that the firm needs in order to continue when business is at its lowest point in the cycle. It is an amount continually necessary that cannot be reduced in the shorter term. It is an amount that remains within the business until such time as the business is dissolved and the assets liquidated for distribution. Exhibit 6.6 illustrates this concept graphically.

Temporary current assets, on the other hand, are directly related to the level of business activity and to the consequences of earlier business decisions. If the business sells more, it needs more working capital to purchase higher levels of inventory and to fund accounts receivable.

CYCLICALITY OF TEMPORARY WORKING CAPITAL

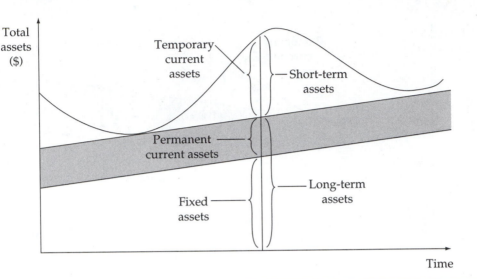

Management of working capital is a dynamic concept and requires some knowledge of the leads and lags inherent in the working-capital cycle. Thus, the management of working capital requires not only a knowledge of the volumes involved but also of the *velocity* of the cycle. Such knowledge enables the manager to synchronize inflows and outflows as efficiently as possible, thus avoiding an enforced trip to the bank requesting credit to finance working capital.

A business is said to be "overextended" where its sales, and hence the need for working capital, exceeds the firm's ability to fund expansion. In addition to undercapitalization, this is perhaps the single biggest cause of small-firm failure. Being overextended is caused by poor management, yet it is one of the easiest small-business sins to rectify.

Due to the cyclical or seasonal nature of many businesses, the amount of temporary working capital required can vary enormously. The greater the seasonality the less permanent capital a firm has in relation to its total requirement in peak periods. Compare the relative size of temporary and permanent current assets in Exhibit 6.6 with those in Exhibit 6.7 to see the effect cyclicality can have.

Cyclical variation is not necessarily a factor that automatically increases the risk of operating outside of optimum levels, its predictability is very important. University book stores have a very busy period at the start of each semester, but the semester cycle is well known and fairly constant. The shop knows approximately how many students there are in each of the courses for

MATCHING ASSET MATURITY TO SOURCES OF FINANCE

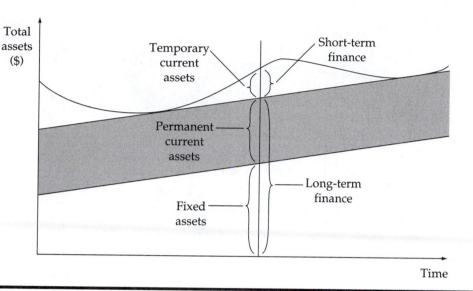

which an essential reading text has been prescribed. Businesses depending upon the weather, such as leisure industries or ice-cream businesses, subject themselves to the vagaries, adverse or otherwise, weather conditions may bring. If their estimates of sales do not coincide with weather patterns, they may find themselves overstocked for some time (or vice versa). The inventory must still be paid for and the additional temporary working capital found from cash reserves or through credit.

FINANCING CURRENT ASSETS

There are two aspects to the financing of current assets:

1. the level, or amount, of short-term finance to use
2. the source of such financing

As a general working principle, assets should be financed from a source with a maturity commensurate with cash-flow generation of the asset. As noted above, the seasonality of some firms requires temporary financing from short-term sources. Long-term assets, including permanent current assets, should be financed from long-term sources. Following from the exhibits shown above, the concept of matching sources of finance to their uses can be understood, as in Exhibit 6.8.

♦ **EXHIBIT 6.9**

CONSERVATIVE FINANCING STRATEGY

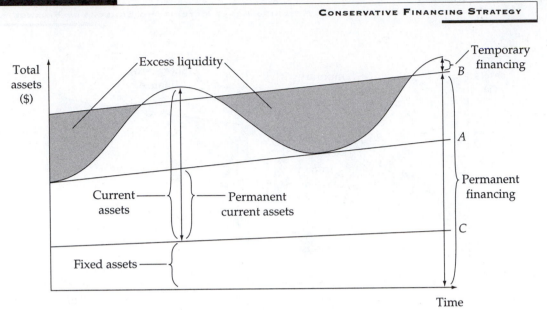

If a firm has to finance permanent current assets, then these assets should be financed with long-term sources of funding.

HEDGING STRATEGIES

The arguments just presented imply a known trade cycle in terms of both volume and velocity. This may be the ideal situation but it is rarely that apparent in real business life. When there is a degree of uncertainty the firm, or owner/manager, consciously or otherwise, proactively or reactively, decides on a course of action to determine the level of assets held. This, in turn, determines the sources of finance required and thus the long-term financial strategy. The three main financial strategies are standard hedging, conservative, and aggressive financing strategies.

The conservative (line B) and aggressive (line C) strategies are illustrated in Exhibits 6.9 and 6.10 and the standard hedging strategy (line A) is where permanent sources of financing just cover the permanent current assets.

Exhibit 6.9 depicts the long-term or permanent financing of assets exceeding the actual permanent current assets from the minimum point on the trade cycle up to the dotted line (line B). As a result, there are occasions when the firm will find itself with surplus cash to invest. The further upward the dotted line goes, the more conservative the strategy is. It would not be advisable to operate with permanent capital beyond the top of the trade cycle

AGGRESSIVE FINANCING STRATEGY

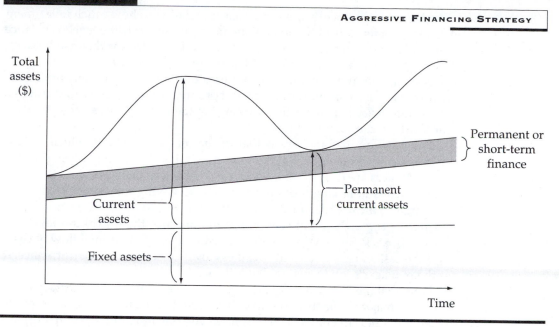

as the firm would always have excess liquidity and there would be significant opportunity costs in so doing.

Theory suggests that the standard hedging strategy (line *A*) is the one to
pursue. This may be true for large firms, but smaller firms will have to establish the fixed costs associated with investing cash in the money markets. Depending upon the size of the cash surplus and the period for which it is held,
it would be better to put the money on deposit with a bank. There is also a
comfort factor in having that little extra surplus, and the firm may wish to
discount the potential income to be earned from the deposit interest against
this factor. Clearly, this decision is dependent upon the firm's management.

On the other hand, a firm may adopt a more aggressive posture in its working-capital policy. This firm is one that permanently relies on short-term financing, even at the lowest point of the cycle. This is illustrated in Exhibit 6.10.

While short-term debt may be cheaper than long-term debt, the firm in
this situation opens itself up to the risks of not being able to find new sources
of short-term finance or of not being able to roll over existing debt. It then
finds itself in a precarious liquidity situation.

In real life, the smaller firm either intuitively or through calculation adopts
a certain target level of liquidity. However, for any firm, the dynamics of
business life will result in the actual situation ranging across all three strategies. The important thing is that the firm maintain that level with which the
owner/manager is most comfortable and that is in keeping with the principles outlined.

STOCK VERSUS FLOW

Stock, in this instance, is the static concept relating to how much investment in current assets a firm has at any one point in time. It is the level or balance associated with each of the current accounts. Thus, stock is the cash held, receivables owed, or inventories held at a single point in time.

Flow implies movement, which necessitates the dynamic element of time. A firm has a flow of working capital, both inward and outward, during its operation cycle. The faster the working-capital cycle revolves, the "harder" the working capital is said to work.

The often-quoted analogy is that of the oil in a machine, which, in this case, is the working capital of the business. If there is no oil in an engine, the consequences are dire. Having too much oil may be just as bad, so there is a cost attached to having too little as well as to having too much. What must be sought is the maintenance of an optimal level of oil to ensure smooth performance, somewhere between the minimum and the maximum levels on the oil dipstick. Similarly, a business must maintain an optimal flow of cash, and the cash must work for the business to ensure its smooth performance. It is the manager's job to ensure that it does.

Now that the terms and concepts have been explored it is necessary to review the major elements of the working-capital cycle, namely cash, accounts receivable, and inventory. There is, however, one remaining pertinent point to make: there exists a very close and interactive relationship between the various elements of working capital. An attempt to optimize one element cannot be done in isolation from other elements. Small-business management in particular requires a holistic approach.

 CONCEPT CHECK

1. *Describe the elements of the working-capital cycle.*
2. *Describe net working capital.*
3. *Describe the conflict between profitability and liquidity.*
4. *How do current assets have an opportunity cost?*
5. *Distinguish between permanent and temporary current assets.*
6. *How and why do we match the maturities of assets and sources of finance?*
7. *Distinguish between aggressive and conservative working-capital policies.*
8. *Describe the formulation and uses (and provisos) of the two major working-capital-oriented ratios.*
9. *Distinguish between the concepts of stock and flow.*

6.3 CASH MANAGEMENT

Cash management involves the administration of both cash and short-term marketable securities (also called near-cash assets). Cash is not only the paper and coin currency physically located on the firm's premises, but also the money held in a bank checking account and payments to and from the firm in transit. Cash is cash from whatever source, or for whatever expenditure, as long as it legitimately relates to the business. Thus cash receipts may originate not only with sales (be they cash or credit) but also from the "sales" of equity and debt. These concepts were first presented in Chapter 3 when the statement of cash flows was introduced. Miscellaneous cash income also derives from such activities as interest received on investments, sales of fixed assets, and so on. Expenditures similarly include cash payments for fixed assets, dividends, taxes, and repayment of loans and interest, as well as operating costs.

Despite the fact that cash is a non-income-producing asset, a business must maintain certain levels of it for various purposes.

REASONS FOR HOLDING CASH BALANCES

John Maynard Keynes advocated three reasons[3] why an individual or firm would hold cash:

✦ The **transactions motive** constitutes the largest component of a firm's demand for cash balances. Cash is held to purchase pre-planned asset acquisitions and to pay bills and other operating expenditures that arise from the normal course of business, both regular and irregular, including payment of dividends and taxes.

✦ The **precautionary motive** for holding cash arises when it is assumed that something *may* happen in the future, but there is considerable uncertainty as to the event and its timing. In other words, cash is held for emergencies. For instance, a strike at a major supplier may cut off the source of a leading profitable line of goods. The small business is therefore likely to experience a significant reduction in sales as it may not be able to substitute other suppliers' goods at short notice. If it cannot replenish its inventory for resale, costs per unit will rise (as fixed costs remain constant in the short term), which will adversely affect liquidity and profitability. Such an event cannot be considered a normal part of business and it may therefore be prudent to hold some reserve in cash or preferably near-cash assets as some protection against such unforeseeable events (sometimes referred to as "hedging"). The amount held for such a purpose will naturally depend upon the industry within which a firm operates and the general political, economic, and social climate. It will also depend upon the credit lines a firm has available to it (the greater the availability of quick credit lines the less the need for short-term cash reserves) and the structure of its balance sheet financing.

✦ The **speculative motive** is the least relevant to most smaller businesses, unless a firm operates in a speculative environment (mainly financial in-

[3]See J. M. Keynes, *The General Theory of Employment, Interest and Money* (New York: Harcourt Brace, 1936), p. 64.

stitutions operating in commodities, stocks and shares, property development, etc.). However, firms that purchase from a notoriously unstable market (for example, certain natural resource markets) may take advantage of lower prices when the market is down. Another speculative use may be the purchase of foreign currency when the exchange rate is unforeseeably favorable (in anticipation of adverse changes in the future). The reduction in the market price must clearly be sufficiently large to offset the opportunity cost of holding the cash for that purpose and the cost of holding inventories. Again, availability of quick credit may reduce the need for such a cash balance, as will the terms of credit received. Smaller businesses are not known for having large cash reserves for this purpose and considerable discretion should be exercised in this area.

CASH CONTROL

So far we have made a brave assumption that has not been made explicit, namely, that the smaller business has an effective and accurate accounting system in place, and that someone within the firm is responsible for it. Elementary as this may seem, it is not always the case. However, assume that the accounting and financial systems installed, manual or computerized, are up to the task of being relied upon to produce meaningful data and that such data is made available to management and to employees according to their needs.

Cash management is made up of four interdependent elements:

1. cash forecasting
2. managing cash flows
3. banking relations
4. investing surplus cash

It is obvious that any firm, small or large, should maintain a good working relationship with its bankers. The investment of surplus cash usually is not an issue of overriding importance to the majority of smaller firms as they rarely have sufficiently large balances to justify the resource expenditure in optimizing short-term investments. Short-term, interest-bearing bank deposits can be a simple and reasonable substitute for money-market investment, especially in the case of small amounts of excess cash. Therefore this section can concentrate on the first two items listed: cash forecasting and managing cash flows.

Cash Forecasting

Cash forecasts are a basic tool in cash management and are usually divided into short-term and long-term forecast categories. Following accounting convention, the point of division is one year. Short-term forecasts are used:

✦ to determine operating cash requirements
✦ to anticipate short-term financing
✦ to facilitate the management of money-market investments

Such forecasts can be quite accurate (if prepared with care and knowledge, of course) and can allow the firm to manipulate its income and expenditure to the best advantage. Given that perfect accuracy of net cash-flow forecasts, and thus perfect synchronization, does not exist, a firm must hold cash as a buffer. The possibility that the management of a typical smaller business has made a positive decision not to operate a cash budget is not a plausible option.

What constitutes an optimal time period for the forecast depends on the firm and the industry within which it operates. The best short-term forecast is most likely the one that relates to the firm's overall short-term planning horizon. If the nature of the industry only allows for a six-month planning horizon then that should be the forecast period. If the industry is quite predictable and stable, it may be possible to construct a detailed eighteen-month period forecast.

Note that the longer-term forecast is less accurate because increasing the time dimension increases uncertainty. A short-term forecast is intended to be detailed enough to enable effective management planning to occur, and, ultimately, the time horizon of the short-term forecast will be dictated by the accuracy that can be imparted over a specified time.

There may be some justification for having several short-term forecasts or forecasts that vary over the analysis period. For example, a firm may require a detailed weekly analysis for three months and a monthly analysis for the next nine. In effect, the firm has three time horizons, quarterly, annually, and a longer-term forecast. The more plans a firm prepares, the greater the input of resources required. It follows that the limiting parameters of the forecast relate not only to the industry and to predictability, but also to the size of the firm and its available resources.

An example of a short-term forecast is given in Exhibit 6.11. Notice that receivables are placed at the top, emphasizing their importance. Forecasting cash sales (if any) and credit sales is probably the most difficult aspect of preparing a cash forecast because of all the factors that impinge upon sales performance: pricing policy, credit-granting policy, credit terms given, competition, the business cycle, government legislation, defaults, etc. Experience has shown that errors in the estimation of sales, and subsequently receivables, can be considerable. Nevertheless, the best effort should be made, whether through historical ratios or projection of trends.

Expenditures can usually be estimated with a far greater degree of accuracy than is the case for sales. However, for those firms that purchase inventories in a fluctuating market, say raw materials, accurate forecasting can also be a problem. There is a good argument for suggesting that all small businesses should evaluate different scenarios. It is not uncommon to find three scenarios per forecast produced: optimistic, expected, and pessimistic. "What-if" situations are examined, say, the pessimistic solution is viewed and the cash requirement is then based upon that projection. Should the expected situation be used and it falls short of reality such that additional financing is required, then the same problems and difficulties as before arise.

SHORT-TERM CASH FORECAST ($ IN THOUSANDS)

	Quarter 1	Quarter 2	Quarter 3	Quarter 4	Year
Cash receipts forecast:					
Cash sales	$106	$ 93	$120	$111	$ 430
Credit sales	397	346	378	353	1,474
New loans		100			100
Interest received					
Miscellaneous				15	15
Total cash receipts	$503	$539	$498	$479	$2,019
Cash payments forecast:					
Trade purchases	$153	$168	$138	$150	$ 609
Operating expenses	225	239	252	248	964
Capital expenditures	30	150			180
Taxes		30		30	60
Dividends	25		25		50
Loan repayments			25	25	50
Interest paid	10	10	20	18	58
Total cash payments	$443	$597	$460	$471	$1,971
Net cash flow	$ 60	$−58	$ 38	$ 8	$ 48
Plus: beginning cash balance	−26	34	−24	14	22
Ending cash balance	$ 34	$−24	$ 14	$ 22	$ 70

Showing all three scenarios to the bank at least indicates the *most* cash that *may* be required.

Exhibit 6.11 uses quarterly data to make the figures manageable. In practice, this would typically be monthly for the first year, and even weekly for months one through three as aggregate monthly figures may hide peaks and troughs in the month(s). For example, payment of payroll on the first of the month, receipts from sales at the end, and so forth. The cash budget draws in the figures from other budgets: the sales budget, the capital-expenditure budget, the operating-expenses budget, and others, if produced. All of these "subbudgets" will be more detailed, and only the summary budget is provided in what follows.

The cash budget shown in Exhibit 6.11 also shows two tax payments; this is country-specific. There are also two dividend payments, an interim and a final, which are firm-specific. The firm here has a problem in quarter two when it has a net cash flow deficit of $58,000, with an ending negative balance of $24,000. This may be due in part to the capital expenditure and it would have been advisable to take a $125,000 loan rather than $100,000. Perhaps the financing source would only finance two-thirds from longer-term funds, or perhaps the firm was confident that short-term cash receipts would cover the deficit and did not wish to borrow more long-term funds. Generally, the firm is keeping a low cash threshold and paying off its loans (note that there must already have been a sizable loan, as interest was running at $10,000 in the first two quarters).

Both cash receipts and expenditures are subject to the effects of inflation. While the early 1990s have seen inflation reduced to quite low levels in many countries, inflation may increase once more and the firm may have to adjust for this accordingly.

Clearly, the damage arising from the need to seek financing for short-term, unanticipated shortfalls in cash cannot be overemphasized. Even if the financing body, usually the bank, grants a temporary facility, the mere fact that the business has needed it does not engender confidence in the management of the business. Sometimes there may be a very good reason, but too often such borrowing is the result of poor forecasting. Other things being equal, notifying the bank in advance that a loan is required at some point in the near future gives the bank more confidence in the business and in its management.

Short-term forecasting may also be applied to check the accuracy of the longer-term forecast and to assist in the planning of repayment of short- and long-term debt and in the acquisition of capital assets. As noted above, seasonal businesses are particularly at risk from external vagaries and, while the cash plan may suffer a greater risk of being inaccurate, it is very important that such businesses undertake the exercise. If the purchase of inventories does not correlate with receipt of cash arising from their subsequent sale, the business will find itself in difficulties from which it may not be able to extricate itself.

The cash forecast also guides the firm in a growth situation. It will guide its credit-granting policies and influence the decision on cash discounts given and received. The compilation and use of cash forecasts will certainly significantly reduce the likelihood of a firm running into insurmountable problems through overextending.

Constructing an effective system for the compilation of cash forecasts is only the first step in the management process. The second step is to compare the budgeted figures with actual results incurred, noting the variances between them. Many small businesses today have computerized systems and there are many software packages for personal computers that do this job. A decision has to be made regarding the level of variance that is acceptable for each of the variables analyzed. If the decision is to live with a variance of 2 percent down and 5 percent up on sales, then if the variance falls within that range that is acceptable. If it falls outside the range, the figure should be examined for the underlying cause of the variance. It is important to examine favorable variances as well as unfavorable so that any lessons learned can be implemented in the future. Should the variances be consistently outside the parameter range determined, then the firm should re-examine the system and the bases upon which the forecast is produced.

The longer-term cash forecast is not intended to impart the same degree of detail as the short-term forecast. For the smaller business the time horizon is typically from one to three years, depending on the type of business. The first year of this plan may be segmented monthly but thereafter quarterly is typical. It is used to give the manager an idea of when large inflows and outflows are expected so that they can be managed in the most expeditious manner. Typical of the uses for the longer-term forecast is the acquisition of capital assets, actual or estimated payment of future tax liabilities, and even highlighting of trends. Long-term projections assist in the planning of the financial structure, perhaps indicating that repayment schedules should be speeded up, if possible, to allow for asset acquisition as a response to new technologies becoming available earlier than expected, etc.

One thing that all forecasts have in common is that they are only estimates of the future. As time passes the estimates must give way to actual results, and revised estimates must be made and entered. It is a continuous process and, as such, needs to be undertaken at regular periodic intervals. The procedure of replacing one period that has been completed with one that is added at the end is a feature that is sometimes referred to as a rolling forecast, or budget. An annual budget, updated monthly, is always twelve months in advance regardless of which month of the year the firm is currently trading.

Naturally, forecasting the future is fraught with difficulties, but a cash budget is such an important tool in the whole process of financial management that the exercise must at least be attempted and constructed as accurately as possible. The computing phrase "garbage in, garbage out," referring to the quality of data used (and hence received), is equally applicable here.

Managing Cash Flows

Cash flow is a dynamic concept because it involves time. The number of owners or managers of a smaller business who do not consider some facet of cash flow, either the receipts, the expenditures, or the cash balance, during each and every working day must be few and far between. For a significant number of smaller businesses, managing cash flow is the single most important preoccupation, as every aspect of business influences, or is influenced by, the cash position. Therefore, problems such as overstocking, payments for unplanned expenditures, inaccurate estimations (most notably taxes and sales figures), and so forth, can arise regularly. Cash management is typically a daily operation. The problem facing the smaller business is that the tendency to "fight fires" means that controlling cash flow is sometimes delayed or overlooked. Failure to bank checks on a daily basis costs money. Inadequate cash-management procedures and controls may result in lost checks, which can be quite embarrassing.

However, having said that, relegating cash management to a lower level of priority is sometimes the correct thing to do; after all, without sales there is no business. The problem is that relegation of priority is all too often the consequence of an inadequate system.

There is also the problem of delegation of responsibility. The system may appear to work well enough, but if the cash controller, be it the owner, the manager, or a clerk, is absent (due to illness or vacation), the system stalls until the individual returns. The business slows down as the "oil" is not circulating (to use the previous analogy). The smaller business frequently does not have a competent deputy who can undertake such management for extended periods. This is potentially a very expensive omission.

Part of the cash-management function is to minimize the time taken by customers to pay their account. One option available is to utilize the lock-box system. For small businesses operating nationally in geographically large countries such as the United States, Canada, or Australia, this system can reduce the time that cash is in transit considerably. The lock box operates by having customers mail their payments to a post office box relatively near to them. A regional bank located near to the post box collects the checks on a daily or more frequent basis and credits the payee's account with that bank accordingly. Once credited, the regional bank then instantaneously transfers funds to the payee's own local bank, thus reducing the time to receive a check (which would otherwise go through the normal postal system) by up to four days. While the regional bank does charge for the service, and it can be expensive, it may still be beneficial because the firm reduces its own receivables handling costs by having the bank undertake some of the administration.

The banking system of each country varies, but typically any transaction utilizing the bank to make wire transfers, or electronic funds transfers, rather than using the postal service, will speed up the collection system, albeit at a cost. Therefore, advice should be sought from the bank about collection procedures.

The guiding principle for making cash payments is to pay them as late as is dictated by normal practice (subject to taking worthwhile cash discounts for early payment). There is no hard and fast rule about accepting discounts for early payment—it depends upon the liquidity of the business. However, it is very important that payment is made from within one accounting system, using one check book, drawn on one checking account. Where there are numerous checking accounts with more than one authorized signatory there is plenty of opportunity to get into a financial mess. It is not unknown for a creditor to be paid twice in a simple system. Where the system becomes more complicated the probabilities of entanglement increases. This is also a good reason for having one person either making the payment (countersigned normally) or being responsible for overseeing the function.

With respect to the actual balance at the bank, it is essential that frequent and regular statements are requested in order to reconcile the bank statement to the cash book (or its computerized version). Large firms tend to undertake this **bank reconciliation,** as it is termed, daily, but smaller firms need do it only weekly or monthly depending upon size and industry. It is rather difficult to have faith in a cash forecast if the bank statement and the cash book do not reconcile!

Banking Relations

The need for a good relationship between the businessperson and the bank should be self-evident. The majority of small businesses have significant support from their banks. For their part, the bank is a good source of advice. The bank needs to be kept informed about the business, its decisions, actions, and results. Consultation with the bank may influence a course of action for the better. The key word is *communication,* how much or how little communication between the businessperson and the banker is dependent upon the parties involved and the state of the business.

The preparation of good forecasts, the implementation of sound operational controls (including, but not exclusively, the accounting and finance function) and communicating these to the banker engenders goodwill. Good forecasting assists both the firm and the bank in determining whether or not a temporary shortfall of cash will occur and thus necessitates funding support. If the business is not getting the support it deserves, it should consider changing banks. Small banks are generally better with smaller businesses than larger banks.

Investing Surplus Cash

For most smaller businesses the possibility of having surplus cash to invest would be considered a luxury. Nevertheless, several points are worth mentioning.

✦ The emphasis of such investment activity should be short term, say up to three months, depending on the information contained within the firm's cash forecasts.

✦ High-risk and (potentially) high-return investments should be avoided. The downside of such investments may be more than the firm can afford to lose. Perhaps the best general option is to put surplus cash on interest-bearing deposit at the bank. For firms with more substantial sums to invest, other marketable securities, such as Treasury bills or certificates of deposit should be considered. A bank can offer advice on this and will endeavor to be objective once the course of action has been determined.

✦ The firm should be aware that there are fixed costs associated with investing in securities (and often penalty clauses for early withdrawal of funds). Such costs reduce the actual return and are particularly relevant for relatively small investments.

CONCEPT CHECK

1. *Why do firms hold cash balances?*
2. *Why does a firm need to control its cash?*
3. *What is the purpose of a cash forecast?*
4. *Why do small businesses have problems managing their cash flows?*
5. *What is a bank reconciliation?*
6. *What four interdependent elements make up cash management?*

6.4 MANAGING ACCOUNTS RECEIVABLE

Accounts receivable (or just receivables) arise from credit sales in the normal course of trading. While clearly dependent on the type of business and the ratio of credit sales to total sales, receivables can be the largest asset on a

CREDIT PROCEDURES

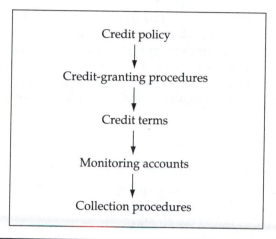

firm's books and is probably the one over which the firm has the least control. Firms operating close to the margin cannot afford to lose a grip on receivables and must be prepared to commit resources and actively manage the asset with a full awareness of the consequences of decisions regarding the granting of credit, discounts, and procedures for collection.

The granting of credit involves a cost, in fact a variety of costs, both in real and opportunity terms. Real costs are those of administration and of bad debts. The costs associated in that part of the administrative function involve screening new customers and failure to adequately implement this procedure will undoubtedly result in a higher level of bad debts. There is also the opportunity cost of funding the credit, and the shorter the credit period the less such costs will be. There is a logical procedure for managing accounts receivable, as shown in Exhibit 6.12.

CREDIT POLICY

Credit policy is of considerable importance as it clearly has a major influence on sales. Credit policy decides to whom the firm will offer credit, the terms of the credit, the procedures to implement, and the personnel to allocate that ensures the policy is being carried out correctly.

For instance, some smaller firms, while allocating all accounts to the "receivables clerk," make it a procedural condition that large or special accounts should be referred to the owner or senior manager before any action is considered. The system may dictate that there are to be no shipments to customers with accounts exceeding sixty days without the express authorization of the owner or manager. Quite often the procedural rules state that two reminders be sent fifteen days apart for accounts exceeding a certain period, say forty-five or sixty days overdue and that all accounts exceeding ninety days overdue go to a credit collection agency or through the generally more expensive legal system.

Procedures are set up not only to automatically make a decision for every contingency, but also to ensure that the system brings to the attention of the decisionmaker that which is at variance with the norm. Owners, managers, and the accounts receivable department get to know longer-standing customers quite well and can make decisions based upon their experience as long as guiding business parameters are not breached.

CREDIT-GRANTING PROCEDURES

It is not good business practice to grant credit without even the most minimal of checks on the potential customer (it may not seem cost-effective to do a background credit check on a customer requesting a minor amount of credit, but a lack of references may become a problem as the value of purchases suddenly increases). A failure to undertake adequate credit checks will merely increase the risk of future bad debts and potentially turn an otherwise profitable firm into an unprofitable one. Rather, the firm should establish credit standards, defined by minimum criteria of creditworthiness an applicant must possess to be acceptable to the firm. Routine procedures with standard forms to assess potential new customers are one way to reduce the all-too-common, and frequently expensive, intuitive approach. Assessment forms contain information provided by the potential customer and also information from third parties regarding their creditworthiness. It is obviously important that this is done before any credit is granted. It may well be too late after goods have been shipped.

The design of the credit application is a matter determined by the individual supplier. One credit form for the customer and one for external verification is not uncommon where credit assessment is undertaken. The answers given in a pre-designed format can then act as the basis for credit scoring. If the credit score achieves a certain level then the firm should accept the customer and grant credit. There are still many firms that do not undertake this type of assessment and it may well be interesting to speculate upon their level of bad debts in relation to those firms that do implement such a procedure.

There is a traditional approach to assessing the creditworthiness of potential customers and the information required is summarized under five headings, known as the "Five Cs" of credit.[4] These are:

---

[4]For a more rigorous treatment of the credit-granting decision and an expansion upon the Five Cs, see F. C. Scherr, *Modern Working Capital Management: Text and Cases* (Englewood Cliffs, NJ: Prentice-Hall, 1989).

1. Capital: the financial strengths and weaknesses of an applicant via extensive ratio analysis. In particular, debt and liquidity ratios should be established.
2. Character: the willingness to pay; a past history of payments to trade suppliers, defaults, desire to pay one's debts as they fall due; and the honesty exhibited by the applicant's management are important factors.
3. Collateral: in the event of liquidation the state of the applicant's assets, mortgages secured against those assets, and level of indebtedness become important. The greater the proportion of secured assets the less the likelihood that funds will be available for unsecured (trade) debts.
4. Capacity: what is the ability of management to run a business and the physical capability of the firm to produce?
5. Conditions: what general business conditions, such as competition and the business cycle, are relevant?

A credit bureau will be able to provide much of this information. Information required from the credit-granting evaluation forms may include the following:

Customer application for credit:

- type of business
- address of registered office
- trading address
- names of directors
- name and address of principal bank
- date of establishment
- authorization to approach the bank for a reference
- name and address of auditor who can provide a copy of financial statements for the last two or three years
- major suppliers
- number of employees
- whether the firm has been refused credit in the past
- amount of credit requested

Supplier's form for external credit verification:

- credit rating from commercial agency (e.g., Dun & Bradstreet)
- check with local credit agency (who may investigate the customer firm's creditworthiness for a fee)
- check with other suppliers
- check with trade associations, if applicable
- check bank references
- analyze financial statements received from auditors
- check regulatory body where accounts are filed for change of name, etc. (a credit agency should provide this information)

Should the information received prove acceptable, the firm can inform the customer, outline the terms, conditions, and the credit limit given. If acceptable to the customer, the order can be processed. There is a strong temptation for the smaller business to bypass these measures in order to gain the sale in case the customer is unwilling to either wait (which is an early sign/excuse of potential defaulters) or submit the information or authorizations requested. It is a temptation that may well prove to be false economy and is to be resisted unless there is a particularly valid (and supported) reason for doing so. The minimum the supplier should do is to make a telephone call to a local credit agency for at least part of the information required.

Even after the credit-granting decision has been made there are a number of firms who then prioritize their customers into categories, say A for the well-proven customer, B for those who pay but may be occasionally late, C for those who pay but are known to be continually late, and D for new customers until they establish a track record. The C and D groups then receive the most attention for early signs of default as they are considered the groups most at risk of default. What constitutes risk is assessed by the credit controller according to the customer's ability and willingness to pay the debt as it becomes due. Other things being equal, the greater the profit margin, the more risk a firm can take on.

Nevertheless, even though a creditor may ultimately pay the supplier there are costs of monitoring and chasing slow accounts, not to mention the time value of working capital to support the outstanding balances until they are paid. Additional costs arise where a default actually occurs and the account balance must be written off as a bad debt. The manager must view the credit-granting policy in light of such costs and perhaps change the terms upon which credit is granted to the group of slow payers.

The point at which a creditor, or group of creditors, should no longer be acceptable as customers is where the costs of granting credit (the opportunity cost of increased sales resulting in higher levels of receivables and a potential lengthening of repayment periods, and also the physical cost of administration) exceed the profit derived from the sale. There is always this trade-off to be made and a balance to be struck. This type of trade-off can be shown by means of an example:

A firm decides on a policy to increase sales and thus profitability. To assist in this process, it changes the credit standards for potential new customers. The result is that the average collection period for new customers becomes sixty days (old customers maintain their previous thirty-day payment practices). Sales increase by 20 percent due to this effort—from $6 million to $7.2 million. The contribution margin of the marginal sales is 30 percent and the opportunity cost of investment in receivables is 15 percent. The firm now wishes to know whether this policy has been profitable. Exhibit 6.13 shows the results achieved by increasing the level of sales.

Exhibit 6.13 can be more fully explained by the following:

1. The additional average investment in receivables is $1.2 million per year, divided by the turnover in receivables per year, six, which results in $200,000

CHANGING CREDIT STANDARDS: THE SALES DECISION

Additional sales (annual)	=	20% × $6 million	=	$1,200,000
Profit on additional sales (annual)	=	30% × $1.2 million	=	$360,000
Additional receivables	=	$\dfrac{\$1.2 \text{ million}}{6}$	=	$200,000
Profitability on additional receivables	=	30% × $200,000	=	$60,000
Required return on investment in receivables[5]	=	15% × $200,000	=	$30,000
Excess profit on investment in receivables	=	$60,000 − $30,000	=	$30,000
Additional annual profit	=	$360,000 − $30,000	=	$330,000

2. The profitability of additional sales is $360,000. Therefore, the profitability of the additional receivables is $60,000

3. While the cost of this investment is only 70 percent of its sale price, or 70% × $200,000 = $140,000, the actual investment in the advance to the new creditors is $200,000 (which includes the profit margin)

4. Required return on investment is: 15% × $200,000 = $30,000

5. Profit on investment less required return is $60,000 − $30,000 = $30,000

As the excess-profit figure is positive (in both approaches), the firm is correct to lower its credit standards. In fact, notwithstanding the qualifications below, the firm should relax its credit standards up to a point where marginal profitability on additional sales equals the required return on the investment in receivables necessary to support those sales.[6]

However, there are some assumptions that must be made when considering changing the credit policy:

◆ sales are constant throughout the year
◆ bad debts are ignored
◆ the firm has the capacity to increase production to meet the new, higher level of sales
◆ increased production is at the same unit cost as production in the pre-expansion period
◆ existing customers do not react to the new customers' collection period

None of the above assumptions is likely to exist in practice but must be included in the analysis judgmentally if not arithmetically. There are mathematical

---

[5] The literature relating to the appropriate figure to which the opportunity cost should be applied exhibits some ambiguity as to whether cost of sales or sales should be used. The authors have taken the view that applying the opportunity cost to the sales figure is the least controversial approach, but it should be pointed out that using the cost-of-sales figure instead is the more conservative approach. If the approach taken is to view the investment in receivables at "cost" rather than "sales," the required return becomes 15 percent of $140,000 ($21,000), and the additional annual profit becomes $339,000.

[6] See footnote 5.

models developed to assist the credit analyst in the larger company[7] that are less appropriate to the smaller firm employing judgmental techniques and have been omitted from further discussion here for that reason.

CREDIT TERMS

Deriving directly from the credit policy a firm adopts, the terms of sale specify the credit period allowed to the customer before payment is due. This may be any reasonable period, but typically from fourteen to ninety days are the norm, depending upon industry, and twenty-eight or thirty days is the most common. The discount allowed is the reduction allowed on the full invoice price for goods sold (discounts are not normally allowed on additional costs, such as freight and insurance) if paid earlier than the standard terms. This is usually expressed on an invoice as, for example, "terms 2/10, net 30," which means that a discount of 2 percent can be taken if paid within ten days, otherwise the full amount of the invoice is to be paid within thirty days. It is not uncommon to find a rate of interest *added* if not paid within thirty days and the invoice will state, for example, "1 percent per month interest on overdue balances."

The terms and discount on credit clearly influence cash flow, and the discount is given to speed up remittances. However, they can play a part in the competitive price positioning of a firm in the marketplace. Those firms that have more attractive terms and/or discount policy may well receive more orders (the goods are, in effect, cheaper). Terms can be lengthened to stimulate demand and shortened to reduce it, as long as the buyer is aware of the changes before a purchase is made. While a firm may better the industry norm for terms and discount, it is unusual to see a firm offer worse terms unless demand for that firm's product is sufficiently strong to overcome such unattractive terms. As usual, there is a trade-off between increasing profits due to additional sales and the costs associated with the terms given to achieve the necessary return on the additional investment in receivables, similar to the example above. Having said that, terms and discounts tend to remain fairly stable in any particular industry and do not appear to be widely used as a competitive instrument.

Credit terms incorporate the **credit period** and the **discount period** allowed for early payment. A firm may wish to change one at a time or both together, therefore they may initially be viewed separately. Using the figures from the above example, suppose that the firm decides that all customers should be allowed a credit period of sixty days and that, as a result, sales increase by $720,000, which is paid after sixty days. The benefit associated with changing the credit period is shown in Exhibit 6.14.

In Exhibit 6.14, the additional investment in receivables associated with new sales is $720,000 divided by six (the receivables turnover rate), giving $120,000.[8] However, there are still the original receivables to consider. Re-

---

[7]See Scherr, 1989, Chapter 6.

[8]If the cost approach is followed (see footnote 5) and the proportion of cost to sales price is 70 percent, the investment in additional receivables would reduce by $36,000 to $84,000 (70 percent multiplied by $120,000).

CHANGING CREDIT STANDARDS: COSTS

Increased investment associated with original level of sales: ($1,000,000 − $500,000)	$500,000
Increased investment associated with new level of sales: $720,000/6	120,000
Total increased investment in receivables:	620,000
The profit on new sales is: $720,000 × 30%	216,000
Total cost associated with new level of sales: $620,000 × 15% (opportunity cost)	93,000
Therefore, net profit on changing the credit period is:	$123,000

ceivables were $500,000, or $6 million divided by twelve (twelve because they were originally collected after thirty days). Clearly, now that they take twice as long to collect, this component of the receivables doubles to $1 million, an increase of $500,000. As the change results in a profit, the firm should consider this an option (always bearing in mind that the assumptions noted above should be taken into account).

The same type of example can be given for a change in the discount a firm allows its customers for early payment. Again, the problem is one of trade-off between the cost associated with the discount and the opportunity cost of putting the cash received to alternative uses. Assuming sales (receivables) of $6 million and a credit period of net forty-five days with no discount given, the average collection period remains sixty days and the average investment in receivables is $6 million divided by six, or $1 million. If the firm now changes its terms to 2/10, net 45, with 60 percent of customers taking advantage of the new terms, the average collection period reduces to one month. The cost of the discount allowed is $6 million multiplied by 0.02, which is then multiplied by 0.6, equalling $72,000. The benefit gained is one month's cost of holding receivables; that is, $500,000 multiplied by 0.15 (required return or opportunity cost of 15 percent as before), or $75,000. Therefore, it is advisable to introduce these new terms as there is a net benefit of $3,000, and a probable reduction in the risk associated with potential defaulters as payments have been made earlier and risk tends to increase with time.

This procedure *may* be followed any number of times to establish a criterion for the introduction of new terms. The problem lies in the fact that the figures are only known after they have occurred and estimation of such figures will be fraught with inaccuracies. If terms have been changed before then the results of that change can be analyzed to give some indication of the utilization of discount terms. Trade magazines may have survey data or other information relating to a specific industry in respect of credit terms.

MONITORING RECEIVABLES

Monitoring receivables occurs at two levels that are obviously related. First, there is the monitoring of individual balances, particularly those that are considered most at risk of default. Second, there is the monitoring of trends and changes in patterns of payment. The smaller firm should monitor individual risky accounts at least weekly but daily is advisable unless there is a particularly strong reason not to do so. Most accounts will run along quite routinely and need little supervision. However, the credit-control department, which can consist of one part-time employee to a supervisor/manager in charge of a department, should hold a summary meeting to update the senior manager on the current situation at regular periodic intervals, perhaps informally every week and formally every month. Some smaller businesses will feel there is no need to do this as they work in close proximity to other members of the staff and communicate very well. Yet, as the firm grows, communication becomes increasingly difficult and changes in the organization will necessitate more formal structures.

It is clear that a receivable is not a receivable until the invoice is dispatched. Some firms save their invoices and send them out at the end of the month or wait until the goods are dispatched, perhaps even sending them with the goods. There is no reason to do so. As long as the goods leave the seller's premises within a reasonable time, the invoice can be sent at the same time the delivery order is filled out. There is a cash value on time, so every effort must be made to send out the invoices as early as possible to reduce the time lag. If payment is made by a customer on their end-of-month balance, rather than on invoice date, invoices sent late may fail to be processed by the customer in that month. The seller can effectively lose one month's use of the invoice value of the cash. Compounded over more than one account, this can be very expensive.

There is one invaluable technique to assist the firm in monitoring process of both individual accounts and trends and patterns, called the **receivables aging schedule**. This schedule can be produced at any time: daily, weekly, or monthly. A monthly aging schedule will show each individual account name and reference, the credit limit designated by the credit-granting procedures, the total amount owed, and then how long each element of the debt (invoice amount in full or part) has been outstanding; for example, thirty days (current accounts), up to sixty days, ninety days, one hundred twenty days, and over one hundred twenty days. A cumulative percentage of debt in each period may also be shown. This schedule is the work horse of the credit-control department and is used on a daily basis to check off overdue amounts as they come in and to identify slow-paying customers. An example of an aging schedule is shown in Exhibit 6.15.

Like the cash forecast, the receivables aging schedule is a management tool that any self-respecting business *must* construct *and use*. There are many software programs that will take the drudgery out of this operation and the information is available at the press of a key (or click of a mouse).

The schedule gives immediate access to those accounts that are overdue. It can signal those accounts that are falling behind, those accounts that are up to their credit limit (or beyond if the credit department has been lax), and inflows of cash. It can reiterate previous input as to action taken and future action suggested. A computerized system can also be instructed to produce reports on those accounts that are overdue and require action from the re-

◆ **EXHIBIT 6.15**

AGED RECEIVABLES SCHEDULE

Account name	Date account opened	Credit limit ($)	30 days past due	31–60 days past due	61–90 days past due	90+ days past due	Total due
Oshefsky, Inc.	5/64	$ 5,000	$ 873	$ 253	$ 0	$ 0	$ 1,126
Builders Inc.	9/71	20,000	3,750	6,250	212	0	10,212
C. Ment Founds.	6/77	15,000	6,450	3,200	0	0	9,650
D. Igger & Sons	1/69	3,000	1,547	512	398	105	2,562
X. Cavators, Ltd.	5/87	5,000	3,280	0	0	0	3,280
Sylvia Mandelbaum	6/90	30,000	3,400	0	0	0	3,400
G.O. Round Paints	11/93	2,000	1,215	658	317	34	2,224
Total			$20,515	$10,873	$ 927	$139	$32,454

ceivables clerk or manager on a regular, say weekly, basis. The records can be interrogated at any time. In addition, external auditors will find their job greatly simplified if the firm produces a year-end aging schedule. The time cost savings would probably justify the purchase of not only the software but the computer as well. The bad debts to be written off at year-end and the provision for doubtful accounts will in part be derived from this schedule. Monitoring the aging accounts receivable schedule is a particularly useful technique in the management of accounts receivable.

Another useful way of monitoring receivables is to construct trends over a period of time. Such trends may be derived from any one of the following:

◆ average collection period
◆ percentage of receivables in each of the aging periods
◆ ratio of bad debts to credit sales

The average collection period formula is:

$$\text{Average collection period} = \frac{\text{Receivables} \times \text{days}}{\$ \text{ credit sales per year}}$$

By calculating this ratio each month the firm has a trend with which to view its overall credit procedures. For example, consider a firm with an average level of receivables of $750,000 on an annual sales base of $6,000,000 and credit terms of thirty days net. The average collection period would be:

$$\text{Average collection period} = \frac{\$750,000 \times 365}{\$6,000,000} = 45.6 \text{ days}$$

The firm may consider the figure of 45.6 days as reasonable or not. Nevertheless, if the same firm's receivables increased to an average of $900,000 instead of $750,000, then the average collection period becomes 54.75 days. This is an adverse trend (although a trend normally has more than two reference points) and the firm should take steps to speed up the collection period. Note that, while an increase in receivables may indicate an adverse trend, there may be an associated increase in sales, in which case the above formula should be implemented.

The percentage of receivables in each of the aging categories is quite straightforward: just compare the percentages obtained from each month's aging schedule with those of previous months and observe any changes. This is quite adequate to give the smaller firm the information it requires.

Similarly, the ratio of bad debts to credit sales can be monitored and the information derived informs management about trends. Any non-random variation in the trend, adverse or positive, begs investigation and the firm must ask why these bad debts came about (or, indeed, why bad debts have been reduced) and whether it is due to one particular large bad debt that unduly biases the trend, or due to signs that the economy is moving toward a recession. Reasons for bad debts include:

✦ poor credit standards
✦ poor credit terms
✦ inadequate monitoring and collection procedures

There is a fundamental problem when trying to monitor aggregate bad-debt trends, namely that they are "lumpy," that is, they come at different times, in different amounts. Matching a bad debt to date of origin is often difficult because bad debts sometimes creep up incrementally rather than have one invoice amount unpaid. Numerous invoices over a long period make this a difficult type of analysis and one that has grave limitations. A statement such that all debts are bad after one hundred twenty days eases the calculation but may not be true. Taking a quarterly perspective alleviates this problem a little but still retains some of the problems inherent in the monthly calculation. (A rolling quarterly assessment may be made and the bad-debt figures plotted on a graph with the dollar value of bad debt on one axis and time on the other. A line of best fit can be drawn by eye or the data can be run using a statistical computer package for regression analysis.) It is a trade-off between accuracy and resources.

Trends may be influenced when the industry changes its payment characteristics, which, in turn, may be influenced by increasing competition leading to a change in terms. Increased competition may mean lowering credit standards to maintain sales levels, which, in turn, is likely to affect bad-debt levels. Perhaps the industry is restructuring into larger firms through acquisition and merger, leaving the existing non-merged firms in a worse competitive position. Such micro and macro economic influences can significantly impact trends. The causality of trend changes is not always easy to unravel.

A cautionary note should be heeded before leaving the subject of monitoring of accounts receivable. It is human instinct on the part of the credit controller to want to lower the average collection period and reduce bad debts.

COLLECTION PROCEDURES

Account is overdue by:	Action
14 days	gentle reminder
30 days	stronger reminder
45 days	telephone call
60 days	strong letter stopping supplies
75 days	telephone and letter threatening transfer of matter to a collection agency or legal proceedings
90 days	transfer matter to collection agency or begin legal proceedings

Certainly, if only the very best-rated companies are accepted as customers, this can be done. However, if the firm has gone through the steps above to arrive at a credit policy outlining credit standards and terms, then this policy should be adhered to. The controller would, in effect, be turning away profitable business if the policy terms were open to interpretation such that they could be more stringent than was intended. It is not always good business to see bad debts at 0.01 percent and collection periods averaging thirty days—it may not be optimal (or not in keeping with firm policy).

COLLECTION PROCEDURES

The assumption has already been made that there is an effective and efficient accounting system, manual or computerized, in operation. Consequently, those accounts that are regularly paid on time are of little concern. More important are the slow payers and potentially delinquent accounts and the procedures for dealing with them. Each firm will have its own view on how to deal with overdue accounts, but one thing is certain, there should be a firmness without hostility in both the procedures within the firm and in dealings (e.g., letters) with the delinquent customer. Hostility is often equally as counterproductive as is being too accommodating. A firm should establish appropriate procedures and stick with them. An example of the collection procedure is shown in Exhibit 6.16.

The collection procedure can be influenced by the firm's knowledge of the customer. The more risky a customer may be, the more quickly the above steps can be implemented. The receivables clerk or the owner/manager should attempt to establish the cause of the late payment and take steps appropriately. Gentle handling of a long-term customer in temporary difficulties will yield greater benefits than abrupt letters. The steps taken to induce a recalcitrant customer to pay will be influenced by a rather different set of factors. If the customer has funds, but will not pay, then much stronger collection procedures should be implemented. If a customer has no funds, then there is no point in spending money to retrieve nothing. It would be better to put the debt into the hands of a debt-collection agency and provide for it in the income statement. Another alternative is to **factor** (or sell) the accounts receivable. The factoring firm will charge a percentage for this service (perhaps up to 60 percent of the potential collection depending on the default risk). However, the factor is selective and it may not be a viable option for many small businesses.

Notwithstanding the judgment that must be exercised by senior management, it is still important that the firm does not waver in its resolve to implement a procedure already established. It cannot be a very encompassing procedure if it is continually subject to change. Being fair but firm gains respect, having lax procedures does not.

CONCEPT CHECK

1. *What are the five steps in establishing credit procedures?*
2. *What are the major factors that need to be considered in developing a credit policy?*
3. *What are the Five Cs and why are they important?*
4. *What items must be considered when evaluating a change in credit standards?*
5. *What is a receivables aging schedule?*
6. *Why is the average collection period important?*
7. *What elements should be considered before sending a delinquent debtor a nasty letter?*

6.5 INVENTORY MANAGEMENT

Nearly every small business holds inventory to a greater or lesser extent: greater if it needs to hold stock for production; lesser if it is a service firm. The importance of inventory management is directly related to the firm's investment in inventory and is consequently quite industry-specific. It is up to the owner/manager to devise the policy, procedures, and levels of inventory for the efficient running of the business. Policy tends to be based upon the aggressive or conservative working-capital characteristics of the firm, as well as of the industry. Inventory-management procedures can range from the simple to the mathematically complex. The optimal level of inventory held originates from the policy and the procedures together with the cyclical nature of the business. As inventories are significantly more important to manufacturing (and also to specialist distributors) this section will view inventories from a manufacturing perspective. For the most part, what follows is applicable across a range of industries.

Inventories are typically categorized under three headings:

✦ Raw materials: these are the deliveries from a supplier and comprise such items as raw materials (flour for a baker and wood for furniture), through

metals and manufactured inputs (batteries or silicon chips for computers). Whatever their physical characteristics, raw materials have not yet
entered the firm's own production processes.

+ **Work-in-progress (WIP):** WIP comprises the raw materials that have
been taken into the firm's production process and to which some value
has been added.

+ Finished goods: as the name implies, finished goods are units that have
completed the production process and are ready for sale. One firm's finished goods may well be another's raw material. Take the wool industry
as an example. Wool from the sheep farmer is sold to a bleacher, who
bleaches it. The wool is then sold to the comber, who combs it. The finished combed wool is the raw material for the spinner, who then sells it to
the dyer. The dyer dyes it and sells it to the weaver, who then sells it to the
garment wholesaler, who then makes a variety of articles from it. Depending upon the integration of the industry, more than one task may be
completed by the same firm but the principle remains intact.

Clearly, there is a need to keep a certain level of inventory in all of these
categories because inventory is required to facilitate a consistent flow of
production to meet the orders for the final product. Raw materials allow
the production process to start and continue: work-in-progress inventory
is needed throughout the production process to buffer differing demands
at different times and allow re-scheduling when unforeseen events arise; a
finished goods inventory may be kept because of cyclicality, or knowing
that surges in demand may occur, either predicted or unpredicted.

There are serious consequences to running out of stock; so inventories of
finished goods that are held as a buffer against this contingency are known
as **safety stock**. All categories of inventory may be kept either as a hedge
against adverse events such as disruption in the supply chain, malfunctions
and strikes, or, if a favorable purchase price has been obtained, as a consequence of such things as bulk discounts. The more stable the industry and
relations between supplier and buyer, the more confidence a purchaser has
in the security of raw-material supply and the less inventory a firm may perceive it requires.

Inventory management provides yet another illustration of the need for
balance—the balance between the cost of holding inventory (which can be
very costly considering the flexibility and security it provides), and the
risk (and therefore cost, known as **stock-out costs**) of having insufficient
inventories anywhere in the production or distribution chain. Perhaps
more than any other area, the competing facets of sales, purchasing, and
production ally themselves to the cause of holding large inventory stocks
throughout all the processes with which the firm is involved. It is only the
financial arguments that may dampen and sway this exuberance via the
analysis of the costs associated with holding levels of inventory in excess
of optimum.

At this point, the argument returns to the concept of stocks and flows. Levels of inventory are stocks, but it takes time to move the initial input through

the production and distribution processes, which implies a flow, a dynamic element. The *velocity* of inventory turnover strongly influences the level of investment such that the greater the velocity, the smaller the stock required to be held for the same risk profile. Up to a point, the greater the velocity, the lower the attributable fixed cost per unit of inventory. Thus all facets of running a small business, i.e., purchasing, sales, production, and finance, come together and present themselves to the owner/manager, inducing him to take a holistic and integrative view of the internal workings of his firm.

INVENTORY-MINIMIZING ALTERNATIVES

As with cash, inventories must flow in order to adequately lubricate the business machine. For the most part, inventory management deals with trying to achieve solutions to the problem of risk and uncertainty. Inventories are kept as one solution to the problem, whether the risk derives from the internal factors or external markets. However, the small business should keep a broad perspective. For instance, firms that use significant amounts of raw materials may wish to enter into private arrangements with the producer rather than continually purchasing on the open market. Some small brewers have arrangements with local hop growers, agreeing to purchase either the total crop or a specified amount. The vagaries of weather introduce an element of risk but the price to the brewer will be lower and any shortfall in the harvest can be adjusted for by purchasing on the open market.

Many firms take out futures contracts for raw materials, agreeing to buy a crop next year at an agreed price. Inventory is not required as lines of supply have already been secured. While it is true that larger firms indulge in this type of arrangement, many small firms can also avail themselves of the practice. The small brewer above is only one example. The downside of being contractually "tied" to a limited number of suppliers is that, should a supplier be unable to meet the contractual obligations, the small business will have to seek alternatives on the market. In this circumstance, the necessary supplies may not be available (or not of the right specification or quality) and the lead time involved in obtaining the appropriate supplies could well damage (possibly even prove fatal to) the firm. The firm should be wary of relying upon one or a few supply sources.

Japanese firms have endeavored to reduce inventories by entering into direct contracts with suppliers. The buyer gives the supplier detailed specifications of the products it requires and also stipulates the *exact* time it wants them and in what quantities so that inventories are supplied **just in time (JIT).** The effect of JIT inventory reordering (hourly, daily, or on some other basis) is to reduce the customer's inventories.

Arguably, small firms do not have the critical size to implement this with the effectiveness of larger firms, but the principle of direct relationships with suppliers to provide a demand-based system for the provision/acquisition of critical supplies at a mutually agreed time can result in cost reductions and must therefore be considered beneficial. It is becoming more common to observe orders being placed automatically through computer linkages between customer and supplier, the customer's computer monitoring rate of sales to determine whether existing order dates and quantities need to be changed in light of the rate of sales or production. The number of direct computer linkages in the future will undoubtedly increase, bringing with it further reductions of holding costs.

The point here is that sizable levels of inventory are not inevitable and a broader-based view can suggest ways of inventory reduction other than the standard approaches to minimization of costs suggested below.

METHODS OF INVENTORY MANAGEMENT

Clearly, it is helpful to the smaller business if certain guidelines are available to assist in optimizing inventory management without being engulfed in sophisticated analyses. What the small businessperson needs to know is:

1. the appropriate level of stock to hold
2. the types of inventory costs
3. the level of safety stocks to keep
4. how much stock to order
5. when to order stock

The Appropriate Level of Stock to Hold

The appropriate level of stock to hold is sometimes referred to as turnover analysis and utilizes the inventory turnover measure described earlier in this chapter and is exhibited again below:

$$\text{Inventory turnover} = \frac{\text{Cost of goods sold}}{\text{Average inventory}}$$

For example, a firm with a cost of sales in one year of $1.8 million and an average investment in inventory (valued at cost) of $300,000 will have an inventory turnover of six.

$$\text{Inventory turnover ratio} = \frac{\$1,800,000}{\$300,000} = 6$$

The resultant figure, six, tells the firm how many times in one year the $300,000 inventory is used up and replaced. This means that the inventories will be used and replaced six times per year *on average*. Therefore, approximately two months of stock is held at any time.

One problem associated with this approach is that this measure does not help the manager in deciding which items of stock are moving quickly, and which ones are not. It may lend some assistance when comparing the firm's ratio to other firms in the industry, or as a guide in evaluating trends, but it is not specific. However, given suitable provision of accounting records, there is no reason why the major individual lines a firm carries cannot be treated the same way, merely substituting cost of sales for product A and average inventory for product A. If the firm holds a large range of items, this procedure needs to be computerized to effectively evaluate all lines.

Even if a firm carries many product lines it may be that only a few need to be examined. If there really are too many lines to do this effectively in a manual system, there are a number of industry-specific computer software programs that will undertake these calculations and reorder almost automatically (as well as producing an itemized list of slow-moving lines).

There is nothing in the inventory turnover ratio to suggest anything about optimality, it merely clarifies what the situation is. Referring to the section above on minimizing inventory, alternatives may induce the smaller business to review the approach taken to inventory management and reflect upon direct contracts and JIT techniques.

Optimal stock levels depend on the type of industry in which a firm finds itself and on the type of product with which it deals. What is optimal depends in part upon:

1. the costs associated with the size of the order (and also economic shipment volumes)
2. the frequency of orders placed
3. the necessary levels of safety stock deemed prudent by the management

Fundamentally, the smaller business should keep the minimum amount of inventory commensurate with the demand for the units held.

Types of Inventory Costs

Inventories have actual costs attached to them, and it is usual practice to break them down into **ordering costs** (the costs of administration, handling, transport, and purchase) and **carrying costs** (storage, **insurance,** security, spoilage, obsolescence, and financial costs, such as interest on loans raised to fund inventories).

Carrying costs tend to be, although not always, directly proportional to the level of inventory held, while ordering costs tend to be disproportional and vary more with the number of times an order is placed than with the actual volume of inventory. There is an inverse relationship between these two costs: *the key to the inventory-management problem is to find the point at which the costs are equal*. This will be covered further when the **economic order quantity** is discussed.

Stock-out costs are more difficult to quantify. For example, the immediate profit and cash flow lost as a result of a stock-out, and the costs associated with physical changes due to interruptions in the production processes (such as retooling or rescheduling), or perhaps trying to perform some type of damage limitation action, are not easily established in advance.

As with cash and receivables there are also opportunity costs associated with stock-outs. These comprise the profit foregone and subsequent loss of goodwill and may result from a stock-out of final products or insufficient inventory during the production process, which inhibits the restocking of finished goods to desired levels. In addition, there is the opportunity cost of the value of the inventories themselves, i.e., the return on investment that an equivalent value could yield if put to an alternative use of similar risk.

The Level of Safety Stock

If demand is certain, the firm can plan accordingly and no safety stock is necessary. As business is not conducted in a certain environment, safety stocks are required. The greater the uncertainty, the greater the level of safety stocks. The question then arises as to the most appropriate level of inventory to be held. The requirement is to balance the probability and cost of a stock-out against the costs associated with carrying sufficient safety stocks for all contingencies. Unless large safety stocks are carried there will presumably be times when demand is in excess of what the firm can supply. The firm can make some estimate of likely sales, based upon an extrapolation of past sales levels (not necessarily linear), and it will know what it produces on, say, a monthly basis. It is then possible to construct an approximation of the relationship between the various anticipated costs associated with a certain level of safety stock. For example, assume that a firm's past records indicate that units of inventory used in a month emulate the following pattern:[9]

Inventory demanded	100	200	300	400	500
Probability	0.10	0.50	0.25	0.10	0.05

If a firm has a typical production batch of two hundred units, and the stock-out cost has been estimated at $10 per unit, while the carrying cost is calculated at $2 per unit. Exhibit 6.17 shows the computation of the level of safety stock the firm should maintain.

If three hundred units of buffer stock are kept, there is no possibility that a stock-out will occur (batch production standing at two hundred units plus the three hundred equals five hundred inventory units, the maximum demand the firm believes it will potentially have to meet), the only cost being the carrying cost (three hundred multiplied by $2 equals $600).

If that stock safety level is reduced to two hundred units, a stock-out of one hundred units *may* occur (four hundred units are covered with safety stock included, therefore the probability of requiring five hundred units is 5 percent, from the pattern illustrated above). The cost of a stock-out is therefore $10 per unit multiplied by the number of units, one hundred, equals $1,000. *But* the probability of this occurring is 0.05, the expected value of the

---

[9]The approach taken in this example is similar to that taken in the text by J. Dewhurst and P. Burns, *Small Business: Planning, Finance and Control,* 2d. ed. (London: Macmillan, 1989), 373–374.

PROBABILITY AND COST OF STOCK-OUT

Safety stock	Stock-out units	Stock-out cost ($10/unit)	Probability	Expected stock-out cost	Carrying cost ($2/unit)	Total cost
300	0	0	0	0	600	600
200	100	1,000	0.05	50	400	450
100	200	2,000	0.05	100	100	200
	100	1,000	0.10	100	100	200
				200	200	400
0	300	3,000	0.05	150	0	150
	200	2,000	0.10	200	0	200
	100	1,000	0.25	250	0	250
				600	0	600

stock-out cost is 0.05 multiplied by $1,000 which equals $50. Adding the carrying cost of two hundred units ($400) gives a total of $450. The operation is similar for the remaining calculations. However, as the firm's requirement is to minimize total cost, the final column in Exhibit 6.17 indicates that minimum cost is achieved when the balance between costs of carrying and the cost of stock-out is at a safety-stock level of one hundred units. The firm should therefore carry this amount to minimize these costs. This can also be shown graphically, as in Exhibit 6.18.

How Much Inventory to Order

The first step in selecting the optimal order quantity is to determine the type of inventory one is talking about. The types of inventory are:

✦ An ongoing production process requires continuous supplies of the same or similar inputs to produce the same or similar outputs, which appear on the market in a reasonably homogenous manner. Such a process involves **dynamic inventory management** and, in what follows, this is the type of inventory discussed.

✦ There are also inventories that typically have limited, one-time production runs and that require no continuous supplies. For instance, a firm may print and market annual diaries. It determines it can sell one hundred thousand of these, and in August it begins production. It knows it requires one hundred thousand covers, spines, clasps, and so on, plus an appropriate amount of paper. It takes three months to cover the lead times from suppliers. On completion of production in, say, October, the firm begins to sell the diaries. Should the sales strategy prove more than usually successful, by January the total batch could have been sold with demand unsatisfied. The firm can

◆ EXHIBIT 6.18

MINIMIZING COSTS OF CARRYING SAFETY STOCK

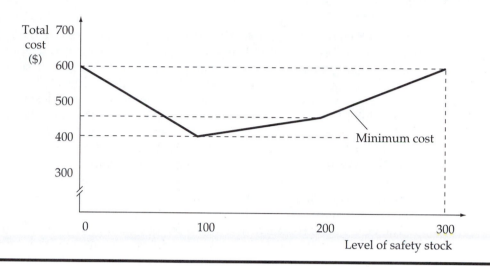

hardly produce any more due to the lead times and set-up costs precluding the availability of the product before May, when nobody wants diaries. The type of process utilized by the firm is referred to as **static inventory management**. It refers to a once-only production run within a finite time span.

◆ A third type of inventory is that produced by the firm itself for input into a major product during the production process. Management of this **intermediate-process inventory** revolves around the concept or technique known as materials requirement planning (MRP). Readers of this text should be aware of MRP, but it is beyond the scope of this text.

The Economic Order Quantity[10]   The economic order quantity (EOQ) deals with the dynamic inventory problem. More complicated versions deal with the static type of inventory but this text is restricted to the simpler model, sometimes referred to as a deterministic model, to the extent that the variable inputs are assumed known, or determined. The assumptions of the model are:

1. demand is known for each inventory item
2. usage of inventory items is a linear function
3. the quantity ordered does not change over time

---

[10]R. H. Wilson wrote a seminal article on economic order quantity in 1934. Consequently, it is sometimes referred to as "the Wilson Formula."

4. unit ordering cost per item is constant
5. variables are fixed over time
6. inventory replenishment is instantaneous when the inventory level reaches zero

The EOQ model has been modified at various times to relieve the restrictive assumptions, the easiest being to incorporate a concept of safety stock, thus alleviating the restrictions of assumptions 1 and 6. Based on assumption 6, if an inventory shipment arrives just as the last unit of inventory has been used, inventory rises from zero to whatever the number of units just received.

In Exhibit 6.19, if a shipment is received every month, then the *average* holding period of each unit of inventory is two weeks, that is, shipment volume divided by two. It follows that while the amount ordered has halved (and therefore the carrying cost), there are twice as many orders involved. If the shipment arrives every two weeks in volumes of one-half the monthly total, the average holding period is one week. This example introduces the "sawtooth" nature of the model.

The EOQ model considers only two types of cost, carrying cost (C) and ordering cost (O). In this instance the monthly delivery results in higher carrying cost and lower ordering cost than the bi-weekly. Fortunately, there is a mathematical formula to work out the optimum balance for the minimization of cost, stated as:

$$Q^* = \sqrt{\frac{2UO}{C}}$$

Where Q^* = economic order quantity (EOQ)

U = units used per year

O = cost of ordering

C = cost of carrying one unit

For example, a small New York importer sells five thousand Norwegian toy trolls in the United States each year. The importer estimates that the cost of each order is approximately $50 to cover clerical costs associated with the order placement, subsequent payment of invoice, and customs clearance, etc. It also costs on average $2 per year to store one troll (plus other miscellaneous warehousing costs). The importer wants to know how many trolls should be ordered at a time. Applying the EOQ formula:

$$Q^* = \sqrt{\frac{2(5,000)(50)}{2}} = 500$$

The importer's economic order quantity is five hundred units. While this is very useful to know, it does not indicate *when* this amount is to be ordered. To extend the EOQ model the analyst needs to relax assumption 6 and look at the lead times involved.

◆ EXHIBIT 6.19

THE PATTERN OF INVENTORY LEVEL

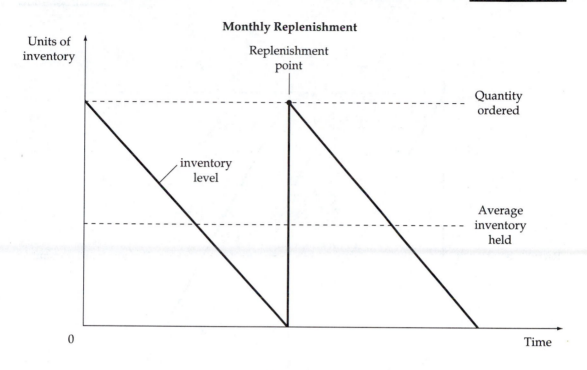

Monthly Replenishment

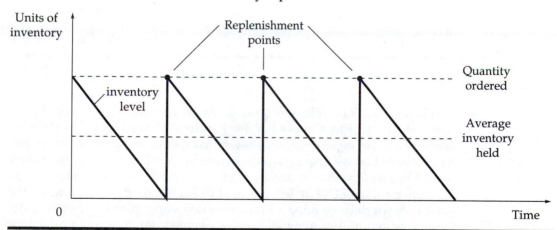

Bi-weekly Replenishment

When to Order

Assume the distributor operates in a fifty-week year, sales will be one hundred per week, and each shipment will last five weeks. From placement of order until arrival in New York takes two weeks. The reorder point is therefore two weeks multiplied by one hundred, which equals two hundred units.

◆ **EXHIBIT 6.20**

INVENTORY ORDERS: SIZE AND TIMING

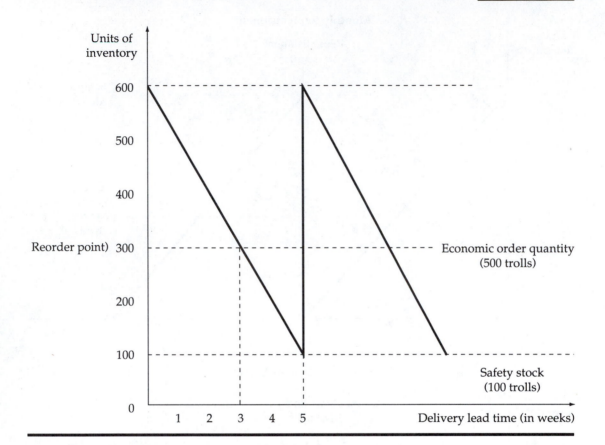

When the stock of trolls gets down to the two hundred level, then the importer should reorder the EOQ of five hundred. However, this provides no safety stock and experience has shown that delays of up to one week can occur due to bad weather or late departure by the ship, etc. Therefore there should be an allowance of one week of safety stock, or one hundred trolls. Consequently, the EOQ (of five hundred trolls) should be ordered when the stock is down to three hundred (one hundred safety plus two hundred delivery lead time). Assuming all goes as planned, the maximum inventory holding of trolls will never exceed six hundred (assuming no early deliveries). This is shown in Exhibit 6.20.

For a stock-out to occur, the safety stock has to be completely used *and* the sloping line then has to extend through the horizontal axis, creating a triangle that indicates the costs of shortage.

ALTERNATIVE FORMS OF INVENTORY MANAGEMENT

Clearly, not all smaller businesses have the resources, capacity, or information to undertake such an analysis as the EOQ above. Priorities have to be set and simpler and quicker ways of controlling inventory must be sought, several of which are outlined below. However, the small-business manager is urged to consider the possibility of utilizing the EOQ method on those product lines that constitute the most important element of the business. EOQ is not appropriate to all businesses, but it can be beneficial if it is.

Visual

The cost of implementation of procedures such as the EOQ model tend to increase with the complexity of the firm's operations. As a result, they are rarely used by the smaller firm. The very smallest firms can often keep a check on their stock by either merely looking around or by taking a mental note of inventory levels each morning, a couple of minutes before the real work of the day begins. Obviously, the number of lines cannot be too large and some knowledge of delivery lag times is helpful.

The Continuous Inventory Method

Very simple in theory, the **continuous,** or **perpetual, inventory method** commences with stock on hand at a given date, adds to it all stock deliveries, and deducts all stock shipments. The balance at any one point in time is the stock on hand. This method was used before the introduction of the personal computer and worked reasonably well if accurately and diligently maintained. A formal inventory count was still required, usually annually, to reconcile records with actual amounts. Pilferage, loss, or damage could then be assessed. With the introduction of the personal computer into business use, and the numerous software packages available, it remains a useful method of determining inventory levels at any particular point in time. In addition, the computer can monitor levels of inventory and issue a reorder reminder at a predetermined level of inventory.

Another useful cost-saving device is the **bar code.** Using a bar-code reader for inventories in and out will save time and therefore money on the recording of stock movements. It also updates the computer records automatically so there is no delay in establishing inventory records. Also, invoices and inventories can be matched and any discrepancy investigated. Retail outlets and even supermarkets now have quite sophisticated accounting records, and it is quite unusual not to have the sales point linked to a computer. This method still requires a physical inventory count, but with a computerized tag, or bar code, the job is much simpler than it once was and is more accurate.

The ABC Method

The **ABC method** simply allocates priority to different product lines or groups. Those products with a priority A classification are the most important items the firm holds and typically have the highest dollar value (price per unit multiplied by annual quantity sold) or the greatest sensitivity to basic product change or design. Priority B products are either less sensitive or have lower dollar value. Priority C products are one step lower on the scale, and so on. The number of priorities allocated depends on the firm but there must not be so many as to defeat the purpose of the exercise—to control inventory in a simple but effective manner. Also, the lowest priority items must not be forgotten, they should merely receive less emphasis in inventory procedures.

The Two-Bin Method

Many smaller businesses adopt a well-tried and often quite acceptable form of inventory control, the **two-bin method.** With this method, the reorder point occurs when the container in which the inventory is held becomes empty and the second container, or bin, is brought into use. The stock controller then orders a new bin quantity. Obviously, the length of time taken to empty one bin must not exceed the time taken from reordering to the arrival of the new stock; in this case the firm may resort to substituting a bigger bin or employing a third bin (in which case, the method should be called a three-bin method). However, the principle is the same. This method of inventory management is very simplistic, but it is very cheap to implement and generally functions well. It is not necessarily optimal, but the costs associated with the utilization of resources to achieve optimality derived from, say, the EOQ model may well offset the additional cost associated with the cost of ordering and the cost of carrying excess inventory.

 CONCEPT CHECK

1. *What are the three types of inventory?*
2. *What fundamental decisions relate to the management of inventory?*
3. *How does the inventory turnover ratio assist the process of inventory control?*
4. *What types of costs are associated with inventory?*
5. *What is a safety stock and what trade-offs are possible when determining its level?*
6. *Why should the velocity of inventory turnover affect a safety stock's level?*
7. *What is meant by the term* dynamic inventories? *What other types of inventory are there?*
8. *What is a stock-out? What two factors combine to reduce the probability of this occurring?*
9. *What are the underlying principles of the EOQ model?*
10. *What alternative, non-computational forms of management do small businesses exhibit in inventory control?*

6.6 LIABILITIES

Short-term sources of funds may be any of the accounts shown in Quadrant 2 of Exhibit 6.1. By far the largest in terms of monetary value for most small businesses is accounts payable, although for some firms bank overdrafts can figure prominently.

Many of the principles embodied in the section on accounts receivable can be seen from the buyer's perspective in accounts payable. There are credit periods and discount terms, often similar to those that the firm experiences on its own credit sales. The balance must once again be struck between the need for this financing and its cost. The cost of foregoing trade discounts can be considerable. For example, a cash (trade) discount is offered at 2/10, net 30. The cost of not taking the cash discount can be calculated as follows:

$$\text{Cost} = \frac{\text{discount \%}}{100 - \text{discount \%}} \times \frac{365}{\text{credit period} - \text{discount period}}$$

At 2/10 net 30, this becomes:

$$\text{Cost} = \frac{2}{100 - 2} \times \frac{365}{30 - 10} = \frac{2}{98} \times \frac{365}{20} = 37.2\%$$

The twenty days of credit from the tenth of the month to the thirtieth is the period in which the purchaser is borrowing from the seller. In this instance, the rate for the annual cost of borrowing is 37.2 percent and the purchaser would do better to pay on day ten, take the 2 percent cash discount, and source the funding from somewhere that offers it more cheaply if possible.

The purchaser may not pay the invoice until day sixty, in which case the equation becomes:

$$\text{Cost} = \frac{2}{98} \times \frac{365}{60 - 10} = 14.9\%$$

If this calculation is done many times over, merely changing the days of credit taken, there results a downward-sloping curve, from the day the discount was foregone. At the same time, there is some opportunity cost of late payment (shown as an upward-sloping dotted line) from the point C* in Exhibit 6.21.

The longer a purchaser can refrain from paying, the better the financial terms, often referred to as "stretching" trade credit. However, there are other less quantifiable (or opportunity) costs of continual late payment. For example, the seller may:

✦ withdraw trade credit
✦ impose harsher terms
✦ not supply at all, even on a cash-on-delivery basis
✦ give the purchaser a low priority, which is particularly true when there is a requirement for technical support

With a particularly bad credit rating the buyer may not be able to obtain credit anywhere, and should a buyer not pay the bill at all, legal action is likely to follow. Nevertheless, stretching may still be a useful tool to employ on the infrequent occasions when it is needed urgently.

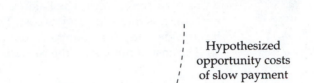

ANNUAL COST OF BORROWING ON TRADE CREDIT

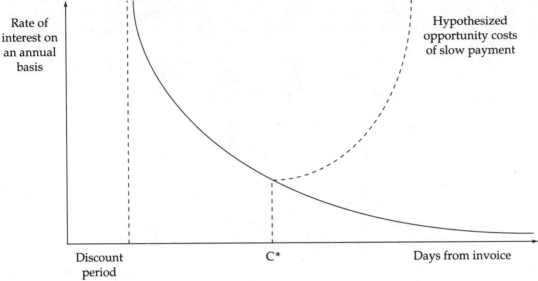

Other things being equal, if payables exceed receivables, then the firm is in a period requiring short-term trade-credit finance. This is a preferable situation to funding receivables from other sources.

 CONCEPT CHECK

1. *What are trade discounts?*
2. *If a trade discount is not accepted, what strategy can be used to minimize the cost?*
3. *What dangers are inherent in consistently paying late?*
4. *Illustrate graphically the costs associated with varying payment dates and discount terms to a firm's supplier.*

SUMMARY

✦ Net working capital is the difference between the cash value of the firm's investment in current assets and the cash debt in current liabilities. Working-capital policy is the overall decision regarding the risk and return trade-offs with which the firm wishes to live. Working-capital management is the way in which current accounts are managed within parameters determined in policy decisions; such policy is determined, in part, by the risk profile of the firm as represented by the senior management.

✦ Arguably, working-capital management is the most important function of small-business management as there is a strong and direct relationship between the management of current assets and the way the firm views that most important of elements for the smaller business, liquidity.

✦ The distinction between temporary and permanent assets and their appropriate sources of finance is essential in understanding the concept of the working-capital cycle. Also of importance is the concept of opportunity cost (the cost of not putting resources to other, more profitable, uses). Liquidity is critical to the success of the smaller firm, but liquidity and profitability are often competing goals.

✦ Three main current accounts (cash, receivables, and inventory) exist within the working-capital cycle. Cash is held to pay for everyday transactions and as a precaution against unforeseeable events. Due to the lack of synchronization between inflows and outflows of cash, a cash balance is held as a buffer. The trade-off is that too little cash involves the prospect of illiquidity, too much involves an opportunity cost and the non-optimization of this resource.

✦ Forecasting cash requirements is of particular importance to a small business and the cash budget is a particularly useful management tool.

✦ Receivables policy involves a trade-off between the higher profit potential of increased sales and the additional costs incurred in the form of bad debts and higher collection expenses. The terms on which credit is granted has a cost and an appropriate balance must be struck when formulating policy. A consequence of selling too much without the necessary working capital to support it leads to overextending and possible bankruptcy. The receivables aging schedule is a useful tool in the monitoring of receivables.

✦ Within inventories, two principal forms of cost are evident: the cost of carrying and the cost of ordering. The simple economic order quantity (EOQ) model illustrates how to attempt to balance these two inversely related items (several assumptions of the simple model can be relaxed). The concepts of stock-out and safety stock are central to understanding the principles of good inventory management.

✦ Current liabilities tend to play a lesser role in working-capital management, but the cost of using trade creditors as a source of short-term finance is potentially high.

✦ Working-capital policy and management are central to operating an efficient business and the firm should try to optimize these accounts not only as separate entities but as integrated, interdependent, and holistic entities. It is important to balance the competing and often opposing aims of each account. The time spent doing so, while sometimes viewed as less productive given the competing claims of other functions in the business, is time well invested. This balance ultimately can make the difference between profit and loss, or even bankruptcy due to illiquidity.

THE CASE—PART SIX

In 2002, Dave increased the capacity of his plant as planned. To finance this move, he passed his dividend, borrowed $20,000 on current account from the bank, and drew out the deposit that he had invested with the bank. The 2002 sales exceeded those of the previous year by about 20 percent, or approximately $100,000, while net operating income increased by 16.7 percent and the "bottom line" by about 22 percent. Despite the percentage increase, Dave has trouble accepting that a sales increase of this magnitude increased the profit by a mere $6,829 and this causes him to worry more about how to streamline the business than how to expand it. The high levels of current assets, such as accounts receivable and inventory, committed about $137,000 at the end of 2002, which Dave believes is too much. Dave wants to reach his potential in 2003.

ASSIGNMENT 6.1

Dave's monthly working capital from December 2001 exhibits the following pattern:

	Current assets	Fixed assets	Total assets	Current liabilities
Dec	$125,324	$ 84,522	$209,846	$42,290
Jan	85,598	144,523	230,121	37,763
Feb	79,934	140,300	220,234	33,121
Mar	59,219	141,483	200,702	31,672
Apr	61,115	139,964	201,079	40,002
May	122,157	138,444	260,601	44,451
June	141,908	136,924	278,832	53,444
July	165,014	135,405	300,419	61,676
Aug	156,241	133,885	290,126	58,610
Sept	137,660	132,366	270,026	62,343
Oct	119,869	130,846	250,715	67,109
Nov	121,297	129,326	250,623	71,123
Dec	147,923	127,807	275,730	70,813

Required

1. What was Dave's net working capital at December 31, 2002?
2. Construct a graph showing the levels of Dave's permanent current assets, temporary current assets, fixed assets, and long-term assets for the period under consideration.
3. Explain what appears to be happening to Dave's temporary current assets.

ASSIGNMENT 6.2

Dave is not happy about the rate of increase of his profits despite the increases in sales. A summary of the firm's performance for its first five years is as follows:

INCOME STATEMENTS FOR DAVE'S BIKES & CO.

	Year				
	1998	1999	2000	2001	2002
Sales	$ 250,000	$ 337,500	$ 438,750	$ 504,562	$ 605,475
Cost of sales	(125,000)	(172,125)	(228,238)	(267,723)	(327,693)
Gross profit	$ 125,000	$ 165,375	$ 210,512	$ 236,839	$ 277,782
Operating expense	(100,000)	(125,000)	(153,300)	(173,094)	(201,314)
Depreciation	(8,900)	(12,330)	(14,713)	(12,535)	(16,715)
Total operating cost	$(108,900)	$(137,330)	$(168,013)	$(185,629)	$(218,029)
Net operating income	$ 16,100	$ 28,045	$ 42,499	$ 51,210	$ 59,753
Interest received	0	0	0	150	0
Interest paid	(4,720)	(4,554)	(7,196)	(7,743)	(6,380)
Earnings (pre-tax)	$ 11,380	$ 23,491	$ 35,303	$ 43,617	$ 53,373
Tax	(3,414)	(7,048)	(10,591)	(13,085)	(16,012)
Earnings (after-tax)	$ 7,966	$ 16,443	$ 24,712	$ 30,532	$ 37,361
Dividends paid	0	0	(9,885)	(12,213)	0
Retained earnings	$ 7,966	$ 16,443	$ 14,827	$ 18,319	$ 37,361

BALANCE SHEETS FOR DAVE'S BIKES & CO.

	1998	1999	Year 2000	2001	2002
Assets:					
Cash	$ 111	$ 79	$ 333	$ 3,401	$ 730
Accounts receivable	31,250	42,188	54,843	63,070	75,685
Inventory	23,438	32,273	42,795	50,198	61,442
Prepaid expenses	5,000	6,250	7,665	8,655	10,066
Current assets	$ 59,799	$ 80,790	$105,636	$125,324	$147,923
Vehicle	24,000	24,000	44,000	44,000	44,000
Accum. depreciation*	(4,800)	(8,640)	(15,712)	(21,370)	(25,896)
	$ 19,200	$ 15,360	$ 28,288	$ 22,630	$ 18,104
Plant and equipment	41,000	79,000	79,000	79,000	139,000
Accum. depreciation	(4,100)	(11,590)	(18,331)	(24,398)	(35,858)
	$ 36,900	$ 67,410	$ 60,669	$ 54,602	$103,142
Fittings		10,000	10,000	10,000	10,000
Accum. depreciation		(1,000)	(1,900)	(2,710)	(3,439)
		$ 9,000	$ 8,100	$ 7,290	$ 6,561
Fixed assets	56,100	91,770	97,057	84,522	127,807
Total assets	$115,899	$172,560	$202,693	$209,846	$275,730
Liabilities:					
Accounts payable	$ 11,250	$ 14,856	$ 19,077	$ 22,041	$ 26,450
Accrued expenses	9,000	11,886	15,261	17,632	21,161
Income tax payable	683	1,409	2,118	2,617	3,202
Short-term bank loan	7,000	30,000	7,000	0	20,000
Current liabilities	$ 27,933	$ 58,151	$ 43,456	$ 42,290	$ 70,813
Long-term loan	50,000	60,000	90,000	80,000	80,000
Total liabilities	$ 77,933	$118,151	$133,456	$122,290	$150,813
Paid-in capital	30,000	30,000	30,000	30,000	30,000
Retained earnings	7,966	24,409	39,237	57,556	94,917
Owner's equity	$ 37,966	$ 54,409	$ 69,237	$ 87,556	$124,917
Total liabilities and owner's equity	$115,899	$172,560	$202,693	$209,846	$275,730

Required

1. Utilizing trend analyses based on percent of sales, explain to Dave where his increase in sales revenue went.
2. Calculate the following ratios for 2001 and 2002. Comment on any differences.
   - a) Current ratio
   - b) Acid-test ratio
   - c) Receivables turnover
   - d) Average collection period
   - e) Inventory turnover

---

*An income statement shows depreciation on an annual basis, but a balance sheet will show accumulated depreciation (total depreciation charged over the life of the asset).

f) Inventory holding period
g) Payables turnover
h) Payables holding period
3. For 2002 determine the number of days in the operating cycle and hence the number of days it takes to convert cash.
4. How well has Dave matched asset maturity to sources of finance over the past five years?
5. Has Dave been conservative or aggressive in his attitude toward working capital?

ASSIGNMENT 6.3

Dave's projections for 2003 reflected the following figures and relationships:

Sales	$ 666,022
Cost of sales	(367,672)
Gross profit	$ 298,350
Operating expenses	(222,845)
Depreciation	(18,591)
Net operating income	$ 56,914
Interest	(7,963)
Earnings (pre-tax)	48,951
Income tax	(14,685)
Net income	$ 34,266
Dividends paid	(13,707)
Retained earnings	$ 20,559

60 percent of operating expenses are fixed and are evenly spread throughout the year
40 percent of operating expenses are variable and are expended in proportion to sales

	Beginning	Ending
Accounts receivable	$75,685	$83,254
Inventory	61,442	68,938
Payables (cost of sales)	26,450	29,526
Net payables (operating expenses)	11,095	12,479
Tax payable	3,202	2,937

Beginning current assets and current liabilities are received and/or paid in the first quarter where relevant

	Receivables	Purchases	Operating expenses
Collected/paid in the quarter accrued	30%	65%	15%
Collected/paid in the next quarter	70%	35%	85%

New loans of $30,000 are raised in the final quarter while dividends are paid in the final quarter as are capital expenditures of $40,000
Interest is paid evenly throughout the year. One-third of tax is paid in the second quarter, two-thirds in the final quarter

	Quarter 1	Quarter 2	Quarter 3	Quarter 4
Sales	30%	10%	20%	40%
Cost of sales	30%	10%	20%	40%
Variable operating expenses	30%	10%	20%	40%

Cash sales, cash operating expenses and cash purchases are all 10 percent of the relevant items

Required

1. Determine the ending cash balance for each quarter.
2. If the bank credit line is $20,000 and is fully drawn at the start of the year, will it be appropriate for Dave's needs?

ASSIGNMENT 6.4

Dave believes that he should shorten the period of credit extended to his debtors.

Required

1. How might Dave accelerate the collection of accounts receivable?
2. What is the downside of accelerating the collection of accounts receivable?

ASSIGNMENT 6.5

Early in 2003 Dave receives a request to extend credit to a new client who offers to purchase $48,000 worth of bikes per year if Dave will extend him credit for two months.

Required

1. Assuming that 40 percent of operating expenses are variable and that Dave's opportunity cost of capital is 15 percent, and using some of the ratios from Assignment 6.3 determine Dave's:
   a) marginal profit before tax
   b) excess profit
2. Does the situation change if the new order is a single, non-repeating order?
3. If Dave's other clients (who are extended credit for only one month) discovered the terms being offered to the new customer, they might also request a two-month credit period. Using the 2003 receivables as a basis, what will the effect be on Dave's profitability?

ASSIGNMENT 6.6

The following information is available concerning Dave's June 2003 listing of receivables.

Account name	Date opened	Credit limit	30 days past due	30–60 days past due	61–90 days past due	90+ days past due	Total
Bikes, Inc.	5/1998	$20,000	$ 9,600	$ 0	$0	$ 0	$ 9,600
Fastbikes	9/1998	20,000	9,600	4,800	0	0	14,400
Bikes 'R' Us	6/1999	20,000	12,000	0	0	0	12,000
Bikes 4 Kids	1/2000	8,000	0	0	0	7,200	7,200
Sam's Bikes	5/2000	10,000	0	9,600	0	0	9,600
Bike-Go-Round	6/2001	20,000	7,200	4,800	0	0	12,000
Bike Suppliers	11/2002	24,000	14,400	0	0	0	14,400
Total			$52,800	$19,200	$0	$7,200	$79,200

Required

1. Describe the nature of any problems that you see, and advise Dave about appropriate action.

ASSIGNMENT 6.7

At the start of 2003 Dave believes that he can sell 520 bicycles during the year. He estimates that the cost of servicing one order is $100 and the carrying cost for a bicycle is $16.25 per year.

Required

1. Calculate the EOQ, the number of orders per year, and the period between orders.
2. If Dave wants to reduce his inventory stock to a four-week supply, graph the pattern of inventory usage for eight weeks and for four weeks.
3. If Dave also wants to keep a safety stock of ten units, what is the effect on his pattern of inventory usage?
4. If there is a strike in the shipping industry that lasts for two weeks at the time that Dave needs to reorder, what will happen?

ASSIGNMENT 6.8

Due to the length of transportation on imports, Dave believes that he is getting a raw deal with his terms of 3/10 net 30 from his overseas supplier.

Required

1. Advise Dave about the credit cost of missing the discount and paying in thirty days as required.
2. Advise Dave on the credit cost of missing the discount and paying in sixty days.

SELECTED ADDITIONAL READINGS

Slow payment problems. 1987. *SBRT Quarterly Survey* No. 11: 20-27.

Belt, B. 1979. Working capital policy and liquidity in the small business. *Journal of Small Business Management* 16 (3).

Brealey, R. A., and S. C. Myers. 1991. *Principles of corporate finance.* 4th ed. (New York: McGraw-Hill).

Brunell, K. T., K. A. Jessell, and D. E. McCarty. 1990. Cash management practices of small firms. *Journal of Cash Management* (November–December): 52–55.

Burns, R., and J. Walker. 1991. A survey of working capital policy among small manufacturing firms. *Journal of Small Business Finance* 1 (1).

Casey, W. 1989. Working capital. *Certified accountant* (October): 36–39.

Chaney, J., H. Custer, and L. Grotke. 1977. Cash management and planning for the small businessman. *American Journal of Small Business* 1 (3) (January).

Dewhurst, J., and P. Burns. 1989. *Small business: Planning, finance and control.* 2d ed. (London: Macmillan).

Devine, W. F., V. J. Wherling, and K. M. Hiltebeitel. 1989. Small business cash management services. *The National Public Accountant* (September).

Dobbins, R. 1993. An introduction to financial management. *Management Decision* 31 (2).

Elliehausen, G. E., and J. D. Wolken. 1992. The use of trade credit by small firms. Paper presented to the 1992 International Research Symposium on Small Firm Finance.

Fisher, D. I. 1973. Cash management. *Conference board report* No. 580.

Fleming, M. M. K., and J. K. Kim. 1989. Where did the cash go? *Management Accounting* (July).

Grablowsky, B. J. 1976. Mismanagement of accounts receivable by small business. *Journal of Small Business* 14 (4).

———— 1978. Management of the cash position. *Journal of Small Business Management* 16 (3).

———— 1984. Financial management of inventory. *Journal of Small Business Management* 22 (3).

Hartgraves, A. L., F. A. Jacobs, and L. H. Beard. 1983. Managing accounts receivable in a small business. *Business* (July–September): 34–40.

Jacobs, F. A., L. H. Beard, and A. L. Hartgraves. 1983. Controlling cash flow in the small business. *Business* (1): 31–36.

Levin, R. I., and V. R. Travis. 1987. Small company finance: What the books don't say. *Harvard Business Review* (November–December).

Lewellen, W. G., and R. W. Johnson. 1972. Better way to monitor accounts receivable. *Harvard Business Review* (May–June).

McMahon, R. G. P. 1986. *Financial management for small business.* (Sydney, Australia: Commerce Clearing House).

McMahon, R. G. P., S. Holmes, P. J. Hutchinson, and D. M. Forsaith. 1993. *Small enterprise financial management: Theory and practice* (Ft. Worth: Harcourt Brace).

Richman, T. 1986. Seeing red. *Inc.* (May) 77–85.

Scherr, F. C. 1989. *Modern working capital management: Text and cases* (Englewood Cliffs, NJ: Prentice-Hall).

Scott, D. F., J. W. Petty, J. D. Martin, A. J. Keown. 1988. *Basic financial management.* 4th ed. (Englewood Cliffs, NJ: Prentice-Hall).

Thompson, R. 1986. Understanding cash flow: A system dynamics analysis. *Journal of Small Business Management* (April).

Van Horne, J. C. 1992. *Financial management and policy.* 9th ed. (Englewood Cliffs, NJ: Prentice Hall).

Wacht, R. F. 1984. Credit insurance: A receivables management tool for small business. *Business* (October–December): 8–15.

Walker, E. W., and J. W. Petty, 1978. *Financial management of the small firm.* 2d ed. (Englewood Cliffs, NJ: Prentice-Hall).

Wilson, R. H. 1934. A scientific routine for stock control. *Harvard Business Review* XIII.

LONG-TERM ASSET DECISIONS

OBJECTIVES

1. *Examine the capital-acquisition environment*
2. *Examine the role of capital budgeting in the context of the small business*
3. *Distinguish between strategic and tactical investments.*
4. *Introduce the nature of project evaluation*
5. *Review the time value of money*
6. *Examine the construction of cash-flow forecasts and how inflation and taxation are incorporated into them*
7. *Introduce the notion of the discount factor and examine the basis for its selection*

7.1   INTRODUCTION

Chapter 6 was concerned with the elements and efficiency of use of the short-term assets in a firm's balance sheet. This chapter is concerned with how the long-lived-asset-acquisition process should be addressed. Long-lived assets are also referred to as **capital assets** because they comprise the physical assets controlled by the firm.

Chapter 1 identified a number of reasons why small businesses are different from larger businesses, and consequently smaller-firm finance differs from larger-firm finance (generally referred to as corporate finance). The basic principles of capital acquisitions are common to all firms but in the case of the smaller firm, problems of relevance and thus application arise. In Chapters 7 and 8 the difference between large and small businesses tends to be one of emphasis.

Capital budgeting is the term given to the process by which organizations make capital investment decisions[1]. Capital budgeting is just as relevant to the small firm as it is to the large firm, although in the case of the former the investment decision is often determined without the benefit of formal analysis. The success of capital-budgeting decisions affects the chances of a firm's future prosperity and survival; that is, a decision to purchase an asset today dictates the future direction and profitability of the firm tomorrow.

It can be argued strongly that major asset-acquisition decisions are significantly more important to the small firm than to the large firm. Capital-investment decisions by larger firms, although frequently larger in dollar terms, tend to be proportionately smaller in relation to their asset base than is the case with the decisions of smaller firms. Consequently, while errors in acquisition are always costly, the cost to a smaller firm is proportionately greater. Nevertheless, many small firms are not capital intensive and these businesses suffer less risk as the result of a poor decision than those that are capital intensive. The rarity of major investment decisions by those smaller firms that do undertake major capital investments increases the risk that can be associated with the decision. Smaller businesses tend to base their investment decisions on an intuitive assessment of the situation; for some firms this works reasonably well, whereas for others it does not.

Risk, in this context, depends on the size of the outlay relative to the size of the firm. Relatively small expenditures are frequently not worth the effort of a formal evaluation and some types of capital expenditures do not lend themselves to the evaluation process at all (e.g., expenditures on furniture and fittings, or an extension of the computer system, or car-park extensions). In fact, the number of capital investments that fall into this category may well exceed those that are amenable to formal analysis.

---

[1]This definition is given in R. Butler, L. G. Davies, R. H. Pike, and J. Sharp, *Strategic Investment Decisions: Theory, Practice and Process* (London: Routledge, 1993), 49.

The general rule, therefore, is that only those investments that have measurable cash flows should be considered as suitable for formal analysis. If one discards those investments that are too small to waste valuable management time on, what is left are acquisitions that can be considered measurable and significantly sizable and costly.

Because smaller firms are often entrepreneurially driven and may tend to be less sophisticated in their acquisition analyses than larger firms, they nevertheless also have need of formal methods of evaluation. Computer-based spreadsheet packages take the hard work out of the process once the data has been entered. All that is needed is to know what data to enter, what to leave out, and how to calculate the required figures from such data, much of which is prompted by the software package used.

As with an individual purchasing a house or a car, capital investment is a major commitment and one with which the individual or firm must live. True, in the short term an individual can sell the house or car and incur minimal losses (or possibly even a profit) but any asset that a firm purchases is designed for income generation and/or wealth creation. It is very rare for a firm that acquires economically inappropriate fixed assets to make a profit on their resale (land being a potential exception). Less income (cash) generation, greater expenditure (not only on the lost investment but also on the amount expended in trying to retrieve the situation), less liquidity, less profit, and potential bankruptcy are the inevitable results of poor investment appraisal.

Small firms particularly, or those firms with little capital investment, will have limited use for what follows in this chapter. However, many small firms do have relatively capital-intensive operations and do utilize formal investment-appraisal procedures to some extent. Whether a firm uses the "back of an envelope" assessment, one-page statements, or a full-blown procedure manual is firm-specific and size-related. The appraisal technique should be relevant to the investment process of the firm.

The remainder of this chapter deals with a discussion about what capital budgeting is and is not and the reasons for capital acquisitions. It then reviews the capital-acquisition procedure and explores each of the steps outlined. The arithmetic evaluation techniques will be presented in Chapter 8. The intent of the discussion that follows is to increase awareness of the need for careful selection of an appropriate technique that may improve the firm's capital-budgeting and investment-appraisal skills.

 CONCEPT CHECK

1. *Why are capital acquisitions more important to the small firm than to the large firm?*
2. *What type of investments are suited to formal analysis?*
3. *What are the results of poor investment appraisal?*
4. *What reasons are often given to negate the use of formal investment appraisal?*

7.2 CAPITAL BUDGETING

The term *capital budgeting* emphasizes the process of decision making, while the term *capital investment* evokes images of analysis of a single project evaluation; the terms will be considered synonymous here.

Capital investment is *not* the investment of cash into paper assets such as stocks and bonds. Although a firm may have stocks and bonds on its balance sheet as an asset, these investments are frequently redeemed within one year. Therefore, no further consideration shall be given to these assets. Instead, capital investment will be considered and will refer to the investment in real physical assets, such as property, plant, machinery, etc., and also the investment in less tangible assets, such as research and development, advertising directed at the long-term awareness of the firm and its products, and so on, with life expectancies typically in excess of one year.

Capital investment also is *not* the cash investment in working capital, such as inventory, that was discussed in the previous chapter, although the change in working capital resulting from the acquisition is reflected in the firm's cash flow and should be accounted for in the evaluation. Capital investment refers to long-lived or fixed assets usually with a life expectancy exceeding one year (following the accounting convention), as opposed to the short-term assets of less than one year life expectancy in working capital.

Among the long-term assets of many businesses is an item called goodwill. It is perhaps the most intangible long-term asset of all and, as such, it also tends to be problematic in business-acquisition evaluations. This is discussed further in Chapter 10 on business valuation and purchase.

In many circumstances, a firm is faced with more than one potential acquisition opportunity competing for the limited investment funds available. Because a firm in this situation normally has to "ration" such funds, one part of the investment appraisal procedure is known as **capital rationing**. As a consequence of funds limitations and competing alternative investments, the owner or finance manager must evaluate the alternatives and include only the most desirable (in terms of financial analysis) ones in the capital budget. However, capital-investment opportunities do not always exceed the available funds. If so, there is no need for capital rationing. In the case of many smaller businesses, there are few significant strategic capital investment opportunities and capital acquisition decisions are therefore infrequent.

There are two key areas in which corporate finance differs in practice from the smaller business. First, smaller firms are more dependent on liquidity. As a result, there are a number of new ideas about the capital-investment decision in smaller firms that concentrate on the liquidity issue. Second, corporate finance typically concentrates on maximizing shareholder wealth; whereas in a closely held firm the desired goals of the owner or manager frequently differ from shareholder-wealth maximization.

For smaller businesses in particular there is a degree of opportunism about the what and when of acquisition. To keep costs down, the small firm may look for used equipment with a reasonable life expectancy, for example, previously owned cars, computer systems, back-up machinery, and so on.

Even if capital acquisitions are second hand they are new to the acquiring firm and the same procedures apply. This makes good sense as, for example, state-of-the-art computing power is not necessarily required for small and relatively simple office tasks. There are a number of firms that purchase equipment from bankrupt companies or resell perfectly usable items to on-going businesses at prices that are considerably below new prices. Such capital-investment purchases may not be required for immediate use, but to take advantage of the opportunity presented, an investment decision may have to be made that is not in accord with the capital-acquisition budget. In extreme circumstances this can affect the firm's future production strategy by dictating the asset configuration of the business. However, such acquisitions made in isolation are very dangerous. It may be that the firm should forego the cost-saving opportunity rather than part with scarce cash resources at an ill-suited time. On balance, capital expenditure planning will always reap rewards.

STRATEGIC AND TACTICAL INVESTMENTS

It is obvious that small businesses in particular are resource-constrained, especially in reguard to the cash resource, and expenditure on long-term assets reduces the availability of cash resources for application in other areas, such as working capital. It is all a question of balance. Not all longer-lived asset acquisitions are of a significant nature. Some acquisitions tend to be what may be called strategic in nature and involve relatively large sums of money, while less significant acquisitions (the result of tactical decisions) tend to commit relatively smaller sums of money.

Strategic investments can be defined as those that lend direction to a firm and tend to involve relatively large sums of money. They include changes in product lines or areas of operation, as well as critical investments that keep the firm going in the same direction.

Tactical investments are those of a more minor nature that involve relatively smaller sums of cash and do not significantly influence a firm's future direction. They include replacement investments with a long duration, for example, enlargement of offices or installation of a new computer. However, strategic decisions cannot be generalized as being relevant to a period in excess of one year. The time period that constitutes whether or not a decision is strategic is industry- and even firm-dependent. What is a strategic time period to a sales organization may not be so in a longer-term manufacturing operation. The link between strategic and tactical capital acquisitions is that they both involve the purchase of an asset, not for resale, but to contribute to the generation of the firm's wealth through the production of goods or services.

A central tenet in finance theory is that all acquisitions should be undertaken if they meet certain value-enhancing criteria (notwithstanding the capital-rationing aspect). This assumes that all costs (not only those specifically addressed in cash-flow calculations, but also those costs associated with the non-optimal choice of projects—or even failure) and benefits, as well as cash-generating ability and market positioning, can be measured. Even large firms cannot completely do this with the resources at their disposal, so it is unreasonable to assume that smaller firms can measure such benefits and costs to the standard required by normative theory.

Consider that the objective function of the owners of the small business is not necessarily wealth maximization. The strategic and technical fit of a new asset that theoretically adds value to the business may not allow for a lack of managerial expertise and compatibility with the desires of the owner. Because strategic investments cost more and tend to have greater relative impact on the business, they are more influenced by non-financial criteria.

Arguably, normative financial-evaluation techniques, such as payback and net present value, are better able to prescribe the investments that the firm should *not* make. The logic being that a smaller firm may possess unique reasons for being in business and can choose a path suggested to it by competing but financially viable alternatives. What the firm cannot do is to select from financially non-viable alternatives. The larger firm does not have this choice available to it. According to financial theory, the larger publicly quoted corporation must select those investments compatible with maximizing shareholder wealth. The infrequency of strategic investments within the smaller firm can also mitigate against formal evaluations.

In larger firms only strategic investments may require investor sanction. Smaller firms tend to have all capital investments sanctioned either by the investment board (if there is one) or, more often, by the owner. This distinction is useful when an investment decision is evaluated on all of its merits and not just on financial criteria.

REASONS FOR CAPITAL ACQUISITIONS

The principal reasons why a business makes a capital investment include:

✦ replacing worn out or obsolete assets
✦ improving the business's efficiency, possibly through cost reduction
✦ acquiring assets for expansion
  (i) of the present business via an existing or new product line, or the setting up of a new venture within or without the existing legal form, or
  (ii) to improve distribution and/or sales channels
✦ acquiring another business
✦ complying with legal requirements (e.g., health and safety)
✦ satisfying work-force (union) demands
✦ environmental reasons

Capital-investment decisions necessitate looking to the future; the longer the projection period, the more forecast estimates can move away from their initial expectations. In addition, unexpected stochastic elements (such as fundamental changes in the economic environment) can also come into play. The process of thinking strategically is less an option and more a requirement.

 CONCEPT CHECK

1. *What is capital investment?*
2. *When does capital rationing occur?*
3. *How do the investment decisions of small firms differ from those of larger firms?*
4. *What are the differences between strategic investments and tactical investments?*
5. *Who makes strategic investment decisions?*
6. *Why do firms make capital acquisitions?*

7.3 THE INVESTMENT PROCESS AND THE CAPITAL BUDGET

The capital budget reflects the strategy a firm is pursuing. In instances where the owner or manager does not subscribe to the process of formalized strategic planning, the capital budget can, in part, redress this omission. To produce an effective capital budget, the management of a firm must take into consideration the future direction of the business in order to plan for asset acquisition and replacement. In other words, the decisionmakers have to consider the firm's future to adequately plan for it and, by doing so, establish their performance criteria and intentions.

While the capital budget feeds into the firm's overall cash budget for whatever the chosen time horizon may be, its construction starts prior to this. The budget itself ideally should include and represent the views of those people within the firm who can make a valid contribution to its construction. Ideas and views must be called for continually across the whole firm and be built into a cohesive plan. Those of a negative disposition would argue that many smaller firms are just too small for this type of idea collection to be effective, or that the firm is small enough for the owner or manager to know intimately the views of all the staff. It is suggested that this argument is fallacious in many instances, tending to be person- or personality-driven and thus unique in every smaller firm. While the degree of formalization may be correlated to firm size, the principle is correct down to the smallest firm. The *process* itself is considerably more important than the formality.

The capital-budgeting decision process moves in two directions from the bottom up and from the top down. It may also be viewed as a circular, or re-iterative, process. To enable this, there must be some channel of communication. The degree of formalization of such a channel depends on the nature, size, and complexity of the business; the channel must be accessible at any

THE CAPITAL-BUDGETING PROCESS

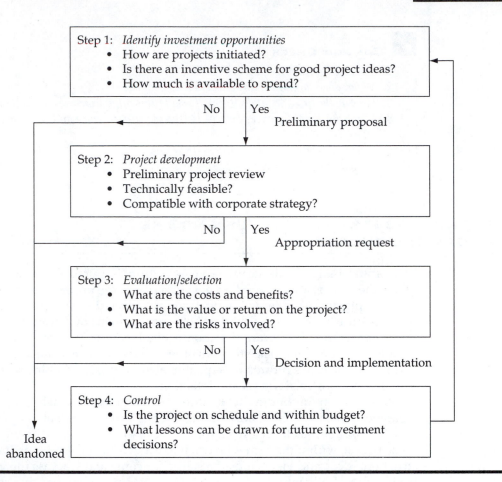

reasonable time. It is also vitally important for decisionmakers to be aware of all of the views and requirements of the staff, and to reward thought and effort. Routine (tactical) capital acquisitions tend to be more amenable to formalized routines while the more strategic and non-routine acquisitions tend to be more informal. Junior employees usually focus on tactical acquisitions, and senior management on strategic matters. But put together, the whole is represented. What a smaller firm's management may *think* is required and what actually *is* required, can frequently be some distance apart. Any process that can narrow this distance must invariably be good business practice. Exhibit 7.1 illustrates the process of investment decisions.[2]

---

[2]Ibid, 52.

STEP 1. IDENTIFICATION OF INVESTMENT OPPORTUNITIES

The first step in the process of investment decisionmaking is very important and, as such, consumes a significant amount of time. Naturally, there are those owners or managers who say they generate ten or one hundred ideas a day. This may be true, but very few of those ideas see the light of day, not necessarily for financial reasons but because most are impractical. Many good business-development ideas are suggested by third parties: customers, suppliers, friends, or colleagues outside the business. Regardless of their source, those firms that fail to generate sufficient useful investment proposals to at least sustain themselves will soon find themselves overtaken in a competitive world.

STEP 2. PROJECT DEVELOPMENT

The second step involves the first screening of ideas, some of which can be discarded after a short discussion and others that require additional input before further development. This stage often has attendant organizational problems; for instance, a proposal by the owner or manager may be given significantly more weight than an equally good or better proposal by a more junior member of the staff. This stage can be bypassed where the owner is also the decisionmaker, but may lead to a less than objective selection of proposals for evaluation. Delegating decisionmaking is not always a smaller firm's strong point. If possible, consultation with and delegation to those affected by such a decision may well prove beneficial.

STEP 3. EVALUATION AND SELECTION

Step 3 results in some form of decision: accept, reject, request more information, or postpone until a following period, etc. The decision depends on the evaluation techniques used. Some form of risk assessment and scenario evaluation, such as sensitivity analysis, should be considered as well. The smaller firm suffers, more than larger firms, from resource constraints, not the least of which are time and knowledge. However, there is no reason why at least some effort cannot be made to gradually introduce techniques and procedures that, in time, will become progressively more sophisticated to aid in the decisionmaking process.

Assuming all the potential capital-acquisition requirements have been submitted and evaluated, the total funds for capital allocation must be decided, i.e., how much can be afforded in the light of present and future financial performance of the firm. Financial performance refers not only to profitability but also, in particular, to the cash flow of the firm. One cannot escape the fact that capital acquisitions have a direct impact on working capital in the smaller firm, hence the inclusion of capital acquisitions in cash-flow forecasts. Both capital expenditures and the flow of cash generated by an investment must be taken into account when cash forecasts are prepared. The accuracy of the cash-flow generation in future time periods is the essence of the investment evaluation and, while it is sometimes difficult to accurately predict cash flows, this step is nevertheless an essential component of the process.

There is always an element of prioritization about capital investments, for example, what is urgent and what can be postponed. Assuming that a ranking of possible projects has been achieved, a cut-off point (e.g., the target return on an investment) should be determined and the potential acquisitions selected, the capital budget can be constructed and integrated into the overall cash budget.

It is of crucial importance to note that depreciation charged to the income statement of the business is merely a nominal figure for tax purposes. Depreciation does not, under any circumstance, provide for a fund with which to purchase new assets. If this is what is required, the firm must set aside a separate fund (sometimes referred to as a sinking fund or an asset-replacement fund) and contribute, on a regular basis, an appropriate sum to pay for the purchase of capital assets at some estimated time in the future. If this is not done, then when the time for asset replacement arrives, the firm may not have the liquidity available to undertake the replacement. Such regular payments result in a decrease in the firm's liquidity in the short term, but significantly reduce the severe impact of large capital maintenance expenditures—what results is many smaller, regular impacts.

When a major capital asset replacement is planned, the sinking fund should be liquidated, and the resultant cash flow should show as a cash inflow in the cash budget and then again as an outflow on the proposed date of acquisition.

The above should not be taken as a universal recommendation to set up sinking funds: the money may have better uses elsewhere. It is to suggest that the absence of such a provision may well result in a visit to the bank and the potential payment of unnecessarily higher rates of interest for a loan.

STEP 4. POST-ACQUISITION CONTROL

Step 4 is often omitted by firms, large and small alike. Once the acquisition is made there is a tendency not to evaluate its ongoing efficiency except in the most superficial way: is it still working/standing/producing? Not many smaller firms would re-evaluate the investment even one year hence and compare it to the original evaluation. If they did so, some valuable lessons could be learned. However, resource constraints, again, come into play. The point is to be aware that such evaluations can be beneficial in the appropriate circumstances.

While stage one is of fundamental importance to the planning process, its success is largely dependent on the type of firm and the personalities within it. In a creative firm new ideas are continually being generated, and the owner or manager is receptive to all reasonable propositions. However, the level of creativity tends to be unique to the individual firm and so general-izations on this basis are difficult.

The level of creativity also affects step 2 of the process. Assuming for the moment that the majority of the strategic capital-acquisition proposals are developed by the firm's senior management, they will be aware of many of the considerations required from an investment. Thus the initial rough screening and technical elements already will be inherent in the decision to discard or to keep alternatives.

Step 3 is less firm-specific. It applies to all projects that make it through the first two steps and, as such, it receives the bulk of the attention in this chapter.

 CONCEPT CHECK

1. *What is a capital budget and how does it differ from a cash budget?*
2. *Describe the elements of the capital-budgeting process.*
3. *What is a sinking fund and how does it work?*
4. *What is the relationship between a sinking fund and depreciation?*
5. *What is the effect of a sinking fund on the firm's budgetary process?*
6. *How does the level of creativity expressed in a firm affect the capital-budgeting process?*

7.4 PROJECT EVALUATION

Investment appraisal is one of the areas where the techniques outlined in this section are similar for the larger and smaller firm. These techniques are standard to most finance and capital-budgeting texts and the reader is re-ferred to those for supplementary reading.[3] While the treatment of basic techniques in this chapter is not intended to be inherently difficult (and can be undertaken on a spreadsheet), mainstream finance texts add significant refinement and sophistication, rendering some techniques quite complex and not relevant to the smaller firm.

ELEMENTS REQUIRED FOR INVESTMENT EVALUATION

The fundamental requirements of investment evaluation are:

+ a detailed statement giving the expected cash inflows and outflows to be assigned to the investment
+ an assessment of the impact of taxation

---

[3]See, for instance: Brealey and Myers, McGraw Hill, 1996; Bierman and Smidt, 1988; Levy and Sarnat, 1986; Lumby, 1991.

✦ a discount rate to account for the time value of money

✦ an additional rate to account for the risk associated with the investment

The crux of standard acquisition appraisal is how to accurately determine the cash flows and the required rate of return, or discount rate. Clearly, the accuracy of the input data has a tremendous effect on the result of the numerical calculation. Even relatively small deviations can affect the numerical "accept/reject" decision. Once the cash flows and discount rate have been determined, the calculation is relatively simple. The resultant figure is then used as a guide for acceptance or rejection of the proposal by management. Here, *guide* is the operative word. The analyses do not of themselves make the decision; management makes the decision. Capital-investment appraisal merely contributes to managerial knowledge about the issue. The starting point is the establishment of the relevant data with which to work before proceeding to the method of calculation.

Before discussing the process of cash-flow determination, this section will first introduce the notion of the time value of money and return to it when the determination of the discount rate is discussed.

CONCEPT CHECK

1. What are the elements required for investment evaluation?
2. What two fundamental things have to be described before an investment appraisal can take place?
3. Why does the outcome of investment appraisal only guide *the decision-making process?*

7.5 TIME VALUE OF MONEY

Any investment analysis that considers time must determine the present equivalent value today of a cash flow that occurs at some future point, i.e., future cash flows must be related to their present equivalent values (or present values, as they are known). The process is a reversal of the notion of compound interest (which starts at the present and moves toward the future).

The compound-interest formula is:

$$\text{Future value of } \$1 = (1 + r)^n$$

where r = rate of interest that can be obtained

n = number of years the money is to be invested

Thus the **present value** of an expected future cash stream, stated with reference to compound interest, is the reciprocal of the compounding formula:

$$\text{Present value of future \$1} = \frac{1}{(1 + r)^n}$$

The factor $1/(1 + r)^n$ is known as the **discount factor** (see Appendix II) where r is the discount rate (the actual percentage of discount required).

Therefore it can be established that:

Present value = future value × discount factor

Note that the discount factor must always be less than 1 because the preference for current consumption means that the owner will only defer consumption if offered more in the future. So the future value of an investment today must always exceed the present cost (or value) of that investment if the owner is to be satisfied. Conversely, the present value of an amount to be received at some time in the future always will be less than that future value.

For example, $100 invested today at an annual interest rate of 8 percent will return $108 after one year. If the owner knows that she is to receive $108 in one year's time, what is it worth today? Fortunately, financial tables assist the analyst in this calculation (although in this example the computation is quite easy). From the financial tables (see Appendix II) one can read the "coordinates": the period equals 1 and interest equals 8 percent. This gives a discount factor of 0.9259. Multiplying $108 by this factor in order to come back to the original amount of $100.

If dealing with time periods extending far into the future, the calculation of the appropriate discount factors can become quite laborious without the financial tables to help. Even with the assistance of financial tables, where cash flows continue for a large number of periods, the calculations can become quite tedious. Fortunately, these types of calculations rarely need to be done by hand today; either a programmable calculator (to store the discount formula and apply it to the relevant data), or a financial calculator (input the cash flows, number of periods, and the discount rate, then press the "PV" button) can be used. The PC-based spreadsheet package is increasingly used for these calculations. However, using the tables is a good place to start because, after a while, the scale of some of the figures is recognized, helping to prevent mistakes when using another medium. However the calculation is done, what is required is the raw input data: the forecasted cash flows, the discount rate (or the discount factor itself), and the time period.

In the discussions that follow, the terms *required rate of return* and *discount rate* are used interchangeably. The rate is based on the current market rate of interest.

The discount rates that are used are fundamentally based on the riskless rate of return (r_f), which is the required rate of return on a riskless investment, such as Treasury bills. This rate rewards the deferral of consumption without reference to any risk associated with the deferral. On the other hand, the discount rate might include an additional premium to reward the risk assumed by the investor. This section is concerned only with r_f and the discussion will return to the consideration of a discount rate inclusive of risk in a later section of this chapter.

Even in a riskless situation, where one is certain that money lent will be repaid at some future point in time, it is most important to understand that $1 today (time period t_0) is different from $1 in the next time period (t_1), which is again different from $1 in the period after that (t_2), and so on (t_n). These cash flows *cannot* be simply added together; they are valued at different time periods. For instance, suppose one goes to a bank and requests $1,000 from one's checking account. It would be more than a little surprising if the bank paid the requested amount in the currency of several different countries all at once. One would have to determine the exchange values of the different currencies before determining whether or not the amount paid was the correct amount.

Similarly, each time period may be viewed as a different type of currency that must be exchanged (discounted) for a common currency. The common currency is the present value of each future time period's cash flow. In much the same way, one might select U.S. dollars to be the common currency against which the values of the other currencies can be measured and exchanged. Adding U.S., Canadian, Australian, and Singapore dollars together makes no sense; neither does adding unadjusted future cash flows together. Only appropriately discounted cash flows can be added together. This difference in time, with certainty of future cash flow, is referred to as the **time value discount rate**.

The discount rate used to adjust for the time value of money under certainty is typically established by reference to the yield associated with investing in three-month Treasury bills. While there are other approaches to the determination of this rate (r_f), this text adopts the Treasury bill alternative, a rate that is regularly reported in the financial pages of newspapers and is therefore easily observable.

CONCEPT CHECK

1. *What is the relationship between the compound rate and the discount rate?*
2. *What is the difference between a discount rate and a discount factor?*
3. *Why can the required rate of return be called a discount rate?*
4. *Why do we need to determine present values?*

7.6 CASH FLOWS

Cash flows are taken into account on the day they are received or paid, and cash-flow budgets are prepared on the basis of the expected date of receipt or payment of cash. Cash inflows are *not* profit and they are *not* income. Cash flows are dollars that go into or out of the firm's cash or bank balance.

Cash flows can change without any change in profit or income and vice versa. Therefore, unlike profit and income, cash flows are *not* subject to:

+ a depreciation deduction
+ the accrual system of accounting
+ determining the appropriate period in which to take revenue
+ the distinction between revenue and capital

CASH FLOWS ARE INCREMENTAL

The concept of incremental (or marginal, as it is sometimes called) cash flows means that all cash inflows and outflows *associated with the project* from the time of its acceptance must be part of the calculation. It is the difference in the cash flows of the firm that are directly attributable to the project that are important. For example, costs already incurred, say in the evaluation of the project before acceptance, are considered sunk costs (irrecoverable whether or not the project goes ahead) and are irrelevant in an incremental framework.

Incremental cash flows include opportunity costs. These relate to the amount that the firm could generate in cash flows if it put some of the resources it already owns to another use, whether or not it is currently contributing to cash flow. For example, if a firm has vacant warehouse or factory space that it is not using, it is not contributing to cash flow. There is a temptation not to take this into account, but that would not be accurate. If that floor space could be rented out to a third party, then the rental income foregone is the opportunity cost and must be offset against the anticipated cash inflows from the proposed investment if that investment required the use of the floor space.

DERIVATION OF APPROPRIATE CASH FLOW

Assuming that the proposed project has passed the rough screening tests of being strategically and technically compatible with the firm's aspirations and its corporate plan (a rather grand expression for something that may only exist in the mind of the owners or managers), the actual process of investment evaluation can begin. This is where many difficulties are first encountered and are often observed as the excuse for the owners or managers of smaller firms for not undertaking numerical techniques of evaluation. Where do the figures come from? What should be included? What should be left out? What about tax?

What should be included in the cash-flow calculation?

+ all cash inflows associated with the project
+ all cash outflows (costs) *directly* associated with the project
+ opportunity costs

✦ changes in the working capital requirement
✦ installation and removal costs, if applicable
✦ the terminal value (resale or scrap)

What should be excluded from the cash-flow calculation?

✦ depreciation
✦ sunk costs (e.g., management time taken prior to the acquisition in evaluating alternative proposals, regardless of whether the investment was made or not)
✦ existing assets (e.g., vacant floor space, land already owned by the firm), although the opportunity cost of utilizing such assets would be considered
✦ financing charges associated with internally generated funds for the investment

One problem with deriving the appropriate cash flow is that there are a number of ways the calculation can be done. Fundamentally, it is possible for at least three of the four areas listed below to be adjusted either in the cash flow itself or by adjusting the discount rate used on the cash flows. The four main areas that need to be addressed are:

1. taxation
2. time value of money
3. inflation
4. risk

Taxation is typically adjusted for in the cash-flow calculation, cash outflows directly related to the project are accounted for by use of the discount rate, r. Inflation and risk are seen in both the numerator and denominator of the valuation equation. Thus, the computation may be viewed as a tale of two parts, the numerator and the denominator. The numerator details the cash flows associated with a project and the denominator the required adjustment (shown later in this chapter) for risk and time valuation.

First, there is the cash flow, then inflation, and then taxation. It is appropriate to start with **gross cash flows,** unadjusted, then adjust for inflation and taxation. Finally, some consideration needs to be given to the discount rate and what constitutes an appropriate rate of interest considering risk and the time value of money.

CASH-FLOW CALCULATION

Like a good story, the project cash-flow calculation has a beginning, a middle, and an end. The beginning is the calculation of the cash flows relating to the acquisition cost of the investment, the middle is the annual ongoing cost associated with its operation, and the end is the cost associated with its disposal. Acquisition and disposal cash flows tend to be directly associated with the investment and thus are relatively straightforward. If the investment has no impact on the cash flows of other aspects of the business then this too is relatively straightforward. If, however, the new investment replaces an item that itself generated cash flows, then only the difference between new and old item cash flows are relevant, and this increases the complexity of the calculation. This difference is seen primarily in the middle part of the story, i.e., the ongoing cash flows associated with the operating costs, and is termed the **differential cash flow**.

As this discussion concentrates on the practical application of investment appraisal for the smaller business, some of the technical arguments can be foregone for inclusion or non-inclusion of some items. In general it is appropriate here to ignore income, profits, and accounting principles. Concentrate purely on cash flows (most texts assume after-tax cash flows but the taxation adjustment follows the unadjusted cash-flow calculation later in this chapter).

An example, based on a real company but with name and details changed, will help to clarify this approach.

EXAMPLE: NITTER, INC.

Nitter, a small firm with fifty employees manufactures surgical dressings for the medical industry, mainly hospitals. New technology is available to produce technically superior dressings by means of knitting instead of the traditional weaving method. This is considered a radical departure from the knowledge base within the company and the senior managers are keen to ensure a thorough evaluation by utilizing capital-investment procedures. They have already undertaken market-research analysis, which suggests a viable market of an additional one million units per year. In-hospital trials have been conducted by means of leasing the knitting machine for six months before a decision to buy is contractually required.

The acquisition cost of the machine will be $200,000 and the cost of transporting it to the firm's premises will be $12,000. The estimated life of the machine is five years and is to be depreciated on a straight-line basis down to zero. The labor and material costs (supplied by the firm itself) for installation will amount to $6,000. Initial training costs will be $15,000. The new machine will replace one of the weaving machines, which will be placed in storage for a cost of $6,000. The old machine will hedge against project failure and the new machine will occupy the same space as the machine it replaces. It is estimated that the initial increase in working capital is $20,000. The additional working-capital requirements will cover any increases in new inventory required, in accounts receivable resulting from increased credit sales, or even additional cash required to sell the additional products.

In the first year it is estimated that increased sales will amount to approximately $120,000, while materials and consumables will increase by $10,000. The variable overheads can be allocated to production, $15,000, and to sales, $30,000, for a total of $45,000. Expectations for subsequent years project an

◆ EXHIBIT 7.2

NITTER, INC. PROJECT-EVALUATION WORKSHEET

NITTER, INC.
PROJECT K: REVISED CASH FLOWS CALCULATION (YEAR 1)

At the start of the project:
Acquisition costs:

1.	Machine	$(200,000)	
2.	Transportation cost	(12,000)	
3.	Installation (labor and materials cost)	(8,000)	
4.	Training costs	(15,000)	
5.	Increase in working capital	(20,000)	
	Total installed cost		$(255,000)

During the life of the project:
Differential operating cash flows (year 1):

6.	Increased sales revenue	$ 120,000	
	Differential operating costs:		
7.	Labor (no change)	0	
8.	Materials	(10,000)	
9.	Variable overheads:		
	Production	(15,000)	
	Sales	(30,000)	
10.	Old machine storage costs	(6,000)	
	Year one operating cash flow		$ 59,000

At the end of the project:
Terminal (disposal) cash flow:

11.	Removal costs—labor	$ (3,000)	
12.	Liquidation of initial working capital	20,000	
13.	Sale of machine	5,000	
	Total terminal cash flows:		$ 22,000

increase in sales volume of 20 percent per annum and operating costs will increase proportionately. Labor will be unchanged.

At the end of the machine's life it is expected that it can be sold for $5,000, less a removal cost of $1,000 (excluding opportunity costs). The increased working capital required by the project initially can be liquidated at the end of the five years for an estimated $20,000.

To determine whether this project is financially sound, the firm wishes to construct a project-evaluation analysis based on the above figures. Assuming no inflation and only the initial outlay period (t_0) plus an initial one-period estimation at t_1, Exhibit 7.2 shows the outcome of the first part of the analysis. The positive numbers are cash inflows and the negative numbers are cash outflows.

Explanation of Items 1 to 13 in Exhibit 7.2

Acquisition Costs

1. The machine—The machine will be invoiced at a price that is assumed to cover all the capitalizable elements associated with it, including peripheral components such as fuse boxes, software necessary to run it, etc. Since leasing costs were incurred prior to the decision to purchase, they are considered a sunk cost and have no impact on incremental cash flows. They are therefore ignored in the calculation.

2. Transportation cost—Will the transport be supplied by an external party (a haulage firm for instance) or by Nitter itself? If an external party (or the supplier) provides transport and invoices Nitter, then that is a valid expense in this section. If Nitter supplies the transport, then an assessment of the opportunity cost of doing so must be made. Item 3 below (installation) illustrates the opportunity-cost concept.

3. Installation—One possible option is not to capitalize materials and labor associated with installation, but rather to account for them as expenses. Labor and materials are applied to the installation at cost. But what figure should be used in the analysis? In this instance, some of the costs of the labor and materials are known so insert that cost plus (and this is very important) the opportunity cost of the time taken by labor that could be used productively elsewhere. Only then can one say that, despite the vagaries of accounting procedures, one has taken account of the cash flows associated with the plant installation.

   Opportunity cost is based on the argument that, if three people are employed for one week to install the machine then they cannot be employed doing something that contributes cash flow to the firm. If the firm makes a net cash-flow increment (say, gross margin) of 200 percent on those people in one week, then the project has to "reimburse" the firm for that lost cash flow. As an example, consider the role of student accountants in a professional accountancy firm. They may receive 25 to 30 percent of the rate at which they are charged out to clients, and therefore utilizing them for internal administration is very costly when the opportunity cost is considered. In Nitter's case, the new project will remove internal resources from a more lucrative use. Resources consumed should be entered as "cash out" (or "in," where resources are generated in addition to sales). The cost of the labor, including any opportunity cost associated with the installation phase of the project is estimated at $6,000, plus the $2,000 opportunity cost; that is, $8,000.

4. Training costs—Training costs are associated with acquisition costs. While they comprise an incremental cost (and will not be incurred if the machine is not purchased), training is not an ongoing differential cost associated with the new machine over the old. Therefore training should be shown as part of the cost of acquisition and not each year over the life of the machine. Ongoing training, however, may be separated from

labor but it is more likely to be reflected in labor costs. Assume here that no ongoing training will take place because the previous (existing) machine requires a similar amount of training.

5. Working capital—It will be necessary to increase working capital by $20,000 in the initial time period after which it will become proportional to increased sales (remember that the ongoing inventories of the old machine will have been run down and a new buffer stock will be required). So the initial increase in working capital can be included as an acquisition cost. A separate figure for the increased requirements should be included in differential costs in future time periods.

Differential Annual Operating Cash Flows

6. **Differential sales revenue**—The concept of differential operating cash inflows and outflows was outlined earlier in this chapter. The new machine should potentially generate annual sales of $400,000, which means that, if the previous machine generated sales of $280,000, the incremental annual contribution of the new machine is $120,000. If the investment was a straight expansion without impinging on other cash-flow elements of the firm's resources then one would enter $400,000 and there would not be a differential.

    It is worth mentioning at this point that this figure is clearly very difficult to estimate and the marketing and production departments (or equivalent if the business is not departmentalized, or the manufacturing sector) have to work closely and meticulously together to stand any chance of being reasonably accurate in their forecasts. Anyone who has constructed cash budgets is aware of the fact that sales are extremely difficult to forecast accurately, while projecting costs is not as difficult a task.

7. Labor—The figure shown assumes that the same labor hours are required for the proposed machine's operation as for the old machine and that consequently there is no change in the operating cash flows. Any reduction or increase in labor payment (cash flow) associated with the new machine over the old is entered here.

8. Materials and consumables—A negative $10,000 is shown because this is how much more the new machine will use in the first year. The item could be grouped under working capital but is kept separate here. Naturally this is an estimate and the production department (if there is a separate department so named) and the person or department responsible for management accounting must confer in the construction of this figure.

9. Variable overheads—Expected increases in variable production overheads and variable sales overheads are similarly included as differential operating costs. The estimated increase in sales will be a result of extra time and effort on the part of the sales team to generate not only sales of the new product, but also increased awareness of the new product amongst hospital staff who are not directly related to the purchasing function.

Note that there is no mention of **fixed overhead costs** because, by definition, they are fixed, and will therefore have to be paid regardless of whether the new machine is installed or not. For instance, factory lease or rental payments will remain unchanged because the new machine will occupy the space currently used by the old machine.

Neither is there any mention of depreciation. As has been seen, depreciation is not a cash flow, it is an accounting concept, a book entry only. Depreciation will be considered when taxation is introduced.

10. Storage cost—It is easy to overlook that the old machine is being stored while the new one is sitting, literally, in its place. Is this a direct project cost or an overhead because of the managerial decision not to sell it? It could be either (and an illustration of creative accounting for or against a project depending on the evaluator's viewpoint) but here the incremental view is opted—that it will not be stored unless the new machine is bought.

Terminal Cash Flows

11. Removal costs—The analyst needs to know the basis on which this figure is derived. If it is the direct payment of labor to dismantle and remove the machine, then one must add into this the opportunity cost of alternative employment associated with the labor (if the alternative is to be laid off due to a slack period, then the cost is actually the direct payment, as there is no alternative use for the labor). Assume the 200 percent margin on labor's time mentioned earlier; the figure should then be $1,000 actual cost plus $2,000 opportunity cost, a total of $3,000.

12. Working capital—At termination, any working capital contributed during the life of the project will be recovered. This constitutes a cash inflow. Assuming that the value of inventory, etc., is recoverable at cost, this is $20,000.

13. Sale of machine—The figure shown, $5,000, represents the receipt from the sale of the machine.

Note that, in a real cash-flow projection, partial years would be taken into account, so that if a machine operates for six months in the final year then the annual anticipated cash flows in that year will be half (six months) plus the terminal cash-flow values.

The next step in the process is to expand the sales and cost estimates out to a five-year time horizon. This necessitates consideration of the projected 20 percent growth rate in sales and the direct relationship predicted between sales and many of the cost items. In fact, the only cost item that will not increase proportionately with sales is item 10, the storage cost of the old machine. In addition, the increase in sales will also necessitate a matching increase in working capital (previously, only the initial working capital requirements were considered). Assuming that the initial working-capital requirement of $20,000 needs to increase at the rate of sales growth and that

◆ EXHIBIT 7.3

NITTER, INC., GROWTH PROJECTIONS AT 20 PERCENT ANNUALLY

NITTER, INC.
PROJECT K: DIFFERENTIAL OPERATING CASH-FLOW FORECAST TO YEAR 5
(CASH VALUE—$ IN THOUSANDS)

Year	0	1	2	3	4	5
Sales revenue	$0	$120.0	$144.0	$172.8	$207.4	$248.8
Variable costs		55.0	66.0	79.2	95.1	114.0
		$65.0	$78.0	$93.6	$112.3	$134.8
Working capital			4.0	4.8	5.8	6.9
Storage cost		6.0	6.0	6.0	6.0	6.0
Differential cash flows	$0	$59.0	$68.0	$82.8	$100.5	$121.9

the first impact of this will be seen in the second period, Exhibit 7.3 shows the resultant projections of the differential cash flows.

INFLATION

The third step in the project-evaluation analysis is to introduce an expected inflation rate (of 5 percent per annum) for each of the next five years. Note that time period 1 does not require adjustment, not because it is not subject to inflation, but merely because one can assume that the figures shown already incorporate inflation.

Inflation can be defined as a general rise in the market price levels. Focusing on the specific price rises, or on the inflation associated with a particular project is less relevant than the general level of inflation confronting the economy. Referring back to the three-month Treasury bill, or T-bill, remember that this was deemed to be a riskless asset. Assume that the T-bill is priced today to provide a yield of 8 percent (per annum). This yield (or market rate of return) comprises a **real rate of return** for foregoing consumption and an additional component return to cover inflation during the period to maturity. If the market yield of the T-bill is 8 percent per year, then it may be that 3 percent of this return is the real return required by investors for foregoing consumption of the amount invested in the T-bill. Therefore, 5 percent annually is the estimation of inflation during the period. Because yields on investments always reflect these two components, analysts usually include both (at least initially) in the required rate of return, r, that is applied in **discounted cash-flow (DCF) analysis.**

Thus, one may say that the cash flows are subject to a rate of discount that has the following components (in this instance, 3 percent and 5 percent):

$$r = \text{real return required} + \text{return required for anticipated inflation}$$

Technically, the nominal rate is not the sum of the real rate plus inflation. In fact, it is based on a geometric progression such that:

$$(1 + r) = (1 + k)(1 + i)$$

where r is the nominal rate, k is the real rate, and i is the inflation rate. Thus:

$$r = (1 + k)(1 + i) - 1$$

and:

$$k = (1 + r)/(1 + i) - 1$$

Some analysts argue that, if the risk-free rate is to be applied to a project, the duration of the appropriate risk-free asset should reflect the duration of the project itself rather than the shorter-term view that this discussion has taken to this point. In Nitter's case, the project's duration is five years. Assume, instead, that five-year Treasury notes have an expected yield of 8 percent per annum. This yield is the geometric average of the expected annual yields, each of which is, in turn, a function of the expected real rate for the relevant period and the expected inflation for that period. If one wants to determine the expected annual real return on this security, begin by annualizing the inflation expectations. Suppose inflation is expected to be 5 percent for the first three years and then declines to 4 percent in year 4 and 3 percent in year 5. If, as in Exhibit 7.5, one assumes a constant inflation rate of 5 percent, then one can say that the *average* inflation rate is 5 percent (i.e., equals the constant). However, if the inflation rate is *not* constant, one cannot merely arithmetically average the rates (e.g., [5 percent + 5 percent + 5 percent + 4 percent + 3 percent]/5 = 4.4 percent). Instead, the geometric average needs to be found—the nth root of the products of the factors (minus 1).

$$r = n\sqrt{\prod_{t=1}^{n}(1 + i)^t} - 1 = {}^5\sqrt{(1.05)(1.05)(1.05)(1.04)(1.03)} - 1$$

In this case, this is [the fifth root of $1.05 \times 1.05 \times 1.05 \times 1.04 \times 1.03$] − 1, which equals 4.397 percent. The difference between the arithmetic and geometric averages is very small in this case, but if the figures were larger, or the duration longer, the difference would be greater.

So if:

$$(1 + r) = 1.08 \quad \text{and} \quad (1 + i) = 1.044$$

then:

$$(1 + k) = \frac{(1 + r)}{(1 + i)} = 1.0345$$

FIVE-YEAR FORECAST (5 PERCENT CONSTANT INFLATION RATE)

NITTER, INC.
PROJECT K: CASH-FLOW FORECAST TO YEAR 5
(NOMINAL CASH VALUE—$ IN THOUSANDS)

Year	0	1	2	3	4	5
Acquisition costs	$(255.0)					
Differential annual operating cash flows:		$59.0	$68.0	$82.8	$100.5	$121.9
Add inflation adjustment		0	3.4	8.5	15.8	26.2
Nominal operating cash flows		$59.0	$71.4	$91.3	$116.3	$148.1
Terminal cash flows						43.5
Add inflation adjustment						3.6
Nominal cash flows	$(255.0)	$59.0	$71.4	$91.3	$116.3	$195.2

and the expected real return over the five-year period is 3.45 percent. Exhibit 7.5 will return to variable inflation rates. However, the analyst must always remember that nominal discount rates (those including the inflation component) can only be applied to nominal cash flows (which must also include inflation), and that real discount rates can only be applied to **real cash flows** (those that include no allowance for future expected inflation). To do otherwise would result in double counting. One method is not superior to the other, and in many circumstances, as shall be seen, it is necessary to apply both methods to the same problem. In some cases it is easier to forecast cash flows in nominal prices (because they reflect the actual cash flows that are expected at the time of receipt or payment) and adjust for inflation by applying a nominal discount rate.

The cash flows estimated for the five-year period (Exhibit 7.3) were real figures. The first year's figures were extrapolated into the future without adjusting for inflation (although growth was adjusted at a 20 percent rate). If the analyst wants to apply a nominal discount rate to these figures, they should be converted to nominal cash flows. This process is illustrated in Exhibit 7.4. Notice that the first year's figure has not been adjusted to reflect the expected inflation of 5 percent though. Inflation already was included in this figure when the initial estimates were made.

The way to establish the inflation adjustment is to use the expected inflation rate as the basis for a compound factor $(1 + i)^n$. Hence, the adjustments are:

For year 2	$(1.05 - 1)$	$\times$	68.0	$=$	3.4
For year 3	$(1.05^2 - 1)$	$\times$	82.8	$=$	8.5
For year 4	$(1.05^3 - 1)$	$\times$	100.5	$=$	15.8
For year 5	$(1.05^4 - 1)$	$\times$	121.9	$=$	26.3

Because the analyst inflation-adjusted the ongoing increases in working capital (as a component of the differential operating cash flows shown in Exhibit 7.4), the recovery of working capital should reflect this. Also, the salvage value of the machine ($5,000) less removal costs ($3,000) must be adjusted to reflect the impact of inflation during the five-year period between installation and salvage. Note that the initial contribution of working capital ($20,000) would be recovered at its book value only and is not subjected to an adjustment for inflation. The computation of the adjustment is therefore:

Working capital	$[(1.05 - 1)4] + [(1.05^2 - 1)4.8]$
	$+ [(1.05^3 - 1)5.8] + [(1.05^4 - 1)6.9]$
Plus: salvage value	$+ [(1.05^5 - 1)(5 - 3)]$
Inflation adjustment	$= 3.6$

The terminal cash flow comprises:

Sale of machine	5
Removal costs	(3)
Initial working capital	20
Ongoing increases in working capital (4 + 4.8 + 5.8 + 6.9)	21.5
	43.5

To make the problem a little more complicated, assume that, just as the analyst finished the previous computation, he received new economic forecasts showing that, while the 5 percent rate of inflation is expected to pertain to the next three years, inflation is then expected to decline by 1 percent per year for the last two years of projections. It follows that the appropriate inflation factors are now:

For year 2	1.05	=	1.0500
For year 3	(1.05)(1.05)	=	1.1025
For year 4	$(1.05^2)(1.04)$	=	1.1466
For year 5	$(1.05^2)(1.04)(1.03)$	=	1.1810

and the inflation adjustments are therefore:

For year 2	1.0500 − 1	=	5.00%
For year 3	1.1025 − 1	=	10.25%
For year 4	1.1466 − 1	=	14.66%
For year 5	1.1810 − 1	=	18.10%

Exhibit 7.5 illustrates these effects. Note that the calculations in year 5 are:

Working capital	$[(0.05 - 1)4] + [(0.1025 - 1)4.8]$
	$+ [(0.1466 - 1)5.8] + [(0.181 - 1)6.9]$
Plus: salvage value	$+ [(1.05 - 1)0.1810(5 - 3)]$
Inflation adjustment	$= 3.3.$

FIVE-YEAR FORECAST—VARIABLE INFLATION RATES

NITTER, INC.
PROJECT K: CASH-FLOW FORECAST TO YEAR 5
(NOMINAL CASH VALUE—$ IN THOUSANDS)

Year	0	1	2	3	4	5
Acquisition costs	$(255.0)					
Differential annual operating cash flows		$59.0	$68.0	$82.8	$100.5	$121.9
Add inflation adjustment		0	3.4	8.5	14.7	22.1
Nominal operating cash flows		$59.0	$71.4	$91.3	$115.2	$144.0
Terminal cash flows						43.5
Add inflation adjustment						3.3
Nominal cash flows	$(255.0)	$59.0	$71.4	$91.3	$115.2	$190.8

The analyst now has a cash-flow estimate as accurate as we can reason-ably expect. The next thing to do is to adjust for taxation.

TAXATION

Deriving cash flows and adjusting for taxes is not such an easy task for the smaller business where the degree of competence or sophistication in finan-cial analysis may not be as great as in the larger firms with more specialized personnel or resources. Taxation is a complex business that affects all aspects of the firm's financial activities and only more elementary generalizations can be outlined here. Taxation is also nation-specific. It further complicates matters when taxation rates and rules change at least annually. Nevertheless, after-tax cash flows are the fundamental elements in the equation and must be prepared as accurately as is reasonable to expect within the resource con-straints of the smaller firm.

The largest component of the tax adjustment is the method of deprecia-tion employed to offset the standard business income-tax rate levied on a firm's profits. If one assumes this rate is 35 percent, all that has to be done is to reduce the cash flow by the 35 percent tax rate. Needless to say, while the principle is simple, the details are far from it. Remembering that one is dealing with cash flows, the actual timing of the tax burden as it relates to one specific investment may not coincide with the generation of the cash inflows. Six or nine months after the firm's financial year end may elapse before payment, and the inclusion of tax-related cash flows into the cash-flow budget should reflect this delay. Due to the tax rules and regulations, a firm can show pre-tax profits of $1 million and after-tax profits of $900,000 in the audited accounts.

Then there is the problem of what tax rate should be used. If a firm incurs an overall loss, but the new acquisition is itself generating positive cash flows, should the project be taxed as though it contributes profit to the firm, or should it take the firm's overall marginal rate? Should the rate then be 10 percent? The firm should adopt the marginal rate of tax on the incremental profits earned by the project. If it is incurring losses, these losses can be offset against the income from other activities resulting in an incremental cash inflow. If there are no other profits against which to offset a loss, the loss can be carried forward to offset the profits of future years, and no tax is payable (a zero rate) until some time in the future. In other words, the tax rate selected should actually reflect the marginal tax rate that will be paid (or received in the circumstance of a loss) on the profit (loss) of the marginal project.

To the extent that depreciation reduces tax payable, it results in an inflow of cash and therefore must be included in the cash flows associated with the project. To the extent that the market value and the actual depreciated value (which is only known when an asset is disposed of at the end of its useful life) do not match, some adjustment must be made at the termination of the asset's life, usually when sold or scrapped.

There are additional tax aspects to the payment of dividends but this discussion will conveniently ignore these because first, it is a complex issue, and second, in the case of unincorporated firms, no dividends are paid anyway.

There are many different tax regulations and it is not possible to cover them all. The argument that follows assumes that there is a straight-line depreciation policy to be followed (e.g., 25 percent per year for four years).

Another common method of depreciation, **declining balance,** depreciates at a rate of, say, 25 percent for the first year, 25 percent of the remaining balance in the second, 25 percent of that balance, and so on. Any adjustment necessary is made at the time of sale of the asset. The depreciation method commonly applied in the United States (**accelerated cost recovery,** or **ACRS**) can be viewed as a type of **diminishing-value** method of depreciation, and the **first-year allowance** can be viewed as a rather extreme version of this method in which the entire cost of the asset is depreciated in the first year of its life.

Exhibit 7.6 shows the impact of the depreciation. Again, because the tax allowances (25 percent straight line) and the firm's own accounting depreciation charges (20 percent straight line) have resulted in the same zero book value for the plant at the end of the budget period, the effect (but not the timing) has been the same. However, if the asset is sold part way through its life then there would be a discrepancy between the firm's depreciation rate and the 25 percent rate of the tax authorities. This would require an adjustment to be made.

By adding up all of the after-tax cash flows, it will be found that, regardless of which depreciation method is used, they total $141,600. But, while there may not appear to be a difference between the sums of the after-tax cash-flow figures, one can see that the timing of the cash-flow streams is very different.

◆ EXHIBIT 7.6

25 PERCENT STRAIGHT-LINE DEPRECIATION

NITTER, INC.
PROJECT K: NOMINAL CASH FLOWS ADJUSTED FOR TAX ($ IN THOUSANDS)

Year	0	1	2	3	4	5	6
Acquisition costs	$(255)						
Nominal operating cash flows		$59.0	$75.6	$96.6	$121.9	$152.1	
Tax @ 35%		0	(20.6)	(26.5)	(33.8)	(42.7)	$(53.2)
25% after-tax depreciation adjustment ($200,000 × 25%) × 35%			17.5	17.5	17.5	17.5	
Tax on disposal proceeds $5,000 × 35%							1.8
After-tax cash flow	$(255)	$59.0	$72.5	$87.6	$105.6	$126.9	$(55.0)

Assuming that:

1. the analyst is now reasonably confident that the initial capitalized price of the machine is correct,
2. the cash flows are estimated as accurately as possible, and
3. there are no taxation anomalies which would change this figure,

the analyst can now proceed with the process of adjusting for time and risk.

 CONCEPT CHECK

1. *In what ways does the cash-flow approach differ from conventional accounting?*
2. *Why are only incremental cash flows important?*
3. *What items should be included and/or excluded from a cash-flow calculation?*
4. *How is working capital handled in the context of cash-flow analysis?*
5. *How does one adjust for inflation in cash flows?*
6. *Distinguish between real cash flows and nominal cash flows.*
7. *How does depreciation affect cash flows?*

7.7 THE DISCOUNT FACTOR

Recall that, when the nature of inflation was discussed, it was established that there are two components to the required rate of return: the real return required to forego present consumption in favor of future consumption at some time and an adjustment for the anticipated rate of inflation. These two components are rarely separated except for explanatory purposes and are jointly referred to as the **risk-free rate of return**. Now the discussion can attempt to adjust for the more problematic element of risk.

The discount factor is the denominator of the present-value equation and equals $[1/(1 + r)]$. Remember that the discount rate, r, forms the basis for the discount factor. The discount rate can be divided into two parts:

1. that which takes into account the time value of money, including the inflation element
2. that which is assigned to reflect the risk and uncertainty associated with the project

In other words, r is a function of both time and risk such that:

$$r = \frac{\text{risk-free rate of return}}{\text{(Treasury bills)}} + \frac{\text{rate of return required for risk}}{\text{(intuitive assessment)}}$$

It could be argued that time contributes to uncertainty because, as one projects cash flows further into the future, one becomes less sure of their values. The counterargument is that there is a learning process associated with time, and thus future cash flows become more certain. The standard approach considers time and risk independently. Naturally, in practice only one rate is quoted, but at least now it is apparent that r is a function of several components.

However, rather than merely say it is too difficult to evaluate the risk associated with a capital investment and therefore it should not be bothered with it at all (a sentiment often expressed by the managers of many smaller firms), it is suggested here that some intuitive assessment of relevant risk be made and a further premium to reflect this risk be added to the risk-free rate of return.

ADJUSTING FOR RISK (UNCERTAINTY)

The evaluation and derivation of risk and uncertainty becomes quite a complex matter in many standard corporate finance texts, and understandably so; it is a complex issue. It should be noted that some of the ideas expressed below will be revisited in Chapter 10 when the valuation of the smaller business is discussed.

RISK VERSUS UNCERTAINTY

Risk relates to the set of unique consequences of a given decision to which probabilities can be assigned; uncertainty is a situation in which such probabilities cannot be assigned. The distinction is not critical and, unless specifically stated, the term *risk* will refer to both risk and uncertainty in the discussion that follows. What risks does the business face?

Business risk is the risk that is related to the variability of operating cash flows before interest and taxes. It is really a statement about how well the firm is using its assets to service its market. More fixed assets tends to mean less flexibility, which, in turn, may increase riskiness, i.e., business risk is related to operating leverage and break-even points. Business risk is also therefore related to the industry in which a business operates. This concept was first introduced in Chapter 4.

Financial risk represents the additional risk associated with the use of debt. Whereas business risk reflects how well the firm is performing in its external markets via the comparative efficiency with which it uses its assets, financial risk is almost totally internal to the firm. The more debt a firm takes on, the greater the debt-servicing charges (a fixed cost until the capital is repaid). This reduces flexibility and thus tends to increase the variability in earnings. This was also discussed in Chapter 4.

Project risk reflects the variability of a capital project's future cash flows. The more volatile the firm's markets, or perhaps technologies, the greater the risk associated with the forecasted cash flows.

The reader may therefore conclude that the total risk of a firm (or a project) is determined by the variability of its cash flows. The greater the variability, the greater the risk. There are a number of ways to adjust for risk, but they tend to fall into two groups:

1. by adjusting for risk in the discount rate that is then used to calculate NPV (net present value), i.e., the **risk-adjusted discount rate,** and
2. by adjusting the NPV based on a risk-free discount rate. This group involves a number of techniques that will be described in another section of this chapter.

The use of a risk-adjusted discount rate makes intuitive sense. A more risky project should provide a greater reward than a less risky project because most investors are considered **risk averse**. If one applies this intuition, it is obvious that a project that carries more risk requires a higher return for assuming that risk, one is left with the problem of determining the appropriate rate for assuming a risk that is not easily identified, not to mention capable of measurement. Even if the risk variables to be evaluated can be identified, and many cannot, the weight to be attached to each variable may prove impossible to objectively determine.

The additional premium for risk is an allowance for exposure to those variables that impinge on cash flows, such as:

✦ the internal state of the firm (product quality, labor relations, customer support, delivery times, reliability, etc.)
✦ firm-specific external factors (the state of the industry, expected growth trends in the market, the nature of competitors, how competitors react to aggressive advertising, and so on)
✦ non-specific external factors (the general state of the economy, the level of business confidence, expected inflation and expectations regarding future interest rates—all of which affect the market for the goods or services of the small firm)
✦ project-specific, asset-related factors (reliability, exposure to technological change, and the need for the retention of appropriately qualified people)

The list is almost endless. Gaining a good "feel" for the firm's overall economic situation will undoubtedly produce a more realistic and appropriate discount rate than not making any effort at all.

Remember that r is the opportunity cost of capital invested in the project under consideration. It is the rate that the firm could obtain by investing in an alternative but similar risk profile investment opportunity whether or not that investment is in capital assets (for instance, it may be in paper investments, such as stocks and shares). There is no point in setting a discount rate equivalent to that of Treasury bills when the market a business faces is considerably more risky than such an investment. There are some benchmarks out there for the analyst to consider, such as other firms' performance, industry norms, and figures obtained from trade journals.

Quite clearly the owner or manager of the smaller firm with non-traded equity can set whatever required rate of return is desired. However, should a required rate of return be set that is significantly below some reasonable estimate of the market's view of a realistic risk-adjusted discount rate, and the return on investments closely approximate the lower rate, the firm will not survive very long. It follows that, if the firm is still in existence, then previous acquisitions cannot have been disastrous, but possibly they could have been better. Past experience will also provide a useful guide to the sort of risk–return tradeoffs that previous projects have achieved (for instance, through the variability of cash flows). Be warned, though, the relevant rate of return for a new project is not necessarily equivalent to those rates that previous investments have achieved. The relevant rate is the opportunity cost associated with the risk of the new project. It is related to the risk of the new project, not to the risk of the firm's existing business.

This brings the discussion back to the objective function. While the owner or manager of a business can be reasonably independent about her goals, be they lifestyle-oriented or wealth-oriented, the firm itself must operate within the economic parameters of the market. For the purposes of investment appraisal, though, the analyst needs to utilize the premise that the owner or manager actively pursues some objective function related to the maximization of wealth (or sales, or profit) that leads to a financially viable rate of return.

The main criticism of the intuitive derivation of the required-rate-of-return approach is that it is too casual, too intuitive, and too subjective. Rates of return that have been previously achieved on the firm's existing assets are often adopted for future projects; this approach is wrong. However, there are certainly problems faced when trying to identify **proxy firms** (firms that are of a similar risk class to the project under consideration and for which the rate of return can be established) in a risk class similar to a new project and then trying to make sense of the financial data of these proxies. Alternative models, such as the capital asset-pricing model, are not really appropriate for application to the smaller firm. This text shall return to this argument once the reader is familiar with the NPV (net present value) technique.

CONCEPT CHECK

1. *Distinguish between risk and uncertainty.*
2. *What types of risk does a business face?*
3. *What is the effect of risk aversity on the investment-appraisal process?*
4. *What factors affect the risk premium?*
5. *How is a required rate of return set?*
6. *What is the role of the proxy firm in investment appraisal?*

SUMMARY

♦ The long-term asset decision, also known as the capital-budgeting decision, is a very important part of the small-business finance tool kit for those firms that have reason to purchase large and significant assets. It is perhaps more important for smaller firms because they do not have the resources to draw on should an acquisition error occur. As a consequence, such decisions are usually important strategic decisions and must be viewed in light of the firm's whole operating environment and not just in relation to its financial aspects.

♦ Capital budgeting is an organizational process, of which the financial evaluation and associated techniques form only a part. Investment appraisal also communicates direction and purpose to the individuals who comprise the firm, its financiers, and its markets. As such, it performs more than one role in the organization.

♦ The essential elements in project evaluation are the accurate derivation of expected nominal or monetary cash flows arising from a project over its life and the determination of the appropriate discount rate to use in each of the periods in which a change is expected. These two elements together form the crux of capital-investment analysis.

♦ Taxation is of crucial importance as the relevant cash flows are the after-tax cash flows. While this complicates the calculations, tax rates are reasonably steady in the near term, and, once a forecast has been set up on a spreadsheet, changes are relatively easy to implement.

♦ The discount rate, or at least some observable optimal discount rate, is more difficult to be precise about as smaller firms tend to be either not publicly quoted or closed companies. There is often little assistance from financial markets for help in its determination. Nevertheless, building the various components does lend some structure to its derivation, even though, ultimately, the final rate is more intuitive than science.

THE CASE—PART SEVEN

Toward the end of 2002 Dave recognizes that his business is in a static sales situation at about 420 units per year. At about the same time, he is offered the opportunity to sell bicycles overseas. This entails additional expenditure on plant and machinery (including its installation by the supplier) of approximately $40,000. No new training expenditure is required. He is seeking advice about how he should go about evaluating the investment so he can appraise the potential correctly. The investment will be made at the start of 2003.

Dave anticipates that he will sell an additional sixty bikes at a price of $1,200 in 2003, one hundred bikes in 2004 and one hundred and ten thereafter. These sales are included in the 2003 financial reports and the projections from 2004 on. The profit margin will remain unchanged. Variable operating expenses will increase by 24 percent of the marginal sales while fixed operating expenses will increase by $3,000.

Dave will borrow an additional $30,000 to finance the project, the balance to be funded from internal cash flows.

The new machinery should last for an indeterminable period if maintained and, as a consequence, its salvage value can be ignored.

ASSIGNMENT 7.1

Required

1. Suggest the logical process that Dave should follow in the appraisal of his new project.

ASSIGNMENT 7.2

Required

1. Using the projections below (and the outcome of 2003) and assuming that the past relationships between sales and receivables and sales and payables (i.e., working capital) hold for the new project. Assume that the total installed cost of the new project is $40,000 plus an increase in working capital, calculate the cash flows derived from the additional investment for the years 2004, 2005 and 2006.

BALANCE SHEETS FOR DAVE'S BIKES & CO.

	Actual	Projections		
	2003	2004	2005	2006
Assets:				
Cash	$ 10	$ 842	$ 421	$ 246
Accounts receivable	83,254	92,410	98,417	99,894
Inventory	68,938	76,522	81,496	82,718
Prepaid expenses	11,142	12,171	12,748	12,890
Current assets	$163,344	$181,945	$193,082	$195,748
Vehicle	$ 44,000	$ 84,000	$ 84,000	$ 84,000
Accum. depreciation	(29,517)	(40,413)	(49,130)	(56,104)
	$ 14,483	$ 43,587	$ 34,870	$ 27,896
Plant and equipment	179,000	189,000	199,000	199,000
Accum. depreciation	(50,172)	(64,055)	(77,550)	(89,695)
	$128,828	$124,945	$121,450	$109,305
Fittings	10,000	10,000	10,000	10,000
Accum. depreciation	(4,095)	(4,686)	(5,217)	(5,695)
	$ 5,905	$ 5,314	$ 4,783	$ 4,305
Fixed assets	$149,216	$173,846	$161,103	$141,506
Total assets	$312,560	$355,791	$354,185	$337,254

(continued)

(BALANCE SHEET CONTINUED)

Liabilities:				
Accounts payable	$ 29,526	$ 32,577	$ 34,480	$ 34,948
Accrued expenses	23,621	26,061	27,585	27,958
Income tax payable	2,937	3,210	3,897	4,391
Short-term bank loan	1,000	16,000	3,000	4,000
Current liabilities	$ 57,084	$ 77,848	$ 68,962	$ 71,297
Long-term loan	110,000	110,000	90,000	40,000
Total liabilities	$167,084	$187,848	$158,962	$111,297
Paid-in capital	$ 30,000	$ 30,000	$ 30,000	$ 30,000
Retained earnings	115,476	137,943	165,223	195,957
Owner's equity	$145,476	$167,943	$195,223	$225,957
Total liabilities and owners' equity	$312,560	$355,791	$354,185	$337,254

INCOME STATEMENT FOR DAVE'S BIKES & CO.

	Actual	Projections		
	2003	2004	2005	2006
Sales	$ 666,022	$ 739,285	$ 787,338	$ 799,149
Cost of sales	(367,672)	(408,115)	(434,643)	(441,163)
Gross profit	$ 298,350	$ 331,170	$ 352,695	$ 357,986
Operating expense	$ 222,845	$ 243,428	$ 254,961	$ 257,795
Depreciation	18,591	25,370	22,743	19,597
Total operating cost	$ 241,436	$ 268,798	$ 277,704	$ 277,392
Net operating income	$ 56,914	$ 62,372	$ 74,991	$ 80,594
Interest received	0	0	0	0
Interest paid	(7,963)	(8,879)	(10,038)	(7,419)
Earnings pre-tax	$ 48,951	$ 53,493	$ 64,953	$ 73,175
Tax	(14,685)	(16,048)	(19,486)	(21,953)
Earnings after tax	$ 34,266	$ 37,445	$ 45,467	$ 51,222
Dividends paid	(13,707)	(14,978)	(18,187)	(20,489)
Retained earnings	$ 20,559	$ 22,467	$ 27,280	$ 30,733

CASH FLOWS FOR DAVE'S BIKES & CO.

	Actual	Projections		
	2003	2004	2005	2006
Cash sales	$ 658,454	$ 730,127	$ 781,332	$ 797,672
Cash purchases	(373,630)	(414,173)	(438,665)	(442,151)
Cash operating expenses	(219,924)	(240,490)	(253,065)	(257,329)
Income tax at 30 percent	(14,951)	(15,775)	(18,798)	(21,459)
Cash flow from operations	$ 49,950	$ 59,689	$ 70,804	$ 76,733

(continued)

(CASH FLOWS CONTINUED)

Interest paid	$ (7,963)	$ (8,879)	$(10,038)	$ (7,419)
Dividends paid	(13,707)	(14,978)	(18,187)	(20,489)
Equity	0	0	0	0
Debt	11,000	15,000	(33,000)	(49,000)
Cash flow from financing	$(10,670)	$ (8,857)	$(61,225)	$(76,908)
Deposits	$ 0	$ 0	$ 0	$ 0
Vehicles	0	(40,000)	0	0
Plant	(40,000)	(10,000)	(10,000)	0
Cash flow from investing	$(40,000)	$(50,000)	$(10,000)	$ 0
Change in cash	$ (720)	$ 832	$ (421)	$ (175)
Opening cash	730	10	842	421
Closing cash	$ 10	$ 842	$ 421	$ 246

ASSIGNMENT 7.3

Dave believes that the book values of the assets of the business are approximately equal to their market values and that, at this point in time, there is no goodwill element associated with the business.

Required

1. Using the information provided in Assignment 6.2 of the previous chapter and in Assignment 7.1 above, calculate Dave's pre-tax and post-tax return on assets and return on equity for the five years 1998 to 2002.

2. Assume that there has been no inflation during Dave's time in business. If Dave perceives that a pre-tax risk premium of 3 percent should be associated with foreign activities, determine the real required rate of return on the new project if the sales arising from the new project are all to be exported and his domestic cost of capital is based on your answer to question 1.

ASSIGNMENT 7.4

The figures exhibited in Assignment 7.2 can be considered "real" because Dave made no allowance for the effect of inflation.

Required

1. If operating costs and revenues are expected to suffer inflation of 10 percent per annum from (and including) 2004, determine Dave's projected cash flows for 2004, 2005 and 2006.

ASSIGNMENT 7.5

Dave has always applied straight-line depreciation to his assets in the past, however he is prepared to consider utilizing a different basis for the new asset if it is worthwhile.

Required

1. If, for taxation purposes, Dave is able to choose between 20 percent straight-line depreciation, 20 percent diminishing-value depreciation, and a first-year allowance of 60 percent followed by two years of 20 percent straight line, determine the taxation effect of each policy and advise Dave of the most beneficial choice.

SELECTED ADDITIONAL READINGS

Belongia, M. T., and M. R. Garfinkel, eds. 1992. *The business cycle: Theories and evidence.* (Boston/London: Kluwer).

Bhandari, B. S. 1986. Discounted payback: A criterion for capital investment decisions. *Journal of Small Business Management* 24 (2) (April) pp. 16–22.

Bierman H., and S. Smidt, 1988. *The capital budgeting decision.* 7th ed. (New York: Macmillan).

Brealey, R. A., and S. C. Myers. 1996. *Principles of corporate finance.* 5th ed. (New York: McGraw-Hill).

Butler, R., L. G. Davies, R. H. Pike, and J. Sharp. 1993. *Strategic investment decisions: Theory, practice and process.* London: Routledge.

Farragher, E. J., 1986. Capital budgeting practices of non-industrial firms. *The Engineering Economist* 31 (4) (summer) pp. 293–303.

Grablowsky, B. J., and W. L. Burns. 1980. The application of capital allocation techniques by small business. *Journal of Small Business Management* 18 (3) (July) pp. 50–58.

Kudla, R. J. 1980. Capital rationing in small businesses. *Journal of Small Business Management* 18 (4).

Lumby, S. 1991. *Investment appraisal and financing decisions.* 4th ed. (London: Chapman & Hall).

McInish, T. H., and R. J. Kudla. 1981. A new approach to capital budgeting in closely held firms and small firms. *American Journal of Small Business* V (4) (spring).

McIntyre, E. V., and J. D. Icerman. 1985. The accounting rate of return—Appropriate for small business? *American Journal of Small Business* IX (3) (winter).

McIntyre, E. V., and N. Coulthurst. 1987. Planning and control of capital investment in medium sized UK companies. *Management Accounting* 65 (3) (March).

McMahon, R. G. P., S. Holmes, P. J. Hutchinson, and D. M. Forsaith. 1993. *Small enterprise financial management: Theory and practice.* (Sydney, Australia: Harcourt Brace).

Osteryoung, J. S. 1979. *Capital budgeting: Long-term asset selection.* 2d ed. (New York: Wiley & Sons, Inc.).

Pike, R. H. 1989. Do sophisticated capital budgeting approaches improve investment decision-making effectiveness? *The Engineering Economist* 34 (2) (winter).

Pike, R. H., and R. Dobbins. 1986. *Investment decisions and financial strategy.* (Deddington, Oxfordshire: Philip Allan Publishers).

Poapst, J. V. 1986. Capital investment decisions in the small firm. *Business Quarterly* 51 (1).

Runyon, L. R. 1983. Capital expenditure decision making in small firms. *Journal of Business Research* 11 (3).

Schall, L. D., G. L. Sundem, and W. R. Geijsbeek. 1978. Survey and analysis of capital budgeting methods. *Journal of Finance* XXXIII (1) (March).

Scott, D. F., O. L. Gray, and M. M. Bird. 1972. Investing and financing behavior of small manufacturing firms. *MSU Business Topics* 29 (3) (summer).

Wacht, R. F. 1989. Capital investment analysis for the small business. *Business* 39 (4).

Walker, E. W., and J. W. Petty. 1978. *Financial management of the small firm.* 2d ed. (Englewood Cliffs, NJ: Prentice-Hall).

FINANCIAL INVESTMENT EVALUATION TECHNIQUES

OBJECTIVES

1. *Describe conventional evaluation techniques, including both those traditional techniques that do not adjust for the existence of time and those techniques that do adjust for time*

2. *Discuss the difficulties imposed by the use of time-adjusted techniques*

3. *Examine the peculiarities of the smaller firm in relation to capital budgeting*

4. *Examine risk in the context of probabilities*

5. *Describe procedures for post-acquisition evaluation*

8.1 INTRODUCTION

There are primarily two groups of techniques that can be applied to investment appraisal; the simpler "not theoretically correct" group, which does not take into account the time value of money, and the more "theoretically correct" group that does. The former group includes the payback and accounting rate of return methods, while the latter group is made up of the net present value and internal rate of return methods.

8.2 INVESTMENT TECHNIQUES IGNORING THE TIME VALUE OF MONEY

The **accounting rate of return (ARR)** approach to investment appraisal is also known as **return on funds employed (ROFE)**, or accounting return on investment. Despite their severe theoretical limitations, both techniques are still prevalent today, no doubt due to their simplicity.

THE PAYBACK METHOD

The **payback method** is commonly used by small businesses as an investment-appraisal technique. It determines how many time periods (e.g., years) it takes for an investment to repay the initial cash outlay on its purchase and associated costs. These costs include outlays on new asset purchases, transport, installation, and retraining. While the simplicity of the payback method and its demonstration of the time taken for the investment to be recouped confer obvious advantages on the approach, it contains two fundamental flaws:

1. it ignores the time value of money, and
2. it ignores all cash flows beyond the pre-determined cut-off point.

As a consequence there is absolutely no relationship between the benefit a project may contribute to a firm over the whole life of the project and its cost. On the positive side this technique is very popular purely because it is easy to use.

With respect to risk consideration, some would argue that this method takes no account of risk at all, while others maintain that payback accounts for the riskiness of the investment by laying the emphasis upon the speed that the initial outlay can be recovered. The longer the time period until costs are fully recovered, the greater the risk associated with the project. Alternatively, more risky projects could be required to have shorter payback periods than safer projects. The view taken here is that payback does incorporate an element of risk adjustment but in such a non-rigorous manner that it remains a bit of a hit-and-miss affair.

Some firms use the payback method as an initial screening technique, but even this is not to be recommended, as explained in the following example.

◆ EXHIBIT 8.1

MACTOOL PAYBACK EXAMPLE: TRUNCATED LIVES

	Project 1	Project 2
Initial outlay	$45,000	$45,000
Cash flows associated with the projects:		
Year 1	20,000	25,000
Year 2	23,000	20,000

◆ EXHIBIT 8.2

MACTOOL PAYBACK EXAMPLE: FULL LIVES

	Project 1	Project 2
Initial outlay	$45,000	$45,000
Cash flows associated with project:		
Year 1	20,000	25,000
Year 2	23,000	20,000
Cut-off point		
Year 3	25,000	15,000
Year 4	25,000	12,000
Year 5	25,000	10,000

Consider Mactool, Inc., a small manufacturing firm with twenty employees that is considering the purchase of a new tooling machine. This is a project that has intuitive appeal because it fits the firm's future direction and technical requirements. There are two competing alternatives, both of which involve an initial purchase costing $30,000 plus $15,000 associated costs. The owner or manager has determined the cut-off payback period as two years. Exhibit 8.1 depicts the first two years' cash flows.

Given the two-year cut-off point, project 2 will be accepted—it repays its initial costs within two years, whereas project 1 does not. But, what if one looks beyond the two-year time horizon? Exhibit 8.2 shows what happens if the projections are extended over the projects' lives and the assumption is made that each machine will be worthless after five years' use.

It is now obvious that a mistake would be made if project 1 was rejected. Its undiscounted contribution is $118,000, whereas the initial choice, project 2, contributes only $82,000. Even discounting does not change the conclusion that project 1 is ultimately the better project.

If it was known that project 1 had a projected life of five years but project 2 had a projected life of only four years (i.e., project 2 would have no cash flow after year 4), the difference would be even larger because project 2's cash flows would only total $72,000.

ACCOUNTING RATE OF RETURN

The accounting rate of return determines the average profitability of an investment over its anticipated life. This method is particularly flawed as an investment appraisal technique because it depends on incremental profits rather than incremental cash flows. Any capital investment-appraisal technique that is dependent upon profit for its analysis must be unacceptable as an appropriate guide to the investment decision. The three rules for capital investment appraisal are: cash flow, cash flow, and cash flow again.

In Chapter 4 on financial ratio analysis it was explained that the ratio of a firm's income to the book value of its assets was an appropriate and frequently used ratio to measure the performance, or efficiency, of a firm. The same principle underlies the application to individual project analysis but is considerably less useful in this role. Not only does it not take into account the time value of money, but it also ignores both the timing of the inflows and the associated risk of the investment. The greater the variation in the timing of cash flows over the life of the asset, the more inappropriate this method becomes.

This method of evaluation is based on the relationship between the average forecasted profit after depreciation and taxes accruing to the project and the average cost of investment:

$$\text{Accounting rate of return} = \frac{\text{sum of annual after-tax profits/years}}{(\text{investment outlay} + \text{salvage value})/2}$$

$$= \frac{\text{expected average after-tax profit}}{\text{average investment}}$$

Apply this to the Mactool example and assume that depreciation is charged at 20 percent per year on a straight-line basis and that taxes can be ignored (for simplicity). Remember that the initial outlay is $45,000. Therefore, the average investment outlay over the life of the project is $45,000 divided by 2, or $22,500. This is the same as the average net book value and can be seen in Exhibit 8.3. The marginal profit for project 1 over its five-year life is shown in Exhibit 8.4.

Substituting into the ARR equation one gets:

$$\text{ARR} = \frac{(11,000 + 14,000 + 16,000 + 16,000 + 16,000/5}{(45,000 + 0)/2} = \frac{14,600}{22,500} = 65\%$$

While this shows a healthy rate of return, once the analyst adjusts for time, the true return on the investment drops significantly, as will be seen.

◆ EXHIBIT 8.3

MACTOOL PROJECT 1 DEPRECIATION

	Year					
	0	1	2	3	4	5
Gross book value	$45,000	$45,000	$45,000	$45,000	$45,000	$45,000
Less: accumulated depreciation	0	(9,000)	(18,000)	(27,000)	(36,000)	(45,000)
Net book value	$45,000	$36,000	$27,000	$18,000	$ 9,000	$ 0

◆ EXHIBIT 8.4

MACTOOL PROJECT 1 MARGINAL PROFIT

	Year					
	0	1	2	3	4	5
Net cash flow	$0	$20,000	$23,000	$25,000	$25,000	$25,000
Less: depreciation	0	9,000	9,000	9,000	9,000	9,000
Less: taxes	0	0	0	0	0	0
Net annual cash flows	$0	$11,000	$14,000	$16,000	$16,000	$16,000

In summary, it may be said that the payback method is a rough, although often-used, measure, but is not really adequate, even for an initial evaluation of potential investment opportunities. The accounting rate of return is too flawed to be worthy of serious consideration for individual project appraisal and it is advisable not to use it. The competition from, and the effectiveness of, the discounted cash-flow techniques that follow is far too strong.

CONCEPT CHECK

1. *What are the strengths and weaknesses of the payback-period technique?*
2. *What are the strengths and weaknesses of the accounting rate-of-return technique?*

8.3 TIME VALUE TECHNIQUES

Any investment analysis that considers time must determine today's value of cash flows that arise at some future point in time, i.e., they must be discounted back from the future. The principal techniques that take this into account are **net present value (NPV)** and **internal rate of return (IRR)** methods. It is important to remember that all of these techniques are based on cash flow and not on profit.

For a quick review of the present-value formula, assume a person's generous grandparent promises to pay them $5,000 should they complete one year at a university. What is the value of the gift in today's dollars if *r* is assumed to be 10 percent?

$$\text{present value (PV)} = \text{discount factor} \times \text{future value (FV)}$$

$$PV = \frac{1}{1+r}(FV) = \frac{1}{1.10}(\$5,000) = \$4,546$$

Rather than calculating 1 divided by 1.10, one can look it up in the present-value tables in Appendix II, where number of years equals 1 and *r* equals 10 percent. The figure shown is 0.9091. Multiplying $5,000 by 0.9091 gives the answer $4,546.

NET PRESENT VALUE

Net present value is a method of capital appraisal that results in one of three possible outcomes:

1. Positive—return is greater than cost (accept)
2. Negative—cost is greater than return (reject)
3. Zero—return is equal to cost (indeterminate/accept)

The altruistic grandparent example needs to be expanded a little because it considered one period, and hence is known as a **single-period model.** Naturally, longer-term capital investments result in cash flows for more than one year. These are referred to as **multi-period models.**

Each time the discount rate changes, a new time period comes into effect. If *r* changes every month for a year, there are twelve time periods to consider. However, assume that *r* remains constant over the period of one year, but can change if required, on a year-to-year basis. The principle is not affected by the length of the time period and is really no problem because each year is cumulative; that is, the resultant present value from the calculation in year 1 can be added to the resultant present value in year 2 and so on for the expected life of the asset.

Apply the discounted cash-flow technique to Mactool's project 1 and assume that the relevant risk-adjusted discount rate is 10 percent per annum. Exhibit 8.5 shows the calculation. The NPV is $43,570. This is the difference between the present value of discounted future cash flows and the investment cost of $45,000. As this NPV is positive, the investment is financially acceptable.

The difference between the discounted future cash flows and the investment cost also reflects the present value of the earnings of the project over

♦ EXHIBIT 8.5

MACTOOL, INC., DISCOUNTED CASH-FLOW ANALYSIS AT 10 PERCENT

	Year	Cash flows	Discount factor	Discounted cash flow
Initial outlay	0	$(45,000)	1.0000	$(45,000)
Cash flows:				
	1	20,000	0.9091	18,182
	2	23,000	0.8264	19,007
	3	25,000	0.7513	18,783
	4	25,000	0.6830	17,075
	5	25,000	0.6209	15,523
Net discounted cash flow over expected life of the asset				$ 43,570

♦ EXHIBIT 8.6

MACTOOL, INC., DISCOUNTED CASH-FLOW ANALYSIS AT 22 PERCENT

	Year	Cash flows	Discount factor	Discounted cash flow
Initial outlay	0	$(45,000)	1.0000	$(45,000)
Cash flows:				
	1	20,000	0.8197	16,394
	2	23,000	0.6719	15,454
	3	25,000	0.5507	13,768
	4	25,000	0.4514	11,285
	5	25,000	0.3700	9,250
Net discounted cash flow over expected life of the asset				$ 21,151

and above the 10 percent required rate of return. If the project had an NPV of zero, it would have earned exactly the 10 percent required.

This calculation has a generalized expression:

$$NPV = \sum_{t=1}^{n} \frac{CFt}{(1 + r)}$$

where: CFt = expected cash flow in some future period t

r = required rate of return over period t

Now, suppose that, on reconsideration of the risk characteristics of project 1, it is decided that the 10 percent opportunity cost is too low and that 22 percent is considered more appropriate. Exhibit 8.6 shows the effect of

MACTOOL, INC., REVISED NET PRESENT VALUE

	Year	Cash flows	Discount rate	Discount factor	Discounted cash flow
Initial outlay	0	$(45,000)		1.000	$(45,000)
Cash flows:					
	1	9,091*	0.25	0.8000	7,273
	2	10,455**	0.22	0.6719	7,025
	3	11,364	0.19	0.5934	6,743
	4	11,364	0.16	0.5523	6,276
	5	11,364	0.19	0.4190	4,762

Net discounted cash flow over expected life of asset $(12,921)

$$\text{*where: } \$9,091 = \$20,000 \times 0.4546 \text{ or } \frac{20,000}{2.2}$$

$$\text{**and: } \$10,455 = \$23,000 \times 0.4546 \text{ or } \frac{23,000}{2.2}$$

the recalculation. Note that while the NPV is still positive at $21,150 it is rather less than the $43,570 originally obtained using a discount rate of 10 percent. However, it is still a financially acceptable project.

The owner of Mactool is still not satisfied, though. A review of the basic data has disclosed an error: pound weights have been confused with metric weights (this has actually happened). To make matters worse, a recently received economic forecast for the next five years indicates changes in interest rates for each of those five years. Rather than the constant rate assumed initially, the owner now wants the calculation adjusted to reflect the error and to take into account the percentage change differences observed in the forecast.

Therefore the estimates of the cash flows from production must be lowered by approximately 2.2 times, and r must be adjusted by +3 percent, 0 percent, –3 percent, –6 percent, and –3 percent (the percentage changes obtained from the forecast, by year from the original estimates). The results of this analysis are shown in Exhibit 8.7.

This clearly changes the situation, as Exhibit 8.7 shows; there is now a negative NPV of $12,921. Assuming the figures are now as accurate as could reasonably be expected, the decision must be to reject the investment proposal. It is a moot point whether the owner was correct in inferring such a direct relationship between the anticipated changes in interest rates and the risk of the project, but it serves to illustrate the point that a different discount rate can be chosen for each time period without disrupting the basic mechanics of the technique.

The Mactool example merely supports what is already known: the answer is only as accurate as the data considered. Consideration of the external economic environment is extremely important because it always influences the expected cash flow. It is the risk and uncertainty inherently associated with forecasting the environment that can cause problems.

The mechanics of NPV analysis are quite straightforward once the cash flows associated with an investment are known and the discount rate has been determined. Many spreadsheet software packages, such as Excel, Quattro Pro, or Lotus 1–2–3, contain simple commands that enable the computation of an NPV (once the cash flows are recorded, of course). One needs to establish the cash flows arising from a marginal investment regardless of the appraisal technique chosen, so why not calculate the NPV?

If the NPV has a failing in its applicability to the smaller firm, it is the derivation of the required rate of return. It was noted in Chapter 1 that small firms are typically closely held businesses, i.e., their shares are not publicly traded. Thus, they neither publicly report their profitability nor utilize a public market for exchanging their equity. This means that it is very difficult to find objective information about the performance of small firms that might, in turn, provide the necessary evidence to justify the use of a particular discount rate. However, Chapter 10 explains why investors or owners expect a high rate of return for investing in small private firms. For the majority of these investors, they expect a rate of return around 30 to 50 percent per year. Therefore, the discount rate for capital projects must be sufficiently high to generate these returns to the equity investor. As there normally is some debt in the capital structure of small business, a lower discount rate might be acceptable. However, a firm on a consistent basis must be able to yield enough to cover its cost of debt and equity. For the majority of small businesses, therefore, the minimum acceptable discount rate must be in excess of 20 percent.

The problem is that small firms are generally short of both knowledge and resources. Despite these constraints, capital investment is a critical area with long-term consequences, and due time and effort must be allocated to making the best judgments possible with limited information.

THE INTERNAL RATE OF RETURN

The critical NPV is zero because this is the point at which decisions are made. An owner accepts a project with an NPV greater than zero and rejects anything less than zero. NPV is a dollar figure; it shows how much value the addition of the marginal project should add to the value of the business. If the NPV is positive, the project is earning more than the discount rate. If the NPV is negative, the project is earning less than the discount rate. The internal rate of return (IRR) technique seeks to determine just what it is (in percentage terms) that a project will earn. The IRR is the discount rate that will set the NPV equal to zero.

The decision rule arising from this technique is to accept a project where the IRR (or **yield**) exceeds the required rate of return (or required yield). This circumstance will also result in a value-adding positive NPV.

Thus there is a close relationship between NPV and IRR; one is only an arithmetic rearrangement of the other. The generalized formula for the IRR is:

$$\sum_{t=1}^{n} \frac{CFt}{(1 + IRR)^t} = 0$$

This equation must be solved in order to determine the IRR. In the simplest two-period case the calculation is relatively easy. Consider the example of project X:

Cash flow in year 0 = −$150,000

Cash flow in year 1 = $180,000

Note that the cash flow in year 0 is negative. It is the initial outlay on the cost of project X. Now, substitute these figures into the IRR equation:

$$- 150,000 + \frac{180,000}{1 + r} = 0$$

Multiplying both sides by $(1 + r)$ gives:

$$- 150,000(1 + r) + 180,000 = 0$$

$$30,000 = 150,000r \text{ and } r = 20\%$$

If the project involves more than two time periods, the solution must be derived using polynomial equations, none of which can be explained or calculated here. Then how is IRR calculated in practice? The answer is either via the use of financial calculator (or a computer-based spreadsheet package, such as Lotus 1–2–3) or by trial and error using the interpolation process. Remember, the IRR is the discount rate that sets the NPV to zero—this is what the analyst is aiming to find.

Interpolation involves considering extremes and then working inward. For example, assume the discount rate is zero, then the NPV is simply the cash flow generated minus the initial outlay. For project X, this is $30,000. Next, assume a very high discount rate in relation to the project, say 40 percent. The NPV is therefore:

$$- 150,000 + \frac{180,000}{(1 + 0.4)} = - 150,000 + 128,571 = - 21,429$$

The NPV at 40 percent is negative and therefore zero NPV lies somewhere between the discount rates of zero and 40 percent. This guide is a little too coarse for reasonable interpolation, so choose another couple of points somewhat closer together and try again to find the NPV of zero. If one arbitrarily decides on 15 percent and 25 percent and repeats the equation for 15 percent and 25 percent one gets:

$$At\ 15\%: - 150,000 + \frac{180,000}{(1 + 0.15)} = - 150,000 + 156,522 = 6,522$$

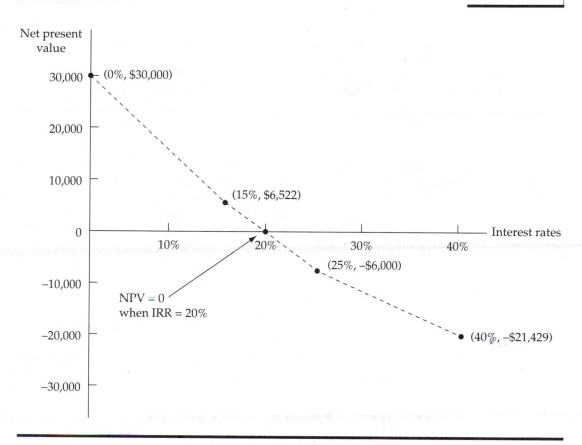

$$\text{At } 25\%\colon\; -150{,}000 + \frac{180{,}000}{(1 + 0.25)} = -150{,}000 + 144{,}000 = -6{,}000$$

The next stage could be to choose another couple of discount rates and do the calculation again, say 18 percent and 22 percent, 19 percent, and 21 percent. However, given the difficulties of estimating r in the first place, it is equally as accurate to draw the above four plots on a graph that has NPVs on the vertical axis and interest rates on the horizontal axis. By joining the lines together and reading where NPV equals zero, as shown in Exhibit 8.8, one can determine the IRR.

From the line crossing the horizontal discount rate axis one can read a figure of 20 percent (determined in the earlier example). This 20 percent discount rate is the IRR of the project. Note the relationship between NPV and IRR. When NPV equals zero, IRR equals 20 percent. If one calculates the NPV of the project using a discount rate of 20 percent one comes back to the fact that NPV equals zero. NPV and IRR are two sides of the same coin.

NITTER, INC., INVESTMENT-RELATED CASH FLOWS

NITTER, INC.
PROJECT K: CASH FLOWS ADJUSTED FOR TAX ($ IN THOUSANDS)

Year	0	1	2	3	4	5	6
After-tax cash flow	−$255	$59.0	$72.5	$87.6	$105.6	$126.9	−$55.0

However, here is where some confusion may begin to creep in. The term *discount rate* has been used interchangeably for *IRR* and also for *required rate of return* determined by the firm's management. The *IRR* refers to the rate of return that the project itself generates. This can be compared with the required rate of return that the firm's management deems acceptable (i.e., the opportunity cost of capital), the same *r* dealt with when discussing NPV. If management decides a project should earn at least 15 percent, this is the required rate of return that is used in the NPV process. If the project generates a return of 20 percent then it is considered an acceptable project as it exceeds what is frequently referred to as the **hurdle rate,** the rate the project must generate to get to the next stage of the evaluation process.

IRR does have a few inherent problems that NPV does not and these will be reviewed presently.

NITTER, INC., PROJECT EVALUATION

These techniques can now be applied to the case of Nitter, Inc. Exhibit 8.9 repeats part of Exhibit 7.6 (this involved the cash flows after 25 percent straight-line depreciation allowance).

Payback Period
Cash inflows in the first three years total $219,100 and for the first four years total $324,700. These can be compared with an investment cost of $255,000. The difference between $255,000 and $219,100 is $35,900. If the fourth year earns $105,600 and the cash flow is evenly distributed throughout the year, it will take 35,900/105,600 = 0.34 of a year, or approximately 4 months to earn the difference. Therefore the payback period is 3 years and 4 months.

Net Present Value
Nitter's management has decided that a discount rate of 16 percent on after-tax cash flows is appropriate for the risk associated with the new plant, and therefore the NPV of the project is expected to be approximately $2,000

◆ **EXHIBIT 8.10**

NITTER, INC., NET PRESENT VALUE

NITTER, INC.
PROJECT K: CASH FLOWS ADJUSTED FOR TAX ($ IN THOUSANDS)

Year	0	1	2	3	4	5	6
After-tax cash flow	−$255.0	$59.0	$72.5	$87.6	$105.6	$126.9	−$55.0
Discount factor	1.000	0.8621	0.7432	0.6407	0.5523	0.4761	0.4104
Discounted cash flow @ 16%	−$255.0	$50.9	$53.9	$56.1	$58.3	$60.4	−$22.6
Net present value = 2.0							

◆ **EXHIBIT 8.11**

NITTER, INC., INTERNAL RATE OF RETURN

NITTER, INC.
PROJECT K: CASH FLOWS ADJUSTED FOR TAX ($ IN THOUSANDS)

Year	0	1	2	3	4	5	6
After-tax cash flow	−$255.0	$59.0	$72.5	$87.6	$105.6	$126.9	−$55.0
Discount factor	1.000	0.8597	0.7390	0.6353	0.5461	0.4695	0.4036
Discounted cash flow @ 16.325%	−$255.0	$50.7	$53.6	$55.7	$57.7	$59.6	−$22.2
Net present value = 0							

($2,079 to be exact) as shown in Exhibit 8.10. The project should be accepted. Given the small NPV (relative to the cost of the investment) the accuracy of the figures should be re-examined to ensure that they present the most fitting scenario.

Internal Rate of Return

Using a spreadsheet, an analyst can establish that the IRR for the project is expected to be 16.325 percent. This can be checked (although intuitively it makes sense because it must be slightly more than the 16 percent r that provided the positive NPV) by using 16.325 percent as a discount rate and seeing what the resultant NPV is. This is especially necessary in this case because there are two sign changes. Exhibit 8.11 shows the IRR.

Note that one cannot look up a discount factor for 16.325 percent in the financial tables, it needs to be calculated. This can be done easily on a standard calculator—divide 1 by 1.16325, then multiply twice for the first period, then continue to multiply (hit the "equals" button) for subsequent periods.

CONCEPT CHECK

1. *What decision criteria are used with the NPV technique?*
2. *How is the future discount rate determined in circumstances where the appropriate discount rate is increasing with time?*
3. *What is the relationship between the NPV and IRR methods?*
4. *What is the decision criterion under the IRR technique?*
5. *Distinguish between the IRR, the discount rate, and the hurdle rate.*
6. *How does the discounted payback technique adjust for*
   (i) the timing of cash flows?
   (ii) the risk of cash flows?

8.4 DIFFICULTIES WITH DISCOUNTED CASH-FLOW TECHNIQUES

While the mechanics of the discounting process are relatively simple, there are a number of problems associated with project selection based on DCF analysis. These include:

✦ mutually exclusive projects,

✦ interdependent projects,

✦ unconventional cash-flow patterns, and

✦ capital rationing.

MUTUALLY EXCLUSIVE PROJECTS

A business is often faced with the choice between investments and/or projects for which the choice of one means that any other selection is excluded. A simple example is the choice of a car—one can only drive one car at a time, so if one is chosen, all others are excluded. The opposite problem is interdependence; an example of this would be that the car selected requires servicing— the driver has to articulate the two projects concurrently.

Another real-life company, Dyer, Inc. (name and details have been changed, of course) printed dyes onto cloth from customers' direct orders. The machine that mixed the basic colors was called a "kitchen." However, there were two elements to this kitchen, one was the mechanical part and the other was the computer control. From an initial information-gathering exercises regarding machines, which, in its own casual way, took about one year, there emerged five possible machine choices. The general consensus after technical evaluation was that two should be struck off the list of possibilities. The problem with the remaining three was that none of them combined engineering "elegance," as the evaluators put it, with the required reliability and sophistication.

DYER, INC., PROJECT ANALYSIS

	Year	Project A	Project B
Acquisition cash	0	$100,000	$60,000
Cash inflows	1	$ 60,000	$36,000
	2	$ 60,000	$36,000
	3	$ 60,000	$36,000
NPV		$ 39,300	$23,580
IRR		36.3%	36.3%

One option was to separate the machine from its computer control and attempt to match the better control with the better machine. Naturally, this was very difficult and, in addition, they already had a computer control that, although outdated, performed well. The problem was that the programming was significantly different from the new controls offered. To add to the problems, some machines could be operated manually and at least one could not. The cost of the machines varied quite significantly and the costs of the machines and controls were not proportionate across the options. Eventually, two options remained. The concept of using in-house programming disappeared with the resignation of a senior evaluator over the issue. These two options are called A and B. Exhibit 8.12 shows the analysis, assuming that Dyer's required rate of return was 14 percent.

The first issue relating to the size of the project is that A is preferable to B, as it generates more wealth for the firm. The opposite side of the coin is that one does not know what alternative projects the $40,000 not invested in project B could be invested in instead. If the potential earnings for other projects exceeded 36.3 percent, then logic indicates investing all of the $100,000 in those alternatives because the "kitchen" investment would be sub-optimal. Naturally, the interdependence of projects ultimately would have an input on the decision.

Note that the ranking of projects would change if project B increased its anticipated cash flows by as little as $1 each year. This would increase B's IRR, while project A's remains constant. Using NPV as a decision criterion, project A would be selected; using IRR as a decision criterion, project B would be selected. The analyst would also choose project B if it could be coupled with a project that earned an NPV greater than $15,730 for an initial outlay of $40,000 so that the sum of the NPVs of the two projects (B and an alternative) exceeded $39,320.

The firm was faced with the problem of estimating the cash flows of each machine and control separately, evaluating the various configurations by adding each of the NPVs associated with the respective machine and control, and selecting the best mix on the basis of financial criteria. Evaluation of the existing control mechanisms provided an added problem because nobody knew initially which machine would be better suited to in-house programming.

Evidently, the general principle of selecting the project with the highest NPV was looking a bit jaded to the evaluators. The technical decision debarred any other option from being implemented so there was not really a choice other than either A or B. The final decision was made on the basis of the perceived relative riskiness of the alternative projects. This was intuitively grounded on the "feel" of the configuration that had not been explicitly recognized by the chosen discount factor. Personal relationships and trust with the various suppliers also played a big part. Not a very financial approach, one might say, but, as discussed previously, capital-budgeting techniques generally help rather than dictate to the manager.

INTERDEPENDENT PROJECTS

It is not too common to find a project that stands alone and is not interdependent to some extent on the forward or backward (even sideways) processes of the firm's activities. One project's cash flows influence, and are influenced by, other investments in the firm. In the case of Nitter, the new project was a large machine that knitted surgical dressings. The project was accepted. However, what was not apparent to the company at the time was that the machine needed to be housed in a new building because it was unexpectedly too large. In addition, the bleaching processes were a little different from those currently used, entailing extra expenditure; additional sterilization of the product required even more expenditure. To make matters worse, because the new machine was located on a different site than the weaving machines, the production department (where the expertise lay) was physically removed from the production process. The company did learn a great deal about capital-investment appraisal after this rather disastrous first attempt. The machine was ultimately transferred out of the company within two years.

In Nitter's case, they actually had one large and several smaller capital-investment decisions to make. The difficulty and time requirements involved in evaluating each project—machine, building (which also involved a lease-or-build appraisal), and other process investments—would have been so prohibitive that any smaller firm would have thrown in the towel. What was required was a combined appraisal of all the interdependent projects.

In general terms, if there are two **interdependent projects,** then three appraisals are required: project A, project B, and project A plus B. Often the whole is greater than the sum of the parts.

THE PATTERN OF CASH FLOWS

The majority of capital investments have what is termed **conventional cash flows** where there is an initial outlay, followed by positive inflows for the remainder of the project's life. However, some investments may have **unconventional cash flows** where there is an initial outflow, followed by years in which the cash flows may be positive or negative. Thus, conventional cash flows have one change of sign, from negative to positive, whereas unconventional cash flows have more than one change of sign. Unfortunately, the IRR changes at each change of sign, so that, broadly speaking, there are as many IRRs as there are changes in sign. This problem is dealt with in standard corporate-finance texts under the heading **multiple IRRs.** For the smaller business, the differences between NPV and IRR will not be too great and is thus not worth pursuing, except to say that the IRR can be checked by discounting the cash flows at the IRR to prove that the NPV (at this rate) is zero. If the NPV is not zero, the correct IRR of the project has not been determined.

Another problem with the appraisal of cash flows is that, depending on their pattern and discount rate, and even given the same initial outlay and life expectancy, the NPVs can offer different solutions, sometimes preferring one alternative over another. The changes have to be fairly large to significantly affect the probable outcome of a decision, but, technically, it is possible.

CAPITAL RATIONING

Capital rationing occurs whenever the firm is constrained in its profitable (i.e., positive NPV) activities by funding restrictions. Corporate-finance theory suggests that the firm should accept *all* positive NPV projects (because they are value-adding) and raise any funding required in the capital markets. However, where sufficient capital (debt or equity) does not exist to finance theoretically acceptable investments, some form of rationing must take place. The corporate-finance discipline has developed many models to guide this process, and the reader should refer to a corporate-finance text if interested in learning more about the topic.

In practice, smaller firms face more barriers to finance than larger firms because, generally, they do not, for one reason or another (typically their small size and perceived high risk), have access to additional equity financing and are rarely prepared to seek it out even if it is available. Many small-business owners argue that they would never take in another partner; but history has shown that, when presented with a profitable-enough project, they usually change their minds. It is all a matter of price.

One of the difficulties with the application of the various DCF techniques is that while (at least in the raw state examined so far) they indicate whether or not a project is acceptable, they will not rank projects.

For example, consider the case of two equally priced but mutually exclusive projects, project A and project B. Project A has an IRR of 45 percent and a hurdle rate of 25 percent; project B has an IRR of 35 percent and a hurdle rate of 10 percent. Project A earns more, but is more risky. The "excess return" on project A is 20 percent, while that of B is 25 percent. The situation is made even more complicated if one considers that project A costs $1,000,000 while B costs $100,000. Examining only the IRRs does not help (examining the NPVs might, in this case). The IRR technique has a problem with scale.

There are similar problems with the NPV approach. Consider two other projects, this time projects X and Y. Project X has an NPV of $100,000 while project Y has an NPV of $20,000. One might think that X should be preferred without argument. But what if the cost of X is $800,000 while that of Y is $50,000? What if the firm only has $50,000 to invest?

If there is no capital restriction, but the projects are mutually exclusive, one can calculate the **profitability index** (also known as the **excess present value index** and the **benefit–cost ratio**) to assist with the decision:

$$PI = \frac{\text{Present value of future cash flows}}{\text{Investment cost}} = \frac{NPV + I_0}{I_0}$$

where: PI = the profitability index
I_0 = the present value of the investment cost

In this example, the profitability index of the project X is $900,000 divided by $800,000, or 1.125, while that of project Y is $70,000 divided by $50,000, or 1.4. The second project is more profitable on this basis (determined by the IRR method), but the first project will add more value to the firm. If the projects are mutually exclusive, and there is no capital restriction, the project with the highest NPV should be accepted. If the projects are independent (both can be chosen at the same time) and there is no capital restriction, both should be chosen. But if funds are restricted to, say, $300,000 what should be done? It might depend on the potential use of the $250,000 that would be left over if one invested only in project Y (if it alone was selected). It might depend on whether there is any chance of "sharing" project X with another firm (e.g., a joint venture of some type). Necessity is the mother of invention, and, if a project is good enough, a firm will generally find the capital to finance it somehow.

Nevertheless, despite the foregoing discussion, while techniques such as the use of profitability indices and NPV profiles may be of assistance to the smaller business, its funding problems usually run too deep to warrant the use of more sophistication. For small firms, the best projects are usually those with positive NPVs that can be afforded.

 CONCEPT CHECK

1. *Distinguish between independent and interdependent projects.*
2. *What is a mutually exclusive project?*

3. *How are projects ranked?*
4. *What is capital rationing and what is its effect?*
5. *Why do small businesses suffer from funding restrictions?*
6. *What is the profitability index of a project?*

8.5   RISK REVISITED

Earlier it was assumed that risk could be assessed through an intuitive assessment of the environment and could then be accounted for by the risk-adjusted discount rate, r. However, it is also possible to take account of risk once the risk-free discount rate has been applied to the net after-tax cash flows. Such techniques revolve around the estimated **probabilities** of achieving the forecasted cash flows in the face of risk and uncertainty. While this text will not dwell on the statistical aspects, it is essential that the reader understands a few terms.

It has been mentioned previously that sales are the most difficult element to calculate when compiling an accurate cash forecast. The general state of the economy may have as much to say about sales as the quality and desirability of the product or service being sold. Nevertheless, given that the firm has arrived at its best estimate of net cash flows after tax, there is the possibility (rather, a probability) that the forecasted cash flows will not be accurate. They may be less than expected or more than expected, i.e., they are dispersed around the expected cash flow in some way.

The best estimate of the future cash flow (the expected cash flow) is a measure of central tendency, which is called the **mean.** The dispersion, deviation, or variance (they are all similar in nature) around the mean can be measured by taking the square root of the variance, called the **standard deviation.**

THE EXPECTED NET PRESENT VALUE

Many small firms seek the advice of "professional" people at some time, be they consultants, bankers, or accountants. It would be unusual to present them with a single point forecast of expected cash flows, and here *expected* is the operative word. If not already presented to them, these professionals will usually ask for the projections to be based on an *optimistic* view of potential cash flow and, perhaps more important, for a *pessimistic* view of the business's fortunes as reflected in its cash-flow projections. The optimistic and pessimistic scenarios are the result of analyzing the probabilities that good or bad events may happen. The probabilities embedded in those forecasts reflect the risk associated with deviating from the **expected net present value (ENPV).**

ENPV is supported by the assumption that it is inaccurate to rely on a single estimate of what will occur. Instead, a preferred alternative is to weight the three NPV scenarios (best, worst, and normal outcomes) by their probabilities of occurrence so that a mean, or combined, figure can be established (the ENPV). This figure can then be evaluated (as with single-point NPVs) and

BIGBLOCK CASH FLOWS

Year	Scenario		
	(1) Boom	(2) Normal	(3) Slump
0	$(10,000)	$(10,000)	$(10,000)
1	5,000	4,000	3,500
2	7,000	5,000	3,000
3	9,000	6,000	2,500

BIGBLOCK SCENARIO ANALYSIS

Year	Scenario		
	(1) Boom	(2) Normal	(3) Slump
0	$(10,000)	$(10,000)	$(10,000)
1	4,167	3,333	2,917
2	4,861	3,472	2,083
3	5,208	3,472	1,447
	$ 4,236	$ 277	$ (3,553)

will lead to a positive or negative decision. In this context, a positive decision is favorable (invest) while a negative decision is unfavorable (do not invest).

Consider Bigblock, a small firm that cuts stone, tiles, and blocks for the local construction industry. New laser technology is replacing traditional cutting techniques. It is more automated and cheaper to run but the initial purchase is more expensive. Leasing such technology is not yet available. The cost of a new laser machine is $10,000, with associated cash flows as shown in Exhibit 8.13. The useful life of the machine is unknown, but is estimated at three years. Disposal value can be considered as nil. One must now attempt to adjust for the variability inherent within the construction industry through a weighting process that takes into account the probability of booms, slumps, and normal trading.

Bigblock has selected a required rate of return of 20 percent on this type of capital investment, since this approximates the performance figures of other similar firms in the construction industry (based on a recently published construction trade-magazine article). For each of the scenarios independently, the NPVs are shown in Exhibit 8.14.

♦ EXHIBIT 8.15

BIGBLOCK ENPV CALCULATION

Scenario	Probability					NPV
(1) Boom	20%	×	$4,236	=		$847
(2) Normal	60%	×	277	=		166
(3) Slump	20%	×	−3,553	=		−711
Expected net present value						$302

The trade journal further reports that there is considerable uncertainty within the economy and that the probability of a normal industry environment is approximately 60 percent, while the prospects of a boom or slump are split evenly: 20 percent and 20 percent. Using these figures, Bigblock calculates the ENPV (the arithmetic mean) as shown in Exhibit 8.15.

The project may be accepted as the expected NPV is positive.

Naturally, the above example is a little simplistic to the extent that a boom or slump rarely occurs evenly over a number of years; in fact, the ongoing process of booms and slumps is referred to as the **business cycle,** and by definition a cycle is not linear.[1] The probabilities are frequently subjective rule-of-thumb estimates, at least for smaller businesses. Larger businesses can spend quite a lot of time, effort, and cash on sophisticated forecasts, but even government predictions are never perfect and often the actual outcome is not even close to the forecast. The discount rate, as already discussed, is also subjectively determined. Nevertheless, such a calculation is much preferred to the alternative of failing to adjust for scenario probabilities, and it will undoubtedly impress those from whom the small business seeks additional sources of capital.

DECISION TREES

Even if only three scenarios are possible and each scenario, in turn, has three variables associated with it, then there are nine possibilities. There is a limit to what can be handled manually before computing power is required. If each year (of three) has three options of boom, normal, or slump, there are three possibilities in the first year, nine in the second, and twenty-seven in the third.

---

[1]For those who are not familiar with the business cycle, it is suggested that some reading and research in this area will pay handsome dividends. People make fortunes on the accurate forecasting of the business cycle (and also lose fortunes because of ignorance or inaccuracy). Many small firms (and some large ones) have prospered or sunk without a trace after mistiming the economy's movements.

PROBABILITIES AND EXPECTED CASH FLOWS

	Year 1			Year 2			
State	Probability (p)	Cash flow (CF)	State	Probability (p)	Cash flow (CF)	p(CF)	Expected cash flow
			A	0.3	$900	$270	
A	0.2	$800	B	0.4	700	280	
			C	0.3	600	180	$730
			A	0.2	700	140	
B	0.6	600	B	0.6	600	360	
			C	0.2	400	80	580
			A	0.1	400	40	
C	0.2	500	B	0.8	200	160	
			C	0.1	100	10	210

For example, assume that, for the first year of a project, three states of nature exist, A, B, and C, each with assigned probabilities of 0.2, 0.6, and 0.2, respectively. These states may be related to the economy, marketing success, or other business factors. The expected cash flow in state A is $600, in state B is $400, and in state C is $200.

Also assume that the owner wants to examine the potential over a two-year period in which state A in the first year may be followed by state A (again) with a probability of 0.3, state B with 0.4, or state C with 0.3. Similarly, state B in the first year may be followed by state A with a probability of 0.2, state B (again) with 0.6, or state C with 0.2. State C in the first year may be followed by state A with a probability of 0.1, state B with 0.8, or state C (again) with 0.1. Exhibit 8.16 depicts these states together with the potential cash-flow consequences for each of the states of nature in each year. Note that level of cash-flow and hence a particular state are both estimates, but are clearly correlated.

Exhibit 8.17 summarizes the likely cash flows given the states of nature that might occur.

The expected cash flows in year 1 and year 2 as well as the expected NPV are shown in Exhibit 8.18. Assuming a 15 percent discount rate and an initial outlay of $850, as shown in Exhibit 8.18, the expected NPV is $95 (or, more accurately, $94.20) and, because the expected NPV for the project is positive, it can be considered financially viable.

We sometimes find managers who, in similar circumstances and faced with an expected NPV of 5 or even larger, may be tempted to say "that's not enough, we had better not proceed." This is an incorrect way of looking at the problem. As long as the procedures have been accurately thought out and the calculations properly made, then risk is accounted for within the numbers. It

◆ **EXHIBIT 8.17**

	Probability	Year 1 cash flow	Year 2 cash flow
State A	0.2	$800	$730
State B	0.6	600	580
State C	0.2	500	210

◆ **EXHIBIT 8.18**

Year 1 state	Probability	Year 1 cash flows	Present value of cash flows in year 1 (0.870)	Year 2 cash flows	Present value of cash flows in year 2 (0.756)	Present value of cash flows in years 1 and 2	Net present value (NPV)
A	0.2	$800	$696	$730	$552	$1,248	$398
B	0.6	600	522	580	438	960	110
C	0.2	500	435	210	159	594	−256

Year 1 state		NPV	×	Probability		
A		$398	×	0.2	=	$80
B		110	×	0.6	=	66
C		−256	×	0.2	=	−51
ENPV						$95

is the *sign* that is the important thing. The rule is: if the NPV is positive, go for it. If the NPV is negative, reconsider the numbers and the probabilities. If the NPV is still negative after reconsideration, reject the project.

Note that only in the case of evaluating similar risk projects will ENPV give some help in choosing amongst them. If projects are of different risks, either or both the discount rate and the probabilities will be different. After adjusting for those differences, comparison of the expected NPV can be made.

There is an alternative way of undertaking this analysis. It involves the use of the **decision tree.** Exhibit 8.19 demonstrates this method. In this form of analysis, the net present values for each of the expected cash flows are estimated (in this example, the nine cash flows are each represented by a branch of the "tree") and then the branch NPV is multiplied by the joint probability of occurrence (the product of the probabilities) to provide the expected NPV for each branch. The sum of these expected net present values is

DECISION TREE

Cash inflow	Probability year 1	Cash flow	Probability year 2	Cash flow	Branch NPV	Joint probability	ENPV
			0.3	$900	526	0.06	31.56
		$800	0.4	$700	375	0.08	30.00
			0.3	$600	299	0.06	17.94
	0.2						
			0.2	$700	201	0.12	24.12
($850)	0.6	$600	0.6	$600	125	0.36	45.00
			0.2	$400	−26	0.12	−3.12
	0.2						
			0.1	$400	−113	0.02	−2.26
		$500	0.8	$200	−264	0.16	−42.24
			0.1	$100	−340	0.02	−6.80
						Expected NPV	$94.20

the expected net present value of the project. As can be seen, it provides the same answer as the earlier demonstration.

SENSITIVITY ANALYSIS

The example in the previous section considered three states of nature (scenarios) that were based on three "point" estimates of the state of the economy. However, cash-flow construction involves many variables to consider including the effects of different states of nature on individual cost items and revenue items and that if such variables are subject to change, then each variable is inherently risky. For example, if sales are expected to be $1 million in year 1, but there is a probability, say 20 percent, that sales may actually only achieve $900,000, how will this affect the calculation of the cash forecast and consequently the NPV? If the investment proposal is still acceptable (i.e., has a positive NPV), it is a fairly robust project.

To the extent that a small change in any one of the items has a high relative impact on the NPV of the project as a whole, one concludes that the NPV is "sensitive" to unit changes in that particular item.

To try and assess the impact of such changes on the project's NPV the analyst can ask the question "What if . . . ?" For example, "What if the cash inflow figures for year 1 or 2 or 3 are changed?" and so on. Or, "What if the cost of distribution, supplies, overheads, labor, or any other variable cost changes?" This type of analysis is best suited to the application of a computer spreadsheet package, such as Excel, Quattro Pro, Lotus 1–2–3, or any similar software package.

Once the forecast is set up in spreadsheet form, one variable at a time can be changed while holding all others constant over a range of values associated with that variable. For example, sales can be allowed to increase or decrease by 1 percent or 2 percent or some other appropriate amount in line with the expectations of the extent and probability of such an event occurring within the domain of the small business's perceived risk profile.

For instance, what if the manager is 90 percent confident that changes in cash inflows (or outflows) will not produce a negative NPV? In these circumstances, one may say "expected sales are $1 million, with 90 percent confidence that they will generate at least $800,000." Therefore, anything below $800,000 will be discarded in terms of a sensitivity analysis. However, there are many points in between the $1 million and the $800,000, and one may wish to know the effect of a sales decrease to $950,000. It is easy to find out when working with a spreadsheet.

Using a spreadsheet package, a cash-flow forecast can link directly to the NPV. This means that one can easily view the end result of a change in the value of a single variable. For example, consider the cost of labor: a 5 percent increase is input and computed, the NPV is still positive; 10 percent and 20 percent result similarly; but 25 percent makes the NPV negative. It is easy to determine that the project can only stand a 23 percent rise before the NPV turns negative and becomes financially unacceptable. This is an example where other inputs may be held constant.

Some variables affect many others though, and this increases the complexity of the programming. For example, consider the effect of an increase in price of oil to a firm that manufactures plastic. First, the cost of power is likely to rise; so too is the cost of raw materials, the cost of living, and, consequently, the cost of labor. The effect of an increase in oil prices will also affect the performance of competitors, who may have production facilities powered by oil. However, some of the competitors may be powered by electricity from hydro, nuclear, or coal stations, while one's own firm buys electricity from a predominantly oil-burning utility. The price of the firm's products cannot merely increase just because costs increase; competition from firms that are not facing the environmental cost increases will prevent that. The "what if" scenarios are endless and common sense must prevail as to what adjustments should be reviewed.

Once familiar with spreadsheet packages and entering figures, they provide a very quick and easy way of examining as many risk scenarios as can be imagined, which can be projected as far forward as is useful. Spreadsheets are a very widely used tool since personal computers are now so prevalent in smaller businesses.

 CONCEPT CHECK

1. *How does the expected NPV differ from the NPV?*
2. *How can decision trees assist with the accept/reject decision?*
3. *What is sensitivity analysis?*

8.6   POST-INVESTMENT AUDIT

Assuming the firm has made an investment decision and then purchases and installs an asset, this should not be the end of the story. How does the firm know if it made the right choice? Some firms are not very bothered about this—it is viewed as spilled milk. However, there are a number of good reasons why the audit process should continue after the acquisition is made. For example:

1. Knowing that a review will take place, say, one year after acquisition, tends to curb overenthusiasm and overoptimism. If a manager undertakes both the evaluation and review it may be thought that there is no reason to have a post-investment audit. Wrong on at least two counts:

   ✦ First, the manager will observe whatever bias may have been inherent within the final evaluation and, hopefully, will analyze any variances to seek the causes.

   ✦ Second, if it is the manager who undertakes both tasks, the owner should review both the initial project evaluation and the post-investment audit. If it is the owner/manager who does both, then that person should have sufficient interest to learn from what has been done. There is an argument that these two roles (planning and review) should be kept distinct and should be undertaken by different individuals. If that is not possible, the process could be supervised by a second person or an outside party, such as an auditor or an independent consultant.

2. The knowledge accumulated from **post-investment audits** continually improves future evaluations, and learning from mistakes leads to continual improvement. As part of the post-investment audit the analyst may question:

✦ Were sufficient data were gathered to adequately support the estimates?

✦ Where did the main errors lie?

✦ Was there a procedure manual or guideline to follow? (If not, should there be one? If there is, were the procedures followed?)

✦ Were the assigned risks adequately assessed?

3. Perhaps most importantly, did the investment meet its intended objectives? Owner/managers are prone to keeping things in their heads and face a personal conflict between being very closed or very open about the more intimate finances of the business. Capital investment appraisals do not require secrecy and it is only the potential embarrassment of having committed objectives and goals to paper if anything goes wrong that causes such things to be locked away, uncommunicated.

Having said that, many of the more efficient smaller businesses:

✦ use a variety of the above audit techniques

✦ tend to operate along prescribed guidelines

✦ have manuals

✦ utilize post-investment audits

✦ usually feel the benefit

Many firms do not follow these guidelines, of course, and, naturally, there are also varying degrees of sophistication in such an evaluation. A post-investment audit should not be viewed as a post-mortem but rather as a constructive dissection.

Should a smaller firm be in doubt as to how to undertake either a capital investment-project evaluation or its subsequent review, the manager can always seek the advice of a qualified professional or firm.

 CONCEPT CHECK

1. *What is a post-investment audit?*
2. *What are the advantages of post-investment audits?*
3. *Why is there reluctance to undertake post-investment audits?*

SUMMARY

✦ The simpler evaluation techniques, such as payback and ARR, are not as helpful as their extensive use would suggest. The more theoretically correct techniques of NPV or IRR are preferable tools of analysis because they consider the time value of money.

✦ When reviewing a project on a stand-alone basis, expected NPV provides a useful technique to assess a limited number of scenarios. Sensitivity analysis takes this approach further and allows numerous scenarios to be evaluated before a decision need be made.

- Not least is the recommendation to perform post-audits on investments under-taken so that planners can learn from the process by analyzing variances be-tween the estimates on which the decision was based and the actual outcome some time later.

- Overall, experience has shown that, while such techniques often meet resistance in smaller firms for a variety of reasons, if employed, these techniques provide invaluable information upon which to base a decision. They are not decision-making tools in and of themselves, the final decision must always rest with the owner/manager and the management team.

THE CASE—PART EIGHT

The last installment of the story (part seven) described how Dave was interested in investigating the possibility of investing an additional $40,000 in plant and machin-ery. He believes that the new machinery should last for an indeterminable period if maintained at a cost of $6,000 per year. Projections for the years 2004, 2005 and 2006 were presented in Assignment 7.2. Dave believes that a 25 percent return (after tax) is appropriate for this project and that the 2006 figures represent a steady-state scenario.

ASSIGNMENT 8.1

Required
1. Calculate the following:
   a) payback for the project
   b) the average rate of return on the project
   c) the net present value of the project
   d) the internal rate of return on the project

ASSIGNMENT 8.2

While Dave is reasonably confident in his projections (the price of a bicycle will be $1,200) he nevertheless realizes that this is an expected figure and that prices can change.

Required
1. If there is a 60 percent probability of receiving the $1,200 price and a 20 percent probability of receiving either $1,100 or $1,300, determine the expected net pre-sent value.

ASSIGNMENT 8.3

Dave is interested in taking his analysis to the next step. He believes that the follow-ing probabilities are likely:

	Year					
	2004			**2005 and forward**		
State	Probability	Cash flow		State	Probability	Cash flow
A	0.2	$1,100		A	0.3	$1,100
				B	0.4	1,200
				C	0.3	1,300
B	0.6	1,200		A	0.2	1,150
				B	0.6	1,200
				C	0.2	1,250
C	0.2	1,300		A	0.1	1,200
				B	0.8	1,300
				C	0.1	1,400

Required

1. Forecast the expected receipts for 2004, 2005 and 2006.
2. Forecast the expected marginal cash flows for 2004, 2005 and 2006.
3. Determine the expected net present value if the initial outlay is $40,000 and the discount rate is 25 percent.

SELECTED ADDITIONAL READINGS

The suggested additional readings listed at the end of Chapter 7 apply equally well to this chapter.

OBTAINING FUNDS

OBJECTIVES

1. *Describe the problems faced by the smaller business in acquiring necessary funding*
2. *Describe the sources of equity for the small business and relate those sources to each stage of the firm's life cycle*
3. *Describe the sources of long-term and short-term debt for the small business and demonstrate the different terms applying to various categories of debt*
4. *Describe the nature of the capital-structure decision in the case of the small business with particular reference to liquidity*
5. *Introduce the complication of dividend policy as it applies to the smaller firm and demonstrate the conflict between internal and external liquidity*

9.1   INTRODUCTION

Regardless of whether the small business is owned by a sole proprietor or is organized as a partnership or a corporation, it will fall into one of two types: lifestyle or entrepreneurial (growth). The principal reason for existence for the lifestyle business is to provide a wage for its owners. Examples include professional services and many retail outlets. On the other hand, the purpose for which the owners invest time and money in the entrepreneurial, or growth, business is to create wealth. While the distinction between the two types is clear enough, businesses often change from one type to another depending on the stage of the life cycle of the owner. Lifestyle-oriented businesses may have less funding problems than growth businesses.

For example, a small business may begin its life as a sole professional practitioner, say a doctor or a dentist. It may stay this way for some time before it is merged with other similar businesses to form a central practice owned by a partnership. Following this growth phase, there may be no future growth at all; the business returns to its lifestyle orientation.

Generally, small businesses require funds for four fundamental purposes:

1. start-up costs, inventory, and human resources
2. capital equipment
3. working capital that is required to fund the ongoing operations of the business
4. growth corporations require funding in the future for expansion

It is in the area of obtaining funds that the differences between large and small businesses become most apparent. In the case of the large business, funding for the profitable business is often readily available through either **public equity markets** or **public debt markets.** In the case of the small business however, these markets do not exist. This chapter considers sources of equity, sources of debt, and the nature of the **capital-structure decision** as it applies to the small business.

9.2   SOURCES OF EQUITY

Small businesses are private firms. The sources of equity in these circumstances usually are comprised of the contributions of the owner/managers themselves, their family, and their friends. In the case of the lifestyle firm, there is a need for an introduction of equity at the beginning of the life of the business. Once this firm is consolidated it continues to supply a living for the owners of the business. However, especially in the case of the growing business, one can observe problems with the acquisition of funding. The original owners provide the initial equity, but that is not enough. As outlined in previous chapters, growth requires funding. If critical ratios, such as the debt-to-assets ratio, are to be maintained within a particular range during a growth phase, there need to be regular contributions of equity.

Retained earnings are capable of providing some of this additional equity, but any additional investment must be provided directly by the owners of the business.

In many cases small businesses begin their lives as backyard industries. The owners work in another business or as wage and salary earners and regularly contribute funds from these sources to the business itself. As the business grows and the owners' contribution in terms of time becomes such that one or more is unable to continue to earn money elsewhere, it becomes necessary to locate other equity sources. The difficulty in the case of many of these businesses relates as much to control issues as to finding the equity itself. Usually the owner has a very personal ownership stake in the formative stages of the business and understandably does not want to lose control of the vision and the strategies that have predicated its future growth. As a consequence, the equity of such businesses is usually held by a very close circle of family and friends.

At some stage in the life cycle of the growth business, it is likely that growth will outstrip the personal abilities of this small circle to provide the required equity funding. It is in this particular circumstance that the difficulties arise. Where are the funds to come from? The owners have only two choices. First, they can borrow to finance the anticipated growth; or second, they can take in new equityholders. While increasing financial leverage is often the first choice, with additional debt comes additional financial risk and at some stage, if the financial risk of the firm is to remain at a realistic level, the owner needs to seek additional external equity funding. This decision may, of course, be imposed by lenders who perceive that further borrowing will expose their positions to increasing risk of default.

Additional external equity funding is not often easy to find. Four possibilities exist:

1. funds might be contributed by a **venture capitalist**
2. funds might be raised from a **private placement**
3. funds may be contributed by another business
4. if the business is large enough, funds may be raised via an initial public offering

The venture capitalist is a person or firm with surplus funds to invest in the equity of attractive (and risky) growth businesses. It is frequently difficult to locate such a provider due to their lack of formal structure; however, there is a growing information network listing such individuals that is often accessible by contacting professional accounting and legal firms.

Venture capital is provided by two distinct types of entities. Venture-capital firms are businesses that specialize in investing in entrepreneurial small businesses. Normally these firms only consider investments in excess of $2,000,000. "**Angels**" are private individuals who provide funds (usually less than $500,000) in the early phases of a firm's growth. Normally, an angel will enter during the early stages of business growth and then, after a firm has proved that it has a successful product and a viable market, a venture capital firm steps in.

Venture capitalists normally provide both expertise and financial backing to the firm. In return for these benefits the firm must give up in some manner a portion of control of the business. This is normally done by structuring deals that protect both the income and capital of the venture capitalist. Most deals worked out between the entrepreneur and the venture capitalist provide that the firm issue a package of securities (both debt and equity) to the venture capitalist and, normally, a seat on the board of directors of the business.

Venture capital is an important engine in the economy of the United States. A study undertaken by Coopers & Lybrand[1] reports statistics from five hundred young, venture-backed companies for the 1989 to 1993 time period. In this study they found that venture-backed firms created one hundred and fifty-two jobs per company, spent almost $9 million in research and development, and had export sales worth $4 million. Most of these firms were in high-growth areas, such as biotech and computer software. The venture-backed firms considered in this study were rapidly growing, with a compound growth rate of sales during 1989 to 1993 of 41 percent, whereas the *Fortune* 500 firms had a compound growth rate of 2 percent and firms in Japan had a sales growth rate of 6 percent.

While firms clearly need equity, and venture capital provides an alternative source for these funds, they are very costly. Most venture capitalists try to obtain a return of 50 percent per year on any funds invested in a business with as much control of the firm as possible to protect the investment. Chapter 12 goes into venture-capital financing in a great deal more detail.

Private placements are another way for firms to issue either stock or debt to investors by selling securities to investors without taking an active role in the management of the business. However, private placement is also a way for the firm to issue securities to a venture capitalist. A good way to think about this is that venture capitalists are normally active participants in the entrepreneurial firm, whereas the private placement is just a means to issue a particular security. In other words, private placements are associated with the issue of a security, while venture capitalists are associated with a specific type of investor. One can frequently see private placements issued to venture capitalists.

An alternative source of equity funding is available where the business is in a position to offer some advantage to another business. It is often the contractual relationship that is sought by the new contributor, and the less money invested to gain that relationship, the more attractive the deal. In many cases, most of the advantages arising from a full acquisition may also be available to an acquiring firm, which takes less than a 100 percent stake in a business. Common examples of this type of arrangement occur where the small business owns patents, human resources, geographic presence, or

---

[1]Coopers & Lybrand L.L.P. and National Venture Capital Association, *Fifth Annual Economic Impact of Venture Capital Study* (Arlington, VA: Coopers & Lybrand L.L.P. and National Venture Capital Association, 1995).

marketing arrangements that can benefit the new contributor. Naturally enough, if the new contributor is to continue funding the growth of the business, the two firms need to be "non-competitors."

It should be pointed out that control of a business does not necessarily follow from ownership of the majority of equity in a corporation. Internal rules of many family corporations contain a **governing director's clause** that allows for the person who (for the time being) is the governing director of the business to unilaterally make decisions that are binding on the business. Or, there may be two different classes of ordinary equity: voting and non-voting. These are all examples of formal control structures; there are also informal control structures that arise in the circumstances of **asymmetric information** (or when one party has more information than the other party).

The acquisition of a minority interest in a small business can be fraught with danger. It is common for the original owners (who maintain effective control not only because of their majority interest, but also because they are managers of the business) to see the new equityholder's stake rather like an interest-free loan of undetermined duration. In these circumstances, not only might no dividend be paid to the new stakeholder, but any increase in profitability can find its way into the pockets of the original owners through perks, higher wages, bonuses, and so on. The final dilemma arises with the eventual desire of the new stakeholder (who, by this time, has had enough) to realize the investment; she has earned nothing and is likely to earn nothing in the future, and she is incapable of controlling the business. It is of little value (regardless of the initial investment) to any purchaser, and will probably be bought by the remaining shareholders for a minimum amount.

This very unpleasant circumstance is very common and is exceptionally difficult to guard against. Contracts with management that spell out rights and obligations (especially with respect to remuneration) are essential where there are shareholders. Formulas for the valuation of shares in the event of withdrawal of the new "partner" may also be of assistance, as can be buy-out arrangements using **call options** and **put options.** A call option allows one party to purchase the stake of the other at the discretion of the purchaser; it might be exercised if the business proves more profitable than anticipated. A put option allows one party to sell its stake to the other at the discretion of the seller. It may be used to force a full buy out by one party and is often used as an "escape clause" by the new contributor to permit an effective exit from the arrangement (for example, if the business proves less profitable than anticipated). One must always be aware that the owner of the growing small firm is in a relatively weak position (funding is essential), while the contributor is in a relatively strong position (funding and other resources are more readily available), and this situation can force the owner into an untenable position.

It should be also noted that many countries have legislated some form of minority protection against the excesses of unscrupulous shareholders. Unfortunately, as in all court actions, the cost of litigation often outweighs the potential benefit.

So, adding a new shareholder is potentially dangerous to both the new shareholder and to the original owners. The best that can be done is to attempt to protect both sides from the actions of the other in advance of the new contribution.

Forty-two states have approved a SCOR (small corporate offering registration). SCORs were instituted in 1988 in the state of Washington as an efficient way for small firms to issue up to $1,000,000 in equity over a twelve-month period. Under Securities and Exchange Commission (SEC) rules, small issues are left for governance to individual states. With SCORs, the offering process has been standardized with an offering circular, commonly called a U-7. With this document, a small business may apply to issue securities in many different states. As these offerings are very small, firms must be able to sell the underlying securities themselves without the help of an underwriter. A SCOR offering, frequently referred to as a DPO (direct public offering), requires that the firm go out and sell the securities. Preliminary statistics indicate that a firm will incur issuance costs of around 10 percent for a SCOR offering.

Firms that typically have the best chance of a successful SCOR offering are those operating a business in which they have wide customer appeal. Minibreweries, restaurants, and golf courses are all examples of types of firms that have had a successful SCOR offering.

The final source of equity for growth is the initial public offering, or IPO. The decision to **go public** is the final decision that the owner of the small business will make that relates to the *small* business. By definition, once the business is publicly listed, it becomes a large business, with access to the funding mechanisms that are available to such firms.

IPOs are very important from the perspective of the negotiability of the firm's stock. Privately held stock is frequently difficult to sell, particularly if a minority interest is held. IPOs provide liquidity. Many studies have shown that the privately held stock will increase in value by 30 percent when it goes public through an IPO. The initial public offering is an especially important consideration for the entrepreneurial firm. For venture capitalists who have been involved in the affairs of the business, going public allows them to exit the business. A venture capitalist likes to get in and out of a business within a five-year period, and an IPO is a frequently used exit strategy by entrepreneurs.

The process of going public varies from country to country; however, some basic principles apply across all borders. The first step in the process is finding an underwriter that is willing to orchestrate the offering. From that point on, the owner of the business places himself in the hands of expert managers of such processes and will largely be used to furnish the information that is required to facilitate the eventual production of the prospectus and the offering itself.

 CONCEPT CHECK

1. *What are some primary sources of equity for small business?*
2. *What is venture capital?*
3. *Would you want to purchase a majority interest in a small business?*

9.3 SOURCES OF DEBT

The critical attribute that separates the small from the larger business is the personal exposure of the owners of the former to the creditors of the firm. Small businesses are firms for which the liability of the owners is unlimited. Even if the firm is technically owned by a corporation, the owner will have to personally guarantee the formally arranged debts (especially the long-term debts) of the business.

However, despite this personal exposure, in the absence of available equity funding, the only other alternative the small business has for its funding is debt. Debt can be divided into short-term and long-term. The former is reported in the current liabilities section of the balance sheet of the business and forms the basis for the firm's working capital, the latter is reported in the long-term liabilities section.

Exhibit 9.1 presents a framework for the analysis of debt financing. It depicts debt as being either long-term or short-term and also shows how debt can be either unsecured or secured in one of two different ways.

Long-Term Debt

There are two fundamental types of collateral security for the long-term (or permanent) debt financing available to the small business: security over a particular specified asset (or assets) of the business; or, security over the business as a whole.

Specifically Secured Debt
The first type of security is exemplified by the mortgage securing real estate. Repayment terms for mortgages become important in the case of the small business because of their impact on cash flow.

Fully Amortized Loans The terms for **amortized loans** specify the payment of a periodic annuity (i.e., the same total amount each period) composed of both interest (the proportion of which declines over time) and principal reduction (the proportion of which increases over time). Payments may be monthly, quarterly, or, increasingly rarely, on a longer periodic basis. With this partial payment plan, part of the principal plus interest on the unpaid balance is paid each period. This type of loan is generally only available through large institutions, and then only for longer terms, such as five to twenty-five years.

For the analysis of the cash flows associated with each of the three categories, assume that Newford Booksellers is a well-established family business that owns its own retail premises. The owners have decided to raise $80,000 against the real estate for the purpose of refurbishing the shop. They have been offered three different loan terms by three different lenders: a fully amortized loan, a **reducing-balance loan**, and an interest-only loan. The $80,000 fully amortized loan bears fixed interest at a rate of 8 percent and is for a term of twenty-five years. Payments will be made once each year (an unlikely assumption, made in the interest of simplicity). Present-value tables

◆ EXHIBIT 9.1

DEBT-FINANCING FRAMEWORK

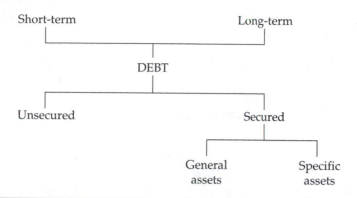

(or a financial calculator) provide the annuity of $7,494 per annum. Similarly, present-value tables (or a financial calculator) can be used to determine the balance of principal outstanding at any time.

There are many advantages to an amortized loan. In the context of budgeting, the job is made a little easier in that there is a constant cash outflow required for each payment. Also, there is the psychological feeling that the borrower is getting ahead; the balance outstanding is being reduced.

Despite the advantages, there are some disadvantages to amortized loans. Where the loan has a fixed interest rate, general interest rates may decline during the term of the loan, to the disadvantage of the borrower. If this happens, the borrower is faced with the choice of refinancing the loan on more favorable terms elsewhere. This decision becomes a trade-off between the costs of refinancing, such as loan application and appraisal fees, and the advantage of a cheaper interest rate. The very fact that the loan is being compulsorily reduced may not be to the advantage of the borrower. If the interest rate on the loan is lower than other prevailing rates, the borrower would be losing a relatively cheap source of money. Under conditions of inflation it may also be argued that it is easier to repay the loan in the future (with inflated money) than to repay it now. Of course the lender makes a trade-off between the interest rate and the inflation rate that is supposed to account for this factor. Where funds are tight, as in the case of the growing firm, compulsory principal reductions adversely affect cash flow; the owners of the business could be using the money required to meet contractual principal reductions for the further development of the business instead of for repaying debt.

Declining-Balance Loans The **declining-balance loan,** or **installment loan,** requires the repayment of a constant periodic amount of principal accompanied by a decreasing amount of interest. Unfortunately, both this type of loan and the amortized loan are commonly described as "amortized loans." The

INSTALLMENT-LOAN STRUCTURE

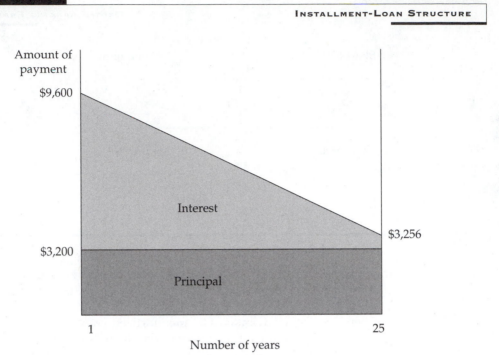

analyst needs to be aware that the terminology of "the street" does not necessarily convey the correct description.

Exhibit 9.2 depicts the cash-flow structure of the loan offered to Newford Booksellers and is based on a loan of $80,000 for twenty-five years bearing 8 percent interest. Under these circumstances, 4 percent of the loan (one hundred divided by twenty-five) must be repaid every year.

As seen in Exhibit 9.2, the installment loan offered is similar to the amortized loan in all respects except for the repayment plan. In this case interest is similarly paid on the outstanding balance of principal, but the periodic repayments of principal are of fixed equal amounts instead of increasing amounts as in the former case. Installment loans vary from short-term to long-term. The balance of principal at any time is the original loan times the proportion of the term that is unexpired. For example, after seven years 28 percent of the loan has been repaid, leaving 72 percent (or $57,600) outstanding.

The advantages of the installment loan are similar to those of the amortized loan: the borrower feels that, because debt is being repaid, the business is progressing favorably, and there is no refinance problem. However, there are some possible disadvantages relating to the acceleration of the repayment pattern. If the interest rate on the loan is lower than the rate that is in

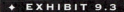

◆ EXHIBIT 9.3

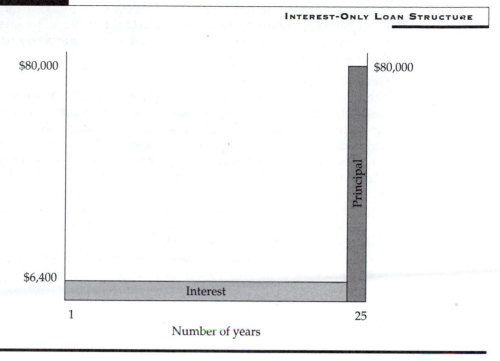

general current use, then there is even faster repayment of a cheap source of finance (note that, if the rate on the loan is higher, then the borrower should attempt to refinance at the cheaper rate). In addition, larger pre-tax profits are needed to fund the increased repayments, and this further handicaps the ability of the business to develop in its early years.

Interest-Only Loans The interest-only loan is one for which interest is paid periodically, and there are no contractual principal reductions until the final payment. Interest-only loans are evident across a wide range of durations, but form the majority of short-term lending. Exhibit 9.3 portrays the cash profile for the interest-only loan of $80,000 at 8 percent with a five-year term that has been offered to the owners of Newford Booksellers.

The advantages of the interest-only loan relate first to its flexibility and second to its effect on cash flows. The knowledge that the loan term is short often encourages lenders to charge less due to the increased flexibility that they have. At the same time, due to the lack of contractual principal reductions, the interest-only loan is easier on the cash flow than either of the types of amortized loans. It allows money that would be otherwise used for repayment to be used for funding growth in the business. These loans may be refinanced on an infinite basis (as long as there are lenders), and under inflationary conditions, inflation reduces the effective value of the principal outstanding.

The disadvantages of interest-only loans include the uncertainty relating to both the costs, terms (interest rate, duration, etc.), and availability of refinance funds. Additionally, the borrower lacks the feeling of progression with respect to debt reduction, even though money *could* effectively be put aside on a regular basis for debt reduction.

Generally Secured Debt

The second type of permanent financing is only available to those small businesses that are structured as corporations. In these cases, it may be possible for the business to raise money via the issue of a debenture, or bond. The bond security gives the lender a general security across all the assets of the business. It is not the same as a mortgage, in which case the deeds of ownership may be transferred to the lender for security, it is a general security over residual assets. It ranks behind mortgages and formal collateral security over the chattels (equipment) of the business. Despite an apparently adequate security margin, the lender in these circumstances will require the personal guarantees of the owners of the equity in the business to provide the creditor with access to the personal assets of the owners in the event of default. Most small businesses, however, are not of the size to successfully issue a bond or debenture.

SHORT-TERM DEBT

The usual sources of short-term debt for the small business range from **trade credit** through formal bank borrowings on a short-term basis.

Trade credit is readily available for firms that show ability to pay on a regular basis. As previously described, it has the advantage of being free (except when discounts are available but not taken). Trade credit is easily arranged and there are very few costs involved in the documentation process. Trade credit has one other advantage in that it is usually unsecured. For some types of small businesses, trade credit is the major contributor to debt financing. Retail businesses that, for example, do not own their own fixed assets other than shop equipment, may rely entirely on trade credit for their funding needs.

Bank credit facilities contribute the alternative major source of short-term debt. There are two types of credit-line facilities. With the first type, the borrower pays interest on the full credit line and any surpluses are reinvested wherever the borrower can do that to the best advantage. With the second type, the borrower organizes a credit line for which she pays a small fee and draws down to the extent of that credit line as funds are needed. Interest is only paid on the actual amount drawn.

Short-term formal borrowing, such as that arranged with a bank, generally needs some form of collateral security. Tangible security, such as the assignment of a life insurance policy or a mortgage over real estate, is preferred and is usually accompanied by the personal guarantee of the borrower.

In the case of the small, indebted corporation, the right of the creditor to realize personal assets does not exist, and, in these circumstances, the personal guarantee is of critical importance to the lender. Also, in these cases, a (often termed a floating debenture). This security will rank behind such prior charges as those specifically secured against particular assets (e.g., a mortgage securing real estate), and is therefore effectively security against the equity of the business.

Other sources of debt for the smaller-business owner include such arrangements as those available with **credit cards.** These are usually relatively expensive sources of finance—however, many successful small firms have been financed initially with their owners' credit cards.

 CONCEPT CHECK

1. *Why is debt more favorably viewed than equity by the small-business owner as a source of new funds?*
2. *In what ways can the different forms of debt be secured by the lender?*
3. *What are the different cash-flow patterns associated with the common different types of loans?*

9.4   DEALING WITH A BANKER

Most small businesses will approach a banker for a loan or a line of credit at some time, and it is important to understand how the bank makes decisions. Essentially, the bank wants to receive interest payments as they fall due and to recover the principal as it falls due with the least risk possible (this is the reason they frequently require personal guarantees). Bankers' requirements therefore relate fundamentally to collateral security and to the firm's ability to meet charges.

Bankers typically evaluate the "Five Cs" (as mentioned in Chapter 6) of credit analysis in determining if a loan should be granted.

1. Capital: What is the capital being provided by the business? Is the bank putting more money in this business than the owner (a sure sign of too much risk for the bank)? Are the debt ratios of the firm in line with similar types of firms in the industry?
2. Character: Has the business been prompt in repaying other loans and obligations? Can the business be trusted to do what it says?
3. Collateral: Collateral security ensures that if the business cannot repay the loan out of its operating activities, the bank can exercise repayment by realizing the collateral. Once a bank decides to grant a loan (because the firm has a high probability of repaying it on a timely basis), it will try to secure the loan with as much collateral as possible. For example, the bank will probably require personal guarantees and a lien, or security interest, in all of the firm's assets. While the bank is trying to protect itself, the collateral arrangements are frequently very flexible.
4. Capacity: Does the business have the capacity to repay the loan? Here lenders are concerned with the pro forma income statement or the cash

budget. Does the firm have a high probability of being able to repay its debt obligation to the bank?

5. Conditions: The banker is concerned with the conditions of the industry and of the economy in which the firm is operating. Is the industry growing? Is there too much competition? There is no incentive for a bank to loan funds if the firm has little chance (no matter how good the idea or past experience has been) of success or survival.

One of the most important things a firm can do when requesting a loan from a bank is to have a well-documented business plan as part of the loan application. This should highlight the accomplishments and planned accomplishments of both the firm and its owners. The pro forma cash budgets, which show if and when a firm can repay the loan, are a very important part of this document. These pro formas are critical—they must be realistic; loan applications are frequently declined by bankers because they know the forecast of cash flows is unattainable, no matter what the pro forma estimate states.

Obtaining debt financing is not always easy. One means of obtaining debt capital is through the use of the Small Business Administration (SBA). The most common type of arrangement with the SBA is its provision of a loan guarantee. By this mechanism, the SBA guarantees payment to a commercial bank where the firm cannot meet its obligations. In order to use this facility, the firm must demonstrate that it has been turned down by a commercial lender. Once this has been demonstrated, the firm can apply to the SBA for a guarantee of up to 90 percent of a $155,000 loan. For loans exceeding $155,000 but below $750,000 (maximum loan size) the loan guarantee percentage is 85 percent. On the provision of the guarantee, the loan is applied for at a commercial bank. The rate charged for these loans typically runs about three percentage points over the prime rate.

 CONCEPT CHECK

1. *What are the "Five Cs" of credit?*
2. *What is the SBA loan-guarantee scheme?*

9.5 LEASING

Leasing is an important element in financing[2] because, in many instances, it provides an alternative to debt financing. For the small business, leasing is an integral part of its means of acquiring assets. There are many tax implications of leasing. If the purchase of an asset is financed by borrowing, the owner is able to claim depreciation as a tax-deductible expense and therefore

[2] See J. S. Osteryoung and D. E. McCarty, *Analytical Techniques for Financial Management* (New York: John Wiley & Sons, 1985), 170–183.

ANALYSIS OF A LEASE

Year	NIC	L_t	$L_t T$	$D_t T$	Yearly cash flow
0	$10,000				$ 10,000
1		$ – 3,000	$900	$ – 750	– 2,850
2		– 3,000	900	– 750	– 2,850
3		– 3,000	900	– 750	– 2,850
4		– 3,000	900	– 750	– 2,850

tions of leasing. If the purchase of an asset is financed by borrowing, the owner is able to claim depreciation as a tax-deductible expense and therefore gains the advantage of the tax shield on depreciation. In the case of a lease, the lessee (i.e., the firm gaining the use of the asset) does not *own* the asset and consequently neither depreciates the asset, nor gains the advantage of the tax shield on depreciation. Consequently, when comparing purchasing and leasing, the loss of the depreciation tax shield must be considered a cost of leasing as the lessee does not get this benefit.

To evaluate a lease, one must look for the internal rate of return[3] that equates the cost of the asset with cash flows associated with the leasing cost. In mathematical terms, this is:

$$NIC = \Sigma[L_t(1 - t) + D_t(T)]$$

where: NIC = net initial cost of the asset being acquired

L_t = the lease payment in year t

D_t = depreciation in year t

T = tax rate of the business

For example, assume that a firm is considering the acquisition of an asset that will cost $10,000. The terms of the lease will be: lease payments for four years of $3,000. Depreciation will be $2,500 per year if the asset is purchased. The firm's tax rate is 30 percent. Exhibit 9.4 depicts the figures on which the analysis is based.

The signs depicted in Exhibit 9.4 need some clarification. First, the NIC is positive since this is a net benefit that will be gleaned from leasing. The tax shield from leasing is positive as this reduces the cost of leasing; the depreci-

[3]Internal rates of return are discussed in depth in Chapters 7 and 8. At this point, the reader should consider the IRR as the *yield* on the project.

The IRR of the yearly cash flows is 5.46 percent. If the after-tax cost of borrowing is more than this, then leasing is preferred. If the after-tax cost of borrowing is less than 5.46 percent then debt is preferred.

If the bank is going to charge this firm 10 percent for borrowing to finance the asset, then the firm should lease as the after-tax cost of borrowing is:

$$7\% \, [10\% \, (1 - 0.3)]$$

Overall, leasing is an important way a firm can finance its assets. However, it is critical to evaluate the cost of leasing in a systematic way.

 CONCEPT CHECK

1. *Why is leasing an important option in the financing of the firm?*
2. *Why is the loss of the depreciation tax shield considered to be a cost of leasing?*
3. *What are the critical components of a lease evaluation?*

9.6   THE CAPITAL STRUCTURE DECISION

The standard finance text generally relates to corporate finance and public equity and will maintain that there may or may not be an optimal capital structure that should be effected via the issue of debt or equity securities. In Chapter 4 the concept of the weighted average cost of capital (WACC) was introduced (from the investor's viewpoint). The objective of capital-structure management is to minimize the weighted average cost of capital.

Corporate-finance theory suggests that, because the cost of debt is less than the cost of equity, increasing the amount of debt in the capital structure will reduce the WACC of the firm. However, the optimal capital structure is not one that utilizes 100 percent debt. Beyond a certain point (the **optimal capital structure**), the incipience of "distress costs" (ranging from the loss of discounts and trade credit to bankruptcy costs) results in increases in the costs of both debt and equity to the extent that the WACC of the firm increases. The target WACC is the optimal point at which the WACC is minimized.

In the case of the publicly listed firm, additional debt and additional equity can be raised via the issue of new bonds and stocks; however, in the case of the small business the owners have little choice but to raise funds where available. As previously stated, the initial funding for the small business will be internal; it will be contributed by the owners of the business either as specific personal contributions of equity or via the retention of profits. This internal funding is not costless and the owners of the business should expect a return on their investment in the business in the same way the owners of publicly held equity demand a return on their investment. In other words, just as the cost of equity for the public corporation is a mirror image of the return on investment earned by investors in publicly traded equities, there is also a cost that can be associated with the private equity contributed in the case of the small business. The owner of the small business has a choice between investing in the business and investing in alternative securities, i.e., the owner faces an opportunity cost. As described by financial theory, such a cost must relate to the risks faced by the small business.

With respect to debt financing, and as in the public arena, the cost of debt will always be less than the cost of equity and the cost of debt has the added attraction of being tax deductible. However, it should never be forgotten that the addition of debt to the capital structure increases the financial risk of the business because it increases the fixed costs of the business and raises the break-even point. This is especially important when contractual arrangements for principal reductions are entered into by the business because these have an adverse effect on the **free cash flows** of the business and add to its liquidity problems. It is therefore of critical importance in the budgeting exercise that all of the charges associated with borrowing are included, both interest and principal reductions. As a rule of thumb, repayment terms should be extended for the maximum period possible; unless interest rates are falling and the advance bears fixed interest, most lenders, especially banks, prefer to see windfall reductions in their advances. It is far better to give the bank a "bonus" than to have to inform the manager that the business cannot meet its contractual commitments for repayment.

The **pecking-order theory** of finance describes the order in which funding is preferred by the owners of businesses. It suggests that firms initially prefer **internal funding,** i.e., funding from profits retained by the business to fund its growth. The second choice is debt, since debt is cheaper than equity both in terms of public costs and in terms of its interest cost. Thirdly, there will be a preference for new equity.

For the small business, the pecking-order theory needs some adjustment to reflect the difficulties associated with financing its activities. Initially there will be a preference for start-up equity and retained earnings. Once the business proves its creditworthiness, debt financing becomes an option. It is in the area of the third preference, that for equity, that the small business differs from its larger cousin. While equity is publicly available, at least in theory, in the case of the large business, it is rarely available to the same extent for the small business. However, the order of preference remains the same for both large and small firms.

Essentially, however, the capital-structure decision must be regarded as *residual* in that the owner of the small business does not have the choices available to larger firms with access to public capital markets. The small business finances where it can, always attempting to minimize the cost of that capital, but it is constrained by its limited access.

 CONCEPT CHECK

1. *What financial theories may apply to the smaller business in the context of capital structure?*
2. *What is the pecking-order theory of finance?*

3. *Why is the capital-structure decision residual in nature?*
4. *Why is the capital-structure decision so difficult to make in the case of the small business?*

9.7 THE COMPLICATION OF DIVIDEND POLICY

In the case of the large publicly held corporation, the dividend is easily identifiable as the amount of profit paid out from time to time to the shareholders of the business. In the case of the small business, however, the dividend needs to be defined differently. The owners of the small business withdraw funds from the business through a variety of mechanisms. The preference for these mechanisms will often depend on relative tax rates.

This topic was introduced in Chapter 2 when the ways in which owners can withdraw funds from a small business were described as including drawings; wages; the provision of perks to the owners; and, in the case of a small corporation, dividends and directors fees. It is important for the analyst to distinguish between payments made to the owners to recompense them for their human-resource inputs and payments made to the owners to compensate them for their capital contribution. Dividends reward the capital contribution.

As is the case with their larger cousins, the dividend policies of small businesses exhibit the **clientele effect.** Different owners of the small business or different groups of owners have different requirements. Some of the owners will be working for the business, others will be passive investors. In these cases, the determination of whether payments are made as wages, perks, directors' fees, or dividends will depend on the needs of those individuals.

 CONCEPT CHECK

1. *What is the impact of the dividend decision on funding the small business?*
2. *What is the clientele effect?*

SUMMARY

✦ This chapter described the difficulties faced by the smaller business in locating its funding, especially in the case of the growing firm.

✦ Equity sources include retained earnings and additional contributions by the original owners, but, eventually, the needs of the firm can outstrip the ability of its owners to contribute. Under these circumstances, the firm either ceases to grow or new contributors are located.

✦ The problems associated with new contributors (and with original owners), especially in the area of control, were discussed and a number of recommendations suggested. Because the potential set of problems is as large as the number of people involved, it is very difficult to suggest a comprehensive list of "dos and don'ts."

owners to contribute. Under these circumstances, the firm either ceases to grow or new contributors are located.

✦ The problems associated with new contributors (and with original owners), especially in the area of control, were discussed and a number of recommendations suggested. Because the potential set of problems is as large as the number of people involved, it is very difficult to suggest a comprehensive list of "dos and don'ts."

✦ The types of debt financing, the cash-flow patterns associated with each, and the problems associated with the allocation of payments between interest and repayment were described and various methods of computation were described.

✦ The needs of the banker were described and the "Five Cs" of credit were identified.

✦ The capital-structure decision was examined for the case of the small business, and the objective of minimizing the weighted average cost of capital was introduced. Pecking-order theory was held to apply to both larger and smaller businesses.

✦ The complication of the need to withdraw funds for current consumption and its commensurate impact on the funding of the business was described.

✦ The role of leasing and its importance in the case of the small business were identified and the method of comparison with borrowing presented.

THE CASE—PART NINE

In early 2002 Dave's Bikes & Co. is approached by a large local mountain-bike retailing firm that wants Dave's Bikes to become their sole supplier. Dave has the productive capacity to cope with the increased manufacturing needs; however, he requires extra funding for taking on a part-time assistant, purchasing raw materials, etc.

ASSIGNMENT 9.1

Required

1. Describe the types of problems Dave will possibly encounter as a small business seeking new funding.
2. How would your answer to question 1 differ if Dave's Bikes was a large business?
3. What sources are available to Dave for acquiring new funding? Which of the sources do you expect Dave to prefer?
4. Do you expect Dave to seek long-term or short-term funding? Explain.

ASSIGNMENT 9.2

In 2002 Dave considers borrowing against his house and using these funds to finance the business.

Required

1. What different types of loans are available? Explain the advantages and disadvantages of each.
2. At this stage of growth in the business, which type of loan do you expect Dave to be interested in? Justify your answer.

ASSIGNMENT 9.3

In 2002 a national corporation expresses interest in buying 40 percent of Dave's Bikes & Co.

Required
1. Advise Dave of the likely benefits and problems that could be faced in such an arrangement.
2. If the corporation is interested in purchasing 65 percent of Dave's business, would your answer remain the same? What other factors should Dave now consider?

ASSIGNMENT 9.4

In considering his funding needs for 2002 and beyond, Dave examines the prospects of borrowing short-term funds only.

Required
1. Explain to Dave the sources of short-term debt.
2. Which of the sources that you identified have the least cost attached?
3. Advise Dave on which source(s) of short-term debt you believe are most appropriate to fund his increased output.

ASSIGNMENT 9.5

Dave has heard the term *optimal capital structure* used when businesspersons discuss debt and equity, but is not quite sure what the term means.

Required
1. Explain to Dave what an optimal capital structure is.
2. Why might Dave's business not be able to achieve an optimal capital structure? Who are the people imposing the limits?

ASSIGNMENT 9.6

At the beginning of 2002, Dave needs to make a decision about how he is to be reimbursed for his activity and his investment. One of the options that he considers is the payment of a larger dividend.

Required
1. Explain how a dividend paid to Dave differs from his wages.
2. Describe the clientele effect as it pertains to small businesses.

SELECTED ADDITIONAL READINGS

Beedles, W. L. 1992. Small firm equity cost: Evidence from Australia. *Journal of Small Business Management* (January): 57–65.

McMahon, R. G., S. Holmes, P. J. Hutchinson, and D. M. Forsaith. 1993. *Small enterprise financial management theory and practice.* (Sydney, Australia: Harcourt Brace): 397–423.

Osteryoung, J. S., and D. E. McCarty. 1985. *Analytical techniques for financial management.* (New York: John Wiley & Sons): 170–183.

Stoll, H. R., and A. J. Curley. 1970. Small business and the new issues market for equities. *Journal of Financial and Quantitative Analysis* 5(3): 309–322.

BUSINESS VALUATION

OBJECTIVES

1. *Examine the reasons why business valuations need to be undertaken*
2. *Describe the role of comparable information in the valuation process*
3. *Discuss the general factors affecting business values*
4. *Examine asset-based and income-based methods of valuation*
5. *Describe how cash flows and the appropriate discount rate can be estimated*
6. *Describe the adjustments that need to be made in the cases of minority and controlling holdings*

10.1 INTRODUCTION

If someone owns one hundred shares in IBM, their value can be readily obtained by looking at the morning newspaper or watching a financial news program on television. However, if one owns a small business there is no convenient way to ascertain the market value of its equity. This chapter's purpose is to develop a methodology for the valuation of a small business.

In Chapter 1 and Chapter 9 a small business was described as one without access to public equity markets (i.e., not publicly traded). It is this lack of marketability that substantially differentiates a small business from a large one. In the case of the publicly listed corporation, regulatory agencies place many restrictions on accounting, management behavior, and financial reporting. However, in the case of many small firms, many of these formal requirements exist only superficially, so that not only is the current value of the business unknown, but also the information a person relies on in making a valuation is less than ideal.

The theory of finance implies that the objective of financial management is to maximize the value of a firm, thereby maximizing the value of the owners' equity. While this may be an insufficient goal in the case of the small business (because many small-business owners are lifestylers rather than value maximizers), nevertheless it remains an underlying tenet of business valuation and suggests the importance of assessing any periodic change in value of a firm. For example, if a firm's value is declining over time, the owner should be given the option of taking action. It is not uncommon to see a firm's value decline (e.g., as a result of increased competition) without any recognition of this on the part of the firm's owners until the firm faces financial distress. If the owner of such a firm had realized that its market value was falling, steps could have been taken to mitigate the problem—the firm could either have been liquidated while some value still existed or, alternatively, steps could have been taken to counter the fundamental problem, thus reversing the diminution of its value.

The theory of finance also suggests that the value of any business is equal to the present value of its future cash flows. Therefore, there are two critical elements to be considered in the valuation process:

1. the estimation of future cash flows
2. the estimation of a required rate of return

While this discussion will use the present value of future income as a benchmark, there are many cases in which businesses sell at values either higher or lower than the present value of the future income. A business can sell below the present value of its income if there is some urgency associated with its sale, for example, as a consequence of the death of a key person (a person whose performance is critical to the success of the business).

There may also be some unique supply-and-demand elements that result in a business not selling for the present value of its future cash flows. These supply-and-demand elements normally come into consideration at two times in the life cycle of an industry. First, when an industry begins growing rapidly in its infancy one will often see firms selling for a higher price than the present value of their cash flows. Second, when an industry is declining, one will often see businesses selling for less than the present value of their future cash flows.

There are many reasons why a small firm might need to be valued, including the following:

♦ changes in the ownership of a business
♦ ascertaining if goals are being met
♦ taxation
♦ seeking finance
♦ legal reasons

CHANGES IN THE OWNERSHIP OF A BUSINESS

A contemplated change in ownership is one of the events that predicates the need for a valuation of a business. In the case of an "open market" purchase and sale, it is likely that both the purchaser and the vendor will want to know just what it is that they are buying and selling, respectively.

If a business is incorporated, then it is possible that the equity of the firm will be the object of sale rather than its assets. However, this is rarely the case with small-business debt. If there is debt in the capital structure, it is likely that it will be secured, among other things, by the personal guarantees of the owners of the business. Because these guarantees are personal to the owner at the time, it is unlikely that lenders will transfer their rights directly to a new owner.

If the business is not incorporated (i.e., is a sole proprietorship or partnership) then it will certainly be the assets that are being bought and sold rather than the equity, because there is no legal vehicle for equity in these circumstances—there are no equity securities (shares) to be transferred.

It is important to distinguish between the two types of sales, not only because of fundamental differences between assets and equity, but also because of the rights and obligations that are being transferred at the same time. For example, a ski resort in New Zealand recently changed ownership. The previous owner had sold lifetime lift passes to a number of people. The new purchasers refused to honor the obligation incurred by the previous owner. How can this be so? The new owners purchased the assets from the previous (corporate) owner. They did not buy the liabilities (both the equity and the obligation to honor the contingent claim). Had the new owners bought the firm's equity they would have had to meet the obligations of the company.

For most small businesses that are sold, the purchaser generally will buy the assets rather than the equity. Equity, as was demonstrated above, is fraught with difficulties. If there is an old tax liability of the business and the business is sold with equity, then the new equityholders are still liable, even though they were not party to the act. If a product liability suit comes forward that was incurred many years ago, then the new equityholders are still liable. As a general rule, it is always best to purchase the assets and not the equity of an existing business.

ASCERTAINING IF GOALS ARE BEING MET

Increasingly, one sees performance awards conferred on the management of a business to encourage their performance. These may take the form of cash bonuses or share options. Where a manager is in control of a "profit center," one of the performance measures is often some chosen element (such as divisional profit) divided by another element (such as the value of business). In these circumstances, both elements need to be determined objectively.

In addition, as already suggested, the owner of a business needs to know how it is performing, both temporally (over time) and comparatively (compared to similar firms).

TAXATION

The federal and state governments levy taxation on value in many different ways. Depending on the particular state in which the business operates, taxes on transfers, gifts, or inheritances may be levied. Capital gains and **property taxes** may also apply.

Where open-market transfers occur at "arm's length," the price of the transfer is generally accepted by the revenue authority as the taxable value, but where the transfer is less than at "arm's length" (e.g., within a family) it is always desirable (or necessary, as the case may be) to obtain a valuation of the assets being transferred.

SEEKING FINANCE

Borrowing money is a major reason for appraising the assets of a business. Lenders seek confirmation of two things when considering whether or not to advance money to a business. They want to ascertain the ability of the business to service the commitments associated with the loan (the pro formas assist here) and the security margin provided by the underlying assets over which they hold security. This latter requirement means that they need to know the value of those assets.

While the financial statements of the business provide the intending lender with a considerable amount of information, the constraints of the accounting process preclude the inclusion of assets at market values (unless they are lower than book values). Also, new businesses do not have financial statements that they can supply to the lender.

LEGAL REASONS

Divorce settlements and the distribution of estates to beneficiaries provide two family orientated reasons why a business might need to be valued. Non-family reasons for valuations include the settlement of damage claims, claims arising through broken contractual arrangements, and claims for compensation, where assets are taken by the government. This latter area includes claims where real property is taken for a public purpose, such as widening a road or installing a pipeline, and this governmental function is a fruitful source of income for real-estate appraisers.

 CONCEPT CHECK

1. *Why is value maximization an insufficient descriptor of the behavior of the small-firm owner?*
2. *What events, other than life-cycle stages, might result in a business selling for a price that differs from the present value of its cash flows?*
3. *Why do privately held businesses need to be valued?*
4. *What impediments are there to the sale of the equity of an indebted proprietorship?*
5. *In the ski resort example mentioned earlier, why did the new owners not have to meet the obligations of the original owners?*

10.2 THE ROLE OF COMPARABLES

COMPARABLE SALES

When undertaking the valuation of any asset, it is always a good idea to find comparable sales. These are assets or resources that are similar to the asset or resource being valued. Possible sources of this information are local business brokers and the Institute of Business Appraisers.[1] However, it is often very difficult to find truly comparable sales. While the analyst may be able to ascertain the price of the transaction, with most transactions there is just not enough other information available to draw meaningful comparisons.

Some analysts like to compare the equity of small privately held companies with public firms. However, this is not a valid approach to the valuation of most small businesses. First, the financial performance of large firms[2] is significantly different from that of small firms, and second, the equity of

---

[1]The Institute of Business Appraisers is located at Suite 15, 112 South Federal Highway, Boynton Beach, FL 33435.

[2]See J. S. Osteryoung, R. L. Constand, and D. Nast, 1992, 35–46.

public firms seem to be approximately 30 percent[3] more valuable than that of equivalent private firms. This phenomenon occurs because public firms offer investors liquidity in their investment; investors in public companies can easily exchange their equity holding for cash. Investors do not have this liquidity opportunity in the case of the private firm. It is therefore almost impossible to compare the values of small businesses with those of public corporations.

Publicly traded firms are frequently used for valuation purposes. However, these firms are *not* comparable in that the public firm has liquidity and generally has a well-diversified customer base. Additionally, the large firm has the ability to attract employees with a great deal of specialization (e.g. human-resource manager). For these reasons, it is normally not a good idea to compare small businesses with large public companies.

 CONCEPT CHECK

1. *Why is it necessary to observe the transactions of comparable businesses?*
2. *State some reasons why, for valuation purposes, small businesses should not be compared to public companies.*

10.3   GENERAL FACTORS INFLUENCING VALUE

THE ECONOMY

The future earning potential of the business depends on both economy-wide and industry-specific factors (as well as firm-specific factors, of course). While many small firms' earnings vary with general economic activity, the earnings of most small businesses will be more closely related to the local or regional environments in which the business operates than to national economic activity. However, local and regional environments will, in turn, be influenced by general economic conditions.

What does this mean for the appraiser of the small business? Simply that when a small business is valued, the appraiser must be cognizant of the economic conditions of the area in which the business operates.

THE INDUSTRY

While the economy is an important factor to be considered, the growth conditions pertaining to the industry in which a business operates are even more important. In 1985, the future for video-rental stores looked rosy, with

---

[3]See J. D. Emory, 1992, 208–212.

excellent growth anticipated in the industry. However, by 1994, the growth for small businesses in this sector was severely truncated by the large chains entering and capturing the market (e.g., Blockbuster Videos). Clearly, a video store in 1985 with a given level of earnings would have been valued much higher than the same firm with the same level of earnings in 1994.

One very good source of information on industry and economic forecasts is the *U.S. Industrial Outlook* developed by the Department of Commerce and published each year by the Government Printing Office. This publication provides historical statistics as well as forecasts for each industry and the economy.

Understanding the product or service rendered by a business is very important in the valuation process. For example, many "pet" stores do not carry pets, but rather pet supplies. Grocery stores really are no longer grocery stores but a combination of drug stores, delicatessens, restaurants, and traditional grocery stores. It is important to define the product or service being provided to ensure that valuation is focused on the correct sources of the firm's income.

Market potential and competition are linked together. The size and growth of the market and of the competition a firm faces or will face in the future in that market are important considerations in the appraisal of a business. When assessing the competitive environment, one must consider both existing and potential competitors. For example, suppose a general store is operating in a given market area without any competition. If it is highly probable that Wal-Mart will begin to compete in this market in the near future, then it is imperative that this information be incorporated into the valuation by allowing for the effects of a potential reduction in sales revenue and the consequent effect of this decline on the earnings of the business.

Information relating to the market size can sometimes be provided by the local chamber of commerce. Additionally, someone (usually at a university) in most states publishes local statistics. For example, the *Florida Statistical Abstract* is published annually by the University of Florida and provides county-by-county demographics. This demographic information is important if the firm's income is sensitive to demographic factors. For example, if a firm's principal customers are individuals over age sixty-five, then demographic information will help to ascertain market size and growth potential. By obtaining data for this age group over time and comparing it to the firm's financial performance, one gains useful information about how sensitive the firm has been to changes in this demographic factor.

 CONCEPT CHECK

1. Why is it necessary to consider economic events when valuing a small business?
2. What is the effect of potential competition on the value of the small business? Why does this effect occur?
3. Why is the industry sector in which a small business operates an important factor to consider in the appraisal context?

10.4 METHODS OF VALUATION

While there are many different ways of categorizing the major approaches to the valuation of a business, most techniques can be classified as either asset-based or income-based.

ASSET-BASED VALUATION METHODS

Asset-based valuations are predicated on the notion that, if the assets of the firm can be valued, the value of equity can be established by deducting the value of existing debt from the value of the firm's assets. The usual appraisal method in these circumstances is to value the firm's assets individually (for example, real estate, plant, and machinery) and add them up to give the value of the firm. For example, if valuing a farm, it is best to apply an asset-based appraisal method.

Appraisers commonly apply three fundamental asset-based approaches to the valuation process: book value, replacement value, and liquidation value.

Book Value

Book values of assets are based on their historical costs, which bear no relationship to either value at the time of purchase or replacement cost today. The allowance of depreciation is a subjective assessment of the reduction in value of the assets arising from their use. Therefore, book values are of historical interest only.

Despite this, book values do provide a guide to the types of decisions that have been made in the past and provide an objective listing of the assets of the business insofar as the list records the assets that have been purchased and may still be in existence.

Replacement Value

The replacement value approach considers that the value of a business is related to the cost of replacing its assets with alternative, but similar, assets. If an asset-based business is for sale for $600,000 but the assets can be replaced for $400,000, then the market value should reflect the replacement value of $400,000. For example, if one needs to value a manufacturing business, he might compare the firm under consideration to comparable firms that have recently sold. The valuation of some types of machinery is likewise sometimes relatively easily ascertained by following machinery auctions or contacting dealers who specialize in used machinery.

Unfortunately, it is not always so easy as the above discussion might suggest. In some circumstances, machinery (and even real estate) may have been "custom-built" and comparable sales may not be evident. In these cases, it is difficult to be quite so objective and values may have to be related to replacement cost (i.e., a new asset) less depreciation.

Of course, this method ignores any goodwill that might be associated with a particular business that cannot be related to its assets. So, the replacement value method, if applied to the valuation of the firm, is only really applicable if the firm does not have any significant goodwill. It is only applicable to the valuation of net **tangible assets**.

Liquidation Value

Appraisers frequently discover that a business is worth less in use (as a going concern) than it is when liquidated. The **value in use** (also called the **going-concern value**) assumes that the value is predicated on the continued existence of the firm as a viable business. The value of any business is the higher of its value in use or its value in liquidation. For example, if the value in use of a business is $200,000, while the liquidation value of the business is $300,000, then the business must be worth the $300,000. After all, a potential investor always has the option of purchasing the business and then liquidating it.

INCOME-BASED METHODS

The Principle

The fundamental principle underpinning income-based valuation methods is that *the value of any asset is equal to the present value of its estimated (pro forma) future cash flows*. The price of a bond, the price of a shopping center, or the price of a small business must all be related to the present value of future income streams. Recall the basic valuation equation:

$$\text{Value} = \sum_{t=1}^{n} \frac{\overline{CF_t}}{(1 + r)^t}$$

where: CF_t = the expected cash flow in period t
r = the required rate of return, discount rate, or opportunity rate
n = the final period of the analysis

This equation states that the value of a business is the present value of all future income (i.e., cash) flows. As with most things, however, there are many decisions and much analysis to be done in order to operationalize this equation.

Three Techniques

The Discounted Cash-Flow Technique The basic valuation equation exhibited above leads to two techniques of application. The first technique must be applied where the periodic cash flows to be discounted cannot be regarded as annuities (i.e., they differ). Under these circumstances, the only option available to the appraiser is to develop a set of pro forma statements and, from the information thus supplied, discount each periodic cash flow separately.

How many periods into the future should the forecasted cash flows of a business be extended? The answer depends on the stability of the revenue stream and the viability of the industry. While these items are subjective, most professional appraisers use five to seven years as the outer limit for their pro formas. This rule of thumb is not based on any theoretical tenet, however, it does seem reasonable that, as a forecast is expanded over a longer time period, the confidence in the forecast decreases. In addition, the discounting process itself rather dilutes the impact of distant cash flows because the discount factor decreases with time. Therefore, the period of time between five to seven years seems reasonable for an appraisal.

While five to seven years seems reasonable for the forecast period, the business does have value *after* that point. The value of the business after the forecast period is called the **terminal value.** There are two ways to compute the terminal value of the business. First, one can use the liquidation value of the business expected at the end of the time-frame under consideration, or, second, the last year's free cash flow can be considered a perpetuity and should therefore be capitalized. The terminal value must then be discounted back to a present value. The discount rate that applied in this step of the process should be an after-tax rate because the terminal value is capital and is not taxed (ignoring any capital gains tax). Before- and after-tax rates will be discussed later.

For example, if the before-tax free cash flow in the last year of the projections was $60,000 and the appropriate pre-tax discount rate is 30 percent, the terminal value is $60,000 divided by 0.3, or $200,000. This value appears in the last year of the forecast period and can then be converted back to its present value by discounting it at the appropriate post-tax discount rate (say, 20 percent) for the appropriate number of periods (seven) to give a present value of $200,000 multiplied by 0.2791, or $55,820.

The Capitalization Technique In circumstances where the expected periodic cash flows of a business are constant in the form of an annuity the formula below can be used:

$$\text{Market value} = \frac{\text{annual cash flows}}{\text{required yield}}$$

The required yield can be determined via the observation of the earnings yields of similar firms.

For example, consider valuing a small business with annual cash flows that are predicted to be $90,000 into the foreseeable future, when firms of this type have observed yields of 30 percent.

$$\text{Market value} = \frac{\$90,000}{30\%} = \$300,000$$

One of the deficiencies of the **earnings-yield method** as applied in this form is that it ignores growth—it capitalizes a constant annuity—and it is therefore best suited to mature, non-growth firms.

The other major deficiency inherent in this method is that it assumes that the future maintainable profit is a perpetuity (i.e., runs forever). How important is this assumption? If one uses a 20 percent rate as the basis for investigation of this problem, and there is a set of discount tables available, look at the present value of annuity table for 20 percent. Over time the factor tends toward 5, which is the reciprocal of the interest rate. At period nine, the factor is 4. So if the future maintainable profit will not last beyond period nine, its value (assuming no terminal value) will be overstated by about 25 percent. However, if one looks at the factor for twenty periods, it is about 4.8, in which case, as long as the future maintainable profit lasts for twenty periods, the extent of the overvaluation will be slight.

The higher the discount rate, the less the overvaluation effect of this method. The lower the discount rate, the greater the overvaluation effect. Check the 10 percent and 30 percent tables to observe this effect.

Note that, from this point forward, this text will use the terms *discount rate* and *capitalization rate* interchangeably, but the reader should remember that the techniques that employ them are fundamentally different.

The Perpetual-Growth Technique Where there is some evidence that the growth rate of cash flows is likely to be constant into the foreseeable future (which must be reasonably far into the future), the perpetual-growth model can assist in the discounting process. This model is of the following form:

$$V = \frac{CF_1}{r - g}$$

where: g = the predicted constant growth rate
CF_1 = the cash flow occurring at the end of period 1
r = the appropriate discount rate

This model assumes constant growth forever! If this assumption is not relevant, then the discounted cash-flow method is the more accurate method of determining a value.

Reconsider the video store example given earlier. The reason that its value has fallen is that the g component of the formula has diminished. Consider that value is inversely proportional to the denominator in the formula; then the smaller the denominator $(r - g)$ the larger the value. A decrease in g will increase the size of the denominator and result in a lower value. The lesson to be learned from the video store example is that appraisers should be conservative in their estimates of future growth. Nothing attracts competition more than perceived high growth, and thus the growth on an individual-firm basis is usually much less than the industry growth rate.

Firms tend to grow quickly early in their life cycles. At the extreme, sales grow from a zero base to "something" in the first year—an infinite growth rate, at least in arithmetic terms.

◆ EXHIBIT 10.1

TWO INCOME-BASED APPROACHES

Ownership	Approach
Unincorporated	Net operating income
Incorporated	Net income

WHICH CASH FLOW SHOULD BE CAPITALIZED?

As with many of the points discussed here, there are two fundamental approaches to the definition of relevant cash flow. The unifying economic concept is that *the cash flow that is to be valued must accrue to the asset being valued.*

Exhibit 10.1 depicts the two approaches and the types of ownership that could predicate their application.

Net Operating Income Approach

When valuing a business that is not incorporated, it is extremely unlikely that its equity can be sold separately from its debt. Not only is there no formal vehicle that represents the ownership of equity in an unincorporated business (no equity "security"), but also the debt funding of such a business is personal to the owners at the time and they do not have the right to transfer it. In this case, to determine the value of equity, the firm must be valued first, then the value of any debt must be deducted in order to arrive at the value of equity. At that point, the value of equity can naturally be compared with the net income accruing to equity in order to derive the expected return on equity.

For example, consider the case of Ramirez Manufacturing, a firm with a future maintainable net operating income of $45,000 for which the appropriate dicount rate is determined to be 15 percent. The value of the firm is therefore $300,000. If the present debt is $100,000, bearing 10 percent interest, then one can say that the value of equity is $200,000 and that the return on equity (ignoring taxes) is $35,000 divided by $200,000, or 17.5 percent. Firms that are strongly asset-based (such as real estate and farming) tend to be valued in this way.

Net Income Approach

On the other hand, when valuing a business that is incorporated, it is theoretically possible for its equity to be sold separately from its debt (although the debt instrument may contain covenants that restrict this right). In this case, to determine the value of equity, the firm need not be valued first. It may be possible to value the debt and equity separately and then add them together to arrive at the value of the firm. This is the approach usually taken when valuing larger publicly listed companies where the value of equity can be readily established by reference to its publicly determined price.

Reconsider the case of Ramirez Manufacturing, with its future maintainable net operating income of $45,000 and future maintainable earnings of $35,000. In this case the appropriate discount rate for equity has been determined to be 17.5 percent. The value of equity is therefore $200,000. If the present debt is $100,000, bearing 10 percent interest, then one can say that the value of the firm is $300,000, and the return on assets (ignoring taxation) is $45,000 divided by $300,000, or 15 percent.

Firms that are strongly income-based (such as service industries) tend to be valued in this way if they are incorporated. Overall, though, it should not matter which method is applied, one should arrive at the same division of assets into debt and equity. Which method is chosen will depend largely on the types of comparable information that is available.

REVENUE MULTIPLIER METHOD

The last approach to valuation is the use of a revenue multiplier. This technique relates the value of a firm exclusively to its revenue. If a firm has revenue of $50,000 and the multiplier is 4, then the value of the business is $200,000. Obviously, this approach has many serious deficiencies. First, two firms can have the same revenue but significantly different profits and yet are given the same value by application of this technique. Second, this valuation approach ignores any future income or cash-flow changes. It is not a very good approach to use in the valuation process.[4]

 CONCEPT CHECK

1. *When should an asset-based method be used to value a small business?*
2. *Why shouldn't the book values of assets be used as the basis for a valuation?*
3. *When should the liquidation value be used as the basis for an appraisal?*
4. *What difficulties do appraisers face when attempting to use the discounted cash-flow technique?*
5. *Describe the strengths and weaknesses of the capitalization technique.*
6. *Describe the strengths and weaknesses of the perpetual-growth technique.*
7. *Compare and contrast the use of the net operating income and the net income approaches.*
8. *Why shouldn't appraisers use revenue multipliers?*

---

[4]For those wishing to pursue the nature of the revenue multiplier further, Shannon Pratt's text, *Valuing a Business,* deals with this subject in some depth.

10.5   STEPS IN THE VALUATION PROCESS

The valuation of a small business is a five-step process:

1. Define what is being valued
2. Specify the purpose of the valuation
3. Adjust prior earnings and cash flows to represent financial performance
4. Develop a pro forma statement for the future financial performance of the business
5. Choose a valuation approach that is relevant to the business being valued

The first step is to understand what is being valued. This may be either the assets of the business or its equity (assuming it is a corporation). The great majority of the sales of small businesses involve sales of assets rather than sales of equity. Remember that if the purchaser of a business buys its equity then the new owner may be responsible for all of the obligations of the business, no matter when they were incurred. So, if a firm has an outstanding lawsuit that began three years ago, the new owner of the equity would be responsible for any outcome of that litigation. But, regardless of whether it uses the assets of the business or its equity, a valuation may still be based on the present value of the expected future income stream.

The second step is to define the purpose of the valuation. There is a very rational reason for this step. Consider two examples. In the first example, a firm is being valued for a divorce litigation with the existing owners remaining in place. Assuming that the business is performing well, it will clearly have more value under these circumstances than if an unrelated third party was to take over the business. This situation occurs because profitability often declines (although perhaps only temporarily) when a new owner takes over. However, if, as the result of a divorce proceeding, an existing owner stays in place, a decline in profitability is less likely.

The second example relates to the ability of businesses to carry the losses from previous years' operation forward to be offset against future income. Depending on the relevant legislation, it is possible that this right could be foregone with a change of ownership. If the business is unincorporated, the tax losses accrue to the individual proprietors and therefore the sale of the business does not affect their rights. But if the business is incorporated and it is the equity that is the object of the transfer, the advantage may be lost. If one is valuing the latter business, the purpose of the valuation would affect the approach taken. In other words, if the equity of such a business is valued for a potential purchaser, the tax losses may have no value; whereas if it is valued for the existing owners (e.g., a periodic valuation where there is no intent to sell), the tax losses do have value.

ESTIMATING CASH FLOWS

The first step in an earnings-based valuation is to calculate the expected (pro forma) income that is to be capitalized. This income figure should be based on the free cash flow that is expected for each future period. Recall that the development of pro forma statements was covered in Chapter 5.

The most difficult step in the valuation process is associated with the adjustment of the earnings, or cash flow, to represent the true economic performance of the firm. In the case of nearly all small businesses, it follows that reported earnings (or cash flows) will have to be adjusted for some or all of the following reasons before an earnings or cash-flow figure that can be used in valuation can be established.

✦ salary paid to the owner/manager
✦ perquisites paid to the owner/manager
✦ wages paid to owner/managers' relatives
✦ financing expenses
✦ expenses that would be different under a new owner
✦ cash revenues are not recorded

As the reader proceeds through this section, remember the principle—one is trying to establish the true level of earnings or cash flows of the business.

Owners' Salary

In the case of an incorporated business the owner/manager may draw a salary as well as or in lieu of a dividend. There are many reasons for this, some of which relate to the differential tax rates accruing to wages and dividends, and some of which relate to the multiple ownership situations in which dividends may be paid to non-working owners.

In the cases of partnerships and sole proprietorships, there will not normally be any evident extraction for salary expense in the financial reports. In these cases, tax law does not distinguish the owner from the business, and any income in excess of expenses is considered taxable income to the owner. In other words, the owners of such businesses usually do not indicate any type of salary payments for themselves.

When adjusting the income statement, the owner's salary must be adjusted to reflect a reasonable wage. In the case of an incorporated business, owners can specify whatever salaries they like, although tax laws do set some limits on this. Both the Robert Morris and Associates' (RMA) *Annual Statement Studies* and *Financial Studies of the Small Business*[5] describe the average compensation paid to owners of small businesses. If, according to the RMA *Annual Statement Studies,* the average owner/manager's compensation is 3 percent of sales, then the reported income statement should be adjusted to reflect this level of compensation.

In the example of the XYZ Corporation (depicted in Exhibit 10.2) $60,000 should be adjusted downward to reflect a comparable salary of $30,000.

---

[5]*Annual Statement Studies* is published by Robert Morris and Associates in Philadelphia, PA, and *Financial Studies of Small Business* is published by Financial Research Associates in Winter Haven, FL.

XYZ CORPORATION INCOME STATEMENT

Revenue	$1,000,000
Cost of sales	(600,000)
Gross profit	$ 400,000
Non-owner wages	(200,000)
Owner wages	(60,000)
Overhead expense	(75,000)
Net operating income	$ 65,000
Interest	(40,000)
Net profit before tax	$ 25,000

Consequently, the reported net profit increases from $25,000 to $55,000. Allowances for the owners' wages significantly impact the net profit.

Owners' Perquisites

The adjustments to income (also known as the normalizing process) must account for any perquisites paid to the owner/manager. Examples of this type of reported expense include the personal use of business vehicles, personal expenses that are paid by the business (e.g., fuel, meals, and travel expenses), and personal financing expenses that are paid by the business (such as cheap loans from the business or above-normal interest payments to family members advancing loan capital to the business). The financing expenses in particular will be examined later in this section because, in some circumstances, they can be ignored.

If any of these perquisites exist, they must be eliminated from the expenses of the business in order to produce a true picture of the financial performance of the business. In economic terms, they have already been allowed for in the computation of the owners' reward.

Wages Paid to Relatives

Whenever a relative of the owner works in a small business, financial abuse is likely. The abuse can result in either underpayment or overpayment in relation to the contribution. If this occurs, and it does frequently, then payments to the relative must be adjusted to reflect market conditions and their marginal-value products.

Suppose the XYZ Corporation employs the owner/manager's niece as a delivery person, paying her $5,000 a year for part-time work. Other delivery people in this business working the same number of hours make only $3,000 a year. In this case, the salary expense should be reduced by $2,000 and the earnings before taxes should increase by $2,000.

Expenses That Differ from the Norm

Frequently, a prospective new owner will consider that the existing structure of the firm's expenses is wrong. The appraisal objective is to determine what the market norm would be. If the present expense structure reflects the norm then no adjustments should be made, but to the extent that the present expense structure does not reflect the norm, adjustments should be considered.

However, when valuing a business for a particular purpose, say for an intended purchaser, it may be relevant to include in the expenses those expenses reflecting the new owner's wishes. This will provide the potential owner with a pro forma income statement that accounts for his intentions. However, unless the new owner's intentions imitate the norm, a valuation based on those intentions will not reflect the norm either.

For example, a video store in a small city in Georgia was being valued by one of the authors of this text. As part of this store's operation, it incurred $2,000 of annual expenses that would not normally occur in a store of this type. In this case, the earnings figure was increased by $2,000 to account for these unnecessary expenses.

Cash Revenues That Are Not Recorded

Sometimes small businesses do not report all their revenue in order to avoid paying taxes on them. While this action is not condoned, it is very common, and for this there must be an adjustment. Cash revenues that are not recorded are usually disclosed by the seller of a business, who claims that the reported income statements understate the true position. The validity of these statements can be tested by comparing the number of units purchased to the units sold, or by examining the margins reported. However, it is often very difficult to ascertain just what is passed "under the table."

Financing Expenses

If the valuation is of the assets of the business, then it follows that the adjusted net operating income reflects the value in the firm without any financing considerations. For example, if an analyst was preparing the valuation for the sale of the assets of XYZ Corporation, then the financing mix of any prospective purchaser is irrelevant.

Sometimes, however, financing expenses (interest expenses) will be relevant. Financing expenses are relevant when valuing the equity of a business and, in this case, should be included in the expenses.

XYZ CORPORATION EXAMPLE

Assume that the following adjustments are reasonable in the case of XYZ Corporation (Exhibit 10.2).

+ Overheads include perks valued at $10,000
+ Owners' wages overstate the economic contribution by $30,000
+ Non-owner wages are understated by $2,000 (the niece)
+ Overhead expense includes $5,000 in abnormal expenses
+ Revenues understate the true position by $200 per week taken from the "till" by the owner

♦ EXHIBIT 10.3

XYZ CORPORATION INCOME STATEMENT (AFTER ADJUSTMENT)

Revenue	$1,010,400
Cost of sales	(600,000)
Gross profit	$ 410,400
Non-owner wages	(202,000)
Owner wages	(30,000)
Overhead expense	(80,000)
Net operating income	$ 98,400
Interest paid	(40,000)
Net profit before tax	$ 58,400

Exhibit 10.3 shows this situation. One can see from this that the profits are $33,400 better than that reported. This would have a significant impact on the value of this firm.

FREE CASH FLOW AND TAXATION

Free cash flow can be defined as the cash that is available after paying all relevant expenses. A surplus free cash flow may occur after the adjustments are accounted for, as suggested above.[6] Free cash flow equates to long-term expected net profit adjusted for non-cash charges (such as depreciation, which was included in the overhead expenses in the XYZ Corporation example) and is preferred to profit as a basis for the valuation process.[7] For example, if a firm has a forecasted level of income in period one of $125,000 and depreciation of $10,000, then the free cash flow is $135,000 to use in the valuation equation. If the firm has to purchase new equipment in period one for $5,000, then the free cash flow is reduced further, to $130,000. Adjustments also need to be made for changes in net working capital on the basis that an increase in net working capital reduces free cash flow, while a decrease in net working capital increases free cash flow by the amount of the change.

Should income flows and the free cash flow be reduced by taxes? If the capitalization rate being used is a pre-tax rate, then the question becomes of no importance—the analyst should apply a pre-tax capitalization rate to pre-tax cash flows. However, there is no doubt that some potential purchasers do

---

[6]The definition of free cash flow varies somewhat from person to person. While it is generally considered to be earnings after tax plus depreciation expense plus or minus any changes in working capital, another variation includes provision for capital maintenance.

[7]J. W. Lippitt and N. J. Mastracchio, Jr., 1993, pp. 52–61 suggest that the valuation of a small business will be incorrect if profits are used rather than free cash flow.

look at the "bottom line" after tax. In this case, the discount rate should be adjusted to reflect the taxation effect:

$$\text{Capitalization rate}_{\text{post-tax}} = \text{capitalization rate}_{\text{pre-tax}}(1 - t)$$

where: t = the appropriate tax rate

The difficulty with the after-tax approach is the designation of the appropriate tax rate. In the case of large businesses, analysts usually assume that the appropriate tax rate is the corporate rate; especially in the case of unincorporated businesses the marginal tax rate of the average purchaser is impossible to realistically compute. Therefore, despite the desires of some would-be purchasers to establish an after-tax rate, it is a practical impossibility. At best, it is possible to apply the intending purchaser's tax rate to the expected before-tax income, establish the after-tax profit and then use this (together with the known value of equity, as calculated by capitalizing the before-tax cash flow at a before-tax capitalization rate) to determine that owner's potential after-tax return on investment.

At this point, refer to the discussion earlier in this chapter concerning the discount rate to be applied to a terminal value. Remember that before-tax cash flows should be discounted at a before-tax rate, while after-tax cash flows should be discounted at an after-tax rate (even if this makes the computation more onerous).

ESTIMATING THE DISCOUNT RATE

In general the discount rate for the equity of most small businesses appears to fall between 30 and 50 percent.[8] While this may, at first sight, seem very high, given the intrinsic risk of small businesses and their lack of liquidity both from operations and from the lack of markets for private equity stocks, it is not.

The studies by John Emory, reported in the *Business Valuation Review*,[9] show that the return on the equities of private companies is around 30 percent to 40 percent higher than public companies, reflecting their lower liquidity. This was ascertained by evaluating the return of companies before they went public and then again after they became publicly negotiable. Because of the higher risk and lower liquidity, the discount rate for private firms must be quite high.

The selected rate must also be commensurate with the risk of the business. The higher the risk, the higher the discount rate. The best test of a discount rate is to use the test of reasonableness; ask yourself what rate of return one would have to earn on the small-business investment to adequately compensate for its inherent risk.

---

[8]See W. D. Bygrave, 1994, p. 50.

[9]See Suggested Additional Readings for this chapter.

The discount rate to be used to relate the future cash flows to the present value of the business must represent a reasonable return to the owner of the business. This opportunity rate must reflect the risk and the required rate of return for any business in the same risk class.

One approach to finding such a discount rate or capitalization rate is to apply the "build-up method." This method bases the capitalization rate on the long-term Treasury bill rate and an average premium rate applicable to small stocks and a premium for risk and non-negotiability (also—confusingly—known as illiquidity, although it has nothing to do with the liquidity of the business itself, but rather with the liquidity of its capital).

The build-up method calls for the appraiser to subjectively ascertain the premiums for risk and illiquidity. Nevertheless, this method is used frequently.

A study by Ibbotson and Associates[10] of actual equity returns that investors received in different sized firms reported that the equities of the smallest 10 percent of publicly traded companies had an average return (including both dividends and share appreciation) of 20 percent per year over the previous ten to fifteen years. However, small firms (as we define them) do not have the liquidity of publicly traded companies.

With this background knowledge, assume that investors in small businesses expect to gain a return higher by about 30 percent to 40 percent over the 20 percent return reported in the Ibbotson studies. This suggests a return of between 26 percent and 28 percent for the strongest small firms. From this level, the discount rate must be adjusted for both the riskiness of the industry as well as for the specific risk of the firm. These last two adjustments are subjective and shown below are some of the factors that should be considered.

Industry factors	Firm factors
1. health of the industry	1. size of firm
2. growth rate in the industry	2. importance of owner
3. competition in the industry	3. growth rate in sales
4. technological developments in the industry	4. competition
	5. technological developments
	6. customer base

Clearly, the specification of a discount rate must include some judgment. However, that judgment must be based on sound financial tenets.

 CONCEPT CHECK

1. *Why is it important to adjust the financial statements of the business?*
2. *How is the income statement adjusted for the salary paid to the owner/manager?*
3. *Under what conditions are financing expenses relevant in the valuation process?*

---

[10]See Ibbotson and Associates, *Stocks, Bonds, Bills and Inflation, 1993 Yearbook* (Chicago, IL: Ibbotson and Associates, 1992).

4. *Why should conditions in the economy and industry be included in the valuation process?*
5. *What is free cash flow and why is it relevant for the valuation process?*
6. *How should taxation be included in the valuation process?*

10.6 TYPES OF VALUES

While this chapter has suggested that the purpose of a valuation may influence either the approach taken or the composition of the cash flows to be capitalized, the discussion has not yet addressed the issue of whether price equals value.

FAIR-MARKET VALUE AND INVESTMENT VALUE

Fair-market value (FMV) is a standard term that is regularly used to describe a particular type of valuation (either of real estate or of a business). The FMV is defined as the price of the business on a cash or cash-equivalent basis to which both the seller and buyer agree, neither operating under duress or undue time pressure and both having in their possession, or knowing, the relevant facts of business.

This definition of FMV assumes a cash transaction, but if the seller agrees to partially finance the deal, then the cash-equivalent of any advantage contained in this loan must be ascertained. For example, if the agreed terms of a purchase and sale agreement include a cash payment of $50,000 and a loan from the seller to the buyer of $100,000 amortized evenly over a five-year period at a 4 percent interest rate when the market rate for equivalent debt is 8 percent, then there is obviously some advantage accruing to the purchaser. The present value of the loan can be ascertained at $89,687 (the present value of the annuity—comprised of interest and principal repayment—of $22,462 for five years at 8 percent is $89,687); this is its cash equivalent. The fair-market value of this business, with a purchase price of $50,000 cash down and a seller loan of $100,000 at 4 percent for five years and a true market rate of interest of 8 percent, is only $139,687.

The term **investment value** is also used to describe the value of a business to a specific purchaser. It is not the same as the FMV. For example, if the buyer of a small business already owns several similar types of operations and the overhead from this purchase will be significantly less than the current operation, then the value to the purchaser is worth more than the value to the seller. In this case the synergistic gain accrues to the purchaser. This theory ignores the fact that the vendor may be aware of the potential synergy and may attempt to capture some of it by increasing the selling price to that purchaser.

PRICE VERSUS VALUE

While in an efficient market, price should always equal value, the market for small businesses can only be described as inefficient in this respect. Without addressing the assumptions underpinning the efficient-markets hypothesis in any depth, suffice it to say that this hypothesis is based on the notion of many rational buyers and sellers with homogeneous expectations and the inability of the market to support arbitrage profits.

In the case of many small businesses, the nature of an individual business and the perceptions of a relatively small number of potential purchasers shape the price that is paid when a small business is purchased. This suggests that, due to the thin market, small businesses may be underpriced relative to their fundamental values. The corollary to this suggestion must be therefore, that small businesses earn more than their risk-adjusted discount rates imply. This reasoning may form the basis for the value gains observed during the initial public offering (IPO) process and also for the presence of the illiquidity premium.

On the other hand, there are occasions when the reverse holds. For example, following the deregulation of the New Zealand economy and its labor market, many people found themselves jobless, but with a severance pay "nest-egg" burning a hole in their pockets. Many of these people went in search of small businesses (in relatively short supply) and were quite content to accept a relatively low return on their investment (some would say zero) in return for the provision of a job to go to and a regular income. They could be considered to be either working for nothing (and receiving a return on their capital investment) or receiving a low or zero return on their capital investment (and receiving a return for their labor and management). Many purchasers of small business are predominately purchasing an income stream, with little thought about the return on their investment.

The valuation of a particular small business, with all its firm-specific attributes and specializations, is a very daunting task when one considers that price may not equal value.

 CONCEPT CHECK

1. *Explain the difference between fair-market value and investment value.*
2. *Why doesn't price always equal value in the case of the small business?*
3. *Explain why values increase with an IPO.*

10.7 THE KEY-PERSON DISCOUNT

Personal goodwill is associated directly with the notion of the **key-person discount.** This is a discount from the present value of the firm that relates the value of a key person in a business.

Generally, the key person is the owner/manager and, the smaller the business, the more important the key person. This situation arises in a small business because the customer contact and majority of the major decisions are made by the owner/manager. If that person leaves the business, either through death or retirement, then the income of the business can decline even if a replacement manager can be found (there is always a learning curve for a new proprietor, even when the new person is highly skilled). A study by Lerch[11] evaluates the decline in value of public corporations after the unexpected death of the owner. It shows that the value, on average, of the firms investigated fell by about 30 percent.

While Lerch was looking at large public corporations, small private businesses are much more vulnerable to the loss of a key person. Therefore, any reduction for the loss of a key person in a small business is likely to be greater than the 30 percent reported in the Lerch study.

There are numerous ways to reduce the impact of the loss of a key person. Clearly, with an unexpected death, it is impossible to avoid this type of loss of value. However, in the case of a normal sale of a small business in which the owner has also been the manager, the loss of the key person can be significantly lessened by having the seller work in the business for some period following the change of ownership. This allows a gradual transition for both employees and customers from the old owner to the new. Similarly, the new purchasers can work in a business before it is purchased to reduce the key-person loss effect; or the new owner/manager can have the vendor establish specific operating procedures for the business. By following the operating procedures, the key-person loss effect can be minimized.

 CONCEPT CHECK

1. *What is the economic basis for dividing goodwill between that "belonging" to the business and that "belonging" to the owner?*
2. *What is the key-person discount and how is it incorporated into the valuation process?*

10.8   THE MINORITY DISCOUNT AND THE CONTROL PREMIUM

A business appraiser is frequently called on to evaluate either a minority or a controlling interest in a business. A minority interest is held when the owner of the interest holds less than 50 percent of the voting rights of the business; a controlling interest is held when the owner of the interest holds more than 50 percent of the voting rights. When two owners each own 50 percent, the control structure resembles that of a partnership where both parties own an equal interest; therefore this situation is referred to as the valuation of a *partnership interest.*

---

[11]See M. A. Lerch, 1992, pp. 183–194.

A minority interest implies that the owner does not have control of the business, i.e., its associated management and dividend policies. It is common to see an owner who has a controlling interest pay herself an excess salary. This arrangement imposes a cost on the minority shareholder. While abuse of the minority shareholder occurs with some regularity, the courts have held that the majority, or controlling, interest has a fiduciary responsibility to protect the interests of the minority position.[12] But, in spite of legal protection available to the minority shareholder, substantial discounts are routinely observed in the sale of minority interests, called **minority discounts.**

In an empirical study of minority discounts, Lerch[13] found the average discount to be between 24 percent and 27 percent. This means that fair-market value of a minority interest should be reduced by 24 percent to 27 percent. The more able and willing the controlling interest is to abuse the minority interest, the higher the minority discount should be.

The **control premium** provides a mirror image of the minority discount. Its value is related to the loss in value of the minority interest. Because the value of the firm is not changed by the relative control characteristics of its owners, what is lost by the minority interest must be gained by the controlling interest. In other words, any minority discount must result in a corresponding increase in the value of the controlling interest so that the value of the firm does not change.

For example, consider a firm with an appraised value of its equity equal to $600,000, comprising six thousand shares. Assume that the minority interest owns two thousand shares and the controlling interest owns four thousand shares. The value per share is $100 with the value of the minority being equal to $200,000. However, with a minority discount of 30 percent, this value is reduced to $140,000. The controlling interest is $400,000, but, with the control premium being equal to the minority discount, the value of the controlling interest increases to $460,000, or a control premium of 15 percent. The magnitude of the minority-interest discount and control-interest premium in percentage terms is not equal. However, any dollar shift between the minority interest and controlling interest must be equal so that the value of the firm will not change as a function of its ownership.

 CONCEPT CHECK

1. *How do a minority discount and a control premium arise?*
2. *Why is the control premium a mirror image of the sum of the minority discounts?*

---

[12]See F. H. O'Neal, 1986.

[13]See M. A. Lerch, 1991, pp. 7–13.

10.9 EXAMPLE

Assume an appraiser is valuing the assets of a restaurant with 1994 annual sales of $400,000. The firm has been in business for five years under the current management and has a steady following of loyal customers. The firm's growth rate in sales and earnings over the past five years has consistently averaged 5 percent; this is forecast for the next five years also. The market in which this firm operates is not expected to materially change over the next five years.

Exhibit 10.4 depicts a pro forma income statement of the business for the next five years. The period of five years was chosen as the maximum time period for a restaurant as this industry can be quite volatile. The labor cost, as shown, has the owner/manager's salary incorporated into it and it is in line with industry averages. The appraiser can assume that the terminal value at the end of 1999 is $100,000 (which represents the expected liquidation value of the assets at that time). In this example the terminal value has been assumed non-taxable, but where taxation effects exist, they must be allowed for. Because terminal values are often composed of a mixture of taxable (such as depreciation recovered) and non-taxable items, one way of accounting for the terminal value is to determine the after-tax value and enter that figure (whatever it may be) at the point prior to the determination of free cash flows, as depicted. The tax rate is that of the current owner and is assumed to be that of any future owner.

While the pro forma income statement shows the firm's expected profit, the analyst needs to adjust this figure to reflect the free cash flow before undertaking the discounting step. The adjustments include:

1. add back depreciation
2. add increases in working capital necessary to support the increased sales
3. add the estimated terminal value of this business in year 5 (assume that this is not taxable)

Exhibit 10.5 depicts the conversion of the pro forma income statement into free cash flows. The fair-market value is the present value of these free cash flows. Assuming that a 30 percent post-tax discount rate is appropriate for the risk of this business, the present value of this stream of cash flows is $75,757. This figure is the fair-market value of the assets of this business, both tangible (e.g., equipment) and **intangible assets** (e.g., goodwill).

SUMMARY

✦ The purpose of this chapter is to demonstrate the process of valuing a private small business. The process consists of the five steps that follow:

1. Define what is being valued
2. Specify the purpose of the valuation
3. Adjust prior earnings and cash flows to represent financial performance

✦ EXHIBIT 10.4

PRO FORMA INCOME STATEMENT

Item	1995	1996	1997	1998	1999
Revenue	$420,000	$441,000	$463,050	$486,203	$510,513
Food cost	(147,000)	(154,350)	(162,068)	(170,171)	(178,680)
Labor cost	(150,000)	(155,000)	(170,000)	(168,000)	(185,000)
Depreciation	(20,000)	(20,000)	(20,000)	(20,000)	(20,000)
Operating cost	(95,000)	(100,000)	(105,000)	(110,000)	(120,000)
Earnings before tax	$ 8,000	$ 11,650	$ 5,982	$ 18,032	$ 6,833
Tax (34%)	(2,720)	(3,961)	(2,034)	(6,131)	(2,323)
Earnings after tax	$ 5,280	$ 7,689	$ 3,948	$ 11,901	$ 4,510

✦ EXHIBIT 10.5

COMPUTATION OF FREE CASH FLOWS AND VALUE

Item	1995	1996	1997	1998	1999
Earnings after taxes	$ 5,280	$ 7,690	$ 3,948	$11,901	$ 4,510
Depreciation	20,000	20,000	20,000	20,000	20,000
Working capital increases	(5,000)	(6,000)	(7,000)	(8,000)	(8,500)
Terminal value of business					100,000
Free cash flow	$20,280	$21,690	$16,948	$23,901	$116,010
Discount factor	0.7692	0.5917	0.4552	0.3501	0.2693
Present value	$15,600	$12,834	$ 7,714	$ 8,368	$ 31,241
Total present value	**$75,757**				

4. Develop a pro forma statement for the future financial performance of the business

5. Choose a valuation methodology to ascertain the value of the business

✦ There are many reasons for requiring a valuation to be undertaken. These reasons include: changes in the ownership of a business, ascertaining if goals are being met, taxes, seeking financing, and legal reasons.

✦ The valuation methodology suggests that the value of a business is equal to the present value of the firm's free cash flows. This value can be divided among the various stakeholders in the firm without changing its value.

✦ Before any valuation can be undertaken, information is required about the firm itself, the industry in which it operates, and the economy in general.

✦ Valuations can be either asset-based or income-based and, on a different dimension, can be based on the net operating income of the firm (to determine the value of the firm) or on the net income of a firm (to determine the value of equity).

♦ Specific valuation techniques include discounted cash flows, capitalization of annuities, perpetual-growth models, and revenue multipliers.
♦ In the small-business sector, price does not always equal value.
♦ Minority interests per share are worth less than controlling interests. The sum of the two is the value of equity.

THE CASE — PART TEN

At the end of 2003, Dave decides to proceed with his exporting activities and to increase his capacity. Appendix III contains a complete set of his financial statements to the end of 2003 together with his projections for the next three years (these figures are the same as those used in earlier chapters).

In addition to the expenditure on new plant and machinery of $40,000 that is required immediately to service the export order, Dave estimates that he will also need to invest $10,000 in both 2004 and 2005 to replace some of his old plant. He also decides that he will need a new delivery truck that will cost $20,000 and a new car for himself that will cost $20,000. These will be purchased in early 2004.

When he approaches his bank for a term loan of an additional $30,000 to finance these activities (and to reduce his current account loan), the banker suggests that Dave should provide a valuation of the business.

ASSIGNMENT 10.1

You manage to ascertain the following additional information:

♦ Dave pays himself a wage of $63,000 per year
♦ The personal use of the car costs the firm $7,000 per year
♦ Similar firms pay a fully responsible manager $40,000 per year
♦ Similar firms sell on the basis of 4 to 4.5 times post-tax adjusted net operating income
♦ Goodwill is usually calculated on the basis of two years' worth of excess earnings after allowing for an opportunity cost of net tangible assets of 25 percent pre-tax
♦ A discount rate of 28 percent post-tax is applicable for DCF analysis
♦ Net operating income is expected to grow at a rate of 5 percent beyond 2006

Required
Value Dave's Bikes using the following approaches: discounted cash flow and earnings capitalization. Note: You may need to make other simplifying assumptions.

ASSIGNMENT 10.2

Required
1. In order to value Dave's Bikes (in Assignment 10.1) you needed to adjust the income statements. Why is it necessary to adjust the income statements of small businesses when ascertaining their value?
2. In 2004 Dave's Bikes had a forecasted net operating income of $62,372 (equivalent to $46,324 after tax) and yet the cash flow from operations was forecasted to be $59,689.

a) Explain the reasons for this difference.

b) Which figure should be relied on for valuation purposes?

3. Contact a local business broker (someone who specializes in buying and selling small businesses) and inquire about the valuation approach that would be used in practice to value Dave's Bikes. How does this approach compare with the methodologies covered in this chapter? Why the differences?

ASSIGNMENT 10.3

Required

1. To what extent can information be derived from the stock exchange that is useful for the valuation of private small businesses?

2. Are securities that trade on a stock exchange traded with a minority discount? Why? Under what circumstances would a control premium be appropriate?

ASSIGNMENT 10.4

A computer store has annual sales in 1997 of $500,000. Shown below are its 1997 balance sheet and income statement.

Balance Sheet

Cash	$15,000
Accounts receivable	6,000
Inventory	25,000
Current assets	$46,000
Long-term assets	15,000
Total assets	$61,000
Accounts payable	$16,000
Notes payable	40,000
Total debt	$56,000
Equity	5,000
Total liabilities and equity	$61,000

Income Statement

Sales	$500,000
Cost of sales	300,000
Gross profit	$200,000
Operating expenses	80,000
Depreciation	3,000
Earnings before tax	$117,000
Taxes	39,800
Earnings after tax	$ 77,200

The firm expects the sales to increase by the industry growth rate of 5 percent per year and expenses to increase by 4 percent annually. You believe that the appropriate post-tax discount rate is 35 percent and that five years of pro forma statements reflect the time period for this appraisal. At the end of five years you believe that it is realistic to assume that the business will continue at this level into the foreseeable future (i.e., a perpetuity).

Required

1. Making whatever assumptions you feel necessary, ascertain the fair-market value of the assets of the firm.
2. How realistic were the assumptions that you made in question 1?

SELECTED ADDITIONAL READINGS

Bielinski, D. W. 1987. The ERI equity premium selection method. *Business Valuation Review* (September): 124–127.

Bolten, S. E., J. W. Brockardt, and M. J. Ward, 1987. The summary (build-up) capitalization rate factors for retailers. *Business Valuation Review* (March): 6–13.

Brock, T. 1985. More on capitalization rates. *Business Valuation News* (December): 5–9.

Brown, B. R. 1983. Capitalization rates—small businesses. *Business Valuation News* (December): 3–5.

Bygrave, W. D. 1994. *The portable MBA in entrepreneurship* (New York: John Wiley & Sons).

DeThomas, A. R. 1985. Valuing the ownership interest in the privately held firm. *American Journal of Small Business* 9(3): 50–59.

Dietrich, W. C. 1986. A risk premium/growth model to determine the earnings multiple. *Business Valuation News* (March): 10–17.

———. 1985. Capitalization rates—seeing is believing. *Business Valuation News* (December): 3–4.

Emory, J. D. 1992. The value of marketability as illustrated in initial public offerings of common stock. *Business Valuation Review* (December): 208–212.

Gilbert, G. A. 1990. Discount rates and capitalization rates—where are we? *Business Valuation Review* (December): 108–112.

Graham, M. D. 1990. Selection of market multiples in business valuation. *Business Valuation Review* (March): 8–12.

Lerch, M. A. 1991. Quantitative measures of minority interest discounts. *Business Valuation Review* (March): 7–13.

Lerch, M. A. 1992. Discount for key man loss: A quantitative analysis. *Business Valuation Review* (December): 183–194.

Leung, T. S. 1986. Myths about capitalization rate and risk premium. *Business Valuation News* (March): 6–10.

Lippitt, J. W., and N. J. Mastracchio, Jr. 1993. Valuing a small business: Discounted cash flow, earnings capitalization, and the cost of replacing capital sssets. *Journal of Small Business Management* (July): 52–61.

McMahon, R G., S. Holmes, P. J. Hutchinson, and D. M. Forsaith. 1993. *Small Enterprise Financial Management: Theory and Practice* (Sydney, Australia: Harcourt Brace): 107.

McMullin, S. G. 1986. Discount rate selection. *Business Valuation News* (September): 16–22.

Mercer, Z. C. 1989. The adjusted capital asset pricing model for developing capitalization rates: An extension of previous "build-up" methodologies based upon the capital asset pricing model. *Business Valuation Review* (December): 147–156.

O'Neal, F. H. 1986. Oppression of minority shareholders: Protecting minority rights. *Cleveland State Law Review* (winter/spring).

Osteryoung, J. S., R. L. Constand, and D. Nast. 1992. Financial ratios: Large public and small private firms. *Journal of Small Business Management* (July): 35–46.

Peters, J. O. 1989. The effect of ownership and total market value on acquisition-based price/earnings ratio. *Business Valuation Review* (December): 169–171.

Pratt, S. P. 1985. A note on developing a capitalization rate using the capital asset model. *Business Valuation News* (March): 24.

Pratt, S. P. 1989. *Valuing a business: The analysis and appraisal of closely held companies.* (Homewood, IL: Irwin).

Schilt, J. H. 1982. Selection of capitalization rates for valuing a closely held business. *Business Valuation News* (June): 2–5.

Vos, E. A. 1992. Differences in risk measurements for small unlisted businesses. *Journal of Small Business Finance* 1(3): 255–267.

FINANCIAL ASPECTS OF INTERNATIONAL TRADE

OBJECTIVES

1. *Introduce the complexities of international trade*
2. *Describe the types of information required before embarking on a foreign-trade venture*
3. *Examine the documentation required for international trade*
4. *Introduce the methods of payment associated with international trade*
5. *Describe the economic nature of foreign exchange*
6. *Examine the hedging of foreign exchange*
7. *Present the various ways in which international trade can be financed*
8. *Describe the management of cash flows associated with international trade*

11.1 INTRODUCTION[1]

Although most smaller firms have a purely domestic market, international-ization of smaller firms is increasing as world markets move toward greater globalization. The world is becoming ever smaller and the opportunities and threats facing smaller firms will only increase with time: the domestic market no longer has the horizon it once may have.

There are a number of ways in which entry into foreign markets can be made:

+ export (import)
+ strategic alliances (of which joint ventures are a specific case)
+ licensing
+ **foreign direct investment (FDI)**[2]

The elements of this list, taken together, are referred to as the **foreign market servicing decision.**[3]

For those firms actively engaged in international trade and for those con-templating moving into foreign markets, this chapter outlines the more im-portant areas about which the smaller business should be aware.

The international dimension of business adds complexities not found in the domestic environment. As such, there is a greater emphasis on the risk of: foreign currency exchange; granting credit; getting paid; and even politi-cal factors that may necessitate a country-risk analysis. Smaller firms need to know how to reduce the risks foreign trade can bring. Examples of steps de-signed to reduce risk include the evaluation of:

+ payment terms
+ government export-assistance schemes
+ insurance availability
+ sources of finance for international operations
+ consequences for cash flow over and above normal domestic operations
+ foreign-exchange futures markets

The international firm must also take into account ethnic and cultural differences in the foreign market. Differing banking systems and regula-tions lead to difficulties. Most **less developed countries (LDCs)** and emerging-market countries impose restrictions on the exchange of foreign currency. High levels of inflation are endemic in some countries and, with-out appropriate risk management, the exporter may find the real value of

---

[1]The authors would like to thank Dr. Donald G. Ross for his invaluable comments on this chapter.

[2]For an illustration of the smaller firm that undertakes FDI, see Buckley, Newbould, and Thurwell, *Foreign Direct Investment by Smaller UK Firms* (London: Macmillan, 1988).

[3]An excellent book for a general introduction to the world of international operations for small and large firms alike is *Entry Strategies for International Markets* by Franklin R. Root (Lexington, MA: Lexington Books, 1994).

the invoice, if quoted in the buyer's currency, significantly less than expected when exchanged into the exporter's domestic currency. As a consequence, many risk-management techniques impinge to a greater or lesser degree on the finance function.

As most smaller firms engage in an export or import business, this is the type of firm this chapter will discuss. Obviously, the smaller firm wishing to operate internationally would like to do so with the minimum risk associated with foreign trade. As an exporter, this means operating with:

✦ the maximum likelihood of being paid
✦ a minimal delay in payment
✦ payment received in the exporter's domestic currency
✦ if not payment in the exporter's domestic currency, then payment transferred at the most preferential rate of exchange to the domestic currency

In other words, this list indicates that an exporter expects to be paid the same in real terms as would be paid in the domestic market, on the same credit terms, and without any additional bad-debt risk.

An importer expects payment:

✦ at the most favorable rates
✦ with the optimum delay in payment

For the importer, the optimum delay in payment depends on the currency of payment and the anticipated movements in the respective exchange rates.

Fundamentally, the financial aspects of international trade involve an analysis of risk-reduction strategies and actions. So, too, does domestic trade, of course, but there are more factors to take into consideration internationally. Bear in mind that *perceived* risks in foreign trade do not always translate into *actual* risks. With the appropriate credit and payment terms, international trade can be less risky than domestic trade.

Thus, foreign trade may be considered to be a logical process of assessing:

✦ international business risk
✦ the potential of governmental assistance schemes (although, empirically, such schemes are used infrequently)
✦ the documentation process
✦ foreign-exchange risk
✦ sources of finance (mainly, but not necessarily, domestic)
✦ cash-flow aspects

 CONCEPT CHECK

1. *What are the ways a small firm can gain entry into a foreign market?*
2. *What additional risks are associated with international trade compared to domestic trade?*

3. *What financial factors are important to an exporter?*
4. *What financial factors are important to an importer?*
5. *What cultural differences are likely to affect the risk of international trade?*

11.2 INTERNATIONAL BUSINESS-RISK ASSESSMENT

It is just as imprudent for exporters to sell on credit without the appropriate credit and background checks as it is to do so in the domestic market. It is also imprudent to treat all foreign countries as having the same risk profile. For the most part, and especially for those countries more culturally distant from the home market, background research on the country to which sales are anticipated is an essential requirement. Specific elements in the risk assessment of a country are: credit character, financial strength, country risk, and foreign-exchange risk, in that order. Although Japan, for example, is often viewed as culturally distant, it has a very high credit character, therefore cultural distance does not always imply greater risk. In addition, the risk of foreign payment default can actually be less than for domestic payment default because of the types of payment terms available in international trade. There are also a number of private and government sources who will insure the firm against such foreign risk.

For the smaller business, two significant areas relating to foreign trade are **country-risk assessment** and customer/trading partner assessment.

COUNTRY RISK ASSESSMENT

Country risk is the potential loss from political or economic action that affects the transfer of funds from the target market back to the home country. For direct foreign investments, political and economic action may affect the value of the foreign enterprise or its ability to translate that value back to the source country.

It is not suggested that the smaller firm undertake months of research to establish a profile of each country with which it wishes to do business, but an awareness of the trading and general economic climate, the legal and banking structure, and the predominating culture of the export destination will provide a more knowledgeable base from which to assess the prospects and risk in foreign trade. The learning curve associated with this time-consuming assessment could be fatal to the business. In any case, expert foreign-market assessments are made by professional establishments, such as major banks, accountancy firms, and other independent firms. Country-specific requirements and medium-term (three-to-five-year) economic analysis are also usually available. The Department of Commerce, other government agencies, and local chambers of commerce also provide valuable sources of information. The trade department of the exporter's home-country embassy in that market provides a further major source of information about a potential market. The provision of information, some general, some specific, about the country in which the embassy is located, is part of its function, yet it appears to be an underutilized resource and costs a firm only postage to obtain this information. Seeking out local firms that are, or have been, engaged in exporting to a target country is an excellent source of useful information, some of which is not easily found elsewhere.

For the company desiring to sell outside its domestic market, such country risks can be minimized by utilizing a number of insurance schemes available. For those smaller firms actually making a capital investment, whether in production facilities, distribution channels and networks, or sales offices, it becomes far more important to undertake a risk assessment.

For the smaller firm, one way to take political and economic factors into consideration is to obtain as much literature from professional institutions, banks, accountants, etc., as is prudent, and to read and analyze the data with reference to a checklist of points relevant to the firm and its foreign ambitions. The list of factors below can assist in this by providing a basis for assessment. Should the firm wish to be a little more sophisticated, it can weight the factors in its final list according to degree of importance in accordance with its own criteria and judgment. The weighting, or grading, of the topics contained in such a list is somewhat less relevant to the smaller firm than the process of thinking about the issues involved. Export insurance can help reduce the risk of financial loss, but it can be prohibitively expensive.

A generalized checklist of factors is shown below. The list includes elements relevant to FDI, as this is also one form of foreign-market servicing:

Economic Factors

+ market size
+ availability of resources, including labor
+ quality of financial (e.g., banking) and physical infrastructure
+ international trade balance
+ economic growth
+ inflation
+ devaluation
+ taxation (general levels and any discrimination with respect to foreign trade)
+ tariff barriers (and non-tariff barriers)
+ currency convertibility and stability
+ repatriation of currency/funds
+ degree of government influence/restrictions (e.g., joint ventures or currency certificates)
+ government macro economic management (e.g., price controls, control of public and private borrowing)
+ sensitivity to external economic events (e.g., oil prices)

Political and social factors

+ attitude of government to foreign imports/capital
+ relations between source and host governments
+ general levels of political stability (e.g., civil disorder, riots, assassinations, coups, war—or the prospect of it). Knowing the imminence of the Gulf War or the disintegration of the Berlin Wall would profoundly alter the perception of a country's risk)
+ type of government and its stability, opposition factions
+ risk of expropriation
+ government directed/enforced business decisions (e.g., must a firm buy or sell to government agencies only at a predetermined price? Where is the product perishable, physically or technologically?
+ rescheduling of debts by governments and businesses alike
+ freedom of markets and of individuals
+ the role of the military and the opposition
+ social tensions (e.g., ethnic, linguistic, racial, tribal)
+ accounting rules and regulations—true and fair?
+ legal framework regarding contractual relations and appropriate recourse to the courts
+ bribery and the general business ethic

CUSTOMER/TRADING PARTNER ASSESSMENT

Assessing the firm's customers or trading partners, as part of the overall assessment of export risk, is viewed as considerably more important than assessing economic and social factors. The assessment of a foreign customer should be similar to that of the domestic partner assessment except that the information is more difficult to obtain initially, and there are a few different questions to ask about the importing firm. For example:

+ How long has the firm been trading internationally?
+ In what countries has the firm been trading?
+ With whom has the firm been trading?
+ Can it supply details of firms it has traded with in the country of export?
+ What is its payment and delivery record like?
+ How many disputes has it been engaged in (ploy for delayed payment)?
+ Can the company supply unbiased third-party reports on its financial strength and commercial reputation (i.e., credit and character references)?
+ Is the firm unduly influenced by the government?
+ What are the perceived attitudes of the directors or owner/managers?

Firms such as Dun & Bradstreet, for example, offer a service for the evaluation of risk in selected foreign countries. The perception of the business risk can also profoundly influence the decision to use insurance schemes.

EXPORT ASSISTANCE AGENCIES

Most national governments attempt to support firms actively engaged in exporting and other outward flows of goods and services. There are also non-government agencies who may be of assistance. Once the first significant agency has been contacted they will usually advise on other agencies able to offer assistance, either in terms of finance, insurance, or information. Start with the Department of Commerce, local chambers of commerce, International Trade Centers and relevant government departments. See if there is anything equivalent to an Export Development Agency or possibly a generalized small business agency (like the SBA). There are agencies to be found at the local, state, and national level that support foreign trade. The telephone directory and the Yellow Pages should provide some useful contacts initially.

Export credit-guarantee (ECG) agencies (where they exist) provide a risk-reduction option. However, depending on the type of service required and the destination of exports, their use can be quite expensive. Having said that, some governments subsidize their ECG agencies and, as a result, can be seen as an export subsidy to firms. Even so, the ECG will not reimburse a firm for 100 percent of a loss, but only a part. Depending on the scheme, reimbursement may vary from 70 percent to 90 percent, or thereabouts. The question the smaller firm must ask is whether it can, in the worst scenario, afford a total financial loss of the cost of export and can it afford not to insure. Does the cost–benefit ratio favor insurance? It is the firm's decision.

 CONCEPT CHECK

1. *What economic, political, and social aspects should be addressed in a country-risk assessment?*
2. *What economic, political, and social aspects should be addressed in a trading partner assessment?*
3. *Where would you go to find information prior to entering the export market?*

11.3 INTERNATIONAL TRADE DOCUMENTATION

International trade documentation is a collection of forms that are necessary to facilitate international trade. They have evolved, literally, over centuries to perform specific tasks. They are the best compromise as to the division of risk between buyer and seller, the optimal trade-off.

The risks associated with international trade may be viewed as:

✦ the risk of non-completion of a transaction (goods delivery)
✦ the risk of non-payment (financial delivery)
✦ the risk of an unfavorable foreign-exchange transaction

The first two risks may be viewed as complementary (as a transaction is not really completed until it has been paid for). In addition, shipping documents are often intertwined with payment methods, so it makes sense to view the documents as one group, as is done below. Foreign-exchange risk is somewhat different from the non-completion and non-payment risks, although they are related, particularly in methods of payment.

Over the years, a number of documents have emerged as important and have become standard in international trade. These documents are:

+ the **bill of lading (B/L)**
+ the **bill of exchange (B/E)**
+ the **letter of credit (L/C)**

There are alternative methods of payment and secondary documents that are frequently used. Methods of payment include:

+ prepayment
+ collection
+ open account

Secondary documents include:

+ commercial invoice
+ insurance documents
+ certificate of origin
+ packing list
+ certificate of analysis

The invoice and insurance documents are invariably necessary in international trade and the remaining three secondary documents are necessary under certain circumstances.

ESSENTIAL DOCUMENTS

Bill of Lading

The bill of lading (B/L) is primarily a transportation document. It serves as:

+ a *receipt* to the effect that the goods have been received for shipment by the carrier. The carrier has no duty to ensure the accuracy of the contents of the shipment, although there is a duty of reasonable care in the transportation, so only the briefest of descriptions will appear on the B/L.
+ a *memorandum* of the terms and conditions of the contract between the shipper and the carrier for the transportation of goods from the point of loading (and thus transfer of responsibility to the carrier) to the destination (and the transfer of responsibility from the carrier). Clauses relating to alternative delivery ports or circumstances of return may also be included in the B/L.
+ *evidence* of title to the goods, which can be used to obtain payment or guarantee of payment before the goods are released to the consignee.

Where such guarantee is obtained, preferably irrevocably, the B/L can be used as collateral for the advancement of loans to finance the working capital of the exporter.

A B/L contains one important characteristic, whether it is "straight" or "to order." A **straight B/L** does not inherently retain the exporter's title to the goods, it approves delivery of the goods straight to the consignee without a guarantee of payment. Thus, this type of B/L is reserved primarily for prepaid or guaranteed payment of the export. As it does not confer title, it cannot be used as collateral for loans. Exporters wishing to maintain title can issue an **order B/L** addressed to themselves, because the addressee maintains title until endorsement in favor of someone else. As the order bill is negotiable, endorsement is effected only when payment has been made or arrangement for payment is irrevocable (within the terms and limits of the payment instrument).

The B/L can be changed according to prior arrangement or as a function of something happening en route. As a consequence, the B/L may be described as:

✦ clean or foul (indicating damage)
✦ through or direct
✦ on-board or received

A **clean B/L** acknowledges that goods were received by the carrier without "apparent" damage, "apparent" because the carrier is not obliged to check the contents of a shipment in detail, but should inspect the external condition. A **foul B/L** indicates that the goods appear to have suffered damage before responsibility passed to the carrier. Naturally, the receiver has no desire to pay for damaged goods and thus a foul B/L lacks negotiability.

A **through B/L** is a shipping document that provides for the shipment of goods by more than one carrier. A **direct B/L** requires that one vessel carry the shipment to its eventual destination without transshipment.

An **on-board B/L** states that goods have been loaded on board or shipped on a named vessel. A **received B/L** states that goods have been received by the shipper, but does not require that the goods be actually placed on the vessel before the issuance of a B/L.

Bill of Exchange

A bill of exchange (B/E), also known as a draft, is an unconditional order in writing, signed by the drawer, or originator, requiring the person to whom it is addressed to pay on demand (or at a fixed or otherwise determined future point in time) a sum of money to the order of a specified person or bearer (the drawee).

A B/E is used as written evidence of a debt or as a means of securing payment in a court of law. The B/E may be used as a negotiable instrument, in which case it must:

✦ be in writing and be signed by the drawer
✦ contain an unconditional promise or order to pay a specified cash sum
✦ be payable within a determinable future date (a time draft)
✦ be payable to order or to the bearer

If the above conditions are met, the holder of the B/E is termed a **holder in due course,** with the entitlement to receipt of payment regardless of subsequent disagreements. Consequently, this formalization as to the exact nature of the rights and responsibilities of the parties has led to the use of the B/E as an international transaction medium in a number of markets.

As a negotiable instrument, a B/E can also be discounted. For example, if maturity is due in thirty days the exporter can take the B/E to a bank which will give the exporter a proportion of the face value, depending on the time to maturity and whether the bill is written with or without recourse.

Letter of Credit

A bank prepares and issues a letter of credit (L/C) at the behest of an importer in favor of an exporter to provide for payment of goods on presentation of the shipping documents specified in the L/C. This is a popular payment instrument because it utilizes the banking system to receive and check the shipping documents (but not the goods) and guarantee payment. This provides security for both the exporter and the importer. The importer's bank ensures that title has been passed before remitting payment, and the exporter's bank ensures that payment has been arranged before title to the goods is relinquished. There are variations on a letter of credit that can be specified by either party, the importer or exporter, but both have to agree on it.

Banks have strict rules governing L/Cs. For instance, they will only pay against a L/C if the documents stated accompany it, that is, the B/L and commercial invoice plus other documentation, such as insurance certificate, certificate of origin, or any other secondary documentation stipulated. The bank will not act as arbiter in any dispute. The bank, on fulfilling its obligations, has full recourse to the firm requesting the issuance for payment.

L/Cs can be:

+ revocable or irrevocable
+ confirmed or unconfirmed
+ revolving or non-revolving

A **revocable L/C** can be amended or canceled at any time before payment, and thus is of little use as a guarantee of payment. However, it is used between affiliate companies where guarantee of payment is not an issue. An **irrevocable L/C** is the reverse, it cannot be amended or canceled without the consent of all contracting parties. The bank is duty-bound to honor the L/C if all the requirements are met.

A **confirmed L/C** originates when both domestic and foreign banks obligate themselves to the payment; thus, the exporter will receive payment from its domestic bank even if the foreign bank is unable to meet its commitment, as long as all the conditions have been met. An **unconfirmed L/C** is used where only the foreign bank is obligated to meet the debt. The exporter is therefore dependent on the financial viability of that bank, or the political conditions that prevail. If in doubt, get the L/C confirmed.

There are very few **revolving L/Cs** because the risk of exposure is so great. A revolving credit may state, for example, that fixed amounts of money can be drawn every month (or week, or whatever) for a specified period. If that period is three years, at $50,000 per month, then the exporter can draw that amount every month for that period, even if the buyer does not want any more shipments after, say, three months. If the exporter draws less than the full $50,000, it then depends on whether the L/C is cumulative or non-cumulative. If the former, then what is not drawn gets added to the next month. If the L/C is non-cumulative, then the difference is lost and the next month starts afresh, up to $50,000. Consequently, revolving L/Cs tend to be revocable. However, most L/Cs are **non-revolving** and apply to a single transaction.

Exporters prefer to have an irrevocable L/C, if issued by a foreign bank, confirmed by their domestic bank or other reputable third-party bank. Thus, if an American exporter does not like the sound of The People's Revolutionary Bank of Wherever, it may choose to confirm through a London- or Paris-based bank. Alternatively, an irrevocable L/C issued by a domestic bank will serve the purpose. Dealing with a domestic bank does not have the language, cultural, and legal difficulties that may arise with a foreign bank, for example, should payment not be met on the date specified, which all L/Cs require.

The L/C has many advantages for both the exporter and importer:

+ Both parties deal with the bank, thus reducing the distrust that may exist (to a greater or lesser degree) in many export/import transactions.

+ The problem of foreign exchange availability and conversion is dealt with by the banks so both the payment and receipt of cash is facilitated, especially if negotiated domestically or through a third bank.

+ Should foreign-exchange rules be changed by governments, outstanding financial transactions are usually honored. It is unwise for governments to behave dishonorably within the international banking community, whereas there is considerably less at stake for governments when dealing with smaller foreign exporters.

+ An irrevocable L/C can be used as a source of short-term finance.

+ The importer does not have to relinquish any cash until the documents, and often the goods, have arrived, helping her own cash flow as the payment terms may allow a further period of grace before actual payment is required.

Banks are not contractual parties to the L/C. While they have a duty of care to ensure the documents appear bona fide and conform to the conditions and terms of the L/C, banks are not responsible for any aspect relating to insufficiency of documentation beyond that contained in the L/C. The bank must also take reasonable care in dealing with the documentation, not least that they are in fact authentic. Having exhibited this care, the bank is not liable for any losses that may be incurred as a result of, for example, non-authenticity. Banks have no liability with respect to missing or delayed communication, fax, letters, etc., nor for the acts of the contracting parties or any legal responsibilities arising therefrom. In a nutshell, the bank is an agent carrying out instructions and nothing more. Selecting a bank with experience in foreign-trade procedures is preferable to one that has had limited experience with such transactions.

OTHER METHODS OF PAYMENT

The payment method can considerably influence the perceived and actual risk in exporting. In addition to the L/C there are other methods of payment that may be used according to circumstance. These include prepayment, collection, and open account.

Prepayment

If an exporter has received prepayment, then the only risk lies in getting the goods to their destination. The importer assumes nearly all the risk, inasmuch as there may be non-delivery or late delivery where time is of the essence. For some exporters this may be the only way they wish to conduct international business. However, this may leave them at a competitive disadvantage, as importers must also consider their own risks and the effect on their cash flows.

Prepayments carry no credit risk to the exporter and can also provide a valuable source of financing, which assists with cash flow (as discussed in Chapter 6). Prepayments are often seen in contracts for specialized types of equipment where progress payments are a norm in the industry. Responding to a specialized order indicates that the foreign purchaser may be more willing to make such payments to the smaller firm in the knowledge that the firms often cannot carry the financial burden that type of order imposes. However, often the reverse is true and the larger firm uses the smaller firm as a source of short-term funding in respect to working capital. Not surprisingly, prepayments are preferable to small businesses, either because of the perceived risk of the transaction or because the smaller firm needs to fund its own working capital. This form of payment is dependent on the value and type of item being purchased.

The opposite is true for the importer or purchaser who must bear the financing costs. Prepayments may be sensible for the following reasons:

+ if the prepayment is to take advantage of a depreciating domestic currency (i.e., the exporter's currency)
+ if financing costs are significantly lower in the country of export in comparison to the country of import
+ if the exporter has an affiliate or sales office in the target country, transfer of funds may be easier by prepayment to this office as the relationship between exporter and importer are now based in one country, and legislation often requires a parent to be responsible for its affiliate's (subsidiary's) debts

Collection

Collection occurs when the exporter ships the goods and uses the bank to transfer the shipping and payment documents and thus to obtain payment. There is still credit exposure, as there is no specific irrevocable commitment on the part of any bank to pay the exporter on presentation of the documents. However, the exporter can instruct the bank to release the documents only on payment or on receipt of an irrevocable letter of intent to pay, and thus obtain greater credit security.

Open Account

An **open account** can be considered the opposite of a prepayment. The exporter ships the goods *and* passes title to the importer before payment. As a consequence, the exporter is fully exposed to the credit risk until payment is received, thirty, sixty, or ninety days (or longer if the importer delays payment), assuming payment is finally made. The open account is probably the most universal form of payment method. In this instance it is most important to manage the credit risk and financing costs correctly.

In general, few problems are experienced with the procedures and transmission of funds when using the international banking system of the Western world. However, the banking systems of the newly emerging nations of eastern Europe may not have the most sophisticated procedures in place for dealing with international transactions. Stories of next-day transfers actually taking a month or more to be processed in these nations is not uncommon. The same comment applies to a number of other developing countries. The Society for Worldwide Interbank Financial Transmissions (SWIFT) is fast and cheap and is recommended where possible (unless a faster means of transfer is available). The smaller firm should seek the most expedient form of remittance because the costs associated with obtaining faster transfers are generally negligible in relation to other factors.

The choice of payment instrument between importer and exporter is ultimately a trade-off between the marketing benefits and financial costs. On the financial side, the following questions require answers:

+ Can the smaller firm afford to carry a relatively significant element of receivables as exports?
+ Does this require significant provision for doubtful debts in the financial statements?
+ Is the pricing of exports, and thus gross margins, compatible with the perceived increased risk of exporting?
+ Are the fixed and variable cost proportions appropriately aligned with the pricing and risk profile?
+ Is the cost of insurance accurately weighted to anticipated returns?

The marketing side of payment choice similarly poses a number of questions:

+ Is this a one-time order or part of a strategic thrust into the target market?
+ Is the gamble likely to pay off in the longer term so that the costs associated with one or two bad debts should not halt the export thrust completely?
+ What are the conditions in the domestic market?
+ Is it a demand push or a demand pull situation?

+ What are the firm's competitors doing?
+ Is the export market particularly competitive? Are price and terms of trade significant factors in the decision of the importer to take one firm's products rather than another's?

Finally, for the business that does not feel proficient in the documentary procedures of international trade, assistance may be obtained from other firms experienced in this area, for a fee. There are also specialized firms that deal with international-trade documentation, examples of which include shipping agents, freight forwarders, and brokers. Export support agencies should be able to provide a list of firms that support international trade.

SECONDARY DOCUMENTATION

Insurance Policy
The need for an insurance policy is self-evident. Insurance can be arranged directly with the insurer or through a broker and requires consideration of:

+ whether to use a separate policy for each shipment or an overall "open cover" policy for multiple transactions
+ how much coverage is required (and thus the degree of indemnity)

Regardless of customer or country risks, the goods have to get where they are going. Who takes the risks and pays the insurance is the first question. How much coverage is required is the second. If the exporter assumes **CIF (carriage, insurance, and freight),** the exporter pays. Insurance forms part of the terms of trade and it is absolutely essential that each party is clear as to who bears the responsibility for insuring goods at each stage of shipment.

Commercial Invoice
In addition to the usual domestic invoice, an international invoice typically specifies the transportation details, including:

+ shipper
+ dates of shipping
+ amount to be shipped
+ method of payment, including what the payment instrument is
+ in what currency payment is to be made

The invoice also states the terms of trade (which includes a statement as to who is responsible for insurance as noted above).

Other Documents
The exporter should also be aware that a certificate of origin, packing list, and an export license may be required by customs officials, depending on the place of origin and destination. Certain types of exports are subject to specific rules concerning technological content and those not satisfying such requirements will not be granted an export license. Foodstuffs and other items of dubious sanitation may require additional certificates.

CONCEPT CHECK

1. *Distinguish between straight and order bills of lading.*
2. *Distinguish between a bill of lading and a bill of exchange.*
3. *Why is a letter of credit such an important document?*
4. *Describe the various types of letters of credit.*
5. *What advantages does the letter of credit confer on both the importer and the exporter?*
6. *What are prepayments and what advantages do they confer on the exporter?*
7. *What is an open account and what disadvantages does it confer on an exporter?*
8. *What financial and marketing trade-offs need to be made when deciding on the most suitable payment instrument?*

11.4 FOREIGN EXCHANGE

Assuming that the smaller firm is not put off by the political and other risks relating to exporting (and, for the most part, there is no reason why it should) and can find its way around the documentation procedure, it should give some thought to the process of foreign exchange. The bank will usually advise on the various types of payment and carry out the transaction for the firm. However, research ahead of time may help pinpoint unsolicited bank services.

Foreign exchange (F/X) is merely the price of one currency in terms of another, either at the time of the transaction or at some future time period. The exchange relationship between currencies has three main determinants:

1. a nation's balance-of-payments position
2. the level of interest rates prevailing between nations
3. the levels of inflation prevailing within respective nations

The discipline of economics has gone a long way toward providing an understanding of these international financial relationships, but there are still elements that are less well understood. Consequently, uncertainties as to exchange values remain.

In addition to the causes of currency exchange fluctuations there are three more practical aspects of foreign exchange that should be considered:

✦ types of foreign-exchange exposure
✦ foreign-exchange markets
✦ use of hedging as a risk-reduction strategy

TYPES OF FOREIGN-EXCHANGE EXPOSURE

There are generally three types of foreign-exposure risk: transaction exposure, translation exposure, and economic exposure.

Transaction Exposure

Transaction exposure is the predominant type of risk for the smaller firm importing or exporting. It arises when a firm has either receivables or payables denominated in a foreign currency and, therefore, by definition, is not a settled account. Consequently, the account is "exposed" to the possibility of movements in F/X rates until such time as payment is received.

For example: A U.S. firm enters into a contract to export $75,000 of goods to the United Kingdom. The current rate of exchange is £1 = $1.50. If the contribution to net profit is 5 percent, then expected profit is $3,750. The goods are to be dispatched one week hence and the shipment takes three weeks to cross the Atlantic. On arrival in the United Kingdom the purchaser takes collection immediately. The terms of sale state payment is to be made in British pounds (£50,000) thirty days after collection of the goods. In total, this is two months from the date of initiation of the contract. During that two months international events, such as the country's balance-of-payments interactions, conspire to force the value of the pound down to $1.40. The £50,000 is paid on time, but the receipt of cash (ignoring transaction costs, such as bank fees) to the U.S. exporter is now only £50,000 multiplied by $1.40, or $70,000. The foreign exchange loss is $5,000. The contribution to net profit is now actually negative, a loss of $1,250 (–$5,000 plus $3,750).

For the two months between the time the contract is agreed upon and signed and receipt of payment, the exporting firm was "exposed" to exchange-rate fluctuations. The exporter suffered, as the exposure was adverse. It was risky.

Such exposure may also occur where a **forward exchange contract** has been initiated but is not yet settled. Such a contract determines the rate of exchange to be used at some future specified date regardless of what the exchange rate may be on the day the contract terms are to be fulfilled. If a firm uses the forward, or futures, markets they are doing so primarily to hedge, or to cover, their potential risk of exposure. Hedging as a risk-reduction strategy will be discussed later in this chapter.

Translation Exposure

The term *translation exposure* primarily refers to the rate of exchange, and hence the change in value, applied to the historical cost of assets, liabilities, and equity located somewhere other than the parent firm's home nation. For those smaller firms that do have assets and liabilities abroad, there are specific accounting regulations, together with recommendations from government and accounting bodies, that detail how to report on this situation in the most appropriate way. Financial statements, such as the income statement and balance sheet, are historical in nature and thus translation exposure is sometimes referred to as accounting exposure. Such exposure occurs as the financial statements of a firm operating outside the parent company's home nation are consolidated with those of the parent at period end. Line by line, assets, liabilities, equity, revenues, and expenses are converted from the foreign currencies to the domestic currency of the parent company for that period.

Economic Exposure

Economic exposure is the potential *change* that may occur in the net present value of expected future after-tax cash flows. It refers to the overall impact of exchange-rate changes on the value of the firm arising from changes in competitive relationships and the economic impact of transaction and translation exposure. This is, again, of limited application to the indirect import/export firm, but is of greater concern to firms that own an income-earning asset abroad. Direct exporting firms may own sales or distribution channels abroad and thus may be exposed to the variability of exchange rates as they affect the remittance of profits, possibly via dividends, back to the parent.

Tax is sometimes considered a fourth type of exposure, but this mainly affects those firms that hold income-generating assets abroad. Gains and losses are usually only taxable or allowable once they have been realized.

While the various types of foreign-exchange exposure are covered more fully in international financial-management texts that tend to deal with international corporations, there are some small companies that generate 100 percent of their income from exports and other foreign operations, including foreign direct investment.

As far as the U.S. importer is concerned, there is no foreign-exchange risk involved in paying for imports from Norway in U.S. dollars. Likewise, the U.S. exporter has no foreign-exchange problems when demanding from the Norwegian buyer payment in U.S. dollars. Thus the risks of foreign exchange only occur when payment is made in a foreign, rather than in a domestic, currency, as seen in the example earlier in the section on transaction exposure. Therefore, somebody must take the responsibility for negotiating the price, the currency rate of exchange, the denomination, and date of payment. Transportation details are minor in this instance, except with respect to the time taken for delivery and hence the timing of payment (which impinges on cash flow); thus they become an element for negotiation (part of the terms of trade).

Exposure may also arise from borrowing or lending funds internationally, either in relation to transactions, or in an attempt to hedge, or for some other reason. Some years ago in the United Kingdom a scheme was implemented for home buyers to take advantage of low interest rates in Switzerland relative to the United Kingdom, to fund the purchase of domestic property. Unfortunately, the movement in the exchange rate was so adverse with respect to the United Kingdom that the cost of homes financed under this scheme in British pounds nearly doubled.[4] Multinationals often find this a difficult area of operation and the smaller firm simply *must* get professional advice.

CONCEPT CHECK

1. *Compare and contrast the three types of foreign exchange exposure (transaction, translation, and economic).*

---

[4]Recently, Barings, an old and respected London bank, lost approximately $1 billion on the futures market.

2. *What are the determinants of the exchange relationship?*
3. *In what ways is the owner of business assets overseas exposed to foreign-exchange movements?*
4. *Why is the timing element of remittances so important?*

11.5   THE FOREIGN-EXCHANGE MARKETS

The foreign-exchange market is really an interrelated network of dealers throughout the world who conduct business through the use of telecommunications, such as telephone, direct computer link, telex, and fax. Buyers and sellers may be connected from any part of the world where dealers' offices are found, which is in nearly all of the world's major capitals, but predominantly London, New York, and Tokyo. In 1992 the world foreign-exchange market was estimated at $880 billion per working day, with London accounting for 27 percent of that market and the United States for about 17 percent.[5] Looked at another way, this market turns over the equivalent of the combined reserves of every central bank of every country in the world, every working day. In terms of trade, in 1992 this market was fifty-nine times the volume of total world trade. This multiple is expected to increase in the future.

The main players in the market tend to be the dealers employed by the larger commercial banks, investment banks, and finance houses; thus, there can be a direct link between the small firm employing their commercial bank and a resulting foreign-exchange transaction. Most tourists will go to a foreign bank to exchange currency or travelers' checks, or to withdraw local currency on their credit card. Similarly, payment or receipt of moneys to or from abroad is a painless operation in its mechanics, but could be painful if the contractual variables are not precise or adequately favorable.

There are four types of foreign-exchange markets:

1. the spot market
2. the forward market
3. the futures market
4. the options market

These markets are very specialized. While the main determinants of currency fluctuations can be identified, there remain sufficient unknown elements to advise the smaller international firm to seek advice from the foreign section of a reputable commercial bank before committing any significant sum of money to the foreign-exchange market. Smaller firms rarely use the futures or options markets but it is well to be aware of what they are.

---

[5]Information from *The Treasurer*, December 1994.

THE SPOT MARKET

The **spot market,** also known as the **current market,** is where current trans- actions are either bought or sold immediately, or "on the spot." Thus, the **spot rate** is the rate currently prevailing in the international market for for- eign currencies. This is the rate reported in the daily papers. In the United States the British spot rate may be $1 equals £0.67, while in the United King- dom it will be £1 equals $1.50. There are often two rates given, one for buy- ing and one for selling. The difference between the two is the bank's fee for undertaking the transaction. Single-figure middle rates (often found as tourist rates) take the middle point between the buy and sell rates and should be taken only as a guide and not used for contractual purposes. One should seek the bank's advice before entering into a binding commitment.

THE FORWARD MARKET

The **forward market** exists to enter into contractually binding agreements now for performance at some later date. It is a very specific market: the sum involved, the rate of exchange, and the date of completion are all specifically tailored to the needs of the contracting party, buyer or seller. The **forward market rate** is the contractual rate at which two currencies (or occasionally more) must be exchanged some time in the future, typically thirty, ninety, or one hundred eighty days, although it can be arranged for longer periods. Foreign currency is bought today for delivery at some specified future date, although no payment is made at the time the agreement is made. The amount that is agreed to be paid in some future period is contractually bind- ing, regardless of the fluctuations in the exchange rate.

The currency forward market exists as a type of insurance to guarantee that adverse movements in the foreign-exchange rate do not leave the trad- ing firm overexposed to unacceptable losses at some time in the future. The rate quoted by the bank includes what may be called their "fee" for under- taking the risk associated with the uncertainty of future events as reflected in the currency-exchange rate. Managers tend to be risk averse in their com- mercial life, and so it is that the downside risk (losses) are prevalent in their thinking. Any thoughts a firm may have of outguessing the market and speculating in foreign currency is not recommended. Some of the largest and most respected international companies have tried this and failed.

THE FUTURES MARKET

The **futures market** operates on a similar basis to the forward market but tends to involve itself in predetermined currencies, amounts, and periods. The standardization of the futures market differs from the forward market to the extent that, while the former restricts itself to major world currencies, the latter will deal in a whole variety of currencies. In addition, seldom do fu- tures traders "take delivery" of the currency (in contrast to forward market trades, which end transactions in delivery of the desired currency).

THE OPTIONS MARKET

The **options market,** on the other hand, makes it possible for a firm to buy the "right" to buy or sell currency at a specified time in the future at a price contractually agreed upon today. Unlike the forward market, this does not irrevocably commit the firm to taking delivery of the currency. Nor does it expose a firm to the margin requirements of a futures contract. These transactions are dealt with on a specialized options market known as the options exchange.

CONCEPT CHECK

1. *What is the spot market and how does it operate?*
2. *Differentiate between the forward market and the futures market.*
3. *What is a currency option?*

11.6 HEDGING AS A RISK-REDUCTION STRATEGY

The principal operational strategy to reduce transaction exposure is **hedging,** sometimes referred to as **forward hedging** or **covering.** It is merely the contractual relationship where one party purchases, at today's prices, currency in one denomination for delivery at some future specified time, with the payment of currency in another denomination, usually the domestic firm's national currency. Thus, a U.S. firm wishing to purchase yen for payment of a trade debt will enter into a contract specifying the dollar amount to be paid in, say, ninety days, for which the firm will have supplied by the other party a specified amount of yen.

Foreign currency exchange rates can clearly rise or fall. The typical risk-averse firm may well consider hedging as the appropriate strategy. For relatively small monetary amounts, hedging may not be cost advantageous, but as monetary value increases, so the downside risk increases (the upside equivalent rarely carries the same perceived risk weighting as the downside). The smaller firm has no easy task when dealing with the foreign-currency problem. A manager must first understand the concept of hedging, decide whether it is appropriate under the circumstances, and then find a specialized international money-market agent for advice and implementation. Typically, for the smaller firm the bank assumes this role.

For example, consider the U.S. exporter who contracted to export $75,000 worth of goods to the United Kingdom, used only the spot market, and lost $1,250 either due to lack of awareness of the existence of a forward market, or lack of knowledge about it. In any case, its use would undoubtedly incur a cost, which may have been considered too expensive. Assume that, after the loss on the U.K. transaction, the next foray into exporting included a forward market position, i.e., the foreign-exchange exposure was hedged. Also assume that the U.K. importer wanted another delivery of the same amount, and that the British pound had risen back to $1.50.

The bank quotes a price for exchanging £50,000 in two months time into $75,000. The quotation price given is $76,000 (banks will usually give just the quotation price). The exporter, being inquisitive, asks how the bank arrives at that figure. The explanation received is that spot and forward rates are determined by the markets. Deduct one from the other and multiply by the period the forward hedge requires. The premium to be paid by the exporter is then known. For example, assuming the two-month forward rate is £1.52, and the spot rate is £1.50, then:

$$\frac{£1.52 - $1.50}{$1.50}\left(\frac{12}{2}\right)(100) = 8\% \text{ premium per annum}$$

Therefore, the two-month premium is approximately two-twelfths of this, i.e., 1.333 percent, which, when multiplied by $75,000, equals $1,000, and $75,000 plus $1,000 equals $76,000 (or 75,000 multiplied by 1.01333). This equation was for the purpose of illustration only. Currency-exchange dealers are rather more sophisticated about the transaction determinants, but the example contains information readily available to the smaller business (e.g., through the financial press) and will give a reasonable estimation of the costs associated with using the forward market. There will be some additional standard bank fees to pay, of course.

The exporter can now build $1,000 into the costs with assurance that $1,000 will be the total liability. If, instead, the British pound appreciates against the American dollar, then the bank takes the gain.

The general formula that expresses this relationship is:

$$\frac{\text{Forward rate} - \text{spot rate}}{\text{spot rate}}\left(\frac{12}{\text{\# months forward}}\right)(100) = \text{forward premium on a per annum basis}$$

 CONCEPT CHECK

1. *How does hedging work?*
2. *Formulate a hedging problem and solve it, making whatever assumptions you feel necessary.*

11.7 THE ECONOMICS OF FOREIGN EXCHANGE

This section briefly explains some of the underlying causes of movements in the international currency rates of exchange. For the reader of a more practical tendency, this section can be skipped without loss of continuity.

The price of one currency with respect to another lies in the interaction of supply and demand. If the causality of movements in the F/X markets were universally known, then there would be little or no unanticipated movements (although movements would still occur). But, because there are unknowns, it follows that the directions and amounts underlying currency movements are not known with certainty (which, of course, is true for nearly everything concerning the future).

However, although the smaller business is unlikely to be an expert in international economics, a feel for the important factors is important. The main concepts that influence small business are:

+ balance of payments between countries
+ interest rate movements in one country versus another
+ level of inflation in target markets

BALANCE OF PAYMENTS

The **balance of payments** includes:

1. the monetary value of internationally traded goods (shown in the balance of trade statistics), part of the **current account**
2. the monetary value in the international sale or purchase of services (banking, insurance, etc.), part of the current account
3. the movements of capital, the sum of investment and lending, in or out of a country, known as the **capital account**
4. changes in holdings of gold and foreign currencies by official monetary institutions, known as the **official reserves account**

Trade in petroleum and gas products is sometimes itemized separately from the accounts listed above. If a country imports the same value of goods as it exports, then there is a tendency toward equilibrium in the currency markets. When there is an imbalance, this tends to give one currency an appreciation or depreciation in value against another. Thus, in general terms, a worsening balance of payments situation will point toward a weakening currency, other things remaining fairly constant.

One problem is that different countries have different **elasticities of demand** for imports. By elasticity of demand is meant the response in demand to a change in price. Inelastic demand is when a price change will not impact the demand for a product. If imports are fairly inelastic, then even as prices of imported goods rise with respect to the depreciation of domestic currency, then imports will still have a significant impact. One policy the government may adopt is to increase taxes to take money out of circulation in the domestic economy. Inelastic import demand hurts the domestic producer more than the foreign exporter. A lower value of the domestic country's currency internationally makes the price of exports cheaper abroad and should then partially rectify the imbalance of trade by creating greater demand for the domestic currency by foreigners to pay for the imports. Thus, the forces of supply and demand are at work in the goods market.

INTEREST RATE PARITY THEOREM

Interest rates are another determinant of exchange-rate movements. Currencies move on the international exchanges in response to differential rates of interest in other nations. Thus, if comparable investments in the United States and United Kingdom return 10 percent and 5 percent respectively, then funds would flow to the United States for the higher return. However, the argument is that the foreign-exchange market responds to this movement in such a way that the gain in the rate of interest is exactly offset by the change in the values of the currencies (the foreign-exchange rate).

Where $\$r$ and $£r$ are the respective rates of interest in the United States and United Kingdom for comparable investments, and the time period for the forward rate is consistent with the interest rate, the **interest rate parity theory (IRPT)** suggests that:

$$\frac{1 + \$r}{1 + £r} = \frac{\text{forward rate}_{\$/£}}{\text{spot rate}_{\$/£}}$$

Thus, for the 10 percent and 5 percent interest rates for the United States and United Kingdom above and with a known spot rate of $1.50 to £1, this becomes:

$$\frac{1.10}{1.05} = \frac{\text{forward rate}_{\$/£}}{1.50}$$

Therefore:

$$\text{forward rate} = \frac{(1.10)(1.50)}{1.05} = \$1.57/£$$

The investor should then be indifferent to an investment in the United Kingdom or in the United States. In practice, life is not so simple, but for the smaller firm even a cursory knowledge of international interest rate movements may help one determine the way currency is likely to move.

PURCHASING POWER PARITY THEOREM

In an economy that allows free movement of goods, services, and funds, the **purchasing power parity theory (PPPT)** states that there ought to be equilibrium between international prices of goods, i.e., one common international price should prevail. This is a brave assumption, of course, because there are many factors that make this not so; but, as it affects international exchange rates, one may accept the proposition. Consequently, if a product sells for $600 in the United States and the exchange rate is $1.50 to £1, then that product will cost £400 in the United Kingdom (transport and other incidental costs aside). Expressed as an equation, this can be said by:

$$\text{U.K. price (£)} \times \$/£ \text{ spot rate} = \text{U.S. price (\$)}$$

or:

$$\frac{\text{U.S. price (\$)}}{\text{U.K. price (£)}} = \$/£ \text{ spot rate}$$

Assume the United Kingdom has an inflation rate of 5 percent and the United States a rate of 3 percent; then it follows that the price of the goods must change in relation to the movement in the exchange rate. The $600 product in the United States after one year's inflation (3 percent) is $618, and in the United Kingdom, £400 multiplied by 5 percent equals £420. As the system requires some equilibrium, the exchange rate must make a complementary adjustment over a period of time to compensate, which it does by:

$$\frac{\$618}{£420} = \$1.4714/£ \text{ exchange rate expected after one year}$$

In other words, the exchange rate will take up the difference between the inflation rates to maintain a consistent international price—sometimes referred to as the **law of one price**. Shown another way:

$$\frac{1 + \$ \text{ inflation}}{1 + £ \text{ inflation}} = \frac{\text{forward rate}_{\$/£}}{\text{spot rate}_{\$/£}}$$

or:

$$\frac{1 + (.03)}{1 + (.05)} = \frac{\$1.4714/£}{\$1.5000/£} = 0.981$$

which is the same as:

$$\frac{\$600 \ (1.03\%)}{£400 \ (1.05\%)(\$1.50)} = \frac{\$618 \text{ for goods in U.S.}}{\$630 \text{ for goods in U.K.}} = 0.981$$

The effective currency depreciation is therefore:

$$1 - 0.981 = 0.019, \text{ or } 1.9\%$$

This is for a period of one year, but the same type of calculation can be done for any period of time as long as the periods are consistent.

Annual or monthly estimates of inflation rates are available via the financial press and occasionally business programs on television. Once the inflation figures have been obtained, they can be inserted into the calculation for a very approximate guide to exchange-rate fluctuations for the period under review.

Where goods can be traded internationally in a free market, the PPPT will tend to hold, but more in the longer term than in the shorter term. The problem is that the magnitude of the change is not so easy to calculate because there is a requirement to model the interactions of interest rates, inflation, and the associated balance-of-payments movements. In a perfectly rational world all countries should have the same fundamental "real" interest rate with the only difference between their nominal rates being that related to inflation. This is known as the **international fisher effect**.

The real world does allow short-term variations and the above explanations are limited to some extent. Of course the underlying rationale may be of no concern to the smaller business, and as mentioned at the beginning of the section, can be skipped with ease. For those with an additional interest, most international finance texts cover these subjects more thoroughly.

 ### CONCEPT CHECK

1. *What is the balance of payments?*
2. *How do price elasticities affect the balance of payments?*
3. *Describe the impact of differential interest rates on foreign exchange.*
4. *Describe the impact of differential inflation rates on foreign exchange.*

11.8   SOURCES OF FINANCE

Many smaller firms have given serious thought to the prospect of international operations, but may have come to a halt when due consideration has been given to the means by which such expansion can be financed. On the other hand, there are firms that have been oriented toward sales expansion and have undertaken such operations without due consideration to the funding required.

Naturally the method of payment utilized in foreign transactions has a direct bearing on the type and amount of funding required. Where an importer or exporter can bear the financing requirements, it is quite often a bank or other similar institution that supports either or both in the short term.

Some of the potential sources of financing may come from:

◆ the exporter
◆ the importer
◆ the bank
◆ discounting export receivables
◆ export-development agencies
◆ government-aid programs

THE EXPORTER/IMPORTER

It has already been noted that prepayments require that the importer bear all of the financing charges, while open accounts require that the exporter bear all of the financing charges. In between, there is a range of compromises in which the importer and exporter share the costs of financing to a greater or lesser degree, such as in the case of letters of credit. The proportion, or extent, each bears is dependent on the agreed terms within the L/C.

THE BANK

The importing or exporting firm can open what is known as a line of credit with its own bank. This is a short-term funding arrangement whereby the bank will support the requirement for increased working capital in order to fund the export trade. Advances of up to 75 percent of export receivables are not uncommon (depending on various risk factors associated with the exports), no doubt more if there is an export credit guarantee (insurance) in operation and the recovery amount from such a scheme is assigned to the bank. Of course, many factors impinge on this type of arrangement, not the least of which is the past record of the firm requesting the line of credit.

DISCOUNTING EXPORT RECEIVABLES

Export receivables and trade bills can be discounted (factored)—similar in many respects to domestic factoring of accounts receivable. The discounting process occurs when the exporter sells receivables to the bank, or finance house, for cash. The bank may not accept receivables that are considered to have a greater risk than the bank lays down in its guidelines, so pre-negotiation is advisable. Also, the bank may stipulate a minimum level of receivables, so this source of short-term finance may not be appropriate for a small value exporter. However, the required level of export receivables is generally not so large that smaller firms are excluded from this process. The factor's interest depends on the costs associated with the transaction, particularly the fixed costs.

Discounting can be on a **recourse basis** (the exporter guarantees the importer's debt payment) or **non-recourse basis** (the bank accepts the risk of non-payment). Clearly a non-recourse basis offers significant advantages to a small business, such as:

+ protection against a bad debt
+ protection of predictable cash flow in the event of late payment
+ protection against potential losses due to depreciation in the currency exchange rate or adverse movements in interest rates
+ the benefit of immediate cash, thus improved cash flow
+ dispensing with the need to obtain working-capital finance to directly support exports
+ alleviation of one of the firm's fundamental concerns regarding not being paid

Of course, just as in domestic factoring, there is a price to be paid, and it can be quite significant. The same balance of risk and reward must be considered and a decision made in relation to the costs and benefits of the discounting process.

An extension of the above occurs when the bank agrees to lend to the importer/purchaser directly, whereby payment of the export receivable is guaranteed. This is generally of less applicability to the smaller firm but there are instances where it may be appropriate, such as when an international aid or relief agency is purchasing goods or equipment (or contracting for services, such as technical or managerial expertise). Depending on the purchaser it may be worth considering.

SUPPLIER CREDITS

Supplier credit is a useful option available to the smaller firm in the capital-goods sector where normal financing over several years may be required. The finance provider, usually the bank, promises to purchase notes (a generalized term for certain payment instruments, such as promissory notes) that the exporter receives for the goods or services supplied. This is less expensive than some other forms of financing, as the exporter deals directly with the importer/purchaser and the bank acts as a kind of guarantor. This arrangement, in common with many others, must be organized before entering into the export contract, because if the bank declines to enter into such an arrangement, the firm may find itself with cash-flow and other problems.

INTERNATIONAL LEASING

International leasing is not a particularly common form of financing for the smaller business, but it is mentioned here because it does occur and may be relevant. Rather than paying directly for goods, the purchaser may take out an international lease. The form is primarily an extension of the domestic lease but may contain certain aspects of taxation peculiar to international trade or financing.

The cost of leasing is a financial expenditure and appears in the income statement. A lease may yield tax benefits to the **lessee,** depending on the comparative "cost" of equivalent depreciation allowances. Acquisition of capital equipment with a longer life may benefit from the leasing arrangement to avoid being technologically and financially locked in over a number of years. Depending on the business, it is at least worth considering if at all applicable.

EXPORT CREDIT GUARANTEE

Most countries operate some form of government or quasi-government agency to support exporters in their endeavors. Export credit guarantee (ECG) agencies provide insurance for exports to most parts of the world. However, such insurance is expensive and many firms decide that appropriate selection of the payment instrument is a better option even if some sales may be lost in the process.

ECG agencies may also provide a guarantor service to banks that support exporter's financing requirements, and may assist foreign buyers by financing the purchase and therefore assuming the risks of the exporter. However, a particular ECG agency may have hurdle levels of export value that must be attained before they consider it cost-effective to become involved. They may also have predispositions as to the types of industry they are more willing to support—the capital goods industry for one—which is why ECG agencies tend to operate in the medium- to long-term financing of exports. The Organization for Economic Cooperation and Development (OECD) guidelines suggest a limit of 85 percent of the value of goods and services exported, so any higher rate offered is rare and may become proportionately more expensive.

ECG agencies tend to stipulate quite stringent requirements concerning the exporting firm in relation to its financial health and strength, its technical abilities to meet the contractual requirements, and so forth. It is a similar situation with the importer and the country of import. As a consequence ECG agencies tend to be particularly risk averse and their services would not suit a number of smaller companies. However, such agencies may offer a line of credit with local banks to meet the smaller importer's needs, so this would be a line of inquiry to the agency. The recommendation is therefore to approach the relevant agency in the domestic country and undertake a careful evaluation of the costs and benefits, taking special note of the costs relating to the insurance side of their activities.

 ### Concept Check

1. When can the small business seek trade-related finance?
2. How does discounting export receivables work?
3. What are supplier credits?
4. Does your home country operate an ECG agency? If so, what does it offer?

11.9   ALTERNATIVE METHODS OF FINANCING

There are two potential alternatives of financing international trade—consignment and counter-trade.

Consignment

Consignment is a trading arrangement where goods are shipped to an importer without the exporter giving up title of ownership. Because title has not passed, the importer acts as agent and is therefore not required to pay for the goods. The importer then remits the proceeds of sales, less commission and expenses, to the exporter. For the smaller importer this means that the firm can buy in quantities large enough to get the discounts offered for bulk purchases. Also it may contribute to minimizing transport and other costs.

From the exporter's viewpoint, there is more security in the consignment situation because title to the goods has not been transferred. Therefore, they can be returned or sold to someone else. Thus, the risk of a bad debt is potentially lessened when compared with the outright sale of the total consignment to the importer. In addition, the importer has a more impressive range of goods, or of buffer stock, not only to maintain existing markets but to secure new ones (without the financial risk this may otherwise have necessitated if the goods had to be purchased outright).

From the importer's viewpoint, one other potential advantage relating to consignment is that, as the title has not been passed, the goods have not technically been sold. Because any liability of duty is not incurred until the ownership passes, payment of the liability is deferred until sale takes place, or is not paid at all if the goods are re-exported. This, naturally, can be considered a disadvantage to the exporter.

The success of consignment depends on mutual trust and good standard commercial practices, written or otherwise, in the importing country. The potential for fraud or default can be great, with legal recourse difficult in some countries, and expensive in most. The problem for the exporter is primarily the length of time needed to fund the holding, and most require significant amounts of working capital.

For the importer, this form of trading may be ideal, and such an arrangement is, in fact, a very popular distribution channel. For the exporter, it can be very expensive and care must be given to meticulous costing before such an option is undertaken.

COUNTERTRADE

Countertrade is an arrangement where the sale of goods and services to an importer is offset by reciprocal exports from the importing firm or country. If a firm is willing to undertake importing and exporting functions, there is little additional working capital required, and there is greater security of payment as it is in goods, not cash. Countertrade also has a greater profit potential, as profit is inherent not only in the exports, but also on the imports, either in raw material input or as finished goods. One example is the trading of New Zealand dairy products for Russian cars.

This form of trade is not common in the small-business sector, but is often contained within intergovernmental agreements. Ironically, although associated with trade between the east European bloc countries or developing countries, where hard currency for international trade is a scarce resource, the opening up of the eastern European markets can present some significant opportunities for the international smaller businesses of the industrialized world. There are specialist countertrade agents, and the smaller firm is advised to benefit from their experience and seek assistance.

For both importer and exporter, countertrade has the potential to open up new markets with new products (especially technological goods markets), or to facilitate cost reduction through new sources of basic inputs. Naturally, pure exports from developing countries are preferable as they generate foreign currency, but, given the problems of conversion and government controls internally in respect to currency exchange, there still remains mutually beneficial prospects for both the importer and the exporter.

Problems of finding a mutually acceptable currency in which to specify the value of goods or services remain, but this is not too difficult a hurdle to overcome.

CONCEPT CHECK

1. *From the viewpoint of the importer, what are the advantages and disadvantages of consignment trade?*
2. *From the viewpoint of the exporter, what are the advantages and disadvantages of consignment trade?*
3. *What is countertrade and why does it occur?*

11.10 CASH-FLOW MANAGEMENT

As may be expected, there are additional aspects to the planning and management of domestic cash flow (as outlined in Chapter 6) when dealing with international financial transactions. At the outset, it may be wise for the firm to separate cash-flow forecasts relating to such trade from the domestic side of the business. This allows the firm to focus more easily on the international financial aspect of the business and allows for the identification of component variances that would not be evident if the composite cash flow alone is considered. Naturally, once the international cash-flow forecast is prepared it is then incorporated with the domestic, but such separation is very useful for quicker and more specific analysis.

As noted earlier, the complexities of international transactions include:

+ exchange-rate risk
+ existing or potential exchange-rate controls
+ delays in the transfer of funds
+ possible slow collection periods of accounts receivable
+ political risk, especially in relation to capital investment, but also in regard to governmental relations, which may lead to increased tariffs or revocation of import/export licenses

Other elements (in common with domestic elements) that may incur real or perceived increased risk, include:

+ bad debts
+ deliberate strategy of slow payment
+ increased costs and uncertainty of legal recourse if necessitated

✦ likelihood of pilferage

✦ documentation complexities and resulting likelihood of errors

The increased strain on working capital inevitably calls for more financing, and thus a central element in foreign trade is to insure that such financing is in place. The costs of trade indemnity or insurance are, or can be, significant. Cash flow also dictates, to a large degree, the choice of payment instrument. Where working capital is a constraint, fast payment is required, even if there is an additional cost, such as factoring. For larger items or items with a high proportion of sunk costs, prepayments or interim payments are essential. The type of order, in part, dictates the type of credit guarantee or payment instrument. The extent of prepayment is a commercial decision, dependent partly on competition; but, in general, the level of prepayment should be sufficient so the firm is not left financially exposed. If the firm is financially exposed, notwithstanding indemnities, the owner is advised against making prepayment.

SPEEDING RECEIVABLES

Good commercial practice in relation to international trading partners is essential. However, notwithstanding the competitive pressures on the terms of trade, the smaller firm, through judicious choice of payment instrument, can speed up the payment process. The manager should make sure the banks involved have clear instructions so that no delay occurs due to vague documentation. The owner should use fax or telephone, if acceptable, to convey instructions, should ensure the foreign partner has the payment in an irrevocable instrument (preferably with one of the participating banks), and should ensure the paying bank utilizes the fastest payment method. Mail and some inter-bank transfers are not reliable methods and wire transfers can be used instead. Also, have the domestic bank give a written estimate of the time it will take from payment into a foreign bank to crediting the receiver's account.

It may be feasible to use a third bank where transmission links between payer and third bank and receiver and third bank are actually quicker than between the payer's and receiver's banks. The person receiving payment should check with the bank daily from the date of expected transfer where the value is relatively significant. Expecting an international payment on a Tuesday and checking with the bank the following Monday simply because that is the firm's once-a-week reconciliation date leaves the amount as an idle cash balance for six days (assuming that the payment arrives on the expected date).

Discounting receivables is another way of speeding cash flow, as discussed above. However, this is a costly method of receiving immediate cash flow and banks are quite selective in what they choose to discount.

Past experience has shown that the transmission of funds internationally is not without inherent problems. Fund transfers have been known to get "lost" in the banking system for a considerable period of time. This usually results when the importer or exporter does not complete the relevant documentation fully, or perhaps does not use a document that is sufficiently comprehensive. In other words, one should be specific regarding documentary content and meticulous in its completion. In addition, the person receiving payment should note the name of the bank on which payment is drawn and its relevant details: address, bank code number, and so forth.

Cash flow can be affected by countries introducing currency controls. While a slow account receivable should not necessarily be classified as a bad debt, nevertheless, payment is delayed. To get around this potential problem, the exporter and importer may wish to come to an agreement whereby payment for goods or services is placed in a bank with guaranteed fund repatriation. The payment is released on documentary evidence of receipt of goods by the importer. Some of these problems are alleviated if the exporter has a sales subsidiary in such markets where the subsidiary borrows on the parent's guarantee or against receivables, and the subsidiary pays the receivables against the borrowing. Without payment, there can be no export.

 CONCEPT CHECK

1. *What additional cash-flow problems are faced by the exporter (compared to the wholly domestic trader)?*
2. *How can the collection of foreign receivables be accelerated?*

SUMMARY

- ✦ The international smaller firm predominantly imports and/or exports. It also enters into strategic alliances, licensing agreements, and even makes capital investments abroad (foreign direct investments). Many acts of exporting derive from an unsolicited order; therefore, the firm's main preoccupation is with being paid at a rate commensurate with the domestic currency price quoted. As a consequence, the type of payment instrument used and the foreign exposure risk is paramount.
- ✦ The firm's bankers will be of considerable assistance and should be consulted regarding the advantages and disadvantages of the various types of transaction documentation and payment methods to use in particular situations. A letter of credit is not the only relevant document for payment with reduced risk.
- ✦ While the smaller firm will not usually get itself involved in the mechanics of forward exchange, the owners must be aware of the pros and cons of hedging (and its related cost) as well as other instruments of risk reduction, such as export credit guarantees. Exporting is the future for many growing smaller businesses, but it is strongly suggested that the firm seek the advice of the bank, even if it means dealing with the head office, rather than a smaller local branch, in order to get the required expertise.

THE CASE—PART ELEVEN

In 2003, having decided to invest in additional plant and machinery, Dave is beginning to consider more fully the possibilities of the export market. After an initial market survey of the NAFTA countries of Canada and Mexico, he turns his attention elsewhere.

He has bike-riding friends in Spain, South Africa, and several countries in South America who tell him that their homelands may be possible targets for his activities.

ASSIGNMENT 11.1

Required

1. Prepare an initial country-risk assessment on a target country that Dave can use as a screening device to assist him in determining his course of action.
2. What recommendation would you give Dave to assist him in his foreign-market servicing decision?
3. What information should Dave attempt to obtain to reduce the risk of bad debts arising from his exporting activities?
4. Advise Dave about exporting procedures and forms of payment.

ASSIGNMENT 11.2

Required

1. While Dave prefers to be paid in U.S. dollars, he is prepared to consider being paid in another currency. Assume that the United States has domestic inflation of 2 percent per annum, while the country to which he will export is experiencing inflation of 10 percent. The initial consignment is expected to be worth $100,000 in U.S. dollars. Illustrate to Dave the consequences of his decision.
2. Suggest how Dave might reduce his risk by:
   a) using the spot market
   b) using the forward market

SELECTED ADDITIONAL READINGS

Brasch, J. J., and J. Crimmons, 1979. Some observations on small exporter trade credit risk management. *Journal of Small Business Management* 17 (2).

Brealey, R. A., and S. C. Myers. 1991. *Principles of corporate finance.* 4th ed. (New York: McGraw-Hill).

Cannon, T., and M. Willis, 1983. The smaller firm in overseas trade. *European Small Business Journal* 1 (3).

Eiteman, D. K., A. I. Stonehill, and M. H. Moffett. 1992. *Multinational business finance.* 6th ed. (Reading, MA: Addison-Wesley).

Lumby, S. 1991. *Investment appraisal and financing decisions.* 4th ed. (London: Chapman & Hall).

Shen, P. 1980. Cash flow budgeting for the importer. *Management Accounting* 62 (3).

Soenen, L. A. 1983. Foreign exchange management for the small firm. *American Journal of Small Business* VII (3) (January–March).

Valdez, S. 1993. *An introduction to western financial markets.* (London: Macmillan).

FINANCE AND THE ENTREPRENEUR

OBJECTIVES

1. *Distinguish between the financial needs of entrepreneurial- and lifestyle-oriented small businesses*
2. *Describe the stages of financing associated with the development of the entrepreneurial small firm*
3. *Describe the role of venture capitalists and their contribution to financial markets*
4. *Discuss the U.S. regulatory environment as it applies to private placements and initial public offerings*
5. *Introduce the succession and harvest issues that face owners of small family businesses and discuss types of personally difficult conflicts that can arise*
6. *Discuss the philosophy and nature of franchising as a method of assisting the entrepreneurial small firm to expand its operations and as a method of assisting the franchisee to participate in the franchisor's success*

12.1 ENTREPRENEURS AND LIFESTYLERS

Small firms can be classified into those that are entrepreneurial and those that have a lifestyle focus. Chapter 1 introduced the analysis of Petty and Bygrave[1] in which they specified that only 5 percent of small firms are entrepreneurial in outlook. They classified the other 95 percent as "lifestyle businesses." However, the primary focus of this chapter is on the financial needs of entrepreneurial small firms.

From a purely financial perspective, the objective of the entrepreneurial business is more likely to be that of value maximization than that of a lifestyle firm. While lifestyle firms are likely to pursue goals other than value maximization, this does not mean that they ignore value maximization as a goal. After all, no businessperson wants to *lose* wealth, and everybody prefers more wealth to less. It is a matter of degree.

In the pursuit of value maximization, and as seen when venture-capital financing is discussed, the entrepreneurial small firm is more likely to seek the benefits (and face the costs) of public negotiability of its stock. On the other hand, the lifestyle firm is more likely to focus on the need to ensure orderly succession of firm ownership (including intergenerational transfer) than its entrepreneurial counterpart. This is not to say that succession issues can be ignored in the case of the entrepreneurial firm, and, indeed, there are some very large publicly listed "family" firms for which succession issues are very important; again, it is a matter of degree.

Exhibit 12.1 summarizes the relative importance of these issues to the two types of small firms. The direction of the arrow specifies increasing importance.

THE FINANCIAL PROBLEMS OF THE ENTREPRENEUR

Entrepreneurial small firms can be distinguished from other small firms in that they have a much stronger growth orientation. They require financing that takes into account not only the inherent risk of the venture, but also the need for future flexibility so that the financing can adapt easily to the changes that will occur as the firm grows.

Because entrepreneurial firms have a growth focus, they face a set of particular financing problems that are not associated with firms that are not growing rapidly. Earlier chapters of this text provided examples of the problems associated with growth, especially Chapter 5, which demonstrated how to budget for growth and how to calculate the funding needs of the growing firm.

Growth results in two types of funding problems. On the one hand there is a need to fund the purchase of the long-term productive assets (including

---

[1]See W. J. Petty, and W. D. Bygrave, "What Does Finance Have to Say to the Entrepreneur?" *Journal of Small Business Finance* 2(2): pp. 125–138.

◆ **EXHIBIT 12.1**

RELATIVE IMPORTANCE OF OBJECTIVES

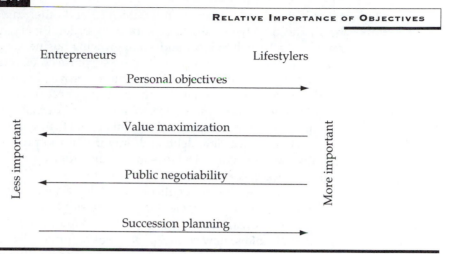

◆ **EXHIBIT 12.2**

LIQUIDITY SHORTFALL

	Original amount	20% growth
Current assets	$200,000	$40,000
Current liabilities	(150,000)	(30,000)
Shortfall		$10,000

research and development) that, in turn, generate growth in sales revenue. On the other hand, there is also a need to finance the growth in working capital that is associated with the growth in sales revenue. As also described in Chapter 5, some of this growth in working capital is spontaneously generated by the proportionate increase in the current liabilities of the firm, but because there is a general need (not in the least from the bank's perspective) to maintain a level of current assets that exceeds that of current liabilities, spontaneous proportionate increases in both current assets and current liabilities will always leave a shortage that requires alternative financing. Exhibit 12.2 shows how 20 percent growth in both current assets and current liabilities results in a shortfall whenever current assets exceed current liabilities. Exhibit 12.2 shows that a 20 percent increase in sales requires the firm to acquire new financing (on top of the spontaneous liability increase) in the amount of $10,000.

Financing the Entrepreneur

How is the shortage shown in Exhibit 12.2 and other capital acquisitions to be financed? Myers[2] suggests a pecking-order theory, which appears to apply equally well to large and small growing businesses alike. He suggests that, first, the firm will rely on its own surpluses (i.e., retained earnings) to provide the needed funding. If this source proves inadequate and the firm needs to consider external financing, it prefers to issue the safest security first. In other words, the preferred source of external finance is new debt; and if, in turn, that too proves inadequate, the firm will issue hybrid securities, such as convertible debt; and only if that too proves to be inadequate will it raise new equity. The reasons for the ordering are related to both cost and control considerations.

While the pecking-order theory provides a neat way of describing the preferences of firm managers, the growing *small* firm faces the added problem associated with lack of access to capital markets. It simply cannot raise new debt, let alone new equity, as easily as a publicly listed firm can. Until it is of a size and level of stability that commends it to the public market, it is forced to rely on private sources to finance its activities.

Stages of Financing

The financing stages are closely related to the stage of development of the firm and can be categorized as follows:

Early Stage Financing
+ Seed financing: The small amount of money that is necessary for product development, building a management team, or completing a business plan
+ Start-up financing: funds needed to facilitate the process of organizing the business structure, facilities and relationships of a firm that is not yet ready to sell any product; this type of financing is associated with firms that are just ready to start conducting business
+ First-stage financing: funds provided to firms that have exhausted their initial capital and require additional funds to initiate full-scale production and marketing

Expansion Financing
+ Second-stage financing: funds provided to operating companies that are expanding and need funds to finance their working-capital increases; these firms may not yet be showing a profit
+ Third-stage (mezzanine) financing: funds provided to firms that are making a profit (or that are close to breaking even); these funds are usually applied to plant expansion, working capital, or the development of an enhanced product

---

[2]See S. C. Myers, 1984, pp. 581–582.

✦ Bridge financing: usually considered temporary until the next round of financing is completed; for example, a firm that plans to go public in the near future may seek bridge financing to meet its immediate needs

With an awareness of the nature of entrepreneurial and lifestyle firms and the financial problems that face the growing small firm, one can proceed to examine two distinctly different ways of organizing the funding of the expanding small business by considering the contributions of franchisees and venture capitalists.

 CONCEPT CHECK

1. *Distinguish between the financial problems of the entrepreneur and the lifestyler.*
2. *What is the pecking-order theory?*
3. *Describe the stages of financing and identify a firm of which you are aware that fits into each stage.*

12.2 VENTURE CAPITAL

Venture capital is a very important source of funding for the entrepreneurial firm. According to Bygrave,[3] the venture-capital market in 1992 contributed approximately $50 billion to U.S. businesses. Venture capital is extremely important to the U.S. economy as a whole. The National Venture Capital Association[4] reports that in the United States, for the five-year period between 1989 and 1993, venture capital-backed businesses produced 152 jobs per company, invested $8.7 million in research and development, and had average export sales of $4 million.

There are two major categories of **venture capitalists:** individuals ("angels") and **venture-capital firms**.

TYPES OF VENTURE CAPITALISTS

Angels
The group of people known as "angels" is made up of those individual investors with a high personal net worth who advance venture capital to entrepreneurial businesses. While it is difficult to gauge the size of this investment group, one estimate is that, every year, 250,000 angels invest $10

---

[3]See W. D. Bygrave, 1994, p. 173.

[4]See study by the National Venture Capital Association, 1995, p. 1.

to \$20 billion in over 30,000 businesses.[5] Angels typically invest between \$100,000 and \$500,000 in the early-stage financing phase of each business that they wish to assist.

Typically, angels are active in charitable and civic affairs and like to take high risk in their pleasures. The potential angel for a particular business is likely to be a person who is familiar with the relevant industry, the technology, and the product under consideration and who is likely to be located in close proximity to the business. Frequently, lawyers and accountants who specialize in new firms and in the financing of growing firms know of angels who specialize in investing in entrepreneurial firms.

Obviously, the problem faced by the firm seeking venture capital from individual investors is to find them. Angels do not have a sign in the front of their office stating "Entrepreneurs Wanted," rather they preserve their anonymity so that they are not bombarded by business plans and requests for funds. **Venture-capital networks (VCNs)** were established for the purpose of overcoming this difficulty. A VCN is an anonymous matchmaking device, its purpose being to provide an investment opportunity for both the entrepreneur and the angel, but with the angel remaining anonymous in the early stages of the process. There are twelve to fifteen VCNs presently operating across the United States.

An entrepreneur seeking finance submits responses to a detailed questionnaire indicating the magnitude of funds needed, type of product, type of market, and the history of the business as well as to a number of other questions concerning the firm's operations and plans. For example, the entrepreneur might be required to submit an executive summary of his business plan. The angel also responds to a detailed questionnaire indicating the type of investment sought including the industry, the amount of funding available, and an indication of any expertise that the angel might be prepared to contribute. Once the information is gathered from both entrepreneur and venture capitalist, a computer program attempts to match the parties involved. When there is a potential match, the VCN sends additional details to the angel. If the angel indicates further interest, the name of the entrepreneur is provided. Usually, at this stage a note is sent to the entrepreneur indicating the name of the angel requesting additional information.

Venture-Capital Firms

Venture-capital firms have existed since the 1940s when the private company American Research and Development (ARD) was founded. In 1957, ARD invested \$70,000 for 77 percent of the common stock of a new company started by four MIT graduate students. In 1971, that investment comprised \$355 million worth of the common stock of Digital Equipment Corporation (DEC). Venture-capital firms have also contributed to the success of Apple Computer, LOTUS, Intel, and Microsoft.

---

[5]See W. D. Bygrave, and J. Timmons, 1992, p. 310.

ALLOCATION OF FUNDS

Stage	Percent financed
Start-up	25%
First	23
Second	18
Third	12
Bridge	6
Leveraged buy-out	16
	100%

The venture-capital firm is a financial intermediary and, as such, organizes the transfer of funds from suppliers of capital to users of capital. More specifically, the venture-capital firm raises funds, invests them in entrepreneurial firms, monitors the performance of the firms, and returns a reward to its own suppliers of funds. This process involves three "players." The first is the investor who invests in a venture-capital pool of funds. The investor is usually a wealthy individual or a financial institution. The second player is the venture-capital firm, which acts as the manager of the investor's funds. The third player is the entrepreneurial firm that needs funds to finance its growth. Today, about $30 to $35 billion annually is under the control of venture-capital firms in the United States.[6]

Most venture-capital firms are structured as limited partnerships in which the management of the firm acts as the general partner and the investors comprise the limited partners. Most partnerships have a life of seven to ten years. Capital appreciation is preferred to income, and a particular venture-capital firm is likely to specialize in certain industries or products. The typical venture-capital firm is a limited partnership with assets in excess of $50 million and over thirty firms that they are currently financing.

Small business investment corporations (SBICs) represent an attempt by the government to generate a venture-capital pool. An SBIC is funded by $4 of low-cost government debt for every $1 of stockholders' equity. Because SBICs need to meet the contractual debt-servicing commitments on this debt funding, they must seek investments that are capable of an annual cash flow that will adequately fit their commitments.

In 1990 Norton surveyed the members of the National Venture Capital Association.[7] Exhibit 12.3 shows where venture capital funds can be invested.

---

[6]See E. Norton, 1994, p. 182.

[7]Ibid, p. 184.

FIRMS RECEIVING VENTURE CAPITAL

Industry	Percentage of firms
Biotech	28%
Software	14
Media/communication	14
Semi-conductors and electronics	12
Medical devices	12
Health-care services	5
Retail	6
Other	9
	100%

The most popular type of financing in this study was preferred stock. Venture-capital firms like to take equity positions, but favor preferred equity because it has prior rights over common stock and is therefore safer, especially when used to finance businesses in the start-up stage.

Most venture-capital funds are invested in relatively high-tech firms, as shown in Exhibit 12.4.[8] This is because venture-capital firms prefer to invest their funds in areas that have the potential for supernormal growth rates, a hallmark of high-tech firms. Of course, this area of investment can also be considered highly risky, but, as in the oil-exploration industry, a single strike can result in a very large payoff, and, by investing in a range of businesses, venture-capital firms obtain the diversification benefits associated with a spread of investments.

EXPECTATIONS OF THE PARTIES

Most venture capitalists want to realize their returns within a five- to seven-year period. Any investor, including a venture capitalist, requires a return that consists of two components. First, the investor seeks a return *on* the investment commensurate with the degree of risk involved. Second, the investor seeks a return *of* the investment itself in the form of either a series of payments (such as is the case with an amortizing loan) or in the form of a single lump sum on the termination of the investment (at which point the total return on investment may also be received). The method by which these components can be **"harvested"** will be discussed in a later section of this chapter.

---

[8]See study by the National Venture Capital Association, 1995, p. 3.

The pattern of the cash flows associated with the two components described above is a matter for negotiation between the parties to the agreement. In general, a venture capitalist seeking **interim payments** (i.e., before termination) is likely to invest in interest-bearing debt or convertible-debt instruments that bear periodic interest payments. On the other hand, a venture capitalist who is less interested in interim payments will either invest in low-interest-bearing convertible debt, or will invest directly in the equity of the firm.

So, the method by which the returns *on* investment and the return *of* investment will be harvested is a critical decision that must be agreed upon by the parties at the outset. The harvest mechanism affects not only the venture capitalist's decision as to how much to invest, but also the decision of the entrepreneur as to the amount of equity to be given to the venture capitalist in exchange for the funding supplied.

For example, consider the case of an entrepreneurial firm needing $1,000,000 in financing for a five-year period. What is the maximum equity to be given to the venture capitalist if the venture capitalist expects a return of 50 percent per year? The future value of the $1,000,000 investment earning a compound rate of 50 percent is approximately $7,600,000, so the entrepreneur must plan to provide the venture capitalist $7,600,000 in year 5. If the expected value of the firm at the end of year 5 is $20,000,000, its present owners should not give up more than 38 percent of its equity or control in the organization ($7,600,000 divided by $20,000,000). In other words, the maximum stake to be transferred to the venture capitalist equals the future value of the venture capitalist's investment divided by the future value of the company.

$$\text{Percentage to be given to investors} = \frac{\text{future value of investment}}{\text{future value of firm}}$$

$$38\% = \frac{\$7,6000,000}{\$20,000,000}$$

Obviously, the venture capitalist wants a return on investment that is a function of the inherent risk associated with the activity and its stage of development. As a firm progresses through these stages, in general its future becomes more certain, and because the rate of return required on investment by the venture capitalist depends on the degree of risk involved, the different stages can be associated with different required rates of return (or from the perspective of the firm itself, with different costs of capital).

Exhibit 12.5 shows the compound annual rate of return that a venture capitalist might expect, given the stage of the enterprise.[9]

As can be seen in Exhibit 12.5, the required rates of return sought by the venture capitalist are very high, especially in the early stages. This is because of the substantial risk the venture capitalist is absorbing.

---

[9]See W. D. Bygrave, 1994, p. 184.

✦ **EXHIBIT 12.5**

STAGE OF FINANCING AND RETURNS REQUIRED

Stage	Annual return required
Seed	80%
Start-up	60
First	50
Second	40
Third	30
Bridge	25

EVALUATION REQUIREMENTS

As with any financier, before committing any funds, the venture capitalist will consider a number of critical factors in an attempt to determine the likelihood of success of the venture and the risk of the investment. These factors are likely to include:

+ history of the business (or the idea, if the business is not yet in existence)
+ assessment of existing and proposed competition
+ qualifications of the management team
+ marketing plan
+ the pro forma income statements and balance sheets over (at least) a three-year period
+ funding requirements of the business
+ assessment of the likelihood of recapture or harvest of funds provided by the venture capitalist together with the necessary return on investment

THE VENTURE-CAPITAL CONTRACT

Because most entrepreneurs are exceptionally reluctant to give a venture capitalist control of their business, the venture capitalist usually will insist that the following elements be addressed in the contractual agreement that forms the basis of the relationship.

+ basis for wealth-sharing and control (percent of ownership and composition of board of directors)
+ period of harvest (when the venture capitalist will exit the firm)
+ termination clause (how the entrepreneur can be removed as head of the business)
+ performance standards (how performance of the entrepreneur will be judged)

Jog et al[10] specify twelve typical clauses that are included in contracts between the entrepreneur and the venture capitalist with the aim of establishing certainty and eliminating potential conflict. These include matters pertaining to:

1. right to nominate directors to the board of directors
2. the need for the board of directors to meet regularly
3. prevention of a unilateral decision to change the firm's accountant
4. prevention of unilateral decisions by management to transfers of shares
5. prevention of unilateral decisions relating to any dividend payment
6. access to financial statements and financial information
7. rights to participate in a new share offering on a pre-emptive basis
8. limitations on management stock-option plans
9. restrictions on transfer and pledging of shares
10. life insurance on principals
11. restrictions on owner/managers' salaries and other compensation
12. specific remedies for non-compliance of any terms of the contract

The purpose of these clauses is to eliminate any agency problem that might exist between the entrepreneur and the venture capitalist.

THE U.S. REGULATORY ENVIRONMENT: PRIVATE PLACEMENTS

The term *private placement* applies to a particular method by which a firm acquires private capital (both debt and equity). Private placements are issues of securities that are sold directly to investors. In the case of private placements, a firm must comply with both federal laws and the securities laws of individual states.

Federal Regulation

Registering securities is a time-consuming and expensive process. **Regulation D** (sometimes referred to as Reg D) was promulgated by the Securities Exchange Commission (SEC) to provide a way for the small business to exempt itself from lengthy and cumbersome registration requirements.

Part of Regulation D is comprised of three rules (Rule 504, Rule 505, and Rule 506) that allow the small business to be exempted from the general registration process in some circumstances. Despite the exemption from the general registration process, the qualifying small business must still file Form D with the Securities and Exchange Commission within fifteen days following the issue of the security. Form D is a brief form requiring general information about the firm and the securities being issued.

---

[10]See V. M. Jog, W. M. Lawson, and A. I. Riding, 1991, p. 12.

Rule 504 **Rule 504** applies to firms issuing less than $1 million in securities over a twelve-month period. It effectively delegates the regulation of small security issues to state regulators by exempting the qualifying business from federal regulations regarding the maximum number of investors or the capability of the investor. It is therefore important to be aware of individual state regulations when applying Rule 504.

Rule 505 **Rule 505** allows the sale of up to $5 million in securities over a twelve-month period to an unlimited number of accredited investors. An "accredited investor" can be one of the following:

1. an institution (e.g., banks and insurance companies)
2. insider of the business (e.g., director and executive officer)
3. an individual or married couple with a net worth in excess of $1,000,000
4. an individual with a net income exceeding $200,000 for the last two years or a couple with income in excess of $300,000 for the last two years

In addition to the provisions relating to accredited investors, Rule 505 permits up to thirty-five unaccredited investors to purchase these securities.

Rule 506 **Rule 506** gives exemption from the general registration regulations to firms wishing to sell an unlimited number of securities to an unlimited number of accredited investors and relatives of existing owners and to up to thirty-five unaccredited investors who must be "sophisticated," i.e., they must have knowledge of the performance of the business.

State Regulation

While U.S. federal regulations provide certain exemptions from securities registration, state laws affecting the sale of securities must also be satisfied. State securities laws are generally known as "blue sky laws" because state legislators wanted to ensure that investors receive more substance than blue sky in their security purchases.

For most entrepreneurial firms, state regulations will be more binding than Regulation D. For this reason, it is critical that state securities laws be investigated before any type of security transaction is undertaken.

 CONCEPT CHECK

1. *Why are venture capitalists important to the entrepreneurial small firm?*
2. *What are the characteristics of angels and venture-capital firms?*
3. *Why are most venture-capital funds invested in the start-up stage?*
4. *What are the expectations of the two parties to a venture-capital investment?*
5. *How does the venture capitalist decide whether or not to invest in a particular firm?*
6. *What are the critical components of a venture-capital contract?*
7. *Describe Regulation D and its exemptions.*

12.3 HARVESTING RETURNS

THE OBJECTIVE

The objective of the harvest is to allow stakeholders of the business to realize their investment in the business in the best way possible where "best" is a function of price, control, and negotiability.

From the perspective of an individual investor wishing to harvest an investment in a small business, there are three methods by which the harvest process can be facilitated:

1. the firm can produce sufficient cash to buy out a group of its investors
2. the firm can be sold to another firm
3. the firm can go public through an IPO (initial public offering)

For the entrepreneurial business, the sums of money required for such an exercise are likely to be considerably larger than is the case with the lifestyler, and the investors are likely to be more "distant" from the entrepreneur. While the entrepreneur's original objective may have been to buy out the stake of any "external" investor, such as a venture capitalist, this objective often conflicts with the growth goal.

In the circumstance in which investors in the business (or at least a significant majority of them) all desire to exit the business, they have two options. The first option applies equally to lifestyle and entrepreneurial small firms and involves the sale, either gradually or in total at a single point in time, of the equity of the business to a new owner. The equity may be exchanged either for cash or for equity in the purchasing firm, although the latter stratagem usually is appropriate only if the buyer is a publicly listed corporation (otherwise the sellers can be trapped in a nightmare situation in which they have neither control nor negotiability).

The second option is to go public. This option realistically applies only to entrepreneurial small firms that are relatively stable in outlook and that are attractive to the general public.

PUBLIC OFFERINGS

When a firm goes public and lists its securities on a stock exchange, its value generally increases by about 30 percent.[11] This added value occurs because shareholders of listed firms enjoy liquidity that private investors do not; their shares are readily negotiable in a public marketplace. So, if a firm wants to increase its value quickly and dramatically, this can be accomplished by a

---

[11]For the reader who is interested in additional material relating to initial public offerings and theories of underpricing, R. G. P. McMahon, S. Holmes, P. J. Hutchinson, and D. M. Forsaith (1993) present an excellent review of the subject on pages 353–360.

public offering of stock; unfortunately, this is an expensive and lengthy proposition.

Initial Public Offerings

The ultimate harvest for an entrepreneur or a venture capitalist takes place when a firm undertakes an IPO and goes public. Because the effect of this decision is to change the fundamental financial nature of the business (including its control structures) it must be made with a great deal of care. Some of the general questions that a business needs to consider prior to an IPO include:

1. the kind of company it will become
2. the amount of capital needed
3. the cost of the issue
4. whether or not going public represents the best financing method
5. whether or not the firm is willing and able to comply with a significant increase in its regulation

Among others, the advantages to the firm of going public are an improved equity position as a result of the cash inflow from the sale of its stock, the negotiability of its securities, the potential use of future issues of its stock to acquire other companies, and an increase in the stature of the business.

However, there are disadvantages in going public. First, there is the loss of privacy. The SEC requires numerous reports and much information that the small firm is not normally accustomed to releasing (such as the salaries of its key executives). Second, going public establishes the need for the board of directors to approve certain types of decisions imposing additional restrictions on management. Third, there is a significant cost associated with going public. Not only is there the initial cost of the IPO itself (an underwriter will frequently charge up to 10 percent for underwriting services, and legal, accounting, and printing expenses can use up another 10 percent of cash receipts from the issue), but also there are the ongoing costs associated with the provision of information that is required by those who monitor the activities of listed corporations.

In general, both entrepreneurs and venture capitalists tend to seek an IPO as soon as it is feasible. The offering provides the investments of both parties with negotiability (and therefore future liquidity) and enables the harvest of the investment to be achieved by the venture capitalist without the rancor that sometimes accompanies the valuation of privately held interests.

Small Corporate Offering Registration

SCOR (small corporate offering registration) was introduced in 1989. This mechanism enables a firm to go public and to raise up to $1,000,000 without the need to adhere to the requirements of Regulation D with respect to the accreditation or number of investors. The issue cost associated with the use of SCOR is much less than a normal IPO (frequently less than $100,000).

SCOR offerings are registered with the state and the majority of states now offer this form of security registration.

CONCEPT CHECK

1. *Why might a firm wish to go public?*
2. *What impediments are there to the small business seeking public negotiability?*
3. *What is a SCOR?*

12.4 FAMILY ISSUES

Harvesting the investment from the family-owned business may be only one of the objectives of the principal owner of the firm (who might also have been its founder). In this circumstance, the principal might also have strong intentions relating to the maintenance of the business in the hands of immediate family. This means that personally difficult decisions often need to be made concerning the firm's future ownership and control, and the equitability of such decisions within the family framework.

Where a small firm, be it lifestyle- or entrepreneur-oriented, is owned, or largely owned, by the close members of an individual family, the mere realization of interests (i.e., the harvest) is often not enough to achieve the intentions of the principal of the firm. Additional factors need to be considered in the long-term planning process. In the discussion that follows, no distinction will be made between the two types of firms and it will be assumed that the principal decisionmaker is both the head of the family and the principal owner of the firm.

The most difficult decision that needs to be made by the principal relates to the question of equitability of distribution. If the principal has no intention of seeing the business controlled by the family, or an individual member of the family, the question becomes one of timing the sale of the business and utilizing the provisions of gift and inheritance-tax provisions to insure that the principal's wealth passes in an equitable manner. Decisions of this type are beyond the scope of this text and the interested reader is recommended to refer to a text on estate planning for further information on this topic.

If the principal has intentions for the firm to remain family-controlled and is interested in the effective intergenerational transfer of both the capital of the business and its control, the size of the problem is related to the number of persons requiring consideration. Ideally (from the perspective of the business itself), one person should be given the opportunity of owning a controlling interest in the firm, but the protection and rights of future minority stakeholders also need to be considered.

If the firm is structured as a sole proprietorship, it may be possible to transfer its equity entirely to one person, but, naturally enough, that person must not only *want* to run the business but *be capable* of doing so. It is also possible to transfer the ownership of such a firm to two or more people, usually siblings, a feature that is commonly associated in particular with family farming businesses. Naturally, the business needs to be economically capable of either providing a living for the "new" partners, or, alternatively, they need access to enough independent income to provide both for their living needs and for the needs of the business, if necessary. Siblings and their immediate families are often in conflict with each other. The principal needs to recognize this and objectively plan for mechanisms (which may involve the exclusion of one or more siblings from the business) that will provide stability for the firm.

One of the major problems associated with the transfer of ownership is that of determining the number of new owners of the business and how to equitably provide for those family members who are excluded from its ownership. If the intention is to provide an environment of stability for the business so that it can continue to grow and prosper, the owners of the business must also be financially stable. Overfragmentation of ownership could leave it in a financially vulnerable state, so the tradeoff is often between the future stability of the business and the equality of the settlement. The decision is obviously a very personal one, and one that can only be taken by the principal of the firm.

Where the business is owned by a family-dominated corporation, the same principles apply. The advantage of the corporate form of ownership is that the stock of the corporation can be transferred with relative ease over a long period of time to the chosen future controller, or controllers. However, the corporate form does not exclude the principal from having to make the "hard" decision concerning future ownership and control.

 CONCEPT CHECK

1. *Why are there likely to be additional management problems in the case of the family firm?*
2. *What is the difficulty associated with giving the "next generation" equal shares in the business?*

12.5 FRANCHISING

THE NATURE OF FRANCHISING

Caves and Murphy[12] define a **franchise** as "an agreement lasting for a definite or indefinite period of time in which the owner of a protected trademark grants to another person or firm, for some consideration, the right to

---

[12]See R. E. Caves, and W. Murphy, 1976, p. 572.

operate this trademark for the purpose of producing or distributing this service."

Franchising plays an important part in the economies of most countries. In the United States there are 550,000 franchised businesses and the number is growing at a rate of 6 percent per year.[13] In 1991, some $758 billion, or 41 percent of total retail sales, were derived from franchised businesses.

Franchising is not a unique type of legal business form, such as a sole proprietorship or corporation. Rather, franchising deals with concept of relationships (or contracts) between the **franchisor** (the firm that developed the product or service) and the **franchisee** (the firm that operates the business) and can be associated with any type of legal form of business entity.

One of the earliest franchises was created in A.D. 957 in England, when King Edgar ruled that there were too many alehouses in each village. He specified one alehouse per village, limited the quantities of ale to be sold, and prohibited sales of ale to priests. He also instituted a monitoring system and imposed fines on violators.

Franchising in the United States began in the 1840s with **product franchising**. These franchises were created by manufacturers in order to bypass the existing distribution system. Normally, product franchising is arranged by a manufacturer who wants to improve the distribution of her products. Automobiles, gas stations, and local bottlers provide classic examples of product franchising.

Business-format franchising was first used in the 1950s by firms wanting to expand their services. This type of franchise allows the franchisee to market products or services using the name, trademark, and, most importantly, the prescribed business format of the franchisor. In return for the use of the name, the franchisee pays a fee (i.e., a royalty payment) to the franchisor.

If measured by sales, the bulk of franchise activity in the United States is the result of product franchising (such as automobiles) rather than business format franchising (such as Kentucky Fried Chicken),[14] however, the number of business format franchises is increasing, while that of product franchises is declining. From the perspective of small-business finance though, the distinction between these types of franchising is not significant in their overall analysis.

THE FRANCHISOR

Franchising, or becoming a franchisor, is appealing for many entrepreneurs. If a businessperson is growth-oriented but is restricted by lack of funds, franchising is one way of expanding the business. Franchising not only spares

---

[13]See U.S. Department of Commerce, *Franchising the Economy* (Washington, D.C.: U.S. Government Printing Office, 1991) p. 32.

[14]See J. Mancuso, and D. Boroian, 1993, p. 14.

the franchisor from having to provide most of the funds for expansion, but also reduces the ongoing cost of monitoring each outlet. With a franchise, the onus is placed on the franchisee to perform, and the franchisor's main concern is the revenue stream of the franchisee because this forms the basis of the royalties received. Naturally, the franchisor earns less in dollar terms than if the expansion was undertaken more directly. The return on investment now has to be shared with the franchisee, who has also contributed capital to the enterprise; but the risk is also shared, the need for funding is less, and the franchisee is expected to perform better than an employed outlet manager.

While the idea of becoming a franchisor appeals to many entrepreneurs, there are significant marketing costs associated with starting the operation. Costs such as drafting the uniform franchise offering circular (UFOC)[15] and the pro forma franchise agreement have to be paid before any solicitation of potential franchisees can be undertaken. As with all investment decisions, the costs and benefits must be compared.

One does not usually consider franchisees as being financial contributors to the franchisor, but if one considers an "organization" as being the nexus of contracts[16] the relationship between the franchisor and the franchisee as comprising an organization can be understood. This organization, which has an objective of delivering a product or service to its user, consists of both the franchisor and the franchisee; they are both stakeholders in a business even though they are financially distinct. The various reasons for the establishment of a franchised operation include the reduction in investment required of the franchisor due to the investment of the franchisee. Thus, the franchisee can be considered a partial funder (in its widest sense) of the operations of the franchisor.

There are, of course, many reasons for the establishment of a franchised operation other than the savings associated with the franchisor not having to fund the establishment of outlets. Rubin explains franchising in an agency context.[17] He suggests that firms (franchisors) will offer franchises when the cost of monitoring management is high, a contention supported by Brickley and Dark.[18]

FRANCHISE AGREEMENTS

The Nature and Purpose of the Agreement

The **franchise agreement,** or contract, is normally for a finite number of years (usually around fifteen) and can customarily be renewed. The franchisee generally prefers a contract for as long a period as possible because

---

[15]The UFOC is defined in the next section of this chapter.

[16]The reader who is interested in the nature of organizations is referred to the seminal work of R. H. Coase, 1937.

[17]See P. Rubin, 1978, p. 225.

[18]See J. A. Brickley, and F. H. Dark, 1987, p. 409.

this effectively minimizes the annualized cost of any initial fees (which will be discussed in the next section of this chapter) and because the royalty fee is locked into the agreement.

Under the agreement, the owner of a protected name or trademark grants to another person or firm the right to use this trademark. It is this central tenet that really provides the rationale for the existence of franchises. If one has a franchise agreement with McDonald's, puts up the golden arches, and puts the McDonald's name on a restaurant, then customers will come because they know the consistency and quality assurances that the McDonald's name and trademark provide.

According to Rubin,[19] franchise agreements have four common clauses:

1. the franchisor provides managerial assistance to the franchisee
2. the franchisee runs the business according to the specification of the franchisor
3. a royalty fee of some sort is paid by the franchisee
4. the termination clause defines the method of exit of owners (although the contract is normally subject to renewal)

The purpose of these four clauses is to ensure that the franchisee is operating in the best interests of the franchisor. The clauses force the franchisee to perform in the manner prescribed by the franchisor. This rigidity has both strengths and weaknesses. On the one hand, it forces conformity (for example, a McDonald's Big Mac in Tallahassee, Florida, tastes the same as a Big Mac in San Francisco, California). This conformity is of extreme value because it eliminates any uncertainty in the mind of a potential customer as to the quality of the product and service. On the other hand, the need for conformity restricts the ability of the franchisee to do anything that is new and creative; the franchisee is locked into doing what the franchisor has agreed he must do.

The Uniform Franchise Offering Circular (UFOC)

As in all areas of business, becoming a franchisee is not riskless. At one extreme there are the reputable franchisors who are interested in developing a long-term relationship with their franchisees. However, at the other extreme, there are those who are merely interested in taking money from naive investors. In an attempt to protect the potential franchisee, the Federal Trade Commission requires that a disclosure document (the **uniform franchise offering circular** or **UFOC**), mentioned earlier, be provided to the prospective franchisee. Among other things, it specifies the fee structure, the territorial right, and the termination arrangements that will be included in the franchise contract that formally establishes the relationship between the franchisee and the franchisor.

---

[19]See P. Rubin, 1978, p. 226.

The **initial franchise fee** is normally required to be paid and received on the signing of the agreement. The size of this fee depends on how attractive the franchise is and varies from time to time, depending on the projected outcomes for a particular franchise. It is normally in the range of $20,000 to $25,000 (for example, Kentucky Fried Chicken has a fee of $22,500 and TCBY [The Country's Best Yogurt] charges $20,000) and is usually paid as a lump sum. From the perspective of the franchisor, these fees are important in that they represent a partial recovery of expenses associated with developing and marketing the franchise.

In addition to the initial franchise fee, the franchisee will be required to pay periodic **royalties** and **advertising fees** (as specified in the agreement). The royalty paid to the franchisor funds the continual assistance needs of the franchisee with any surplus representing the franchisor's return on investment. Examples of royalty rates (as a percent of gross sales) include McDonald's, 3.5 percent; TCBY, 4 percent; Blimpie's (submarine sandwich chain), 6 percent; and Subway Sandwiches, 8 percent.

Advertising fees are also customarily assessed as a percent of gross sales. The advertising services provided by the franchisor must be carefully analyzed by the franchisee. The individual franchisee of a franchise operation that is national (e.g., Subway Sandwiches) will benefit from national advertising, while a franchise operation that does not have a national presence will benefit less from national advertising and more from local advertising. TCBY charges 3 percent of gross sales as an advertising fee. The equivalent rate for Subway is 2.5 percent, Burger King is 4 percent, and McDonald's is also 4 percent.

The **exclusive territory rights** associated with a franchise must also be specified. In general, the franchisee wants the territory to be as large as possible in order to avoid competition for customers within a given area. However, the franchisor wants to keep it relatively small in order to be able to sell more franchises in a given area.

The **termination clause** specifies arrangements relevant to the exit of the franchisee from the business. One of the usual requirements is that the franchisor must approve any sale or transfer of assets. In some cases the contract specifies that the franchisor has a **first right of refusal,** which states that once the franchisee and an intending purchaser of the franchisee's interest have agreed on a sale price, the franchisor has the option of purchasing the business at that price.

While the franchise contract will follow closely the specifications of the UFOC, no intending franchisee should enter into such a relationship without independent legal advice.

THE FRANCHISEE

Benefits and Costs

To understand franchising, it is necessary to understand the basic differences between franchised businesses and other businesses. While the two forms of businesses have many similarities, it is the differences that highlight the distinctive features of a franchise operation. From the perspective of the franchisee, the principal advantages provided by franchising include an improvement in cash flows and a reduction in bankruptcy risk. These two benefits need to be carefully weighed against the additional costs associated with the purchase of a franchisee's interest.

With respect to relative failure rates, the Small Business Administration reports that 24 percent of small (non-franchise) businesses fail within the first two years of operation, and 62.7 percent fail within six years.[20] The Department of Commerce[21] reports a failure rate of less than 5 percent for franchisees (this rate can be disputed in that it only represents franchises that were closed and does not include cases of stressed individuals selling their franchises, either to a new franchisee or back to the franchisor). While it is difficult to make a direct comparison between the failure rates of franchise and non-franchise operations, clearly, franchisees face a lower risk of failure.

The risk of bankruptcy for a franchisee *should* be low. The two major causes of small-business failure are a lack of management skill and a lack of adequate finance, and these are greatly reduced in the case of the franchised operation.

With respect to management skills, before a franchise becomes operational, the franchisee will be well trained in all aspects of the business by the franchisor. The classic example of this is the training at McDonald's "Hamburger U," which lasts about six weeks, but most franchisors run training programs that last about two weeks. The purpose of the training program and the operating plan that the franchisor gives to the franchisee is aimed at ensuring the success of the enterprise.

One reason for the lower rate of failure of the franchise can be associated with the financial screening process of potential franchisees that is undertaken by the franchisor. A franchisor eliminates the risk of insufficient capital by having a personal financial statement submitted with each franchise application. Most potential franchisees have to contribute a significant amount of cash to initially fund the operation. For example, in the case of McDonald's, the total investment is likely to cost $550,000 (including the initial franchise fee of $22,500) of which $100,000 must be represented by a cash contribution. Subway requires an initial franchise fee of $10,000 and a total investment of about $60,000, of which a cash contribution of $30,000 is required.[22] The franchisor eliminates the potential failure problem of insufficient capital by selecting those applicants that have adequate funds.

The other benefit of franchising is that cash flow is usually greater and more quickly realized than is the case with a non-franchised operation. Indeed,

---

[20]See *The State of Small Business: A Report of the President*, 1989, p. 25.

[21]See *Franchising the Economy*, 1991, p. 18.

[22]A very good source of data on franchises is *The Source Book of Franchise Opportunities* by Robert and Jeffrey M. Bond, published by Business One Irwin and available at most book stores.

individuals who pay a premium for a franchise expect these advantages or else they would not pay the premium. Caves and Murphy[23] point out that there are scale economies in the sales promotions of franchises as well as many other revenue and cost advantages. The franchisee *should* get the instant credibility that a non-franchise firm has to earn over time (putting a Subway sign up will draw more customers more quickly than the "No-Name Sub Shop") and this instant credibility, combined with the reduced costs inherent in cooperative advertising, generally produces greater cash flows more quickly than is the case with the non-franchised business.

Evaluation Models

While a franchisee accrues certain benefits, such as higher cash flows and lower failure rates, these must be compared to the cost of franchising (including the initial franchise fee and royalty and advertising payments). Clearly, a decision model is needed to ascertain whether or not a franchise is worth purchasing. This can be done by comparing the franchised operation with its equivalent non-franchised operation. The decision depends on the relativity between the marginal benefits (additional cash flows) that a franchisee receives over a non-franchise operation and the marginal cost (additional costs of the initial and royalty fee payments) of franchising. One can then use the net present value (NPV) model[24] in the evaluation process. A positive NPV indicates that the franchised form of business is preferred to the non-franchised form; a negative NPV implies a preference for the non-franchised form.

The first model suggested below evaluates the franchise by considering the after-tax cash flow improvement alone, while the second model extends the first by incorporating the expected reduction in bankruptcy probability.

A Multi-period Model for Franchise Evaluation The first model that can be applied to the evaluation of a franchise is a multi-period model that ignores the decreased probability of failure that is associated with a franchise.

$$NPV_F = \sum_{t=1}^{N} \frac{CF_t}{(1+r)^t} - \sum_{t=1}^{N} \frac{CNF_t}{(1+r)^t} - LSP - \sum_{t=1}^{N} \frac{(FF)(RF_t)}{(1+r)^t}$$

where NPV_F = marginal improvement in the net present value of the franchised over the non-franchised firm

CF_t = franchised firm after-tax cash flow in period t, or gross revenue of the franchised firm multiplied by the after-tax profit margin in period t

[23]See R. E. Caves, and W. Murphy, 1976, p. 574.

[24]Most of the work in this section on the decision model for franchising was originally developed in "A Valuation Model for Franchises," by J. S. Osteryoung, C. Hodges, and W. Wells, 1993.

ANNA CAVALLINI FRANCHISE ANALYSIS

Year	CF_t	CNF_t	LSP	$(FF)(RF_t)$	Net cash flow	Present value at 20 percent
0			$-25,000		$-25,000	$-25,000
1	$100,000	$-50,000		$-30,000	20,000	16,666
2	100,000	-50,000		-30,000	20,000	13,888
3	100,000	-50,000		-30,000	20,000	11,574
4	100,000	-50,000		-30,000	20,000	9,645
5	100,000	-50,000		-30,000	20,000	8,037
6	100,000	-50,000		-30,000	20,000	6,697
7	100,000	-50,000		-30,000	20,000	5,581
8	100,000	-50,000		-30,000	20,000	4,651
9	100,000	-50,000		-30,000	20,000	3,876
10	100,000	-50,000		-30,000	20,000	3,230
NPV						58,845

r = investor's required rate of return
CNF_t = non-franchised firm after-tax cash flow in period t
LSP = lump-sum payment
FF = franchise fee as a percent of annual gross revenues
RF_t = annual gross revenue of the franchise firm

For example, suppose that Anna Cavallini is considering purchasing a fast-food franchise. The annual revenue of the franchised operation is expected to be $500,000, yielding an annual cash flow of $100,000 (after taxes) for ten years; whereas opening an independent location will only produce an annual after-tax cash flow of $50,000. The lump-sum payment (at time 0) is $25,000 and the franchise fee is 6 percent. The relevant opportunity cost of funds is considered to be 20 percent.

Exhibit 12.6 shows the application of the multi-period model to this problem. Given that the NPV of the franchise (the summation of the last column) is positive, at $58,845, this indicates that Anna should purchase the franchise.

A Multi-period Model for Franchise Evaluation with Bankruptcy Probabilities
To account for the difference in failure rate between franchised and non-franchised firms, the analyst needs a more sophisticated model than that described previously in this chapter.

$$NPV_F = \sum_{t=1}^{N} \frac{(CF_t - CNF_t)(1 - b_f)}{(1 + r)^t} + \sum_{t=1}^{N} \frac{CNF_t(b_{nf} - b_f)}{(1 + r)^t} - LSP - \sum_{t=1}^{N} \frac{(FF)(RF_t)}{(1 + r)^t}$$

ANNA CAVALLINI FRANCHISE ANALYSIS INCLUDING FAILURE RATES

Year	$(CF_t - CNF_t)$	$(CF_t - CNF_t)$ $(1 - B_f)$	(CNF_t) $(b_{nf} - b_f)$	LSP	$(FF)(RF_t)$	Net Cash Flow	PV at 20 percent
0				$-25,000		$-25,000	$-25,000
1	$50,000	$45,000	$10,000		$-30,000	25,000	20,833
2	50,000	45,000	10,000		-30,000	25,000	17,361
3	50,000	45,000	10,000		-30,000	25,000	14,467
4	50,000	45,000	10,000		-30,000	25,000	12,056
5	50,000	45,000	10,000		-30,000	25,000	10,046
6	50,000	45,000	10,000		-30,000	25,000	8,372
7	50,000	45,000	10,000		-30,000	25,000	6,977
8	50,000	45,000	10,000		-30,000	25,000	5,814
9	50,000	45,000	10,000		-30,000	25,000	4,845
10	50,000	45,000	10,000		-30,000	25,000	4,037
NPV							$ 79,808

where: b_{nf} = independent probability of bankruptcy of the non-franchise firm in period t

b_f = independent probability of bankruptcy of the franchise

To see how this refined evaluation equation works, assume that Anna now wishes to include in the decision process the fact that the failure rate of franchises of this type is 10 percent, while for similar, but non-franchised firms, it is 30 percent. Exhibit 12.7 shows that the NPV in this case is $79,808.

Notice that the NPV increased by $20,963 (the difference between the NPVs of the two tables) once the probability of failure and bankruptcy was accounted for. This increase results from the enhancement of the value of the franchise when the probability of failure for a franchise is less than the probability of failure for a non-franchised business.

 CONCEPT CHECK

1. *What is a franchise?*
2. *The definition of a franchise proposed by Caves and Murphy is made up of two components. What are they?*
3. *What is product franchising?*
4. *What is business format franchising?*
5. *What are the major advantages associated with being a franchisor?*
6. *What are the costs and disadvantages of being a franchisor?*
7. *Why can we consider franchising as, at least in part, a funding choice?*

8. What are the four common clauses contained in a franchise agreement, and what is their purpose?
9. What is a UFOC and what is its relationship to the franchise agreement?
10. What are the critical components of a UFOC?
11. What are the major differences between franchised businesses and non-franchised businesses?
12. What are the fundamental costs and benefits of franchising?
13. What are the major components that need to be addressed by franchise evaluation models?
14. Why does the inclusion of a relative failure rate increase the value of a franchise?

SUMMARY

+ This chapter is concerned with the ways in which the entrepreneurial firm can fund its expansion.
+ Venture capitalists seek a return commensurate with the amount of risk that they face, which is, in turn, partially related to the stage of development of the business. Agreement must be reached between the venture capitalist and the entrepreneur that protects and satisfies both parties.
+ Private placement is the process of selling and distributing the financial securities of private firms. This process is governed by the federal and state regulations.
+ Public offerings provide a mechanism for both the entrepreneur and the venture capitalist to harvest their investment in the firm. There are two types of public offerings. SCOR can apply to small firms wishing to issue less than $1,000,000, while the IPO generally applies to much larger issues.
+ Planning the harvest of an investment in a family firm presents additional problems when issues such as future control and equitability of control and distribution need to be considered. The principal of such a firm is often required to make hard decisions that trade personal desires against the need to protect the stability of the business itself.
+ Franchising is suggested as one method of enabling expansion of the entrepreneurial firm.
+ Franchising appeals to the franchisor because it reduces both the capital costs associated with opening an outlet and the ongoing monitoring costs associated with its management. In exchange, some of the return that would normally accrue to the owner of a business is passed to the franchisee.
+ Franchising is appealing to the franchisee for the following reasons:
  1. proven business entity
  2. instant credibility
  3. reduced bankruptcy or failure rates
  4. higher, faster cash flows than non-franchised equivalent operations
  5. exclusive territorial right
+ The obligations of the franchisee include:
  1. payment of the initial franchise fee
  2. payment of ongoing royalty fees and contributions to advertising
  3. set-up costs
  4. restrictions on behavior

✦ The UFOC and the franchise agreement establish the relationship between the franchisor and the franchisee.
✦ Two models for evaluating the decision process relating to franchising were presented. These models evaluate the cost and benefits of franchising.

THE CASE—PART TWELVE

Dave's Bikes has been doing well. The only problem that Dave faces is the usual one, common to all small enterprises that grow quickly—funding. Sandy has suggested two alternatives to Dave, franchising and seeking a capital input from a new equity partner.

ASSIGNMENT 12.1

Dave is considering becoming a franchisor. To do this effectively, he needs to show prospective franchisees that buying a Dave's Bikes franchise is a worthwhile investment.

Required

1. Dave proposes charging a lump-sum payment of $50,000 and a royalty fee of 6 percent. The pre-tax cash flow from a franchise operation is expected to be $80,000 per year (before the royalty payment for fifteen years) based on an expected annual revenue of $300,000. On the other hand, an independent operation is likely to earn a cash flow of only $50,000 per annum. If the prospective franchisee's pre-tax discount rate is 25 percent, and assuming that the failure rate of the franchised firm and the independent firm are similar, is Dave's franchise worth investing in?

2. If your answer to question 1 is no, how much should Dave charge for the lump-sum payment?

ASSIGNMENT 12.2

Dave successfully sells eight franchises to operators in adjacent states. He now needs to raise $400,000 to finance his future expansion plans. If these plans succeed, the future free cash flows that will be generated by the firm are expected to be:

Year 1	$ 240,000
Year 2	350,000
Year 3	500,000
Year 4	600,000
Year 5	900,000
Year 6	1,200,000
Year 7	1,500,000

If Dave borrows the money from his bank, he will have to personally guarantee the advance, and while he is not too happy with that prospect, he is prepared to consider all the alternatives.

Required

1. Should Dave seek new debt or new equity to finance the expansion?
2. What are some likely conditions that a new equity partner capitalist will insist on in funding Dave?
3. If an investor requires a 40 percent annual compound rate of return, and assuming that at the end of year 7 the firm is expected to be worth four times its free cash flow, how much equity does Dave need to offer in exchange for the $400,000 capital injection?

SELECTED ADDITIONAL READINGS

Anderson, E. 1984. The growth and performance of franchise systems: Company versus franchise ownership. *Journal of Economics and Business* (December): 421–431.

Blair, R. D., and D. Kasserman. 1982. Optimal franchising. *Southern Economic Journal* (October): 494–504.

Blair, R. D., and D. Kasserman. 1985. Unanswered questions about franchising: Reply. *Southern Economic Journal* (January): 933–936.

Bond, R., and J. M. Bond. 1995. *The source book of franchise opportunities* (Homewood, IL: Business One Irwin).

Brickley, J. A., and F. H. Dark. 1987. The choice of organizational form: The case of franchising. *Journal of Financial Economics* 18(2): 401–420.

Bygrave, W. D. 1994. *The portable MBA in entrepreneurship* (New York: John Wiley & Sons, Inc.).

Bygrave, W. D., and J. Timmons. 1992. *Venture capital at the crossroads* (Boston, MA: Harvard Business School Press).

Caves, R. E., and W. Murphy. 1976. The choice of organizational form: The case of franchising. *Southern Economic Journal* (April): 572–586.

Coase, R. H. 1937. The nature of the firm. *Econometrica* (November).

Combs, J. G., and G. Castrogiovanni. 1994. Franchisor strategy: A proposed model and empirical test of franchise versus company ownership. *Journal of Small Business Management* (April): 37–48.

Dyl, E. 1989. Financial issues in franchising. Presentation at the Small Firm Research Symposium at California State University, Fresno.

Fratrik, M., and R. Lafferty. 1985. Unanswered questions about franchising: Comment. *Southern Economic Journal* (January): 927–932.

Frew, J., and G. Judd. 1986. The value of a real estate franchise. *AREUA Journal* (summer): 374–383.

Garner, D. R., R. Owen, and R. Conway. 1994. *The Ernst & Young guide to financing for growth* (New York: John Wiley & Sons).

Gladstone, D. 1988. *Venture capital handbook* (Englewood Cliffs, NJ: Prentice-Hall).

Hunt, S. 1973. The trend toward company-operated units in franchise chains. *Journal of Retailing* (summer): 3–12.

Inaba, F. 1980. Franchising: Monopoly by contract. *Southern Economic Journal* (July): 65–72.

Joslyn, A. 1987. Legislative definitions of the franchise relationship. *New York Law School Law Review* (32): 779–793.

Kobak, J. 1987. Significant factors in the franchisor–franchisee relationship. *New York Law School Law Review* (32): 795–817.

Mancuso, J., and D. Boroian. 1993. *How to buy and manage a franchise* (New York: Fireside).

McMahon, R. G. P., S. Holmes, P. J. Hutchinson, and D. M. Forsaith. 1993. *Small enterprise financial management: Theory and practice* (Sydney, Australia: Harcourt Brace).

Mittelsteadt, R., and M. Peterson. 1980. *Franchising and the financing of small business: Studies of small business finance* (Washington, D.C.: The Interagency Task Force on Small Business Finance).

Morris, J., S. Senstein, and A. Knowles, eds. 1992. *Pratt's guide to venture capital sources* (New York: SDC).

Mull, R. 1994. Venture capital, private firms, and the capital acquisition process. *Journal of Small Business Finance* 3(3): 229–248.

Myers, S. C. 1984. The capital structure puzzle. *Journal of Finance* (July): 575–592.

National Venture Capital Association. 1995. *Fifth annual economic impact of venture capital study* (Arlington, VA: National Venture Capital Association).

Norton, E. 1994. Venture capitalist attributes and investment vehicles: An exploratory analysis. *Journal of Small Business Finance* (3)3: 181–198.

Osteryoung, J. S., C. Hodges, and W. Wells. 1993. A valuation model for franchises. *Business Valuation Review* (June): 61–71.

Petty, W. J., and W. D. Bygrave. 1993. What does finance have to say to the entrepreneur? *Journal of Small Business Finance* 2(2): 125–138.

Raab, S. S., and G. Matusky. 1987. *Blueprint for franchising a business* (New York: John Wiley & Sons).

Rhee, T. A. 1991. Tax effects on the value of incentive stock options and the decision to go public. *Journal of Small Business Finance* 1(2): 101–114.

Rubin, P. 1978. The theory of the firm and the structure of the franchise contract. *Journal of Law and Economics* (April): 223–233.

Sahlman, W. (1990). The structure and governance of the venture-capital organizations. *Journal of Financial Economics* 27(2): 473–521.

Serwer, A. E. 1995. Trouble in franchise nation. *Fortune* (March 6): 115–122.

Sutton, D. P., and M. W. Beneddetto. 1990. *Initial public offerings* (Chicago: Probus).

The 1989 state of small business: A report of the president. 1990. (Washington, D.C.: U.S. Government Printing Office).

U.S. Department of Commerce. 1984. *Franchising opportunity book* (Washington, D.C.: U.S. Government Printing Office).

U.S. Department of Commerce. 1991. *Franchising the economy* (Washington, D.C.: U.S. Government Printing Office).

Vesper, K. H. 1993. *New venture mechanics* (Englewood Cliffs, NJ: Prentice-Hall).

GLOSSARY

ABC inventory method Allocates priority ratings to different product lines or groups of a firm.

Accelerated cost recovery system (ACRS) A method of depreciating an asset for *taxation* purposes that is faster than is generally accepted for *accounting* purposes. This method allows the firm to decrease the amount of taxation that is paid early in the life of the asset.

Accelerated depreciation See *Accelerated cost recovery system (ACRS)*.

Account Accounting-system record that details additions, deductions, and balances of individual assets, liabilities, revenues, expenses, and owners' equity.

Accounting entity The entire organization to which the financial statement applies.

Accounting period Time period for which financial statements are prepared.

Accounting-period principle Assumption that the financial statement provides a periodic measurement of performance.

Accounting rate of return (ARR) Method of ranking a project based on its marginal profitability and its average cost.

Accounts payable Money owed by the business to persons who provided it with goods or services.

Accounts payable turnover Determines how many times accounts payable are turned over in one year; calculated by dividing cost of goods sold by accounts payable.

Accounts receivable Money due to a business from persons who purchased goods or services from it.

Accounts receivable turnover Rate at which accounts receivable are generated and received.

Accrual basis Revenues and expenses recognized in the period in which they are incurred rather than received or paid.

Acid-test ratio Short-term liquidity ratio based on near-cash assets and liabilities (also called quick ratio).

Add-on interest Interest added to the principal sum of a debt; the resulting total is divided into equal periodic payments (also called flat interest).

Advertising fees (franchising) Periodic payments based on a percent of sales and paid by a franchisee to a franchisor to defray the costs of centralized advertising paid by the franchisor (see also *Franchising, Royalties*).

After-tax EBIT Earnings before interest and tax (EBIT) multiplied by 1 minus the tax rate.

After-tax measures Conversion of a before-tax item to its after-tax equivalent.

Amortized Annuity payments sufficient to meet current interest requirements and to extinguish a debt at expiration of the loan period.

Amortized loan Type of loan that bears a contractual requirement for periodic payments of interest and principal.

Angel Term used to describe an individual provider of venture capital (see also *Venture capital*).

Annual cash budget Annual schedule of expected cash inflows and cash outflows.

Asset turnover ratio Calculate how effectively a firm uses assets to generate sales; calculated by dividing sales revenue by total assets.

Assets Anything owned by the firm that has probable future economic or exchange value.

Asymmetric information Situation in which one party knows more about a given circumstance than the other party.

Audited statements Reports in which auditors have verified the accuracy of transaction recording and preparation methodology.

Auditor's opinion Statement, provided by an independent person, that expresses an opinion as to whether a financial statement was prepared in a proper fashion.

Average collection period Average length of time for which a business extends credit to its customers. Also called average sales credit period.

Average cost of debt (K_i) Periodic total interest divided by the average debt of the period.

Average purchase credit period Average length of time for which a business borrows on credit.

Balance Closing value of an account at the end of the accounting period.

Balance date Date that signifies the end of the accounting period.

Balance of payments Accounting statement of a nation's international trade and financial transactions over a period of time, usually one year (see also *Current account, Capital account, Official reserves account*).

Balance sheet Statement of the financial condition of a firm at a specific point in time (also known as the statement of assets and liabilities).

Balloon loan Loan having small payments of interest and principal at the start increasing to large payments at the end of the loan term.

Bank overdraft Amount of the credit line extended by a bank that is drawn upon at a particular point in time.

Bank reconciliation Procedure for reconciling the difference between the bank balance according to the bank statement and the bank balance according to the ledgers of a business.

Bear market Stock market that exhibits a relatively slow rate of value increases and turnover.

Benefit–cost ratio See *Excess present value index, Profitability index*.

Bill of exchange (B/E) Also known as a commercial draft, it is an unconditional order in writing, signed by the drawer, to pay a pre-determined sum of money at some future time period (see also *Holder in due course*).

Bill of lading (B/L) Document that serves to provide: (1) a receipt of goods, (2) a memorandum of the terms and conditions of carriage, and (3) evidence of title to the goods being transported. A B/L may be: straight or to order, clean or foul, through or direct, on-board or received.

Bond Interest-bearing certificate of debt where the borrower promises to pay the lender specified amounts of interest on specific dates with the principal being returned to the lender at the end of the period.

Book values Values shown in the financial reports of a business for any asset, liability, or owners'-equity item.

Break-even analysis Process of forecasting break-even points according to the level of sales at which the business operates (also called cost–volume–profit analysis).

Break-even point Point at which a business makes neither a profit nor a loss on operations.

Budget Estimate or plan for a future period of business activity.

Budgeting process Another name for financial planning.

Bull markets Periods of generally increasing market prices.

Business cycle Ongoing process of booms and slumps in the life of a business.

Business-format franchising Process by which a franchisor grants to a franchisee the right to market products or services using the name, trademark, and business format of the franchisor (see also *Franchising, Product franchising*).

Business risk Risk that EBIT will vary due to changes in sales revenue and the costs of expenses other than interest; risk associated with a particular industry sector.

Call options The right, but not the obligation, to purchase a stake in a business in the future.

Capital Stock of accumulated wealth belonging to the owners of a business that is put to economic use (also called equity).

Capital account (international trade) Part of the balance of payments account, it details the movements of capital (investment and lending) in or out of a country (see also *Balance of payments, Current account, Official reserves account*).

Capital assets Physical assets of a firm.

Capital budgeting Process of planning the capital investment activities of a business.

Capital budgeting decision See *Capital investment decision*.

Capital investment decision Decision to commit a firm's resources (capital, people, know-how, etc.) to particular projects with the intention of achieving greater financial and other benefits in the future (see also *Capital budgeting*).

Capital rationing Inadequacy of funds for all financially viable investment opportunities, which forces a firm to prioritize among them.

Capital reserves Undistributed profits resulting from capital transactions.

Capital structure Relative amounts of debt and equity a business has.

Capital structure decision Managerial decision relating to the capital structure of the business.

Carrying costs Costs associated with keeping inventory on hand.

Cash basis Revenues and expenses recognized only when physically received or paid.

Cash-conversion cycle A measure of the period of time between incurring a cash expenditure and receiving cash associated with the sale of goods or services created by the initial expenditure.

Cash flow Sources and uses of a firm's cash funds over a specified period.

Cash-flow budget Statement of expected cash receipts and cash payments, showing the timing of each.

Cash-flow statement Report that summarizes the cash movements of the business (See *statement of cash flows*).

Class of shares Types of shares a firm issues; e.g., ordinary shares, preference shares.

Clean bill of lading Document that acknowledges that goods were received by a carrier without apparent damage (see also *Foul bill of lading, Bill of lading*).

Clientele effect Different people prefer to meet their consumption needs from a business in different ways. Dividend policies can be affected by investors who may prefer capital gains, while others may prefer dividends. (Investor preferences are often determined by the investor's tax bracket).

Collateral security Property that is pledged as security for a loan.

Commercial bills Unsecured short-term loans issued by banks at a discount.

Comparable analysis Comparison of items, or groups of items, in financial statements of different organizations.

Compiled statements Unaudited reports provided by the firm's management.

Confirmed letter of credit A letter of credit in which both the domestic and foreign banks obligate themselves to payment of the instrument (see also *Unconfirmed letter of credit, Letter of credit*).

Consignment Trading arrangement where goods are shipped to an importer without the exporter giving up title of ownership. The importer acts as an agent and remits the proceeds of sales, less commission and expenses, to the exporter.

Constant-money principle Assumption that money is the common denominator used for all financial reporting.

Continuous inventory method Begins with all stock on hand at a given date, adds all stock delivered, and deducts all stock shipped to arrive at a balance. Also called perpetual inventory method.

Contribution margin Amount of every sales dollar that is available to contribute to the payment of the fixed costs of a business.

Control premium Premium price paid by the purchaser of a block of stock over and above its current market value due to the purchaser's association with the provision of control over the activities of the firm.

Conventional cash flows When there is an initial capital investment outlay followed by positive cash flows for the remainder of a project's life (see also *Unconventional cash flows*).

Corporation A form of business organization where each owner of the business is not personally liable for the debts of the business in the absence of any personal guarantee (see also *Limited-liability company*).

Cost-volume-profit analysis (CVP) See *Break-even analysis.*

Countertrade Sales of goods to an importer is offset by reciprocal exports from the importing firm or country.

Country-risk assessment Assessment of the potential risk of loss from political or economic action that affects the transfer of funds from target market back to the home country.

Covering See *Forward hedging.*

Credit cards Charge cards that allow purchases on credit.

Credit period Length of time allowed to a customer before payment is due (see also *Discount period*).

Credit policy Policy with respect to both the type of credit facility offered and the terms upon which credit is given.

Current assets Assets that are cash or are expected to be converted to cash or consumed in the production of other current assets within the normal operating cycle of the firm (usually less than one year).

Current liabilities Liabilities that are expected to be discharged on demand or within the normal operating cycle of the firm (usually less than one year).

Current ratio Measure of liquidity based on the association between current assets and current liabilities of the firm (see also *Liquidity ratio, Working-capital ratio*).

Debenture Formal financial instrument acknowledging the indebtedness of a company. May be fixed, floating, or in series. May be specifically or generally secured with the assets of a business (See *bond*).

Debt Amounts owed by the business to non-equity holders.

Debtholders Individuals or institutions who have a stake in the business by virtue of advancing credit to it.

Debt ratio Total debt divided by total assets (also called leverage ratio or gearing ratio).

Debt-to-assets ratio See *Debt ratio.*

Decision tree Graphical representation of alternative sequential decisions exhibiting the most likely outcomes from those decisions.

Declining balance method of depreciation Method of depreciation where the amount of depreciation declines each year as a function of the book value.

Degree of financial leverage (DFL) Measure of the financial risk of the business.

Degree of operating leverage (DOL) Measure of the business risk of a certain business.

Degree of total leverage (DTL) Measure of the total risk of the business based on the responsiveness of a firm's net profit to changes in sales.

Differential cash flow The incremental cash flows of a project or income-generating asset, in respect to its alternative (often a replacement asset).

Differential sales revenue Incremental cash flows of a project or income-generating asset, as it applies to sales revenue only (see also *Differential cash flow*).

Diminishing value Method of accounting for depreciation where the value of an asset is reduced by a constant rate rather than by a constant amount.

Direct bill of lading Shipping document that provides for one vessel to carry a shipment to its eventual destination without transshipment (see also *Through bill of lading, Bill of lading*).

Directors' fees Monetary sum paid to directors of a company for their services.

Discount factor 1 divided by $(1 + i)^n$ by which a periodic cash flow is multiplied to provide its present value.

Discount period Length of time offered to a customer to pay an invoice in order to obtain a discount on the invoice total.

Discounted cash flow Future cash flows multiplied (adjusted) by discount factors to obtain the present values (see also *Discount factor, Present values*).

Discounted cash flow (DCF) analysis The calculation whereby the future cash flows are multiplied by (adjusted for) the discount factors to obtain the present values.

Discounted payback Investment-evaluation technique used to determine the time taken to repay an initial investment outlay, and then to discount future cash flows to present values (see also *Payback, Discounted cash flow*).

Disposal prices Prices assets are sold for when they are no longer useful to a business.

Dividend Distribution of a portion of the profits of a business to its owners.

Dividend imputation Tax credit attached to a dividend that effectively precludes double taxation of dividends.

Dividend payout ratio Measures the proportion of available net income that is paid as dividends to ordinary shareholders.

Dividend yield Dividend per share divided by the current market price per share.

Dividends per share (DPS) See *Dividend payout ratio*.

Doctrine of objectivity Means that all accounting data is provided by reliable records of all transactions.

duPont expression Used for calculating the return on equity showing the relationships between net income, sales, assets, and debt.

Dynamic inventory management Ongoing production process that requires continuous supplies of the same or similar inputs to produce the same or similar outputs (see also *Static inventory management, Intermediate process inventory*).

Dynastic intentions Intention of the owner(s) of a firm that ownership remains within the family.

Earnings before interest and tax (EBIT) See *Net operating income*.

Earnings before tax (EBT) Net operating income less interest expense.

Earnings capitalization method Method for calculating the current market price showing the relationship between value and earnings yield; i.e., current market price per share is the expected earnings per share divided by the required earnings yield.

Earnings yield Earnings per share divided by current market price per share.

Earnings-yield method Method of valuing a business based on the capitalization of its earnings by a market-indicated discount rate equivalent to the expected earnings yield (see also *Price–earnings method, Earnings capitalization method*).

Economic exposure   Potential change that may occur in the net present value of expected future after-tax flows from an overseas investment (see also *Transaction exposure, Translation exposure*).

Economic order quantity   Mathematical relationship that seeks to optimally minimize the inversely related costs of ordering and holding inventory (see also *Carrying costs, Ordering costs*).

Effective annual interest rate   Rate of interest accruing to a financial instrument based on the price paid for the instrument, the number and amount of coupon payments to be received, the length of time between those payments, and the maturity date.

Elasticity of demand   Measure of the degree of responsiveness of quantity demanded of a particular product to a given change in one of the independent variables that affect demand for that product.

Entrepreneurial businesses   A small firm that is actively seeking growth and value maximization (see also *Lifestyle business*).

Equity   The owners' claim to the assets of a business after payment is made to all creditors.

Equityholders   Individuals or institutions who have contributed equity to a business.

Excess present value index   Method of ranking a project based on the association between the present value of the benefits accruing to the project and the present value of its costs (see also *Profitability index*).

Exclusive territory rights (franchising)   Right granted by a franchisor to a franchisee specifying the territory accruing to the franchisee (see also *Franchising*).

Expected net present value   Expected net present value of a project.

Extra funds needed (EFN)   Additional financing of the business necessary after allowing for periodic profit.

Factor   To sell.

Fair-market value (FMV)   Price of a business (on a cash or cash-equivalent basis) to which both the seller and buyer agree, neither operating under duress or undue time pressure and both possessing all relevant facts regarding the business.

Favorable financial leverage   When the return on assets exceeds the cost of debt, the more debt the firm has, the greater the return on equity invested, and the greater the level of financial risk.

Financial budget   Adds items of a capital nature to the operating budget.

Financial efficiency   How well a business uses its equity to generate profitable returns for its owners.

Financial lease   Rental agreement by which the lessee acquires an ownership right to an asset.

Financial leverage   Process of using debt financing to change the return on equity.

Financial risk   The additional variability of leveraged returns over the variability of unleveraged returns (which reflect business risk only).

Financial transactions   Transactions that involve the disbursement or receipt of a firm's funds.

Financing activities   Transactions of a business that relate to its financing.

Finished goods   End product of the manufacturing process.

Finished goods inventory   Book value of finished goods that is included in the inventory reported in the balance sheet.

First right of refusal (franchising)   Option granted by a franchisee to a franchisor that allows the franchisor to purchase the franchisee's operation at an agreed valuation when the franchisee wishes to sell the operation (see also *Franchising*).

First-year allowance   Provision (for taxation purposes only) that allows an additional deduction of depreciation expense in the first year of an asset's ownership.

Fixed assets   Long-term operating assets used by the business over several years, e.g., property, plant, and equipment.

Fixed cost   Cost that does not vary with the level of output; e.g., rent.

Fixed overheads   Expenses that are constant, regardless of sales volume.

Flat interest   See *Add-on interest*.

Flat loan   Loan having a contractual obligation to pay interest only during the term of the loan with full redemption due at the end of the loan period.

Flow   Movement over time.

Foreign direct investment   Capital investment made by a company in a foreign country.

Foreign exchange (F/X)   The price of one currency in terms of another.

Foreign marketing servicing decision   A firm's choice of the mode of operations it will adopt in order to enter into foreign markets.

Forward exchange contract   Contract that determines the rate of exchange to be used at some future specified date regardless of what the exchange rate may be on the day the contract terms are to be fulfilled.

Forward hedging   Operational strategy to reduce uncertainty (exposure) in foreign exchange markets (or indeed other markets) by undertaking forward sales or purchases of foreign currency. Otherwise referred to simply as hedging or covering (see also *Forward market, Futures market, Options market*).

Forward market   Market in which currency is bought today for delivery at some future specified time (see also *Spot market, Futures market, Options market*).

Forward market rate   Contractual rate at which two or more currencies must be exchanged at some future point in time.

Foul bill of lading   Document that indicates that goods received appear to have suffered damage before responsibility passed to the carrier (see also *Bill of lading*).

Franchise   Agreement in which a franchisor grants to a franchisee the right to use a protected trademark to produce or distribute a product or service that is owned by the franchisor (see also *Franchisor, Franchisee*).

Franchise agreement   Contractual relationship between a franchisor and a franchisee that specifies the terms of a franchise (see also *Franchisor, Franchisee*).

Franchisee   Person who obtains the right to use a protected trademark owned by a franchisor (see also *Franchising*).

Franchising   Process of establishing franchises (see also *Franchise*).

Franchisor   Owner of a trademark who contractually grants the use of this asset to the franchisee (see also *Franchising*).

Free cash flows   Cash that is available to the firm for discretionary use.

Front-end loan fee   Loan fee on a loan for which a premium is discounted at the start of the loan period.

Full capacity   Full utilization; i.e., an increase in production is contingent on an increase in productive assets.

Fully participating   Shares that provide the holder with full rights to voting and profits.

Funds   See *Net working capital*.

Future maintainable profit   Projected stable profit of the business.

Futures market   Market in which currency is bought today for delivery at some future specified time, similar to the forward market in principle but operationally somewhat different (see also *Spot market, Options market*).

Gearing ratio   See *Debt ratio*.

General debenture   Security over the general assets of a business (as opposed to specific assets).

General partnership   Business formed by two or more people, each having the power to bind all other partners by their actions; all partners are jointly and severally liable for the debts of the business.

Go public Process of changing from a private firm to a publicly listed company (see also *Initial public offering*).

Going concern assumption Assumption that a business will remain in operation indefinitely.

Goods and services tax Value-added tax levied on most of the goods and services produced or consumed in many countries outside the United States.

Goodwill Either the excess paid over and above the value of an asset or net assets of the business, or the excess paid over and above the book value of the net assets of the business.

Governing director's clause A clause allowing one person (the governing director) in a company to make unilateral decisions about the affairs of the business without consulting with other interested parties.

Gross cash flow Calculation of cash flows in which no adjustment, such as for inflation, has been made.

Gross margin See *Gross profit margin*.

Gross profit Net sales revenue less the cost of goods sold.

Gross profit margin Gross profit divided by sales revenue (also called gross margin).

Gross return on assets (ROA) Earnings before interest and taxes (EBIT) divided by total assets.

Gross return on equity (ROE) Earnings before taxes (EBT) divided by total owners' equity.

Gross working capital All current assets of a business (see also *Net working capital*).

Growth Circumstances in which sales are expected to increase.

Hedging see *Forward hedging*.

Historical-cost convention Historical cost of a transaction is its basis in any financial statement, not its current value.

Holder in due course Holder of a bill of exchange when all the conditions of the bill have been met and the holder is thus unreservedly entitled to payment (see also *Bill of exchange*).

Hurdle rate Rate of return a project must exhibit to get to the next stage of capital investment appraisal.

Income statement Report that describes the results of the income-generating operations of a business for the period under examination (also called the profit and loss statement).

Independent project Project that does not rely upon any other investment project to complement or link it but stands alone (see also *Interdependent projects*).

Initial franchise fee Amount that is paid by a franchisee to a franchisor on the signing of a franchise agreement (see also *Franchising*).

Initial public offering (IPO) The initial issue of stock in a public market.

Installment loan See *Reducing balance table loan*.

Insurance Contractual arrangement by which an insurance company agrees to reimburse a business for designated contingencies in return for monetary consideration.

Intangible assets Assets that are not tangible including patents, copyrights, and goodwill.

Interdependent projects Projects that are linked to one another and for which the decision to invest in one necessarily results in investment in the other(s).

Interest The charge or cost for the use of borrowed money or credit.

Interest coverage ratio Measures how many times the net operating income of a firm covers its interest expense.

Interest rate parity theory (IRPT) Economic theory that suggests that, based on the assumption of perfect international capital mobility, the forward rate is equal to the expected future spot rate, and that any deviation from that equality will give gains or losses and thus will tend to return the rates back toward equality (see also *Forward rate, Spot rate*).

Interest surplus Economic surplus accruing to suppliers of the funding of a business after rewarding all other factors of production with their economic rents.

Interim payments Payments made more frequently than once a year.

Intermediate process inventory Type of inventory produced by the firm itself for input into a major product during the production process (see also *Dynamic inventory management, Static inventory management*).

Internal funding Funding provided by existing owners of a business, usually by way of retained earnings.

Internal rate of return (IRR) Rate the investment will return if all intermediate payments are reinvested at the IRR (can be referred to as yield).

International Fisher effect A proposition in economics that suggests that nominal interest-rate differentials between countries reflect anticipated rates of change in the exchange rate of their currencies.

Interstatement analysis Analysis comparing figures from the financial statements of two or more businesses.

Inventory Stock of goods on hand that are either ready for processing, are being processed, or are ready for sale.

Inventory carrying costs Actual costs associated with holding inventory, such as the costs of storage, insurance, security, spoilage, obsolescence, etc. (see also *Inventory order costs*).

Inventory order costs Actual costs associated with placing an order for inventory, such as the costs of administration, handling, transport, etc. (see also *Inventory carrying costs*).

Inventory turnover Average number of times inventory is replaced during one

year; determined by dividing the cost of goods sold by the average inventory.

Investment activities Allocation of funds to or from the investments of a business.

Investment tax credits A taxation provision allowing a special deduction (for tax purposes only) and relating to investment in particular designated types of assets.

Investment value Value of a business to a specific purchaser.

Irrevocable letter of credit Letter of credit that cannot be amended or canceled without the consent of all contracting parties (see also *Letter of credit*).

Just-in-time (JIT) inventory management Inventory-management procedure designed to reduce inventory holdings; the buyer gives the supplier detailed specifications of the products required and also stipulates the exact time they are required and in what quantities.

Key person discount Loss of value to a business resulting from the loss of a key person and his or her personal goodwill.

Law of one price (international trade) A proposition in economics that the international exchange rate will take up the difference between inflation rates of different nations to maintain a consistent international price (see also *Purchasing power parity theory*).

Legal entity A thing, other than a person, that can sue and be sued or otherwise be dealt with in the same way as a person.

Lessee Contracting party that undertakes to use an asset under lease in return for a payment to the lessor.

Lessor Contracting party that leases an asset to a lessee but does not give up ownership of the asset.

Letter of credit (L/C) Form of payment instrument prepared and issued by a bank for the purpose of settlement of international trade debts. A L/C may be: revocable or irrevocable, confirmed or unconfirmed, revolving or non-revolving.

Leverage ratio   See *Debt ratio*.

Leveraged buy out   Process by which a small group of investors purchase the equity of a firm and finance the purchase with borrowing both by the firm and personally (see also *Management buy out*).

Liabilities   Debts or obligations assumed by a business.

Lifestyle businesses   Firms that are not seeking value maximization as a primary objective.

Limited partnership   Partnership where one general partner is personally liable for the obligations of the partnership.

Limited-liability company (LLC) Form of business organization in which each owner of the business is not liable for the debts of the business unless they have personally covenanted to accept such an obligation (see also *Corporation*).

Line of credit   Funding advanced by a bank to a business. Credit is drawn as needed, similar to the way personal credit cards are used to fund purchases.

Liquid assets   Cash and other current assets, notably marketable securities, which can be quickly and cheaply turned into cash.

Liquidation value   Value of a firm in dissolution; i.e., in the circumstance when a firm ends its life, realizes all assets, and pays all obligations.

Liquidity   State of having liquid (i.e., easily converted into cash) assets.

Liquidity ratio   See *Current ratio, Working-capital ratio*.

Long-term debt   Debt for which the principal does not fall due for repayment inside a period of greater than one year.

Long-term financial planning   Planning that assists management in planning the funding needs for the future growth of a firm.

Long-term liabilities   Liabilities that are not expected to require repayment within the current accounting period.

Magnification factor   Factor associated with financial leverage that results in increasing degrees of financial leverage being associated with increased returns to assets.

Majority interest   Owning more than 50 percent of a business.

Management buy out (MBO)   Process of "taking a firm private" by which the managers of a firm purchase its equity (see also *Leveraged buy out*).

Marginal-value product (MVP)   Economic rent accruing to a factor of production.

Mark-up   Gross profit divided by cost of sales.

Market value   Value of an asset determined by the supply and demand in the relevant marketplace.

Marketable securities   Securities that can be freely exchanged in a public market.

Matching principle   The basis of accrual accounting where the revenue and costs are recognized if they occur in the same period.

Mean   Measure of central tendency, usually the arithmetic mean or average (see also *Standard deviation*).

Minority discount   Reduction in the value of that part of the equity of a firm associated with its lack of control. Opposite of the control premium.

Monte Carlo simulation   Technique for estimating the probability distribution of outcomes, such as in an investment project.

Mortgage   Financial instrument by which the mortgagor (borrower) gives the mortgagee (lender) a lien over the property being mortgaged in return for a loan until such time as the loan is redeemed in full and the security discharged.

Multi-period model   Method of long-term capital investment appraisal that considers cash flows for more than one time period.

Multiple internal rates of return (IRRs) Occur where there are unconventional cash flows from an investment project that change the sign of the internal rate of return (IRR) more than once; thus each change in sign effectively changes the IRR (see also *Internal rate of return, Unconventional cash flows*).

Mutually exclusive projects The choice of one alternative investment project directly excludes the possibility of any other being chosen.

Near-cash assets Assets that may quickly be converted to cash; e.g., marketable securities.

Net asset backing Residual amount available to shareholders after meeting all contractual obligations of a business.

Net income Amount remaining after deducting from gross income all expenses of a period.

Net operating income Gross profit less net operating expenses (also called operating income or earnings before interest and tax, or EBIT).

Net present value (NPV) Project-appraisal technique that determines the net contribution made by a project by discounting the future cash flows to present values and deducting the initial outlay (see also *Discounted cash flow, Present value*).

Net realizable value Disposal value of the assets of a firm less any obligations associated with those assets.

Net return on assets (ROA) Net income (after a nominal allowance for taxation) divided by total assets.

Net working capital Total current assets less total current liabilities (also called working capital or funds).

Net worth Excess of the firm's assets over the firm's liabilities.

Net-worth ratio Equity divided by assets; also called ownership ratio.

Nominal annual interest rate Interest rate that does not take into account the frequency of payments; i.e., is not compounded. The periodic rate multiplied by the number of periods per annum.

Nominal value Price at which a share is initially recorded in the accounts of a business (also called par value).

Non-operating revenue Stream of benefits accruing to a firm from sources other than sales of products or services.

Non-revolving letter of credit A letter of credit that applies to a single transaction (see also *Revolving letter of credit, Letter of credit*).

Notes to the accounts Notes that help the analyst understand some of the conventions and calculations used in the preparation of financial statements.

Objectives The aims or goals of the business organization.

Official reserves account Documents changes in gold and foreign currencies by official monetary institutions; part of a country's balance of payments.

On-board bill of lading Shipping document stating that goods have been received on board or shipped by a named vessel (see also *Received bill of lading, Bill of lading*).

Open account Form of credit sale account whereby an exporter ships goods and passes title to an importer before receipt of payment.

Operating activities Activities involved in the customary operation of the business.

Operating budget Comprehensive plan of the physical product through the business; the interrelationships of all the physical and financial factors involved and the determination of planned income.

Operating efficiency How efficiently a firm uses its assets in the operation of its business (also called technical efficiency). Closely related to business risk.

Operating income See *Net operating income*.

Operating leases Agreements for the use of an asset in exchange for a periodic payment but with no rights to ownership being transferred to the user.

Operating leverage See *Degree of operating leverage.*

Operating revenue Stream of benefits accruing to a firm from the sales of products or services.

Operating risk Risk of not covering all fixed costs if sales decline.

Opportunity cost Measure of the economic cost of using scarce resources to produce one particular good or service in terms of the alternatives thereby foregone.

Optimal capital structure Mix of debt and equity that either maximizes the value of the firm or minimizes the firm's cost of capital.

Options market Market in which can be exercised the contractual right to buy or sell foreign currency at an agreed predetermined price at any time within three months of the contract date (see also *Spot market, Forward market, Futures market*).

Order bill of lading Shipping document that maintains title of goods with the consignor until endorsement in favor of someone else (see also *Straight bill of lading, Bill of lading*).

Ordering costs Costs of administration, handling, transport, and purchase of inventory.

Ordinary shares Common equity issued by a company that entitles the holder to a share of residual assets if the company is dissolved, to vote at a meeting of the company, and to a dividend if it is declared.

Overhead Costs that cannot be traced directly to the production or sale of identifiable goods and services.

Owners' equity Financial interest of the firm's owners in the assets of the business (also called shareholders' funds in the case of a corporation).

Ownership ratio See *Net-worth ratio.*

Par See *Nominal value.*

Partnership The contractual relationship that exists between two or more persons who agree to combine their expertise with a view to earning profits that will then be shared amongst the partners.

Payback Common investment evaluation technique to determine the length of time it takes to recover the initial outlay on an investment (see also *Discounted payback*).

Pecking order theory Suggests that firms will find a source of funding for their activities in a particular order: 1) internally, 2) from debt, and 3) by raising new contributions of equity.

Periodic rate True periodic interest rate. The compound rate.

Permanent current assets Minimum aggregate level of current assets needed for the efficient running of a going concern during its business cycle.

Perpetual growth method Method of valuation based on the assumption that earnings of a business will continue to grow exponentially forever at a constant rate.

Perquisite ("perks") Any gain or profit accruing to owners or employees of a business that is derived from sources other than wages.

Personal guarantee Collateral security over personally owned assets.

Post-investment audit Analysis of a project's performance after the commencement of operations, in particular to compare prior estimates with actual outcomes.

Precautionary motive Assumption that cash should be held because something may occur in the future, but there is uncertainty as to the event and its timing.

Preference shares Shares that entitle their holders to preference dividends and that rank above ordinary equity on the dissolution of a company.

Preferred dividend Dividend paid only to the holders of preference shares.

Premium Difference between the selling price and nominal or par value of a share.

Present value Discounted value of future cash flows.

Price–earnings method Method of valuing a business based on the application of a market-indicated price–earnings multiple to the expected earnings of the business (see also *Earnings yield method*).

Price-earnings multiple Ratio of market value to earnings used to value shares.

Price–earnings (P/E) ratio Current market price divided by the earnings accrued.

Principal sum The net advance by a lender.

Private placement Process of issuing securities directly to a selected set of investors.

Pro forma balance sheet Projected balance sheet.

Pro forma income statement Projected income statement.

Pro forma financial reports Financial statements that project into the future.

Probabilities Measure of the relative frequency or likelihood of the occurrence of an event (see also *Mean, Standard deviation*).

Product franchising Process by which a franchisor grants to a franchisee the right to distribute a product or service owned by the franchisor (see also *Franchising, Business-format franchising*).

Productive capacity Extent to which a business operates without having to increase the size of its asset base.

Profit and loss statement See *Income statement*.

Profit planning Budgetary process that involves estimating future profit and the sensitivity of that profit to changes in sales and/or expenses.

Profitability Ability of the firm to make a profit from its operations.

Profitability index See *Excess present value index (EPVI), Benefit–cost ratio*.

Profitability ratios Measure of the value of equity owners' shares based on a firm's ability to make profit.

Project risk Reflects the variability of a capital project's future cash flows.

Property taxes A levy imposed on real estate. See also *Rates*.

Proxy firm Firm that is similar to one being analyzed and for which relevant information is known.

Public debt markets Market in which debt instruments of public corporations are traded and new debt is raised.

Public equity markets Market in which equity instruments of public corporations are traded and new equity is raised.

Publicly negotiable equity Equity that can be traded in a public equity market.

Purchasing power parity theory (PPPT) Economic theory of foreign exchange determination that postulates that there ought to be equilibrium between international prices of goods (see also *Law of one price*).

Put options The obligation to sell a stake in a business at a specific price.

Quasi-equity Debt funding advanced to a business that may convert to equity.

Quick ratio See *Acid-test ratio*.

Rates Charges set by local authorities to cover the cost of services provided to the property and property owners. See also *Property taxes*.

Raw materials Materials that are combined in the manufacturing process to produce the end product.

Real cash flows Cash flows that do not allow for future expected inflation.

Real rate of return Nominal rate of return after adjustment for inflation.

Realized capital profit Difference between the realized price of an asset and its cost.

Realized capital reserves Undistributed profits resulting from the accumulation of realized capital profits.

Receivables aging schedule Detailed schedule showing each of a firm's accounts receivable in order to monitor, on a frequent and regular basis, a customer's current status, which, in turn, can highlight potential bad debts.

Received bill of lading Shipping document stating that goods have been received by a shipper (see also *On-board bill of lading, Bill of lading*).

Recourse-basis discounting An exporter guarantees an importer's debt payment.

Reducing balance table loan Regular repayment of a constant amount of principal accompanied by a decreasing amount of interest (also called installment loan).

Refinancing Replacement of existing debt by new debt.

Regulation D A set of rules specifying conditions under which a firm issuing new securities may be exempted from cumbersome registration requirements.

Rent Contractual amount paid for the use of an asset.

Replacement cost Cost of replacing an asset today.

Replacement value Value of an asset based on the cost of its replacement but allowing for its present condition.

Reserves See *Retained earnings*.

Retained earnings Undistributed profits of a business arising from its operations.

Return on assets (ROA) See *Gross ROA* and *Net ROA*.

Return on equity (ROE) ratio Net income divided by owners' equity (see also *Gross ROE*).

Return on funds employed (ROFE) See *Accounting rate of return (ARR)*.

Return on investment (ROI) Periodic economic gain accruing to the owner of an asset from its use.

Revenue reserves See *Retained earnings*.

Reviewed statements Reports based on information supplied by management that are certified as to their reasonableness by a chartered accountant.

Revocable letter of credit A letter of credit that can be amended or canceled at any time before payment is made (see also *Irrevocable letter of credit, Letter of credit*).

Revolving letter of credit Assured line of credit with a bank over a specified time period, usually drawn upon by an exporter in stages (see also *Non-revolving letter of credit, Letter of credit*).

Risk Result of the variability of income.

Risk averse An individual or firm whose behavior or attitude exhibits a conservative approach toward risk taking.

Risk profile Attitude of the owner–manager toward risk in running the business; where an owner falls on a continuum between being risk averse and being a risk taker.

Risk-adjusted discount rate Rate used to adjust future cash flows for the element of risk (see also *Time value discount rate*).

Risk-free rate of return Return required on a riskless investment.

Royalties (franchising) Periodic payments by a franchisee to a franchisor based on an agreed percent of sales (see also *Advertising fees, Franchising*).

Rule 504 Delegates to the state the regulation of small security issues for firms issuing less than $1 million worth of stock.

Rule 505 Allows the sale of up to $5 million in securities over a twelve-month period to an unlimited number of investors.

Rule 506 Exempts from general registration regulations firms under certain circumstances.

Safety stock Level of inventory held as a buffer against the contingency of running out of stock (see also *Stock-out cost*).

Sales tax Tax levied on all sales of output produced by the business.

Schedule of depreciation Schedule detailing the book values and amounts of depreciation accrued during the lives of the assets of the business.

Series debentures Public issue of bonds of a designated amount per bond.

Share premium reserve Accumulation of undistributed profits arising from the sale of equity by a company.

Shareholders' funds See *Owners' equity*.

Short-term assets Non-cash assets listed in the balance sheet that can be expected to be converted into cash in the short term, typically less than one year, such as accounts receivable, inventories, etc.

Short-term financial planning Development and use of a cash budget.

Single-period model Method of capital investment appraisal that considers only one time period.

Small business investment corporations (SBICs) The government uses low-cost debt to fund a venture-capital pool of investors.

Small corporate offering registration (SCOR) Allows a firm to go public and raise up to $1 million without adherence to Regulation D.

Sole proprietorship A business owned entirely by one person (also called sole trader).

Sole trader See *Sole proprietorship*.

Special partnership See *Sub-chapter S corporation*.

Speculative motive Assumption that cash should be held by a business in order to take advantage of a speculative environment.

Spot market Market for the purchase and sale of foreign currency for immediate delivery, that is, "on the spot" (see also *Forward market, Futures market, Options market*).

Spot rate Interest rate currently prevailing in the international market for foreign currencies (see also *Forward market rate*).

Spread In the context of financial leverage, the difference between the cost of debt and the return on the assets purchased with the funds so raised.

Standard deviation Measure of spread, or dispersion, around a mean (see also *Mean*).

Statement of assets and liabilities See *Balance sheet*.

Statement of cash flows Summarizes the cash movements of the business. In other countries, can be called statement of movements in working capital.

Statement of changes in financial position Financial report showing the sources and uses of working capital.

Static inventory management A once-only production run with a finite time span (see also *Dynamic inventory management, Intermediate process inventory*).

Stock How much a firm has invested in current assets at any point in time.

Stock-out When there are insufficient inventories anywhere in the production or distribution chain (see also *Safety stock, Stock-out cost*).

Stock-out cost Cost incurred by a firm for maintaining insufficient inventories in the production or distribution chain (see also *Stock-out, Safety stock*).

Straight bill of lading Approves delivery of goods to a consignee but does not inherently retain the exporter's title and, as such, offers no guarantee of payment attached (see also *Order bill of lading, Bill of lading*).

Straight-line depreciation A method of accounting for depreciation by which the cost of an asset is divided by its years of useful life to provide a constant annual expense.

Strategic investments Significant investments that lend direction to a firm (see also *Tactical investments*).

Strategic liquidity Liquidity that is maintained for the purpose of future investment.

Structural analysis Comparison of items, or groups of items, within a single financial report.

Sub-chapter S corporation (or S corporation) A business that has the limited-liability attributes of a corporation, but for other purposes (e.g., taxation) is treated as a partnership.

Tactical investments Minor operational investments without significant strategic impetus (see also *Strategic investments*).

Tangible assets Assets of a firm excluding intangible and contingent assets such as copyrights, patents, and goodwill.

Tax return Form completed by the business to comply with government tax regulations.

Taxation paid and accrued The periodic total of all tax that has been paid and that which is owed but is as yet unpaid.

Temporary current assets Current assets required over and above the level of permanent current assets as a direct result of the level of business activity (see also *Permanent current assets*).

Terminal value Value of a project at a future point in time; associated with either the project's liquidation (including the recovery of working capital) or its value-in-use at the time specified.

Termination clause (franchising) Clause in a franchise agreement that specifies the arrangements relevant to a franchisee who exits the business (see also *Franchising*).

Through bill of lading Shipping document that provides for the shipment of goods by more than one carrier (see also *Direct bill of lading, Bill of lading*).

Time value discount rate Rate used to adjust future cash flows, which includes the inflation element over time but excludes the risk element. The three-month Treasury Bill rate is commonly used as the proxy for this rate as it is considered riskless (see also *Present value*).

Total value product (TVP) Sum of the marginal value products of the factors of production.

Trade credit Credit advanced to a business by its suppliers of goods or services.

Transaction exposure Situation in which a firm is exposed to the possibility of movements in foreign exchange rates on overseas debts (see also *Translation exposure, Foreign exchange*).

Transactions motive Cash should be held to purchase assets and pay bills during the normal course of business.

Translation exposure Change in historical (or accounting) cost of equity and net assets located abroad when translated back to the domestic currency of the parent firm (see also *Transaction exposure*).

Two-bin inventory method Reorder point for inventory occurs when the first of two bins becomes empty.

Unconfirmed letter of credit A letter of credit in which only the foreign bank is obligated to meet the debt (see also *Confirmed letter of credit, Letter of credit*).

Unconventional cash flows When there is a capital investment outflow followed by periods (years) in which the cash flows may be positive or negative (see also *Conventional cash flows*).

Uniform franchise offering circular (UFOC) Disclosure document that is required by the Federal Trade Commission; specifies the terms of a potential franchise agreement (see also *Franchising*).

Unrealized capital reserves Unrealized profits resulting from the revaluation of assets.

Utility Level of satisfaction accruing to an individual following the pursuit of some action.

Value-added tax (VAT) Tax levied on most of the goods and services produced or consumed in Great Britain and other countries.

Variable costs See *Variable operating expenses*.

Variable operating expenses Expenses that change in direct proportion to the level of sales and production.

Variable operating costs Overhead expenses that vary directly with sales volume.

Venture capital Capital provided to an entrepreneurial firm to fund its future operations and growth (see also *Angel, Venture capitalist, Venture capital firm*).

Venture capitalist Person or institution with surplus funds to invest in the equity of attractive and risky growth businesses.

Venture-capital firm Firm specializing in the provision of venture capital (see also *Angel, Venture capital*).

Venture-capital network (VCN) Anonymous matchmaking device used to introduce venture capitalists to firms seeking capital (see also *Venture capital*).

Wealth maximization The objective customarily attributed to the owners of a business whereby they maximize their utility by maximizing their wealth (i.e., they maximize their preparation for future consumption).

Weighted average cost of capital (WACC) Average cost of capital based on the relative proportions of debt and equity to total assets and their respective costs; i.e., the product of the debt-to-assets ratio and the cost of debt plus the product of the equity-to-assets ratio and the cost of equity.

Work-in-progress inventory (W/P) That part of the reported inventory of a business that comprises work in progress.

Working capital See *Net working capital*.

Working-capital management Management of current assets and current liabilities; the management of the liquidity of a business.

Working-capital ratio Another name given to the current ratio.

Yield (see *Internal rate of return*)

Yield factors General term encompassing factors such as dividend yield and earnings yield.

APPENDIX II

FINANCIAL TABLES

COMPOUND FACTOR

FUTURE VALUE OF ANNUITY FACTOR

PRESENT VALUE FACTOR

PRESENT VALUE OF ANNUITY FACTOR

COMPOUND FACTOR

Period	1%	2%	3%	4%	5%	6%	7%	8%	9%	10%	11%	12%	13%	14%	15%	16%	18%	20%	22%	24%	26%	28%	30%	32%	34%	36%	38%	40%
1	1.0100	1.0200	1.0300	1.0400	1.0500	1.0600	1.0700	1.0800	1.0900	1.1000	1.1100	1.1200	1.1300	1.1400	1.1500	1.1600	1.1800	1.2000	1.2200	1.2400	1.2600	1.2800	1.3000	1.3200	1.3400	1.3600	1.3800	1.4000
2	1.0201	1.0404	1.0609	1.0816	1.1025	1.1236	1.1449	1.1664	1.1881	1.2100	1.2321	1.2544	1.2769	1.2996	1.3225	1.3456	1.3924	1.4400	1.4884	1.5376	1.5876	1.6384	1.6900	1.7424	1.7956	1.8496	1.9044	1.9600
3	1.0303	1.0612	1.0927	1.1255	1.1576	1.1910	1.2250	1.2597	1.2950	1.3310	1.3676	1.4049	1.4429	1.4815	1.5209	1.5609	1.6430	1.7280	1.8158	1.9066	2.0004	2.0972	2.1970	2.3000	2.4061	2.5155	2.6281	2.7440
4	1.0406	1.0824	1.1255	1.1699	1.2155	1.2625	1.3108	1.3605	1.4116	1.4641	1.5181	1.5735	1.6305	1.6890	1.7490	1.8106	1.9388	2.0736	2.2153	2.3642	2.5205	2.6844	2.8561	3.0360	3.2242	3.4210	3.6267	3.8416
5	1.0510	1.1041	1.1593	1.2167	1.2763	1.3382	1.4026	1.4693	1.5386	1.6105	1.6851	1.7623	1.8424	1.9254	2.0114	2.1003	2.2878	2.4883	2.7027	2.9316	3.1758	3.4360	3.7129	4.0075	4.3204	4.6526	5.0049	5.3782
6	1.0615	1.1262	1.1941	1.2653	1.3401	1.4185	1.5007	1.5869	1.6771	1.7716	1.8704	1.9738	2.0820	2.1950	2.3131	2.4364	2.6996	2.9860	3.2973	3.6352	4.0015	4.3980	4.8268	5.2899	5.7893	6.3275	6.9068	7.5295
7	1.0721	1.1487	1.2299	1.3159	1.4071	1.5036	1.6058	1.7138	1.8280	1.9487	2.0762	2.2107	2.3526	2.5023	2.6600	2.8262	3.1855	3.5832	4.0227	4.5077	5.0419	5.6295	6.2749	6.9826	7.7577	8.6054	9.5313	10.5414
8	1.0829	1.1717	1.2668	1.3686	1.4775	1.5938	1.7182	1.8509	1.9926	2.1436	2.3045	2.4760	2.6584	2.8526	3.0590	3.2784	3.7589	4.2998	4.9077	5.5895	6.3528	7.2058	8.1573	9.2171	10.3953	11.7034	13.1532	14.7579
9	1.0937	1.1951	1.3048	1.4233	1.5513	1.6895	1.8385	1.9990	2.1719	2.3579	2.5580	2.7731	3.0040	3.2519	3.5179	3.8030	4.4355	5.1598	5.9874	6.9310	8.0045	9.2234	10.6045	12.1665	13.9297	15.9166	18.1515	20.6610
10	1.1046	1.2190	1.3439	1.4802	1.6289	1.7908	1.9672	2.1589	2.3674	2.5937	2.8394	3.1058	3.3946	3.7072	4.0456	4.4114	5.2338	6.1917	7.3046	8.5944	10.0857	11.8059	13.7858	16.0598	18.6659	21.6466	25.0490	28.9255
11	1.1157	1.2434	1.3842	1.5395	1.7103	1.8983	2.1049	2.3316	2.5804	2.8531	3.1518	3.4785	3.8359	4.2262	4.6524	5.1173	6.1759	7.4301	8.9117	10.6571	12.7080	15.1116	17.9216	21.1989	25.0123	29.4393	34.5677	40.4957
12	1.1268	1.2682	1.4258	1.6010	1.7959	2.0122	2.2522	2.5182	2.8127	3.1384	3.4985	3.8960	4.3345	4.8179	5.3503	5.9360	7.2876	8.9161	10.8722	13.2148	16.0120	19.3428	23.2981	27.9825	33.5164	40.0375	47.7034	56.6939
13	1.1381	1.2936	1.4685	1.6651	1.8856	2.1329	2.4098	2.7196	3.0658	3.4523	3.8833	4.3635	4.8980	5.4924	6.1528	6.8858	8.5994	10.6993	13.2641	16.3863	20.1752	24.7588	30.2875	36.9370	44.9120	54.4510	65.8306	79.3715
14	1.1495	1.3195	1.5126	1.7317	1.9799	2.2609	2.5785	2.9372	3.3417	3.7975	4.3104	4.8871	5.5348	6.2613	7.0757	7.9875	10.1472	12.8392	16.1822	20.3191	25.4207	31.6913	39.3738	48.7568	60.1821	74.0534	90.8463	111.1201
15	1.1610	1.3459	1.5580	1.8009	2.0789	2.3966	2.7590	3.1722	3.6425	4.1772	4.7846	5.4736	6.2543	7.1379	8.1371	9.2655	11.9737	15.4070	19.7423	25.1956	32.0301	40.5648	51.1859	64.3590	80.6440	100.7126	125.3679	155.5681
16	1.1726	1.3728	1.6047	1.8730	2.1829	2.5404	2.9522	3.4259	3.9703	4.5950	5.3109	6.1304	7.0673	8.1372	9.3576	10.7480	14.1290	18.4884	24.0856	31.2426	40.3579	51.9230	66.5417	84.9538	108.0629	136.9691	173.0077	217.7953
17	1.1843	1.4002	1.6528	1.9479	2.2920	2.6928	3.1588	3.7000	4.3276	5.0545	5.8951	6.8660	7.9861	9.2765	10.7613	12.4677	16.6722	22.1861	29.3844	38.7408	50.8510	66.4614	86.5042	112.1390	144.8043	186.2779	238.7506	304.9135
18	1.1961	1.4282	1.7024	2.0258	2.4066	2.8543	3.3799	3.9960	4.7171	5.5599	6.5436	7.6900	9.0243	10.5752	12.3755	14.4625	19.6733	26.6233	35.8490	48.0386	64.0722	85.0706	112.4554	148.0235	194.0378	253.3380	329.4758	426.8789
19	1.2081	1.4568	1.7535	2.1068	2.5270	3.0256	3.6165	4.3157	5.1417	6.1159	7.2633	8.6128	10.1974	12.0557	14.2318	16.7765	23.2144	31.9480	43.7358	59.5679	80.7310	108.8904	146.1920	195.3911	260.0107	344.5397	454.6766	597.6304
20	1.2202	1.4859	1.8061	2.1911	2.6533	3.2071	3.8697	4.6610	5.6044	6.7275	8.0623	9.6463	11.5231	13.7435	16.3665	19.4608	27.3930	38.3376	53.3576	73.8641	101.7211	139.3797	190.0496	257.9162	348.4143	468.5740	627.4538	836.6826
21	1.2324	1.5157	1.8603	2.2788	2.7860	3.3996	4.1406	5.0338	6.1088	7.4002	8.9492	10.8038	13.0211	15.6676	18.8215	22.5745	32.3238	46.0051	65.0963	91.5915	128.1685	178.4060	247.0645	340.4494	466.8752	637.2606	865.8862	1171.3556
22	1.2447	1.5460	1.9161	2.3699	2.9253	3.6035	4.4304	5.4365	6.6586	8.1403	9.9336	12.1003	14.7138	17.8610	21.6447	26.1864	38.1421	55.2061	79.4175	113.5735	161.4924	228.3596	321.1839	449.3932	625.6127	866.6744	1194.9229	1639.8978
23	1.2572	1.5769	1.9736	2.4647	3.0715	3.8197	4.7405	5.8715	7.2579	8.9543	11.0263	13.5523	16.6266	20.3616	24.8915	30.3762	45.0076	66.2474	96.8894	140.8312	203.4804	292.3003	417.5391	593.1990	838.3210	1178.6772	1648.9937	2295.8569
24	1.2697	1.6084	2.0328	2.5633	3.2251	4.0489	5.0724	6.3412	7.9111	9.8497	12.2392	15.1786	18.7881	23.2122	28.6252	35.2364	53.1090	79.4968	118.2050	174.6306	256.3853	374.1444	542.8008	783.0227	1123.3500	1603.0010	2275.6113	3214.1997
25	1.2824	1.6406	2.0938	2.6658	3.3864	4.2919	5.4274	6.8485	8.6231	10.8347	13.5855	17.0001	21.2305	26.4619	32.9190	40.8742	62.6686	95.3962	144.2101	216.5420	323.0454	478.9049	705.6410	1033.5900	1505.2892	2180.0814	3140.3435	4499.8796
26	1.2953	1.6734	2.1566	2.7725	3.5557	4.5494	5.8074	7.3964	9.3992	11.9182	15.0799	19.0401	23.9905	30.1666	37.8568	47.4141	73.9490	114.4755	175.9364	268.5121	407.0373	612.9982	917.3333	1364.3387	2017.0876	2964.9107	4333.6741	6299.8314
27	1.3082	1.7069	2.2213	2.8834	3.7335	4.8223	6.2139	7.9881	10.2451	13.1100	16.7386	21.3249	27.1093	34.3899	43.5353	55.0004	87.2598	137.3706	214.6424	332.9550	512.8670	784.6377	1192.5333	1800.9271	2702.8974	4032.2786	5980.4702	8819.7640
28	1.3213	1.7410	2.2879	2.9987	3.9201	5.1117	6.6488	8.6271	11.1671	14.4210	18.5799	23.8839	30.6335	39.2045	50.0656	63.8004	102.9666	164.8447	261.8637	412.8642	646.2124	1004.3363	1550.2933	2377.2238	3621.8825	5483.8988	8253.0489	12347.6696
29	1.3345	1.7758	2.3566	3.1187	4.1161	5.4184	7.1143	9.3173	12.1722	15.8631	20.6237	26.7499	34.6158	44.6931	57.5755	74.0085	121.5005	197.8136	319.4737	511.9516	814.2276	1285.5504	2015.3813	3137.9354	4853.3225	7458.1024	11389.2075	17286.7374
30	1.3478	1.8114	2.4273	3.2434	4.3219	5.7435	7.6123	10.0627	13.2677	17.4494	22.8923	29.9599	39.1159	50.9502	66.2118	85.8499	143.3706	237.3763	389.7579	634.8199	1025.9267	1645.5046	2619.9956	4142.0748	6503.4522	10143.0193	15717.1064	24201.4324
31	1.3613	1.8476	2.5001	3.3731	4.5380	6.0881	8.1451	10.8677	14.4618	19.1943	25.4104	33.5551	44.2010	58.0832	76.1435	99.5859	169.1774	284.8516	475.5046	787.1767	1292.6677	2106.2458	3405.9943	5467.5387	8714.6259	13794.5062	21689.6068	
32	1.3749	1.8845	2.5751	3.5081	4.7649	6.4534	8.7153	11.7371	15.7633	21.1138	28.2056	37.5817	49.9471	66.2148	87.5651	115.5196	199.6293	341.8219	580.1156	976.0991	1628.7613	2695.9947	4427.7926	7217.1511	11677.5987	18760.5285	29931.6573	
33	1.3887	1.9222	2.6523	3.6484	5.0032	6.8406	9.3253	12.6760	17.1820	23.2252	31.3082	42.0915	56.4402	75.4849	100.6998	134.0027	235.5625	410.1863	707.7411	1210.3629	2052.2392	3450.8732	5756.1304	9526.6395	15647.9823	25514.3187	41305.6871	
34	1.4026	1.9607	2.7319	3.7943	5.2533	7.2510	9.9781	13.6901	18.7284	25.5477	34.7521	47.1425	63.7774	86.0528	115.8048	155.4432	277.9638	492.2235	863.4440	1500.8500	2585.8215	4417.1177	7482.9696	12575.1641	20968.2963	34699.4734	57001.8483	
35	1.4166	1.9999	2.8139	3.9461	5.5160	7.6861	10.6766	14.7853	20.4140	28.1024	38.5749	52.7996	72.0685	98.1002	133.1755	180.3141	327.9973	590.6682	1053.4018	1861.0540	3258.1350	5653.9106	9727.8604	16599.2166	28097.5170	47191.2839	78662.5506	
36	1.4308	2.0399	2.8983	4.1039	5.7918	8.1473	11.4239	15.9682	22.2512	30.9127	42.8181	59.1356	81.4374	111.8342	153.1519	209.1643	387.0368	708.8019	1285.1502	2307.7070	4105.2501	7237.0056	12646.2186	21910.9659	37650.6728	64180.1461		
37	1.4451	2.0807	2.9852	4.2681	6.0814	8.6361	12.2236	17.2456	24.2538	34.0039	47.5281	66.2318	92.0243	127.4910	176.1246	242.6306	456.7034	850.5622	1567.8833	2861.5567	5172.6152	9263.3671	16440.0841	28922.4750	50451.9015	87284.9987		
38	1.4595	2.1223	3.0748	4.4388	6.3855	9.1543	13.0793	18.6253	26.4367	37.4043	52.7562	74.1797	103.9874	145.3397	202.5433	281.4515	538.9100	1020.6747	1912.8176	3548.3303	6517.4951	11857.1099	21372.1094	38177.6670	67605.5481			
39	1.4741	2.1647	3.1670	4.6164	6.7048	9.7035	13.9948	20.1153	28.8160	41.1448	58.5593	83.0812	117.5058	165.6873	232.9248	326.4838	635.9135	1224.8096	2333.6375	4399.9295	8212.0438	15177.1007	27783.7422	50394.5205	90591.4344			
40	1.4889	2.2080	3.2620	4.8010	7.0400	10.2857	14.9745	21.7245	31.4094	45.2593	65.0009	93.0510	132.7816	188.8835	267.8635	378.7212	750.3783	1469.7716	2847.0378	5455.9126	10347.1752	19426.6889	36118.8648	66520.7670				
41	1.5038	2.2522	3.3599	4.9931	7.3920	10.9029	16.0227	23.4625	34.2363	49.7852	72.1510	104.2171	150.0432	215.3272	308.0431	439.3165	885.4464	1763.7259	3473.3861	6765.3317	13037.4408	24866.1618	46954.5243	87807.4125				
42	1.5188	2.2972	3.4607	5.1928	7.7616	11.5570	17.1443	25.3395	37.3175	54.7637	80.0876	116.7231	169.5488	245.4730	354.2495	509.6072	1044.8268	2116.4711	4237.5310	8389.0113	16427.1754	31828.6871	61040.8815					
43	1.5340	2.3432	3.5645	5.4005	8.1497	12.2505	18.3444	27.3666	40.6761	60.2401	88.8972	130.7299	191.5901	279.8392	407.3870	591.1443	1232.8956	2539.7653	5169.7878	10402.3740	20698.2410	40740.7195	79353.1460					
44	1.5493	2.3901	3.6715	5.6165	8.5572	12.9855	19.6285	29.5560	44.3370	66.2641	98.6759	146.4175	216.4968	319.0167	468.4950	685.7274	1454.8168	3047.7183	6307.1411	12898.9437	26079.7819	52148.1210						
45	1.5648	2.4379	3.7816	5.8412	8.9850	13.7646	21.0025	31.9204	48.3273	72.8905	109.5302	163.9876	244.6414	363.6791	538.7693	795.4438	1716.6839	3657.2620	7694.7122	15994.6902	32860.5275	66749.5949						
46	1.5805	2.4866	3.8950	6.0748	9.4343	14.5905	22.4726	34.4741	52.6767	80.1795	121.5786	183.6661	276.4448	414.5941	619.5847	922.7148	2025.6870	4388.7144	9387.5489	19833.4158	41404.2646	85439.4814						
47	1.5963	2.5363	4.0119	6.3178	9.9060	15.4659	24.0457	37.2320	57.4176	88.1975	134.9522	205.7061	312.3826	472.6373	712.5224	1070.3492	2390.3106	5266.4573	11452.8096	24593.4356	52169.3734							
48	1.6122	2.5871	4.1323	6.5705	10.4013	16.3939	25.7289	40.2106	62.5852	97.0172	149.7970	230.3908	352.9923	538.8065	819.4007	1241.6051	2820.5665	6319.7487	13972.4277	30495.8602	65733.4105							
49	1.6283	2.6388	4.2562	6.8333	10.9213	17.3775	27.5299	43.4274	68.2179	106.7190	166.2746	258.0377	398.8813	614.2395	942.3108	1440.2619	3328.2685	7583.6985	17046.3618	37814.8666	82824.0972							
50	1.6446	2.6916	4.3839	7.1067	11.4674	18.4202	29.4570	46.9016	74.3575	117.3909	184.5648	289.0022	450.7359	700.2330	1083.6574	1670.7038	3927.3569	9100.4382	20796.5615	46890.6346								
51	1.6611	2.7454	4.5154	7.3910	12.0408	19.5254	31.5190	50.6537	81.0497	129.1299	204.8670	323.6825	509.3316	798.2656	1246.2061	1938.0164	4634.2811	10920.5258	25371.8050	58144.1389								
52	1.6777	2.8003	4.6509	7.6866	12.6428	20.6969	33.7253	54.7060	88.3442	142.0429	227.4023	362.5243	575.5447	910.0228	1433.1370	2248.0990	5468.4517	13104.6309	30953.6021	72098.7323								
53	1.6945	2.8563	4.7904	7.9941	13.2749	21.9387	36.0861	59.0826	96.2951	156.2472	252.4166	406.0273	650.3655	1037.4260	1648.1075	2607.7949	6452.7730	15725.5571	37763.3945	89402.4280								
54	1.7114	2.9135	4.9341	8.3138	13.9387	23.2550	38.6122	63.8091	104.9617	171.8719	280.1824	454.7505	734.9130	1182.6500	1895.3236	3025.0421	7614.2721	18870.6685	46071.3413									
55	1.7285	2.9717	5.0821	8.6464	14.6356	24.6503	41.3150	68.9139	114.4083	189.0591	311.0025	509.3206	830.4517	1348.2388	2179.6222	3509.0488	8984.8411	22644.8023	56207.0364									
56	1.7458	3.0312	5.2346	8.9922	15.3674	26.1293	44.2071	74.4270	124.7050	207.9651	345.2127	570.4391	938.4104	1536.9922	2506.5655	4070.4966	10602.1125	27173.7627	68572.5844									
57	1.7633	3.0918	5.3917	9.3519	16.1358	27.6971	47.3015	80.3811	135.9285	228.7616	383.1861	638.8918	1060.4038	1752.1712	2882.5503	4721.7761	12510.4928	32608.5153	83658.5530									
58	1.7809	3.1536	5.5534	9.7260	16.9426	29.3589	50.6127	86.8116	148.1620	251.6377	425.3366	715.5588	1198.2563	1997.4751	3314.9329	5477.2602	14762.3815	39130.2183										
59	1.7987	3.2167	5.7200	10.1150	17.7897	31.1205	54.1555	93.7565	161.4966	276.8015	472.1236	801.4258	1354.0296	2277.1236	3812.1728	6353.6219	17419.6101	46956.2620										
60	1.8167	3.2810	5.8916	10.5196	18.6792	32.9877	57.9464	101.2571	176.0313	304.4816	524.0572	897.5969	1530.0535	2595.9187	4383.9987	7370.2014	20555.1400	56347.5144										

Period	1%	2%	3%	4%	5%	6%	7%	8%	9%	10%	11%	12%	13%	14%	15%	16%	18%	20%	22%	24%	26%	28%	30%	32%	34%	36%	38%	40%
1	1.0000	1.0000	1.0000	1.0000	1.0000	1.0000	1.0000	1.0000	1.0000	1.0000	1.0000	1.0000	1.0000	1.0000	1.0000	1.0000	1.0000	1.0000	1.0000	1.0000	1.0000	1.0000	1.0000	1.0000	1.0000	1.0000	1.0000	1.0000
2	2.0100	2.0200	2.0300	2.0400	2.0500	2.0600	2.0700	2.0800	2.0900	2.1000	2.1100	2.1200	2.1300	2.1400	2.1500	2.1600	2.1800	2.2000	2.2200	2.2400	2.2600	2.2800	2.3000	2.3200	2.3400	2.3600	2.3800	2.4000
3	3.0301	3.0604	3.0909	3.1216	3.1525	3.1836	3.2149	3.2464	3.2781	3.3100	3.3421	3.3744	3.4069	3.4396	3.4725	3.5056	3.5724	3.6400	3.7084	3.7776	3.8476	3.9184	3.9900	4.0624	4.1356	4.2096	4.2844	4.3600
4	4.0604	4.1216	4.1836	4.2465	4.3101	4.3746	4.4399	4.5061	4.5731	4.6410	4.7097	4.7793	4.8498	4.9211	4.9934	5.0665	5.2154	5.3680	5.5242	5.6842	5.8480	6.0156	6.1870	6.3624	6.5417	6.7251	6.9125	7.1040
5	5.1010	5.2040	5.3091	5.4163	5.5256	5.6371	5.7507	5.8666	5.9847	6.1051	6.2278	6.3528	6.4803	6.6101	6.7424	6.8771	7.1542	7.4416	7.7396	8.0484	8.3684	8.6999	9.0431	9.3983	9.7659	10.1461	10.5392	10.9456
6	6.1520	6.3081	6.4684	6.6330	6.8019	6.9753	7.1533	7.3359	7.5233	7.7156	7.9129	8.1152	8.3227	8.5355	8.7537	8.9775	9.4420	9.9299	10.4423	10.9801	11.5442	12.1359	12.7560	13.4058	14.0863	14.7987	15.5441	16.3238
7	7.2135	7.4343	7.6625	7.8983	8.1420	8.3938	8.6540	8.9228	9.2004	9.4872	9.7833	10.0890	10.4047	10.7305	11.0668	11.4139	12.1415	12.9159	13.7396	14.6153	15.5458	16.5339	17.5828	18.6956	19.8756	21.1262	22.4509	23.8534
8	8.2857	8.5830	8.8923	9.2142	9.5491	9.8975	10.2598	10.6366	11.0285	11.4359	11.8594	12.2997	12.7573	13.2328	13.7268	14.2401	15.3270	16.4991	17.7623	19.1229	20.5876	22.1634	23.8577	25.6782	27.6333	29.7316	31.9822	34.3947
9	9.3685	9.7546	10.1591	10.5828	11.0266	11.4913	11.9780	12.4876	13.0210	13.5795	14.1640	14.7757	15.4157	16.0853	16.7858	17.5185	19.0859	20.7989	22.6700	24.7125	26.9404	29.3692	32.0150	34.8953	38.0287	41.4350	45.1354	49.1526
10	10.4622	10.9497	11.4639	12.0061	12.5779	13.1808	13.8164	14.4866	15.1929	15.9374	16.7220	17.5487	18.4197	19.3373	20.3037	21.3215	23.5213	25.9587	28.6574	31.6434	34.9449	38.5926	42.6195	47.0618	51.9584	57.3516	63.2869	69.8137
11	11.5668	12.1687	12.8078	13.4864	14.2068	14.9716	15.7836	16.6455	17.5603	18.5312	19.5614	20.6546	21.8143	23.0445	24.3493	25.7329	28.7551	32.1504	35.9620	40.2379	45.0306	50.3985	56.4053	63.1215	70.6243	78.9982	88.3359	98.7391
12	12.6825	13.4121	14.1920	15.0258	15.9171	16.8699	17.8885	18.9771	20.1407	21.3843	22.7132	24.1331	25.6502	27.2707	29.0017	30.8502	34.9311	39.5805	44.8737	50.8950	57.7386	65.5100	74.3270	84.3204	95.6365	108.4375	122.9036	139.2348
13	13.8093	14.6803	15.6178	16.6268	17.7130	18.8821	20.1406	21.4953	22.9534	24.5227	26.2116	28.0291	29.9847	32.0887	34.3519	36.7862	42.2187	48.4966	55.7459	64.1097	73.7506	84.8529	97.6250	112.3030	129.1529	148.4750	170.6070	195.9287
14	14.9474	15.9739	17.0863	18.2919	19.5986	21.0151	22.5505	24.2149	26.0192	27.9750	30.0949	32.3926	34.8827	37.5811	40.5047	43.6720	50.8180	59.1959	69.0100	80.4961	93.9258	109.6117	127.9125	149.2399	174.0649	202.9260	236.4376	275.3002
15	16.0969	17.2934	18.5989	20.0236	21.5786	23.2760	25.1290	27.1521	29.3609	31.7725	34.4054	37.2797	40.4175	43.8424	47.5804	51.6595	60.9653	72.0351	85.1922	100.8151	119.3465	141.3029	167.2863	197.9967	234.2470	276.9793	327.2839	386.4202
16	17.2579	18.6393	20.1569	21.8245	23.6575	25.6725	27.8881	30.3243	33.0034	35.9497	39.1899	42.7533	46.6717	50.9804	55.7175	60.9250	72.9390	87.4421	104.9345	126.0108	151.3766	181.8677	218.4722	262.3557	314.8910	377.6919	452.6518	541.9883
17	18.4304	20.0121	21.7616	23.6975	25.8404	28.2129	30.8402	33.7502	36.9737	40.5447	44.5008	48.8837	53.7391	59.1176	65.0751	71.6730	87.0680	105.9306	129.0201	157.2534	191.7345	233.7907	285.0139	347.3095	422.9539	514.6610	625.6595	759.7837
18	19.6147	21.4123	23.4144	25.6454	28.1324	30.9057	33.9990	37.4502	41.3013	45.5992	50.3959	55.7497	61.7251	68.3941	75.8364	84.1407	103.7403	128.1167	158.4045	195.9942	242.3855	300.2521	371.5180	459.4485	567.7583	700.9389	864.4101	1064.6971
19	20.8109	22.8406	25.1169	27.6712	30.5390	33.7600	37.3790	41.4463	46.0185	51.1591	56.9395	63.4397	70.7494	78.9692	88.2118	98.6032	123.4135	154.7400	194.2535	244.0328	306.6577	385.3227	483.9734	607.4721	761.7961	954.2769	1193.8859	1491.5760
20	22.0190	24.2974	26.8704	29.7781	33.0660	36.7856	40.9955	45.7620	51.1601	57.2750	64.2028	72.0524	80.9468	91.0249	102.4436	115.3797	146.6280	186.6880	237.9893	303.6006	387.3887	494.2131	630.1655	802.8631	1021.8068	1298.8166	1648.5625	2089.2064
21	23.2392	25.7833	28.6765	31.9692	35.7193	39.9927	44.8652	50.4229	56.7645	64.0025	72.2651	81.6987	92.4699	104.7684	118.8101	134.8405	174.0210	225.0256	291.3469	377.4648	489.1098	633.5927	820.2151	1060.7793	1370.2211	1767.3906	2276.0163	2925.8889
22	24.4716	27.2990	30.5368	34.2480	38.5052	43.3923	49.0057	55.4568	62.8733	71.4027	81.2143	92.5026	105.4910	120.4360	137.6316	157.4150	206.3448	271.0307	356.4432	469.0563	617.2783	811.9987	1067.2796	1401.2287	1837.0962	2404.6512	3141.9025	4097.2445
23	25.7163	28.8450	32.4529	36.6179	41.4305	46.9958	53.4361	60.8933	69.5319	79.5430	91.1479	104.6029	120.2048	138.2970	159.2764	183.6014	244.4868	326.2369	435.8607	582.6298	778.7707	1040.3583	1388.4635	1850.6219	2462.7089	3271.3256	4336.8254	5737.1423
24	26.9735	30.4219	34.4265	39.0826	44.5020	50.8156	58.1767	66.7648	76.7898	88.4973	102.1742	118.1552	136.8315	158.6586	184.1678	213.9776	289.4945	392.4842	532.7501	723.4610	982.2511	1332.6586	1806.0026	2443.8209	3301.0300	4450.0029	5985.8191	8032.9993
25	28.2432	32.0303	36.4593	41.6459	47.7271	54.8645	63.2490	73.1059	84.7009	98.3471	114.4133	133.3339	155.6196	181.8708	212.7930	249.2140	342.6035	471.9811	650.9551	898.0916	1238.6363	1706.8031	2348.8033	3226.8436	4424.3801	6053.0039	8261.4304	11247.1990
26	29.5256	33.6709	38.5530	44.3117	51.1135	59.1564	68.6765	79.9544	93.3240	109.1818	127.9988	150.3339	176.8501	208.3327	245.7120	290.0883	405.2721	567.3773	795.1653	1114.6336	1561.6818	2185.7079	3054.4443	4260.4336	5929.6694	8233.0853	11401.7739	15747.0785
27	30.8209	35.3443	40.7096	47.0842	54.6691	63.7058	74.4838	87.3508	102.7231	121.0999	143.0786	169.3740	200.8406	238.4993	283.5688	337.5024	479.2211	681.8528	971.1016	1383.1457	1968.7191	2798.7061	3971.7776	5624.7723	7946.7570	11197.9960	15735.4480	22046.9099
28	32.1291	37.0512	42.9309	49.9676	58.4026	68.5281	80.6977	95.3388	112.9682	134.2099	159.8173	190.6989	227.9499	272.8892	327.1041	392.5028	566.4809	819.2233	1185.7440	1716.1007	2481.3860	3583.3438	5164.3109	7425.6994	10649.6544	15230.2745	21715.9182	30866.6739
29	33.4504	38.7922	45.2189	52.9663	62.3227	73.6398	87.3465	103.9659	124.1354	148.6309	178.3972	214.5828	258.5834	312.0937	377.1697	456.3032	669.4475	984.0680	1447.6077	2128.9648	3127.7984	4587.6801	6714.6042	9802.9233	14271.5368	20714.1734	29968.9671	43214.3435
30	34.7849	40.5681	47.5754	56.0849	66.4388	79.0582	94.4608	113.2832	136.3075	164.4940	199.0209	241.3327	293.1992	356.7868	434.7451	530.3117	790.9480	1181.8816	1767.0813	2640.9164	3942.0260	5873.2306	8729.9855	12940.8587	19124.8594	28172.2758	41358.1746	60501.0809
31	36.1327	42.3794	50.0027	59.3283	70.7608	84.8017	102.0730	123.3459	149.5752	181.9434	221.9132	271.2926	332.3151	407.7370	500.9569	616.1616	934.3186	1419.2579	2156.8392	3275.7363	4967.9527	7518.7351	11349.9811	17082.9335	25628.3115	38315.2951	57075.2810	84702.5132
32	37.4941	44.2270	52.5028	62.7015	75.2988	90.8898	110.2182	134.2135	164.0370	201.1378	247.3236	304.8477	376.5161	465.8202	577.1005	715.7475	1103.4960	1704.1095	2632.3439	4062.9130	6260.6204	9624.9810	14755.9754	22550.4722	34342.9374	52109.8013	78764.8878	
33	38.8690	46.1116	55.0778	66.2095	80.0638	97.3432	118.9334	145.9506	179.8003	222.2515	275.5292	342.4294	426.4632	532.0350	664.6655	831.2671	1303.1253	2045.9314	3212.4595	5039.0122	7889.3817	12320.9756	19183.7681	29767.6233	46020.5362	70870.3298		
34	40.2577	48.0338	57.7302	69.8579	85.0670	104.1838	128.2588	158.6267	196.9823	245.4767	306.8374	384.5210	482.9034	607.5199	765.3654	965.2698	1538.6878	2456.1176	3920.2006	6249.3751	9941.6210	15771.8488	24939.8985	39294.2628	61669.5185	96384.6485		
35	41.6603	49.9945	60.4621	73.6522	90.3203	111.4348	138.2369	172.3168	215.7108	271.0244	341.5896	431.6635	546.6808	693.5727	881.1702	1120.7130	1816.6516	2948.3411	4783.6447	7750.2251	12527.4424	20188.9665	32422.8681	51869.4269	82638.1547			
36	43.0769	51.9944	63.2759	77.5983	95.8363	119.1209	148.9135	187.1021	236.1247	299.1268	380.1644	484.4631	618.7493	791.6729	1014.3457	1301.0270	2144.6489	3539.0094	5837.0466	9611.2791	15785.5774	25842.8771	42150.7285	68468.6435				
37	44.5076	54.0343	66.1742	81.7022	101.6281	127.2681	160.3374	203.0703	258.3759	330.0395	422.9825	543.5987	700.1867	903.5071	1167.4975	1510.1914	2531.6857	4247.8112	7122.1968	11918.9861	19890.8276	33079.8826	54796.9471	90379.6094				
38	45.9527	56.1149	69.1594	85.9703	107.7095	135.9042	172.5610	220.3159	282.6298	364.0434	470.5106	609.8305	792.2110	1030.9981	1343.6222	1752.8220	2988.3891	5098.3735	8690.0801	14780.5428	25063.4428	42343.2498	71237.0312					
39	47.4123	58.2372	72.2342	90.4091	114.0950	145.0585	185.6403	238.9412	309.0665	401.4478	523.2667	684.0102	896.1984	1176.3378	1546.1655	2034.2735	3527.2992	6119.0482	10602.8978	18328.8731	31580.9379	54200.3589	92609.1405					
40	48.8864	60.4020	75.4013	95.0255	120.7998	154.7620	199.6351	259.0565	337.8824	442.5926	581.8261	767.0914	1013.7042	1342.0251	1779.0903	2360.7572	4163.2130	7343.8578	12936.5353	22728.8026	39792.9817	69377.4604						
41	50.3752	62.6100	78.6633	99.8265	127.8398	165.0477	214.6096	280.7810	369.2919	487.8518	646.8269	860.1424	1146.4858	1530.9086	2046.9539	2739.4784	4913.5914	8813.6294	15783.5730	28184.7152	50140.1570	88804.1494						
42	51.8790	64.8622	82.0232	104.8196	135.2318	175.9505	230.6322	304.2435	403.5281	537.6370	718.9779	964.3595	1296.5289	1746.2358	2354.9969	3178.7949	5799.0378	10577.3553	19256.9591	34950.0469	63177.5978							
43	53.3978	67.1595	85.4839	110.0124	142.9933	187.5076	247.7765	329.5830	440.8457	592.4007	799.0655	1081.0826	1466.0777	1991.7088	2709.2465	3688.4021	6843.8646	12693.8263	23494.4901	43339.0581	79604.7732							
44	54.9318	69.5027	89.0484	115.4129	151.1430	199.7580	266.1209	356.9496	481.5218	652.6408	887.9627	1211.8125	1657.6678	2271.5481	3116.6334	4279.5465	8076.7603	15233.5916	28664.2779	53741.4321								
45	56.4811	71.8927	92.7199	121.0294	159.7002	212.7435	285.7493	386.5056	525.8587	718.9048	986.6386	1358.2300	1874.1646	2590.5648	3585.1285	4965.2739	9531.5771	18281.3099	34971.4191	66640.3758								
46	58.0459	74.3306	96.5015	126.8706	168.6852	226.5081	306.7518	418.4261	574.1860	791.7953	1096.1688	1522.2176	2118.8060	2954.2439	4123.8977	5760.7177	11248.2610	21938.5719	42666.1312	82635.0660								
47	59.6263	76.8172	100.3965	132.9454	178.1194	241.0986	329.2244	452.9002	626.8628	871.9749	1217.7474	1705.8838	2395.2508	3368.8380	4743.4824	6683.4326	13273.9480	26327.2863	52053.6801									
48	61.2226	79.3535	104.4084	139.2632	188.0254	256.5645	353.2701	490.1322	684.2804	960.1723	1352.6996	1911.5898	2707.6334	3841.4753	5456.0047	7753.7818	15664.2586	31593.7436	63506.4897									
49	62.8348	81.9406	108.5406	145.8337	198.4267	272.9584	378.9990	530.3427	746.8656	1057.1896	1502.4966	2141.9806	3060.6258	4380.2819	6275.4055	8995.3869	18484.8251	37913.4923	77478.9175									
50	64.4632	84.5794	112.7969	152.6671	209.3480	290.3359	406.5289	573.7702	815.0836	1163.9085	1668.7712	2400.0182	3459.5071	4994.5213	7217.7163	10435.6488	21813.0937	45497.1908	94525.2793									
51	66.1078	87.2710	117.1808	159.7738	220.8154	308.7561	435.9860	620.6718	889.4411	1281.2994	1853.3360	2689.0204	3910.2430	5694.7543	8301.3737	12106.3526	25740.4505	54597.6289										
52	67.7689	90.0164	121.6962	167.1647	232.8562	328.2814	467.5050	671.3255	970.4908	1410.4293	2058.2029	3012.7029	4419.5746	6493.0199	9547.5798	14044.3690	30374.7316	65518.1547										
53	69.4466	92.8167	126.3471	174.8513	245.4990	348.9783	501.2303	726.0316	1058.8349	1552.4723	2285.6053	3375.2272	4995.1193	7403.0427	10980.7167	16292.4680	35843.1833	78622.7856										
54	71.1410	95.6731	131.1375	182.8454	258.7739	370.9170	537.3164	785.1141	1155.1301	1708.7195	2538.0218	3781.2545	5645.4849	8440.4487	12628.8243	18900.2629	42295.9563	94348.3427										
55	72.8525	98.5865	136.0716	191.1592	272.7126	394.1720	575.9286	848.9232	1260.0918	1880.5914	2818.2042	4236.0050	6380.3979	9623.1243	14524.1479	21925.3050	49910.2284											
56	74.5810	101.5582	141.1538	199.8055	287.3482	418.8223	617.2436	917.8371	1374.5001	2069.6506	3129.2067	4745.3257	7210.8496	10971.3731	16703.7701	25434.3538	58895.0696											
57	76.3268	104.5894	146.3884	208.7978	302.7157	444.9517	661.4506	992.2640	1499.2051	2277.6156	3474.4194	5315.7647	8149.2601	12508.3654	19210.3336	29504.8504	69497.1821											
58	78.0901	107.6812	151.7800	218.1497	318.8514	472.6488	708.7522	1072.6451	1635.1335	2506.3772	3857.6055	5954.6565	9209.6639	14260.5365	22092.8839	34226.6264	82007.6749											
59	79.8710	110.8348	157.3334	227.8757	335.7940	502.0077	759.3648	1159.4568	1783.2955	2758.0149	4282.9421	6670.2153	10407.9202	16258.0117	25407.8188	39703.8867	96770.0563											
60	81.6697	114.0515	163.0534	237.9907	353.5837	533.1282	813.5204	1253.2133	1944.7921	3034.8164	4755.0658	7471.6411	11761.9498	18535.1333	29219.9916	46057.5085												

Period	1%	2%	3%	4%	5%	6%	7%	8%	9%	10%	11%	12%	13%	14%	15%	16%	18%	20%	22%	24%	26%	28%	30%	32%	34%	36%	38%	40%
1	0.9901	0.9804	0.9709	0.9615	0.9524	0.9434	0.9346	0.9259	0.9174	0.9091	0.9009	0.8929	0.8850	0.8772	0.8696	0.8621	0.8475	0.8333	0.8197	0.8065	0.7937	0.7813	0.7692	0.7576	0.7463	0.7353	0.7246	0.7143
2	0.9803	0.9612	0.9426	0.9246	0.9070	0.8900	0.8734	0.8573	0.8417	0.8264	0.8116	0.7972	0.7831	0.7695	0.7561	0.7432	0.7182	0.6944	0.6719	0.6504	0.6299	0.6104	0.5917	0.5739	0.5569	0.5407	0.5251	0.5102
3	0.9706	0.9423	0.9151	0.8890	0.8638	0.8396	0.8163	0.7938	0.7722	0.7513	0.7312	0.7118	0.6931	0.6750	0.6575	0.6407	0.6086	0.5787	0.5507	0.5245	0.4999	0.4768	0.4552	0.4348	0.4156	0.3975	0.3805	0.3644
4	0.9610	0.9238	0.8885	0.8548	0.8227	0.7921	0.7629	0.7350	0.7084	0.6830	0.6587	0.6355	0.6133	0.5921	0.5718	0.5523	0.5158	0.4823	0.4514	0.4230	0.3968	0.3725	0.3501	0.3294	0.3102	0.2923	0.2757	0.2603
5	0.9515	0.9057	0.8626	0.8219	0.7835	0.7473	0.7130	0.6806	0.6499	0.6209	0.5935	0.5674	0.5428	0.5194	0.4972	0.4761	0.4371	0.4019	0.3700	0.3411	0.3149	0.2910	0.2693	0.2495	0.2315	0.2149	0.1998	0.1859
6	0.9420	0.8880	0.8375	0.7903	0.7462	0.7050	0.6663	0.6302	0.5963	0.5645	0.5346	0.5066	0.4803	0.4556	0.4323	0.4104	0.3704	0.3349	0.3033	0.2751	0.2499	0.2274	0.2072	0.1890	0.1727	0.1580	0.1448	0.1328
7	0.9327	0.8706	0.8131	0.7599	0.7107	0.6651	0.6227	0.5835	0.5470	0.5132	0.4817	0.4523	0.4251	0.3996	0.3759	0.3538	0.3139	0.2791	0.2486	0.2218	0.1983	0.1776	0.1594	0.1432	0.1289	0.1162	0.1049	0.0949
8	0.9235	0.8535	0.7894	0.7307	0.6768	0.6274	0.5820	0.5403	0.5019	0.4665	0.4339	0.4039	0.3762	0.3506	0.3269	0.3050	0.2660	0.2326	0.2038	0.1789	0.1574	0.1388	0.1226	0.1085	0.0962	0.0854	0.0760	0.0678
9	0.9143	0.8368	0.7664	0.7026	0.6446	0.5919	0.5439	0.5002	0.4604	0.4241	0.3909	0.3606	0.3329	0.3075	0.2843	0.2630	0.2255	0.1938	0.1670	0.1443	0.1249	0.1084	0.0943	0.0822	0.0718	0.0628	0.0551	0.0484
10	0.9053	0.8203	0.7441	0.6756	0.6139	0.5584	0.5083	0.4632	0.4224	0.3855	0.3522	0.3220	0.2946	0.2697	0.2472	0.2267	0.1911	0.1615	0.1369	0.1164	0.0992	0.0847	0.0725	0.0623	0.0536	0.0462	0.0399	0.0346
11	0.8963	0.8043	0.7224	0.6496	0.5847	0.5268	0.4751	0.4289	0.3875	0.3505	0.3173	0.2875	0.2607	0.2366	0.2149	0.1954	0.1619	0.1346	0.1122	0.0938	0.0787	0.0662	0.0558	0.0472	0.0400	0.0340	0.0289	0.0247
12	0.8874	0.7885	0.7014	0.6246	0.5568	0.4970	0.4440	0.3971	0.3555	0.3186	0.2858	0.2567	0.2307	0.2076	0.1869	0.1685	0.1372	0.1122	0.0920	0.0757	0.0625	0.0517	0.0429	0.0357	0.0298	0.0250	0.0210	0.0176
13	0.8787	0.7730	0.6810	0.6006	0.5303	0.4688	0.4150	0.3677	0.3262	0.2897	0.2575	0.2292	0.2042	0.1821	0.1625	0.1452	0.1163	0.0935	0.0754	0.0610	0.0496	0.0404	0.0330	0.0271	0.0223	0.0184	0.0152	0.0126
14	0.8700	0.7579	0.6611	0.5775	0.5051	0.4423	0.3878	0.3405	0.2992	0.2633	0.2320	0.2046	0.1807	0.1597	0.1413	0.1252	0.0985	0.0779	0.0618	0.0492	0.0393	0.0316	0.0254	0.0205	0.0166	0.0135	0.0110	0.0090
15	0.8613	0.7430	0.6419	0.5553	0.4810	0.4173	0.3624	0.3152	0.2745	0.2394	0.2090	0.1827	0.1599	0.1401	0.1229	0.1079	0.0835	0.0649	0.0507	0.0397	0.0312	0.0247	0.0195	0.0155	0.0124	0.0099	0.0080	0.0064
16	0.8528	0.7284	0.6232	0.5339	0.4581	0.3936	0.3387	0.2919	0.2519	0.2176	0.1883	0.1631	0.1415	0.1229	0.1069	0.0930	0.0708	0.0541	0.0415	0.0320	0.0248	0.0193	0.0150	0.0118	0.0093	0.0073	0.0058	0.0046
17	0.8444	0.7142	0.6050	0.5134	0.4363	0.3714	0.3166	0.2703	0.2311	0.1978	0.1696	0.1456	0.1252	0.1078	0.0929	0.0802	0.0600	0.0451	0.0340	0.0258	0.0197	0.0150	0.0116	0.0089	0.0069	0.0054	0.0042	0.0033
18	0.8360	0.7002	0.5874	0.4936	0.4155	0.3503	0.2959	0.2502	0.2120	0.1799	0.1528	0.1300	0.1108	0.0946	0.0808	0.0691	0.0508	0.0376	0.0279	0.0208	0.0156	0.0118	0.0089	0.0068	0.0052	0.0039	0.0030	0.0023
19	0.8277	0.6864	0.5703	0.4746	0.3957	0.3305	0.2765	0.2317	0.1945	0.1635	0.1377	0.1161	0.0981	0.0829	0.0703	0.0596	0.0431	0.0313	0.0229	0.0168	0.0124	0.0092	0.0068	0.0051	0.0038	0.0029	0.0022	0.0017
20	0.8195	0.6730	0.5537	0.4564	0.3769	0.3118	0.2584	0.2145	0.1784	0.1486	0.1240	0.1037	0.0868	0.0728	0.0611	0.0514	0.0365	0.0261	0.0187	0.0135	0.0098	0.0072	0.0053	0.0039	0.0029	0.0021	0.0016	0.0012
21	0.8114	0.6598	0.5375	0.4388	0.3589	0.2942	0.2415	0.1987	0.1637	0.1351	0.1117	0.0926	0.0768	0.0638	0.0531	0.0443	0.0309	0.0217	0.0154	0.0109	0.0078	0.0056	0.0040	0.0029	0.0021	0.0016	0.0012	0.0009
22	0.8034	0.6468	0.5219	0.4220	0.3418	0.2775	0.2257	0.1839	0.1502	0.1228	0.1007	0.0826	0.0680	0.0560	0.0462	0.0382	0.0262	0.0181	0.0126	0.0088	0.0062	0.0044	0.0031	0.0022	0.0016	0.0012	0.0008	0.0006
23	0.7954	0.6342	0.5067	0.4057	0.3256	0.2618	0.2109	0.1703	0.1378	0.1117	0.0907	0.0738	0.0601	0.0491	0.0402	0.0329	0.0222	0.0151	0.0103	0.0071	0.0049	0.0034	0.0024	0.0017	0.0012	0.0008	0.0006	0.0004
24	0.7876	0.6217	0.4919	0.3901	0.3101	0.2470	0.1971	0.1577	0.1264	0.1015	0.0817	0.0659	0.0532	0.0431	0.0349	0.0284	0.0188	0.0126	0.0085	0.0057	0.0039	0.0027	0.0018	0.0013	0.0009	0.0006	0.0004	0.0003
25	0.7798	0.6095	0.4776	0.3751	0.2953	0.2330	0.1842	0.1460	0.1160	0.0923	0.0736	0.0588	0.0471	0.0378	0.0304	0.0245	0.0160	0.0105	0.0069	0.0046	0.0031	0.0021	0.0014	0.0010	0.0007	0.0005	0.0003	0.0002
26	0.7720	0.5976	0.4637	0.3607	0.2812	0.2198	0.1722	0.1352	0.1064	0.0839	0.0663	0.0525	0.0417	0.0331	0.0264	0.0211	0.0135	0.0087	0.0057	0.0037	0.0025	0.0016	0.0011	0.0007	0.0005	0.0003	0.0002	0.0002
27	0.7644	0.5859	0.4502	0.3468	0.2678	0.2074	0.1609	0.1252	0.0976	0.0763	0.0597	0.0469	0.0369	0.0291	0.0230	0.0182	0.0115	0.0073	0.0047	0.0030	0.0019	0.0013	0.0008	0.0006	0.0004	0.0002	0.0002	0.0001
28	0.7568	0.5744	0.4371	0.3335	0.2551	0.1956	0.1504	0.1159	0.0895	0.0693	0.0538	0.0419	0.0326	0.0255	0.0200	0.0157	0.0097	0.0061	0.0038	0.0024	0.0015	0.0010	0.0006	0.0004	0.0003	0.0002	0.0001	0.0001
29	0.7493	0.5631	0.4243	0.3207	0.2429	0.1846	0.1406	0.1073	0.0822	0.0630	0.0485	0.0374	0.0289	0.0224	0.0174	0.0135	0.0082	0.0051	0.0031	0.0020	0.0012	0.0008	0.0005	0.0003	0.0002	0.0001	0.0001	0.0001
30	0.7419	0.5521	0.4120	0.3083	0.2314	0.1741	0.1314	0.0994	0.0754	0.0573	0.0437	0.0334	0.0256	0.0196	0.0151	0.0116	0.0070	0.0042	0.0026	0.0016	0.0010	0.0006	0.0004	0.0002	0.0002	0.0001	0.0001	0.0000
31	0.7346	0.5412	0.4000	0.2965	0.2204	0.1643	0.1228	0.0920	0.0691	0.0521	0.0394	0.0298	0.0226	0.0172	0.0131	0.0100	0.0059	0.0035	0.0021	0.0013	0.0008	0.0005	0.0003	0.0002	0.0001	0.0001	0.0000	0.0000
32	0.7273	0.5306	0.3883	0.2851	0.2099	0.1550	0.1147	0.0852	0.0634	0.0474	0.0355	0.0266	0.0200	0.0151	0.0114	0.0087	0.0050	0.0029	0.0017	0.0010	0.0006	0.0004	0.0002	0.0001	0.0001	0.0001	0.0000	0.0000
33	0.7201	0.5202	0.3770	0.2741	0.1999	0.1462	0.1072	0.0789	0.0582	0.0431	0.0319	0.0238	0.0177	0.0132	0.0099	0.0075	0.0042	0.0024	0.0014	0.0008	0.0005	0.0003	0.0001	0.0001	0.0001	0.0000	0.0000	0.0000
34	0.7130	0.5100	0.3660	0.2636	0.1904	0.1379	0.1002	0.0730	0.0534	0.0391	0.0288	0.0212	0.0157	0.0116	0.0086	0.0064	0.0036	0.0020	0.0012	0.0007	0.0004	0.0002	0.0001	0.0001	0.0000	0.0000	0.0000	0.0000
35	0.7059	0.5000	0.3554	0.2534	0.1813	0.1301	0.0937	0.0676	0.0490	0.0356	0.0259	0.0189	0.0139	0.0102	0.0075	0.0055	0.0030	0.0017	0.0009	0.0005	0.0003	0.0002	0.0001	0.0001	0.0000	0.0000	0.0000	0.0000
36	0.6989	0.4902	0.3450	0.2437	0.1727	0.1227	0.0875	0.0626	0.0449	0.0323	0.0234	0.0169	0.0123	0.0089	0.0065	0.0048	0.0026	0.0014	0.0008	0.0004	0.0002	0.0001	0.0001	0.0000	0.0000	0.0000	0.0000	0.0000
37	0.6920	0.4806	0.3350	0.2343	0.1644	0.1158	0.0818	0.0580	0.0412	0.0294	0.0210	0.0151	0.0109	0.0078	0.0057	0.0041	0.0022	0.0012	0.0006	0.0003	0.0002	0.0001	0.0001	0.0000	0.0000	0.0000	0.0000	0.0000
38	0.6852	0.4712	0.3252	0.2253	0.1566	0.1092	0.0765	0.0537	0.0378	0.0267	0.0190	0.0135	0.0096	0.0069	0.0049	0.0036	0.0019	0.0010	0.0005	0.0003	0.0002	0.0001	0.0000	0.0000	0.0000	0.0000	0.0000	0.0000
39	0.6784	0.4619	0.3158	0.2166	0.1491	0.1031	0.0715	0.0497	0.0347	0.0243	0.0171	0.0120	0.0085	0.0060	0.0043	0.0031	0.0016	0.0008	0.0004	0.0002	0.0001	0.0001	0.0000	0.0000	0.0000	0.0000	0.0000	0.0000
40	0.6717	0.4529	0.3066	0.2083	0.1420	0.0972	0.0668	0.0460	0.0318	0.0221	0.0154	0.0107	0.0075	0.0053	0.0037	0.0026	0.0013	0.0007	0.0004	0.0002	0.0001	0.0001	0.0000	0.0000	0.0000	0.0000	0.0000	0.0000
41	0.6650	0.4440	0.2976	0.2003	0.1353	0.0917	0.0624	0.0426	0.0292	0.0201	0.0139	0.0096	0.0067	0.0046	0.0032	0.0023	0.0011	0.0006	0.0003	0.0001	0.0001	0.0000	0.0000	0.0000	0.0000	0.0000	0.0000	0.0000
42	0.6584	0.4353	0.2889	0.1926	0.1288	0.0865	0.0583	0.0395	0.0268	0.0183	0.0125	0.0086	0.0059	0.0041	0.0028	0.0020	0.0010	0.0005	0.0002	0.0001	0.0001	0.0000	0.0000	0.0000	0.0000	0.0000	0.0000	0.0000
43	0.6519	0.4268	0.2805	0.1852	0.1227	0.0816	0.0545	0.0365	0.0246	0.0166	0.0112	0.0076	0.0052	0.0036	0.0025	0.0017	0.0008	0.0004	0.0002	0.0001	0.0001	0.0000	0.0000	0.0000	0.0000	0.0000	0.0000	0.0000
44	0.6454	0.4184	0.2724	0.1780	0.1169	0.0770	0.0509	0.0338	0.0226	0.0151	0.0101	0.0068	0.0046	0.0031	0.0021	0.0015	0.0007	0.0003	0.0002	0.0001	0.0000	0.0000	0.0000	0.0000	0.0000	0.0000	0.0000	0.0000
45	0.6391	0.4102	0.2644	0.1712	0.1113	0.0727	0.0476	0.0313	0.0207	0.0137	0.0091	0.0061	0.0041	0.0027	0.0019	0.0013	0.0006	0.0003	0.0001	0.0001	0.0000	0.0000	0.0000	0.0000	0.0000	0.0000	0.0000	0.0000
46	0.6327	0.4022	0.2567	0.1646	0.1060	0.0685	0.0445	0.0290	0.0190	0.0125	0.0082	0.0054	0.0036	0.0024	0.0016	0.0011	0.0005	0.0002	0.0001	0.0001	0.0000	0.0000	0.0000	0.0000	0.0000	0.0000	0.0000	0.0000
47	0.6265	0.3943	0.2493	0.1583	0.1009	0.0647	0.0416	0.0269	0.0174	0.0113	0.0075	0.0048	0.0032	0.0021	0.0014	0.0009	0.0004	0.0002	0.0001	0.0000	0.0000	0.0000	0.0000	0.0000	0.0000	0.0000	0.0000	0.0000
48	0.6203	0.3865	0.2420	0.1522	0.0961	0.0610	0.0389	0.0249	0.0160	0.0103	0.0067	0.0043	0.0028	0.0019	0.0012	0.0008	0.0004	0.0002	0.0001	0.0000	0.0000	0.0000	0.0000	0.0000	0.0000	0.0000	0.0000	0.0000
49	0.6141	0.3790	0.2350	0.1463	0.0916	0.0575	0.0363	0.0230	0.0147	0.0094	0.0060	0.0039	0.0025	0.0016	0.0011	0.0007	0.0003	0.0001	0.0001	0.0000	0.0000	0.0000	0.0000	0.0000	0.0000	0.0000	0.0000	0.0000
50	0.6080	0.3715	0.2281	0.1407	0.0872	0.0543	0.0339	0.0213	0.0134	0.0085	0.0054	0.0035	0.0022	0.0014	0.0009	0.0006	0.0003	0.0001	0.0001	0.0000	0.0000	0.0000	0.0000	0.0000	0.0000	0.0000	0.0000	0.0000
51	0.6020	0.3642	0.2215	0.1353	0.0831	0.0512	0.0317	0.0197	0.0123	0.0077	0.0049	0.0031	0.0020	0.0013	0.0008	0.0005	0.0002	0.0001	0.0001	0.0000	0.0000	0.0000	0.0000	0.0000	0.0000	0.0000	0.0000	0.0000
52	0.5961	0.3571	0.2150	0.1301	0.0791	0.0483	0.0297	0.0183	0.0113	0.0070	0.0044	0.0028	0.0017	0.0011	0.0007	0.0004	0.0002	0.0001	0.0001	0.0000	0.0000	0.0000	0.0000	0.0000	0.0000	0.0000	0.0000	0.0000
53	0.5902	0.3501	0.2088	0.1251	0.0753	0.0456	0.0277	0.0169	0.0104	0.0064	0.0040	0.0025	0.0015	0.0010	0.0006	0.0004	0.0002	0.0001	0.0000	0.0000	0.0000	0.0000	0.0000	0.0000	0.0000	0.0000	0.0000	0.0000
54	0.5843	0.3432	0.2027	0.1203	0.0717	0.0430	0.0259	0.0157	0.0095	0.0058	0.0036	0.0022	0.0014	0.0009	0.0005	0.0003	0.0001	0.0001	0.0000	0.0000	0.0000	0.0000	0.0000	0.0000	0.0000	0.0000	0.0000	0.0000
55	0.5785	0.3365	0.1968	0.1157	0.0683	0.0406	0.0242	0.0145	0.0087	0.0053	0.0032	0.0020	0.0012	0.0007	0.0004	0.0003	0.0001	0.0000	0.0000	0.0000	0.0000	0.0000	0.0000	0.0000	0.0000	0.0000	0.0000	0.0000
56	0.5728	0.3299	0.1910	0.1112	0.0651	0.0383	0.0226	0.0134	0.0080	0.0048	0.0029	0.0018	0.0011	0.0006	0.0004	0.0002	0.0001	0.0000	0.0000	0.0000	0.0000	0.0000	0.0000	0.0000	0.0000	0.0000	0.0000	0.0000
57	0.5671	0.3234	0.1855	0.1069	0.0620	0.0361	0.0211	0.0124	0.0074	0.0044	0.0026	0.0016	0.0009	0.0006	0.0003	0.0002	0.0001	0.0000	0.0000	0.0000	0.0000	0.0000	0.0000	0.0000	0.0000	0.0000	0.0000	0.0000
58	0.5615	0.3171	0.1801	0.1028	0.0590	0.0341	0.0198	0.0115	0.0067	0.0040	0.0024	0.0014	0.0008	0.0005	0.0003	0.0002	0.0001	0.0000	0.0000	0.0000	0.0000	0.0000	0.0000	0.0000	0.0000	0.0000	0.0000	0.0000
59	0.5560	0.3109	0.1748	0.0989	0.0562	0.0321	0.0185	0.0107	0.0062	0.0036	0.0021	0.0012	0.0007	0.0004	0.0003	0.0002	0.0001	0.0000	0.0000	0.0000	0.0000	0.0000	0.0000	0.0000	0.0000	0.0000	0.0000	0.0000
60	0.5504	0.3048	0.1697	0.0951	0.0535	0.0303	0.0173	0.0099	0.0057	0.0033	0.0019	0.0011	0.0007	0.0004	0.0002	0.0001	0.0000	0.0000	0.0000	0.0000	0.0000	0.0000	0.0000	0.0000	0.0000	0.0000	0.0000	0.0000

Period	1%	2%	3%	4%	5%	6%	7%	8%	9%	10%	11%	12%	13%	14%	15%	16%	18%	20%	22%	24%	26%	28%	30%	32%	34%	36%	38%	40%
1	0.9901	0.9804	0.9709	0.9615	0.9524	0.9434	0.9346	0.9259	0.9174	0.9091	0.9009	0.8929	0.8850	0.8772	0.8696	0.8621	0.8475	0.8333	0.8197	0.8065	0.7937	0.7813	0.7692	0.7576	0.7463	0.7353	0.7246	0.7143
2	1.9704	1.9416	1.9135	1.8861	1.8594	1.8334	1.8080	1.7833	1.7591	1.7355	1.7125	1.6901	1.6681	1.6467	1.6257	1.6052	1.5656	1.5278	1.4915	1.4568	1.4235	1.3916	1.3609	1.3315	1.3032	1.2760	1.2497	1.2245
3	2.9410	2.8839	2.8286	2.7751	2.7232	2.6730	2.6243	2.5771	2.5313	2.4869	2.4437	2.4018	2.3612	2.3216	2.2832	2.2459	2.1743	2.1065	2.0422	1.9813	1.9234	1.8684	1.8161	1.7663	1.7188	1.6735	1.6302	1.5889
4	3.9020	3.8077	3.7171	3.6299	3.5460	3.4651	3.3872	3.3121	3.2397	3.1699	3.1024	3.0373	2.9745	2.9137	2.8550	2.7982	2.6901	2.5887	2.4936	2.4043	2.3202	2.2410	2.1662	2.0957	2.0290	1.9658	1.9060	1.8492
5	4.8534	4.7135	4.5797	4.4518	4.3295	4.2124	4.1002	3.9927	3.8897	3.7908	3.6959	3.6048	3.5172	3.4331	3.3522	3.2743	3.1272	2.9906	2.8636	2.7454	2.6351	2.5320	2.4356	2.3452	2.2604	2.1807	2.1058	2.0352
6	5.7955	5.6014	5.4172	5.2421	5.0757	4.9173	4.7665	4.6229	4.4859	4.3553	4.2305	4.1114	3.9975	3.8887	3.7845	3.6847	3.4976	3.3255	3.1669	3.0205	2.8850	2.7594	2.6427	2.5342	2.4331	2.3388	2.2506	2.1680
7	6.7282	6.4720	6.2303	6.0021	5.7864	5.5824	5.3893	5.2064	5.0330	4.8684	4.7122	4.5638	4.4226	4.2883	4.1604	4.0386	3.8115	3.6046	3.4155	3.2423	3.0833	2.9370	2.8021	2.6775	2.5620	2.4550	2.3555	2.2628
8	7.6517	7.3255	7.0197	6.7327	6.4632	6.2098	5.9713	5.7466	5.5348	5.3349	5.1461	4.9676	4.7988	4.6389	4.4873	4.3436	4.0776	3.8372	3.6193	3.4212	3.2407	3.0758	2.9247	2.7860	2.6582	2.5404	2.4315	2.3306
9	8.5660	8.1622	7.7861	7.4353	7.1078	6.8017	6.5152	6.2469	5.9952	5.7590	5.5370	5.3282	5.1317	4.9464	4.7716	4.6065	4.3030	4.0310	3.7863	3.5655	3.3657	3.1842	3.0190	2.8681	2.7300	2.6033	2.4866	2.3790
10	9.4713	8.9826	8.5302	8.1109	7.7217	7.3601	7.0236	6.7101	6.4177	6.1446	5.8892	5.6502	5.4262	5.2161	5.0188	4.8332	4.4941	4.1925	3.9232	3.6819	3.4648	3.2689	3.0915	2.9304	2.7836	2.6495	2.5265	2.4136
11	10.3676	9.7868	9.2526	8.7605	8.3064	7.8869	7.4987	7.1390	6.8052	6.4951	6.2065	5.9377	5.6869	5.4527	5.2337	5.0286	4.6560	4.3271	4.0354	3.7757	3.5435	3.3351	3.1473	2.9776	2.8236	2.6834	2.5555	2.4383
12	11.2551	10.5753	9.9540	9.3851	8.8633	8.3838	7.9427	7.5361	7.1607	6.8137	6.4924	6.1944	5.9176	5.6603	5.4206	5.1971	4.7932	4.4392	4.1274	3.8514	3.6059	3.3868	3.1903	3.0133	2.8534	2.7084	2.5764	2.4559
13	12.1337	11.3484	10.6350	9.9856	9.3936	8.8527	8.3577	7.9038	7.4869	7.1034	6.7499	6.4235	6.1218	5.8424	5.5831	5.3423	4.9095	4.5327	4.2028	3.9124	3.6555	3.4272	3.2233	3.0404	2.8757	2.7268	2.5916	2.4685
14	13.0037	12.1062	11.2961	10.5631	9.8986	9.2950	8.7455	8.2442	7.7862	7.3667	6.9819	6.6282	6.3025	6.0021	5.7245	5.4675	5.0081	4.6106	4.2646	3.9616	3.6949	3.4587	3.2487	3.0609	2.8923	2.7403	2.6026	2.4775
15	13.8651	12.8493	11.9379	11.1184	10.3797	9.7122	9.1079	8.5595	8.0607	7.6061	7.1909	6.8109	6.4624	6.1422	5.8474	5.5755	5.0916	4.6755	4.3152	4.0013	3.7261	3.4834	3.2682	3.0764	2.9047	2.7502	2.6106	2.4839
16	14.7179	13.5777	12.5611	11.6523	10.8378	10.1059	9.4466	8.8514	8.3126	7.8237	7.3792	6.9740	6.6039	6.2651	5.9542	5.6685	5.1624	4.7296	4.3567	4.0333	3.7509	3.5026	3.2832	3.0882	2.9140	2.7575	2.6164	2.4885
17	15.5623	14.2919	13.1661	12.1657	11.2741	10.4773	9.7632	9.1216	8.5436	8.0216	7.5488	7.1196	6.7291	6.3729	6.0472	5.7487	5.2223	4.7746	4.3908	4.0591	3.7705	3.5177	3.2948	3.0971	2.9209	2.7629	2.6206	2.4918
18	16.3983	14.9920	13.7535	12.6593	11.6896	10.8276	10.0591	9.3719	8.7556	8.2014	7.7016	7.2497	6.8399	6.4674	6.1280	5.8178	5.2732	4.8122	4.4187	4.0799	3.7861	3.5294	3.3037	3.1039	2.9260	2.7668	2.6236	2.4941
19	17.2260	15.6785	14.3238	13.1339	12.0853	11.1581	10.3356	9.6036	8.9501	8.3649	7.8393	7.3658	6.9380	6.5504	6.1982	5.8775	5.3162	4.8435	4.4415	4.0967	3.7985	3.5386	3.3105	3.1090	2.9299	2.7697	2.6258	2.4958
20	18.0456	16.3514	14.8775	13.5903	12.4622	11.4699	10.5940	9.8181	9.1285	8.5136	7.9633	7.4694	7.0248	6.6231	6.2593	5.9288	5.3527	4.8696	4.4603	4.1103	3.8083	3.5458	3.3158	3.1129	2.9327	2.7718	2.6274	2.4970
21	18.8570	17.0112	15.4150	14.0292	12.8212	11.7641	10.8355	10.0168	9.2922	8.6487	8.0751	7.5620	7.1016	6.6870	6.3125	5.9731	5.3837	4.8913	4.4756	4.1212	3.8161	3.5514	3.3198	3.1158	2.9349	2.7734	2.6285	2.4979
22	19.6604	17.6580	15.9369	14.4511	13.1630	12.0416	11.0612	10.2007	9.4424	8.7715	8.1757	7.6446	7.1695	6.7429	6.3587	6.0113	5.4099	4.9094	4.4882	4.1300	3.8223	3.5558	3.3230	3.1180	2.9365	2.7746	2.6294	2.4985
23	20.4558	18.2922	16.4436	14.8568	13.4886	12.3034	11.2722	10.3711	9.5802	8.8832	8.2664	7.7184	7.2297	6.7921	6.3988	6.0442	5.4321	4.9245	4.4985	4.1371	3.8273	3.5592	3.3254	3.1197	2.9377	2.7754	2.6300	2.4989
24	21.2434	18.9139	16.9355	15.2470	13.7986	12.5504	11.4693	10.5288	9.7066	8.9847	8.3481	7.7843	7.2829	6.8351	6.4338	6.0726	5.4509	4.9371	4.5070	4.1428	3.8312	3.5619	3.3272	3.1210	2.9386	2.7760	2.6304	2.4992
25	22.0232	19.5235	17.4131	15.6221	14.0939	12.7834	11.6536	10.6748	9.8226	9.0770	8.4217	7.8431	7.3300	6.8729	6.4641	6.0971	5.4669	4.9476	4.5139	4.1474	3.8342	3.5640	3.3286	3.1220	2.9392	2.7765	2.6307	2.4994
26	22.7952	20.1210	17.8768	15.9828	14.3752	13.0032	11.8258	10.8100	9.9290	9.1609	8.4881	7.8957	7.3717	6.9061	6.4906	6.1182	5.4804	4.9563	4.5196	4.1511	3.8367	3.5656	3.3297	3.1227	2.9397	2.7768	2.6310	2.4996
27	23.5596	20.7069	18.3270	16.3296	14.6430	13.2105	11.9867	10.9352	10.0266	9.2372	8.5478	7.9426	7.4086	6.9352	6.5135	6.1364	5.4919	4.9636	4.5243	4.1542	3.8387	3.5669	3.3305	3.1233	2.9401	2.7771	2.6311	2.4997
28	24.3164	21.2813	18.7641	16.6631	14.8981	13.4062	12.1371	11.0511	10.1161	9.3066	8.6016	7.9844	7.4412	6.9607	6.5335	6.1520	5.5016	4.9697	4.5281	4.1566	3.8402	3.5679	3.3312	3.1237	2.9404	2.7773	2.6313	2.4998
29	25.0658	21.8444	19.1885	16.9837	15.1411	13.5907	12.2777	11.1584	10.1983	9.3696	8.6501	8.0218	7.4701	6.9830	6.5509	6.1656	5.5098	4.9747	4.5312	4.1585	3.8414	3.5687	3.3317	3.1240	2.9406	2.7774	2.6313	2.4999
30	25.8077	22.3965	19.6004	17.2920	15.3725	13.7648	12.4090	11.2578	10.2737	9.4269	8.6938	8.0552	7.4957	7.0027	6.5660	6.1772	5.5168	4.9789	4.5338	4.1601	3.8424	3.5693	3.3321	3.1242	2.9407	2.7775	2.6314	2.4999
31	26.5423	22.9377	20.0004	17.5885	15.5928	13.9291	12.5318	11.3498	10.3428	9.4790	8.7331	8.0850	7.5183	7.0199	6.5791	6.1872	5.5227	4.9824	4.5359	4.1614	3.8432	3.5697	3.3324	3.1244	2.9408	2.7776	2.6315	2.4999
32	27.2696	23.4683	20.3888	17.8736	15.8027	14.0840	12.6466	11.4350	10.4062	9.5264	8.7686	8.1116	7.5383	7.0350	6.5905	6.1959	5.5277	4.9854	4.5376	4.1624	3.8438	3.5701	3.3326	3.1246	2.9409	2.7776	2.6315	2.5000
33	27.9897	23.9886	20.7658	18.1476	16.0025	14.2302	12.7538	11.5139	10.4644	9.5694	8.8005	8.1354	7.5560	7.0482	6.6005	6.2034	5.5320	4.9878	4.5390	4.1632	3.8443	3.5704	3.3328	3.1247	2.9410	2.7777	2.6315	2.5000
34	28.7027	24.4986	21.1318	18.4112	16.1929	14.3681	12.8540	11.5869	10.5178	9.6086	8.8293	8.1566	7.5717	7.0599	6.6091	6.2098	5.5356	4.9898	4.5402	4.1639	3.8447	3.5706	3.3329	3.1248	2.9411	2.7777	2.6315	2.5000
35	29.4086	24.9986	21.4872	18.6646	16.3742	14.4982	12.9477	11.6546	10.5668	9.6442	8.8552	8.1755	7.5856	7.0700	6.6166	6.2153	5.5386	4.9915	4.5411	4.1644	3.8450	3.5708	3.3330	3.1248	2.9411	2.7777	2.6315	2.5000
36	30.1075	25.4888	21.8323	18.9083	16.5469	14.6210	13.0352	11.7172	10.6118	9.6765	8.8786	8.1924	7.5979	7.0790	6.6231	6.2201	5.5412	4.9929	4.5419	4.1649	3.8452	3.5709	3.3331	3.1249	2.9411	2.7777	2.6316	2.5000
37	30.7995	25.9695	22.1672	19.1426	16.7113	14.7368	13.1170	11.7752	10.6530	9.7059	8.8996	8.2075	7.6087	7.0868	6.6288	6.2242	5.5434	4.9941	4.5426	4.1652	3.8454	3.5710	3.3331	3.1249	2.9411	2.7777	2.6316	2.5000
38	31.4847	26.4406	22.4925	19.3679	16.8679	14.8460	13.1935	11.8289	10.6908	9.7327	8.9186	8.2210	7.6183	7.0937	6.6338	6.2278	5.5452	4.9951	4.5431	4.1655	3.8457	3.5711	3.3332	3.1249	2.9412	2.7778	2.6316	2.5000
39	32.1630	26.9026	22.8082	19.5845	17.0170	14.9491	13.2649	11.8786	10.7255	9.7570	8.9357	8.2330	7.6268	7.0997	6.6380	6.2309	5.5468	4.9959	4.5435	4.1657	3.8458	3.5712	3.3332	3.1250	2.9412	2.7778	2.6316	2.5000
40	32.8347	27.3555	23.1148	19.7928	17.1591	15.0463	13.3317	11.9246	10.7574	9.7791	8.9511	8.2438	7.6344	7.1050	6.6418	6.2335	5.5482	4.9966	4.5439	4.1659	3.8458	3.5712	3.3332	3.1250	2.9412	2.7778	2.6316	2.5000
41	33.4997	27.7995	23.4124	19.9931	17.2944	15.1380	13.3941	11.9672	10.7866	9.7991	8.9649	8.2534	7.6410	7.1097	6.6450	6.2358	5.5493	4.9972	4.5441	4.1661	3.8459	3.5713	3.3333	3.1250	2.9412	2.7778	2.6316	2.5000
42	34.1581	28.2348	23.7014	20.1856	17.4232	15.2245	13.4524	12.0067	10.8134	9.8174	8.9774	8.2619	7.6469	7.1138	6.6478	6.2377	5.5502	4.9976	4.5444	4.1662	3.8460	3.5713	3.3333	3.1250	2.9412	2.7778	2.6316	2.5000
43	34.8100	28.6616	23.9819	20.3708	17.5459	15.3062	13.5070	12.0432	10.8380	9.8340	8.9886	8.2696	7.6522	7.1173	6.6503	6.2394	5.5510	4.9980	4.5446	4.1663	3.8460	3.5714	3.3333	3.1250	2.9412	2.7778	2.6316	2.5000
44	35.4555	29.0800	24.2543	20.5488	17.6628	15.3832	13.5579	12.0771	10.8605	9.8491	8.9988	8.2764	7.6568	7.1205	6.6524	6.2409	5.5517	4.9984	4.5447	4.1663	3.8460	3.5714	3.3333	3.1250	2.9412	2.7778	2.6316	2.5000
45	36.0945	29.4902	24.5187	20.7200	17.7741	15.4558	13.6055	12.1084	10.8812	9.8628	9.0079	8.2825	7.6609	7.1232	6.6543	6.2421	5.5523	4.9986	4.5449	4.1664	3.8460	3.5714	3.3333	3.1250	2.9412	2.7778	2.6316	2.5000
46	36.7272	29.8923	24.7754	20.8847	17.8801	15.5244	13.6500	12.1374	10.9002	9.8753	9.0161	8.2880	7.6645	7.1256	6.6559	6.2432	5.5528	4.9989	4.5450	4.1665	3.8461	3.5714	3.3333	3.1250	2.9412	2.7778	2.6316	2.5000
47	37.3537	30.2866	25.0247	21.0429	17.9810	15.5890	13.6916	12.1643	10.9176	9.8866	9.0235	8.2928	7.6677	7.1277	6.6573	6.2442	5.5532	4.9991	4.5451	4.1665	3.8461	3.5714	3.3333	3.1250	2.9412	2.7778	2.6316	2.5000
48	37.9740	30.6731	25.2667	21.1951	18.0772	15.6500	13.7305	12.1891	10.9336	9.8969	9.0302	8.2972	7.6705	7.1296	6.6585	6.2450	5.5536	4.9992	4.5452	4.1665	3.8461	3.5714	3.3333	3.1250	2.9412	2.7778	2.6316	2.5000
49	38.5881	31.0521	25.5017	21.3415	18.1687	15.7076	13.7668	12.2122	10.9482	9.9063	9.0362	8.3010	7.6730	7.1312	6.6596	6.2457	5.5539	4.9993	4.5453	4.1666	3.8461	3.5714	3.3333	3.1250	2.9412	2.7778	2.6316	2.5000
50	39.1961	31.4236	25.7298	21.4822	18.2559	15.7619	13.8007	12.2335	10.9617	9.9148	9.0417	8.3045	7.6752	7.1327	6.6605	6.2463	5.5541	4.9995	4.5452	4.1666	3.8461	3.5714	3.3333	3.1250	2.9412	2.7778	2.6316	2.5000
51	39.7981	31.7878	25.9512	21.6175	18.3390	15.8131	13.8325	12.2532	10.9740	9.9226	9.0465	8.3076	7.6772	7.1339	6.6613	6.2468	5.5544	4.9996	4.5453	4.1666	3.8461	3.5714	3.3333	3.1250	2.9412	2.7778	2.6316	2.5000
52	40.3942	32.1449	26.1662	21.7476	18.4181	15.8614	13.8621	12.2715	10.9853	9.9296	9.0509	8.3103	7.6805	7.1350	6.6620	6.2472	5.5545	4.9997	4.5453	4.1666	3.8461	3.5714	3.3333	3.1250	2.9412	2.7778	2.6316	2.5000
53	40.9844	32.4950	26.3750	21.8727	18.4934	15.9070	13.8898	12.2884	10.9957	9.9360	9.0549	8.3128	7.6818	7.1360	6.6626	6.2476	5.5547	4.9997	4.5453	4.1666	3.8461	3.5714	3.3333	3.1250	2.9412	2.7778	2.6316	2.5000
54	41.5687	32.8383	26.5777	21.9930	18.5651	15.9500	13.9157	12.3041	11.0053	9.9418	9.0585	8.3150	7.6830	7.1368	6.6631	6.2479	5.5548	4.9998	4.5454	4.1666	3.8461	3.5714	3.3333	3.1250	2.9412	2.7778	2.6316	2.5000
55	42.1472	33.1748	26.7744	22.1086	18.6335	15.9905	13.9399	12.3186	11.0140	9.9471	9.0617	8.3170	7.6830	7.1376	6.6636	6.2482	5.5549	4.9998	4.5454	4.1666	3.8461	3.5714	3.3333	3.1250	2.9412	2.7778	2.6316	2.5000
56	42.7200	33.5047	26.9655	22.2198	18.6985	16.0288	13.9626	12.3321	11.0220	9.9519	9.0646	8.3187	7.6841	7.1382	6.6640	6.2485	5.5550	4.9998	4.5454	4.1666	3.8461	3.5714	3.3333	3.1250	2.9412	2.7778	2.6316	2.5000
57	43.2871	33.8281	27.1510	22.3267	18.7605	16.0649	13.9837	12.3445	11.0294	9.9563	9.0672	8.3203	7.6851	7.1388	6.6644	6.2487	5.5551	4.9999	4.5454	4.1666	3.8461	3.5714	3.3333	3.1250	2.9412	2.7778	2.6316	2.5000
58	43.8486	34.1452	27.3310	22.4296	18.8195	16.0990	14.0035	12.3560	11.0361	9.9603	9.0695	8.3217	7.6859	7.1393	6.6647	6.2489	5.5552	4.9999	4.5454	4.1667	3.8461	3.5714	3.3333	3.1250	2.9412	2.7778	2.6316	2.5000
59	44.4046	34.4561	27.5058	22.5284	18.8758	16.1311	14.0219	12.3667	11.0423	9.9639	9.0717	8.3229	7.6867	7.1397	6.6649	6.2490	5.5552	4.9999	4.5454	4.1667	3.8461	3.5714	3.3333	3.1250	2.9412	2.7778	2.6316	2.5000
60	44.9550	34.7609	27.6756	22.6235	18.9293	16.1614	14.0392	12.3766	11.0480	9.9672	9.0736	8.3240	7.6873	7.1401	6.6651	6.2492	5.5553	4.9999	4.5454	4.1667	3.8462	3.5714	3.3333	3.1250	2.9412	2.7778	2.6316	2.5000

APPENDIX III

FINANCIAL STATEMENTS

DAVE'S BIKES, INC.

Dave's Bikes, Inc.

Income Statements

	1998	1999	2000	2001	2002	2003	2004	Projections 2005	2006	2007
Sales		$250,000	$337,500	$438,750	$504,562	$605,475	$666,022	$739,285	$787,338	$799,149
Cost of sales		(125,000)	(172,125)	(228,238)	(267,723)	(327,693)	(367,672)	(408,115)	(434,643)	(441,163)
Gross Profit		$125,000	$165,375	$210,512	$236,839	$277,782	$298,350	$331,170	$352,695	$357,986
Operating expense		$100,000	$125,000	$153,300	$173,094	$201,314	$222,845	$243,428	$254,961	$257,795
Depreciation		8,900	12,330	14,713	12,535	16,715	18,591	25,370	22,743	19,557
Total operating expenses		$108,900	$137,330	$168,013	$185,629	$218,029	$241,436	$268,798	$277,704	$277,352
Net operating income		$ 16,100	$ 28,045	$ 42,499	$ 51,210	$ 59,753	$ 56,914	$ 62,372	$ 74,991	$ 80,634
Interest received		0	0	0	150	0	0	0	0	0
Interest paid		(4,720)	(4,554)	(7,196)	(7,743)	(6,380)	(7,963)	(8,879)	(10,038)	(7,419)
Earnings before tax		$ 11,380	$ 23,491	$ 35,303	$ 43,617	$ 53,373	$ 48,951	$ 53,493	$ 64,953	$ 73,215
Tax		(3,414)	(7,048)	(10,591)	(13,085)	(16,012)	(14,685)	(16,048)	(19,486)	(21,953)
Net income		$ 7,966	$ 16,443	$ 24,712	$ 30,532	$ 37,361	$ 34,266	$ 37,445	$ 45,467	$ 51,262
Dividends paid		0	0	(9,885)	(12,213)	0	(13,707)	(14,978)	(18,187)	(20,489)
Additions to retained earnings		$ 7,966	$ 16,443	$ 14,827	$ 18,319	$ 37,361	$ 20,559	$ 22,467	$ 27,280	$ 30,773

Dave's Bikes, Inc.

Balance Sheets

	1998	1999	2000	2001	2002	2003	2004	Projections 2005	2006	2007
Assets:										
Cash	$24,000	$ 111	$ 79	$ 333	$ 401	$ 730	$ 10	$ 842	$ 421	$ 246
Accounts receivable	0	31,250	42,188	54,843	63,070	75,685	83,254	92,410	98,417	99,894
Inventory	0	23,438	32,273	42,795	50,198	61,442	68,938	76,522	81,496	82,718
Prepaid expenses	0	5,000	6,250	7,665	8,655	10,066	11,142	12,171	12,748	12,890
Current assets	$24,000	$ 59,799	$ 80,790	$105,636	$125,324	$147,923	$163,344	$181,945	$193,082	$195,748
Vehicles	$24,000	$ 24,000	$ 24,000	$ 44,000	$ 44,000	$ 44,000	$ 44,000	$ 84,000	$ 84,000	$ 84,000
Accum. depreciation		(4,800)	(8,640)	(15,712)	(21,370)	(25,896)	(29,517)	(40,413)	(49,130)	(56,104)
Net vehicles	$24,000	$ 19,200	$ 15,360	$ 28,288	$ 22,630	$ 18,104	$14,483	$ 43,587	$ 34,870	$ 27,896
Plant and equipment	$41,000	$ 41,000	$ 89,000	$ 89,000	$ 89,000	$149,000	$189,000	$199,000	$209,000	$209,000
Accum. depreciation		(4,100)	(12,590)	(20,231)	(27,108)	(39,297)	(54,267)	(68,741)	(82,767)	(95,390)
Net plant and equipment	$41,000	$ 36,900	$ 76,410	$ 68,769	$ 61,892	$109,703	$134,733	$130,259	$126,233	$113,610
Fixed assets	$65,000	$ 56,100	$ 91,770	$ 97,057	$ 84,522	$127,807	$149,216	$173,846	$161,103	$141,506
Total assets	$89,000	$115,899	$172,560	$202,693	$209,846	$275,730	$312,560	$355,791	$354,185	$337,254

Dave's Bikes, Inc.

Balance Sheets

	1998	1999	2000	2001	2002	2003	2004	2005	2006	2007
									Projections	
Liabilities:										
Accounts payable		$ 11,250	$ 14,856	$ 19,077	$ 22,041	$ 26,450	$ 29,526	$ 32,577	$ 34,480	$ 34,948
Accrued expenses		9,000	11,886	15,261	17,632	21,161	23,621	26,061	27,585	27,958
Income tax payable		683	1,409	2,118	2,617	3,202	2,937	3,210	3,897	4,390
Short-term bank loan	$ 9,000	7,000	30,000	7,000	0	20,000	1,000	16,000	3,000	4,000
Current liabilities	$ 9,000	$ 27,933	$ 58,151	$ 43,456	$ 42,290	$ 70,813	$ 57,084	$ 77,848	$ 68,962	$ 71,296
Long-term loan	50,000	50,000	60,000	90,000	80,000	80,000	110,000	110,000	90,000	40,000
Total liabilities	$59,000	$ 77,933	$118,151	$133,456	$122,290	$150,813	$167,084	$187,848	$158,962	$111,296
Paid-in capital	$30,000	$ 30,000	$ 30,000	$ 30,000	$ 30,000	$ 30,000	$ 30,000	$ 30,000	$ 30,000	$ 30,000
Retained earnings		7,966	24,409	39,237	57,556	94,917	115,476	137,943	165,223	195,957
Equity	$30,000	$ 37,966	$ 54,409	$ 69,237	$ 87,556	$124,917	$145,476	$167,943	$195,233	$225,957
Total liabilities and owners' equity	$89,000	$115,899	$172,560	$202,693	$209,846	$275,730	$312,560	$355,791	$354,195	$337,253

Dave's Bikes, Inc.

Cash-Flow Statements

Projections

	1998	1999	2000	2001	2002	2003	2004	2005	2006	2007
Cash sales	$ 0	$218,750	$326,563	$426,094	$496,336	$592,861	$658,454	$730,127	$781,332	$797,672
Cash purchases	0	(142,813)	(179,158)	(236,649)	(273,645)	(336,732)	(373,630)	(414,173)	(438,665)	(442,151)
Cash operating expenses	0	(90,375)	(121,562)	(149,228)	(170,231)	(196,994)	(219,924)	(240,490)	(253,065)	(257,329)
Income tax	0	(2,731)	(6,321)	(9,882)	(12,586)	(15,426)	(14,951)	(15,575)	(18,798)	(21,459)
Cash flow from operations	$ 0	$(17,169)	$ 19,522	$ 30,335	$ 39,874	$ 43,709	$ 49,949	$ 59,889	$ 70,804	$ 76,733
Interest paid	0	(4,720)	(4,554)	(7,196)	(7,593)	(6,380)	(7,963)	(8,879)	(10,038)	(7,419)
Dividends paid	0	0	0	(9,885)	(12,213)	0	(13,707)	(14,978)	(18,187)	(20,489)
Equity	30,000	0	0	0	0	0	0	0	0	0
Debt	59,000	(2,000)	33,000	7,000	(17,000)	20,000	11,000	15,000	(33,000)	(49,000)
Cash flow from financing	$ 89,000	$ (6,720)	$ 28,446	$(10,081)	$(36,806)	$ 13,620	$(10,670)	$ (8,857)	$(61,225)	$(76,908)
Deposits	$0	$ 0	$ 0	$ 0	$ (3,000)	$ 3,000	$ 0	$ 0	$ 0	$ 0
Vehicles	(24,000)	0	0	(20,000)	0	0	0	(40,000)	0	0
Plant and equipment	(41,000)	0	(48,000)	0	0	(60,000)	(40,000)	(10,000)	(10,000)	0
Cash flow from investing	$(65,000)	$ 0	$(48,000)	$(20,000)	$ (3,000)	$(57,000)	$(40,000)	$(50,000)	$(10,000)	$ 0
Change in cash	$ 24,000	$(23,889)	$ (32)	$ 254	$ 68	$ 329	$ (721)	$ 1,032	$ (421)	$ (175)
Opening cash	0	24,000	111	79	333	401	730	9	1,041	620
Closing cash	$ 24,000	$ 111	$ 79	$ 333	$ 401	$ 730	$ 19	$ 1,041	$ 620	$ 445

Dave's Bikes, Inc.

Cash-Flow Statements

	1998	1999	2000	2001	2002	2003	2004	Projections 2005	2006	2007
Net operating income	$ 0	$ 16,100	$28,045	$42,499	$51,210	$59,753	$56,914	$62,372	$74,991	$80,594
Income tax	0	(3,414)	(7,047)	(10,591)	(13,085)	(16,012)	(14,685)	(16,048)	(19,486)	(21,951)
	$ 0	$ 12,686	$20,998	$31,908	$38,125	$43,741	$42,229	$46,324	$55,505	$58,643
Positive cash-flow factors:										
Depreciation	0	8,900	12,330	14,713	12,535	16,715	18,591	25,370	22,743	19,597
Accounts payable	0	11,250	3,606	4,221	2,964	4,409	3,076	3,051	1,903	468
Accrued expenses	0	9,000	2,885	3,375	2,371	3,529	2,460	2,440	1,524	373
Taxes payable	0	683	727	709	499	585	(265)	272	687	493
	$ 0	$ 29,833	$19,548	$23,018	$18,369	$25,238	$23,862	$31,133	$26,857	$20,931
Negative cash-flow factors:										
Accounts receivable	0	31,250	10,938	12,655	8,227	12,614	7,569	9,156	6,007	1,477
Inventory	0	23,438	8,836	10,521	7,403	11,244	7,496	7,583	4,974	1,222
Prepaid expenses	0	5,000	1,250	1,415	990	1,411	1,077	1,029	577	142
	$ 0	$ 59,688	$21,024	$24,591	$16,620	$25,269	$16,142	$17,768	$11,558	$ 2,841
Cash flow from operations	$ 0	$(17,169)	$19,522	$30,335	$39,874	$43,709	$49,949	$59,889	$70,804	$76,733
Cash flow from financing	89,000	(6,720)	28,446	(10,081)	(36,806)	13,620	(10,670)	(8,857)	(61,225)	(76,908)
Cash flow from investing	(65,000)	0	(48,000)	(20,000)	(3,000)	(57,000)	(40,000)	(50,000)	(10,000)	0
Change in cash	$24,000	$(23,889)	$ (32)	$ 254	$ 68	$ 329	$ (721)	$ 1,032	$ (421)	$ (175)
Opening cash	24,000	24,000	111	79	333	401	730	9	1,041	620
Closing cash	$24,000	$ 111	$ 79	$ 333	$ 401	$ 730	$ 9	$ 1,041	$ 620	$ 445

Boldfaced entries indicate key terms.